Lecture Notes in Artificial Intelligence   8575

Subseries of Lecture Notes in Computer Science

LNAI Series Editors

Randy Goebel
  University of Alberta, Edmonton, Canada
Yuzuru Tanaka
  Hokkaido University, Sapporo, Japan
Wolfgang Wahlster
  DFKI and Saarland University, Saarbrücken, Germany

LNAI Founding Series Editor

Joerg Siekmann
  DFKI and Saarland University, Saarbrücken, Germany

T0183279

Angel P. del Pobil   Eris Chinellato
Ester Martinez-Martin   John Hallam
Enric Cervera   Antonio Morales (Eds.)

From Animals to Animats 13

13th International Conference
on Simulation of Adaptive Behavior, SAB 2014
Castellón, Spain, July 22-25, 2014
Proceedings

 Springer

Volume Editors

Angel P. del Pobil
Ester Martinez-Martin
Enric Cervera
Antonio Morales
Jaume I University
Robotic Intelligence Laboratory
Avda. Sos Baynat s/n, 12071 Castellón de la Plana, Spain
E-mail: {pobil,emartine,ecervera,morales}@uji.es

Eris Chinellato
University of Leeds
School of Computing
Leeds, LS2 9JT, UK
E-mail: e.chinellato@leeds.ac.uk

John Hallam
University of Southern Denmark
Mærsk McKinney Møller Institute
Campusvej 55, 5230 Odense, Denmark
E-mail: john@mmmi.sdu.dk

ISSN 0302-9743   e-ISSN 1611-3349
ISBN 978-3-319-08863-1   e-ISBN 978-3-319-08864-8
DOI 10.1007/978-3-319-08864-8
Springer Cham Heidelberg New York Dordrecht London

Library of Congress Control Number: 2014942461

LNCS Sublibrary: SL 7 – Artificial Intelligence

© Cover illustration: Jean Solé

Typesetting: Camera-ready by author, data conversion by Scientific Publishing Services, Chennai, India

Printed on acid-free paper

Springer is part of Springer Science+Business Media (www.springer.com)

Preface

This book contains the articles presented at the 13th International Conference on the Simulation of Adaptive Behavior (SAB 2014), held in Castellón at Jaume I University in July 2014.

The objective of the biennial SAB conference is to bring together researchers in computer science, artificial intelligence, artificial life, complex systems, robotics, neurosciences, ethology, evolutionary biology, and related fields so as to further our understanding of the behaviors and underlying mechanisms that allow natural and artificial animals to adapt and survive in uncertain environments.

Adaptive behavior research is distinguished by its focus on the modeling and creation of complete animal-like systems, which – however simple at the moment – may be one of the best routes to understanding intelligence in natural and artificial systems. The conference is part of a long series that started with the first SAB conference held in Paris in September 1990, which was followed by conferences in Honolulu 1992, Brighton 1994, Cape Cod 1996, Zürich 1998, Paris 2000, Edinburgh 2002, Los Angeles 2004, Rome 2006, Osaka 2008, Paris 2010, and Odense 2012. In 1992, MIT Press introduced the quarterly journal *Adaptive Behavior*, now published by SAGE Publications. The establishment of the International Society for Adaptive Behavior (ISAB) in 1995 further underlined the emergence of adaptive behavior as a fully-fledged scientific discipline. The present proceedings provide a comprehensive and up-to-date resource for the future development of this exciting field.

The articles cover the main areas in animat research, including the animat approach and methodology, perception and motor control, navigation and internal world models, learning and adaptation, evolution, and collective and social behavior. The authors focus on well-defined models, computer simulations or robotic models, that help to characterize and compare various organizational principles, architectures, and adaptation processes capable of inducing adaptive behavior in real animals or synthetic agents, the animats.

This conference and its proceedings would not exist without the substantial help of many people. We had three very interesting plenary talks: "Bionic Learning Network – new inspiration from nature" by Nina Gaissert, "Principles of Robustness in Motion Science of Animals, Animations and Robots" by Robert Full, and "Visuomotor Adaptation at a Microscopic Scale" by Michele Rucci. We would like to thank the members of the Program Committee, who critically reviewed all the submissions and provided detailed suggestions on how to improve the articles. The enthusiasm and hard work of numerous individuals were essential to the conference success. Above all, we would like to acknowledge the significant contribution of Ester Martínez-Martín, Angel Durán, Carlos Rubert, Marco Antonelli, Javier Felip, Cristina Díaz, Roger Esteller and all the members of the UJI Robotic Intelligence Laboratory, who helped with the local arrangements. We also thank, once again, Jean Solé for the artistic conception of the SAB 2014 poster and the proceedings cover.

May 2014   Angel P. del Pobil
                                                                    John Hallam

Organization

From Animals to Animats 13, the 13th International Conference on the Simulation of Adaptive Behavior (SAB 2014) was organized by the Robotic Intelligence Laboratory of Jaume I and the International Society for Adaptive Behavior (ISAB).

General Chairs

Angel P. del Pobil	Jaume I University, Castellón, Spain
John Hallam	University of Southern Denmark, Odense, Denmark

Program Chairs

Eris Chinellato	University of Leeds, UK
Enric Cervera	Jaume I University, Castellón, Spain
Antonio Morales	Jaume I University, Castellón, Spain

Organization Chair

Ester Martinez-Martin	Jaume I University, Castellón, Spain

Local Organization Committee

Angel Durán	Raul Marín
Carlos Rubert	Pedro Sanz
Marco Antonelli	David Fornas
Javier Felip	Tejas Parekh
Cristina Díaz	Oscar Gómez
Roger Esteller	Gabriel Recatalá
Juan Carlos García Sánchez	

Program Committee

Frédéric Alexandre	Minoru Asada	Josh Bongard
Pierre Andry	Christian Balkenius	Nicolas Bredeche
Angelo Arleo	Luc Berthouze	Joanna Bryson

Angelo Cangelosi   Philippe Gaussier   Pietro Pantano
Lola Cañamero   Benoît Girard   Tony Prescott
Francis Colas   Phil Husbands   Mikhail Prokopenko
Luis Correia   Fumiya Iida   Inaki Rano
Ezequiel Di Paolo   Hiroyuki Iizuka   Denis Sheynikhovich
Julien Diard   Toshiyuki Kondo   Olivier Sigaud
Stéphane Doncieux   Robert Lowe   Tim Taylor
Marco Dorigo   François Michaud   Charles Taylor
Boris Duran   Jean-Baptiste Mouret   Serge Thill
Richard Duro   Ryohei Nakano   Eiji Uchibe
Luca Gambardella   Stefano Nolfi   Myra S. Wilson

Sponsoring Institutions

Jaume I University, Department of Engineering and Computer Science
International Society for Adaptive Behavior (ISAB)
Generalitat Valenciana
Robotnik Automation
PAL Robotics
Cyberbotics Ltd.

Table of Contents

Animat Approach and Methodology

A Role for Sleep in Artificial Cognition through Deferred Restructuring
of Experience in Autonomous Machines 1
   *Richard J. Duro, Francisco Bellas, José A. Becerra, and
   Rodrigo Salgado*

Time in Consciousness, Memory and Human-Robot Interaction 11
   Michail Maniadakis and Panos Trahanias

Non-representational Sensorimotor Knowledge 21
   Thomas Buhrmann and Ezequiel Di Paolo

Perception and Motor Control

Self-exploration of the Stumpy Robot with Predictive Information
Maximization.. 32
   Georg Martius, Luisa Jahn, Helmut Hauser, and Verena V. Hafner

Detecting the Vibration in the Artificial Web Inspired by the Spider 43
   Eunseok Jeong and DaeEun Kim

Modelling Reaction Times in Non-linear Classification Tasks........... 53
   *Martha Lewis, Anna Fedor, Michael Öllinger, Eörs Szathmáry, and
   Chrisantha Fernando*

Multiple Decoupled CPGs with Local Sensory Feedback for Adaptive
Locomotion Behaviors of Bio-inspired Walking Robots 65
   *Subhi Shaker Barikhan, Florentin Wörgötter, and
   Poramate Manoonpong*

The Role of a Cerebellum-Driven Perceptual Prediction within a
Robotic Postural Task 76
   *Giovanni Maffei, Marti Sanchez-Fibla, Ivan Herreros, and
   Paul F.M.J. Verschure*

Biomimetic Agent Based Modelling Using Male Frog Calling Behaviour
as a Case Study 88
   *Søren Vissing Jørgensen, Yves Demazeau,
   Jakob Christensen-Dalsgaard, and John Hallam*

Navigation and Internal World Models

Snapshot Homing Navigation Based on Edge Features   98
  SeungMin Baek and DaeEun Kim

Ground-Nesting Insects Could Use Visual Tracking for Monitoring Nest
Position during Learning Flights   108
  *Nermin Samet, Jochen Zeil, Elmar Mair, Norbert Boeddeker, and
  Wolfgang Stürzl*

Adaptive Landmark-Based Navigation System Using Learning
Techniques   121
  *Bassel Zeidan, Sakyasingha Dasgupta, Florentin Wörgötter, and
  Poramate Manoonpong*

Robustness Study of a Multimodal Compass Inspired from HD-Cells
and Dynamic Neural Fields   132
  *Pierre Delarboulas, Philippe Gaussier, Ramesh Caussy, and
  Mathias Quoy*

Learning and Adaptation

Developmental Dynamics of RNNPB: New Insight about Infant Action
Development   144
  Jun-Cheol Park, Dae-Shik Kim, and Yukie Nagai

Simulating the Emergence of Early Physical and Social Interactions:
A Developmental Route through Low Level Visuomotor Learning   154
  *Raphael Braud, Ghiles Mostafaoui, Ali Karaouzene, and
  Philippe Gaussier*

Intrinsically Motivated Decision Making for Situated, Goal-Driven
Agents   166
  Mohamed Oubbati, Christian Fischer, and Günther Palm

An Anti-hebbian Learning Rule to Represent Drive Motivations for
Reinforcement Learning   176
  Varun Raj Kompella, Sohrob Kazerounian, and Jürgen Schmidhuber

Unsupervised Learning of Sensory Primitives from Optical Flow
Fields   188
  Oswald Berthold and Verena V. Hafner

Reinforcement-Driven Shaping of Sequence Learning in Neural
Dynamics   198
  *Matthew Luciw, Sohrob Kazerounian, Yulia Sandamirskaya,
  Gregor Schöner, and Jürgen Schmidhuber*

Rapid Humanoid Motion Learning through Coordinated, Parallel
Evolution   210
    Marijn Stollenga, Jürgen Schmidhuber, and Faustino Gomez

Evolution

Programmable Self-assembly with Chained Soft Cells: An Algorithm to
Fold into 2-D Shapes   220
    Jürg Germann, Joshua Auerbach, and Dario Floreano

Voxel Robot: A Pneumatic Robot with Deformable Morphology   230
    Mark Roper, Nikolaos Katsaros, and Chrisantha Fernando

Task-Driven Evolution of Modular Self-reconfigurable Robots   240
    *Vojtěch Vonásek, Sergej Neumann, Lutz Winkler, Karel Košnar,
    Heinz Wörn, and Libor Přeučil*

A Bacterial-Based Algorithm to Simulate Complex Adaptive Systems . . .   250
    Diego Gonzalez-Rodriguez and Jose Rodolfo Hernandez-Carrion

Online Evolution of Deep Convolutional Network for Vision-Based
Reinforcement Learning   260
    Jan Koutník, Jürgen Schmidhuber, and Faustino Gomez

Collective and Social Behavior

A Swarm Robotics Approach to Task Allocation under Soft Deadlines
and Negligible Switching Costs   270
    Yara Khaluf, Mauro Birattari, and Heiko Hamann

Supervised Robot Groups with Reconfigurable Formation:
Theory and Simulations   280
    Zoltán Szántó, Lőrinc Márton, and Sebestyén György

Coupling Learning Capability and Local Rules for the Improvement of
the Objects' Aggregation Task by a Cognitive Multi-Robot System   290
    *Abdelhak Chatty, Philippe Gaussier, Ali Karaouzene,
    Mohamed Bouzid, Ilhem Kallel, and Adel M. Alimi*

Honeybee-Inspired Quality Monitoring of Routing Paths in Mobile Ad
Hoc Networks   300
    Alexandros Giagkos and Myra S. Wilson

Human Inspiration and Comparison for Monitoring Strategies in a
Robotic Convoy Task   310
    Silvia Rossi and Mariacarla Staffa

Animal Social Behaviour: A Visual Analysis   320
    Ester Martinez-Martin and Angel P. del Pobil

Crowd Emotion Detection Using Dynamic Probabilistic Models   328
    Mirza Waqar Baig, Emilia I. Barakova, Lucio Marcenaro,
    Matthias Rauterberg, and Carlo S. Regazzoni

Author Index   339

A Role for Sleep in Artificial Cognition through Deferred Restructuring of Experience in Autonomous Machines

Richard J. Duro, Francisco Bellas, José A. Becerra, and Rodrigo Salgado

Integrated Group for Engineering Research, Universidade da Coruna, Spain
{richard,francisco.bellas,ronin,rodrigo.salgado}@udc.es

Abstract. This paper is concerned with the exploration of the benefits that can be derived within a cognitive architecture for robots through the application of nature inspired sleep related cognitive restructuring processes. To this end, the concept of Deferred Restructuring of Experience in Autonomous Machines (DREAM) is postulated and applied in the context of the Multilevel Darwinist Brain architecture. This concept implies a series of consolidation, enhancement and internal imaging based exploration processes that can be applied over the experience, in terms of models and behavioral structures, a robot has acquired in its interaction with the world during its lifetime. The result is a re-representation of all of this experience so that the robot becomes more efficient and adaptive in its subsequent interactions with the world. A couple of simple proof of concept experiments demonstrate the capabilities of the approach.

1   Introduction

The role of sleeping and dreaming in human and animal cognition is still an open subject. However, in the last few years, a consensus has been reached, mostly from sleep deprivation studies, whereby the cognitive processes that take place during sleep are of paramount importance for the operation of brains. In fact, many authors have started to study how sleeping affects human memory, especially long-term memory, and, consequently, how this influences cognition.

After interaction with the world, an experience is encoded as a representation within the brain [1], a memory. However, memories are not static [2], and for them to persist in time it is necessary to perform different operations such as consolidation to help stabilize these memories or enhancement to facilitate recollection [3]. Many studies support the hypothesis that sleep is involved in these processes.

It has long been accepted that there is a need for sleep after learning in the case of procedural memories for their subsequent consolidation and enhancement. In the case of declarative memories, it was only in the last decade that the benefits of sleep on these consolidation and restructuring processes have become evident [4, 5]. The mechanisms that lead to these benefits are still under debate [6] and several theories have been proposed such as the hippocampal-neocortical model of memory consolidation [7] or the multiple trace theory [8]. Some authors postulate that several of these

A.P. del Pobil et al. (Eds.): SAB 2014, LNAI 8575, pp. 1–10, 2014.

mechanisms may coexist in different stages of sleep [9] to consolidate these memories, eliminating what is useless and enhancing what is relevant. That is, with the aim of restructuring how experiences are stored making them more accessible and usable.

However, as indicated by Walker [9] "the final goal of sleep-dependent memory processing may not be the enhancement of individual memories in isolation, but, instead, their integration into a common schema, and by this enhancement, the facilitation of the development of universal concepts, a process that forms the basis of generalized knowledge and even creativity". This concept is supported by different experiments [10, 11] that verify that if a subject learns something, she might recall it well after a non-sleep series of hours. However, if there is a sleep interval between learning and recall, the ability to generalize these elements to new cases improves drastically. This provides evidence that processes during sleep are involved in the reinterpretation of prior experience, pointing towards a possible strategy followed during sleep at different time scales [12]. Initially novel individual item episodic memories are consolidated. Then, in a longer time scale and using these item memories before they are forgotten, a process of abstraction in terms of creating links to prior knowledge is started, leading to more adaptive semantic networks.

From another point of view, some of these processes have also been described in terms of the Simulation Hypothesis [13]. Following this hypothesis, metal imagery, such as that arising in dreams, is taken as simulation of perceptions and actions. In other words, the neural structures involved in perception and action are reactivated offline and these perceptions and actions lead to mental images instead of the actual interactions with the world. By means of the predictive associations between simulated perceptions and actions an agent can explore a simulated world [14], learning new behaviors and acquiring and generalizing experience by testing different situations.

Nevertheless, what is really relevant for us is that there seems to be a clear consensus on the necessary role of sleep in the consolidation of procedural and declarative memories. More importantly, sleep may permit building schemas of knowledge that lead to better modeling of the world and the discovery of novel solution insights. In other words, during sleep these processes tend to prepare the knowledge contained in memory to make it more accessible to the cognitive entity that will make use of it.

2   DREAM: Deferred Restructuring of Experience in Autonomous Machines

Assuming that natural cognitive systems work in the way commented above, it would be of great interest to explore whether some of these processes could be useful or advantageous when constructing artificial cognitive systems that can be used as robot brains. Previous work in this area has mostly concentrated on the creation of mental imagery in order to endow robots with planning capabilities. Examples can be found as far back as Mel's robot arm [15] or Nolfi and Tani's work [16]. Intrinsic creation of mental imagery is, in fact, almost a requirement within any advanced cognitive architecture, and there are some examples of cognitive architectures that allow for this property [17, 18]. Nevertheless, most of these architectures limit the use of this capability to planning actions they are going to perform during their online operation.

There are, however, some "proof of concept" papers (to our knowledge, very few) that do try to determine if it is advantageous for a robot to perform dream or sleep like processes in terms of mental imagery. One of the most recent is the work by [14]. These authors create an experimental setup where they investigate different ways of implementing phenomenological aspects of dreams in robots using an e-puck robot simulator and ESN reservoir based neural architectures for controlling them. The authors conclude that periods of dream-like processes make learning based on real inputs more efficient. However, they do not contemplate a complete cognitive architecture for the robots, nor do they address other processes, such as memory consolidation or restructuring that can occur during sleep.

The fact is that the need to act in a timely fashion in real robots running a cognitive architecture imposes constraints on the information available as well as on the computations that may be devoted to deciding actions, producing behavior structures or modeling the world. Thus, the models or behaviors obtained may not be the optimal or most generalizable. However, at the end of the day (or any other extended period of time), the robot will have acquired a lot of perceptual information on the world and on itself and it will have produced several models (often partial) and behavior structures (usually too context dependent) for the different contexts it has been faced with.

If this information and experience is not re-conditioned and generalized for reuse, the robot will have to start from scratch every time it is faced with a situation or context that is not very similar to one it has already seen, compromising its adaptation. Thus, a way to improve the learning capabilities of autonomous machines would be to somehow post process this knowledge to generate representations that can be readily and efficiently reused when facing new situations. This post processing can be thought of as a restructuring process over the knowledge (in terms of behavioral structures or models) and information (in terms of perceptual data) in order to represent it in ways that are more useful to it. This is what we have called Deferred Restructuring of Experience in Autonomous Machines (DREAM) and it seeks improvements with regards to generality, versatility and reusability.

In this paper we will consider an artificial Darwinian based cognitive mechanism, the Multilevel Darwinist Brain (MDB), and we will propose a series of offline mechanisms in the framework of the DREAM approach in order to explore the possibilities of the functionalities provided by sleeping and dreaming in order to make the cognitive architecture more efficient.

3   The Multilevel Darwinist Brain (MDB)

The Multilevel Darwinist Brain (MDB) is a cognitive architecture that allows an artificial agent to learn from its experience in a dynamic and unknown environment in order to fulfill its motivations or objectives. Although its basic features from a cognitive perspective have been tested in several robotic experiments, the MDB is in continuous development and improvement due to the high complexity of the cognitive processes it deals with. For a detailed description of the basic operation of the MDB we recommend [17] and for the last version of the architecture see [19].

Just to provide a brief description here, there are four basic elements in the MDB:

- *Models*: predictor structures acquired by interacting with the world and through evolutionary processes that conform the declarative knowledge an agent has. Three types of basic models are considered here: world, internal and satisfaction models. The world and internal models provide the predicted sensorial value in time t+1 from the sensorial value and the applied action in t. The satisfaction model predicts the satisfaction (degree of fulfillment of the motivations) of the robot that corresponds to a given set of external and internal sensing values.
- *Behaviors*: a behavior is a structure that provides the action to be applied in time t+1 from the sensorial input in t. They can be assimilated to the concept of policy in reinforcement learning terminology.
- *Episodes*: real world samples that are obtained from the robot sensors and actuators after applying an action.
- *Memories*: two main kinds of memory elements are considered: Long-Term (LTM) and Short-Term (STM) [19]
  - The STM is made up of a model memory, which contains models and behaviors that are relevant to the current task, and an episodic buffer (EB) that stores the last episodes experienced by the robot. The EB has a very limited capacity according to the temporal nature of the STM.
  - The LTM is made up of a declarative memory, which contains the models that have been consolidated in the learning process, due to their significance and reliability, together with their contexts, and a procedural memory that stores the consolidated behaviors, or skills.

Fig. 1 displays a functional diagram of the last MDB version, including the DREAM process that is the topic of this work. As we can see, the MDB is structured into three asynchronous time scales, one devoted to the execution of actions in the environment in real time (execution scale), the second to the learning of models (learning scale) and the third one to the processes of model and behavior improvement that we have associated to sleeping. The operation of the MDB (which can be seen in detail in [17] can be described in terms of these scales.

To provide the artificial organism with a fluid interaction with the world, it decides on its actions in the execution time scale by simply executing the current behavior. These actions produce effects on the world that are perceived and these episodes are stored in the STM episodic buffer (EB) if they pass an attention mechanism. In parallel, there is a background learning process (learning time scale) running that uses the STM (representation of reality) as a fitness function in order to evolve the populations of models (internal, world and satisfaction models) for a few generations. Not too many to avoid convergence towards a particular content of the STM. The best evaluated models at a given time are used to construct a simulation of the world that is used in order to evaluate the behavior population, which is also evolved in order to obtain the behaviors that produce the best expected satisfaction. When these behaviors improve on the current behavior, the current behavior is updated.

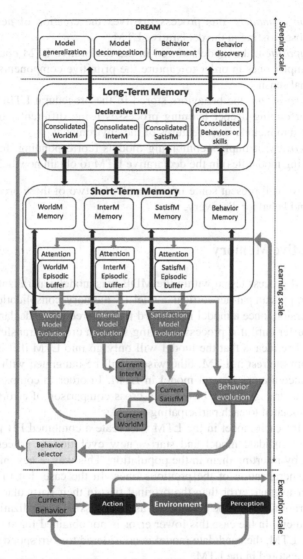

Fig. 1. Functional diagram of the MDB with the DREAM process

Also, whenever a set of models or a behavior have provided a successful and stable response in successive iterations of the MDB, they become candidates to be stored in LTM together with their associated context (EB). The models and their contexts that are finally stored in LTM [19] make up a declarative memory while the behaviors make up a procedural memory (where behaviors can be assimilated to learned skills).

The new scale that is incorporated here is devoted to the DREAM processes, and it can be seen in Fig. 1 denoted as sleep scale. These processes operate with the declarative and procedural LTM, so they depend on the success of the learning processes of the MDB. Four types of general processes have been considered:

1. *Generalization of models*: this process involves the creation of new models by combining those existing in the declarative LTM.
2. *Model decomposition*: the models stored in the declarative LTM could be decomposed into simpler ones in order to capture the primitive components of the external and internal sensing.
3. *Behavior improvement*: the behaviors stored in the procedural LTM could be improved by performing deeper learning processes using different models in LTM that allow them to include more features of the environment.
4. *Behavior discovery*: it implies combining models (corresponding, for instance, to different sensing modalities) in the declarative LTM to obtain new behaviors.

In this paper we will present some initial results for two of these processes: model generalization and behavior discovery.

4   Declarative Memory

The first DREAM process tested within the MDB was model generalization. Using as inspiration the hippocampal-neocortical model of memory consolidation [8], in the current MDB version, once a model is selected to be stored in the declarative LTM, it enters a LTM buffer until it is processed during sleep in order to transfer its characteristics to LTM. The idea is that the model will only go into LTM if it is functionally very distinct from the rest in LTM, otherwise it will be integrated with other models in order to produce a more general model in LTM. In order to compare models, we have developed a strategy that is based on a cross comparison of errors when active over the EBs associated to each participating model.

Specifically, for each model in the LTM we create a combined EB joining its EB with that of the candidate model and start a new evolutionary process using both models as seeds by inserting them in the population. This way, a new model could be obtained as a generalization of the previous ones. In the case that this new model provides a lower average error than the original two in their particular EBs in a low number of generations, it will be considered as a successful generalization and it will replace both of them. In the case this lower error is not obtained for any combination of models in the LTM, the candidate model is considered to correspond to a new context and it will be stored in the LTM.

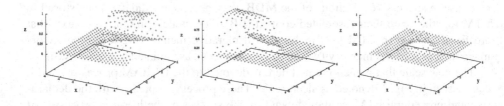

Fig. 2. Modeling provided by the original models (left, middle) and generalization (right)

To show the operation of this generalization process the following experiment has been carried out: we have created a sensorial pattern based on a 3D Gaussian bell function that simulates the world model a robot must learn using the MDB. In a first stage of the experiment, this function is modeled in the MDB using only samples from the left side of the bell while in a second stage only samples from the right side are used. This could correspond to a robotic learning process where an obstacle is partially in the dark from one side or the other depending on the light angle. In both cases, the world model is represented by a multilayer perceptron ANN of 2 inputs (x and y), one hidden layer of 4 neurons and 1 output (z). Evolution is performed using the Differential Evolution algorithm that evolves the weights of the ANN. It is carried out for 800 iterations of the MDB (800 actions are applied) and 10 generations per iteration using an EB of 30 episodes (the Gaussian bell is randomly sampled in each iteration) as the reference. The fitness is given by the error with respect to it. The left image of Fig. 2 contains the modeling provided by the best world model after evolution in the first stage (a continuous sampling of the function is executed in the model) and the middle image the modeling obtained in the second stage. As it can be seen, the models have learned the basic function shape and they are clearly complementary.

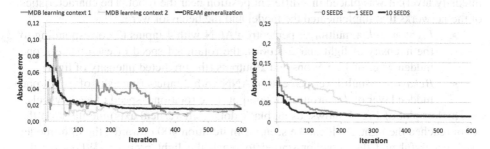

Fig. 3. Absolute error evolution for the DREAM generalization example

Let us assume that the model of the first stage is already in the LTM and the second one has been selected as candidate for entering the LTM in the learning scale of the MDB. The DREAM generalization process in this case implies creating a combined EB with the resulting episodes after the first two stages of evolution and launching a new evolutionary process using this combined EB as fitness while seeding the population with the previous two models. Fig. 3 left displays the evolution of the error in absolute value provided by this generalized model (black line) together with those obtained in the first and second stages of the experiment (dark and light grey lines respectively). If these three lines are compared it can be seen that the absolute error obtained by the generalized model is lower than the original ones on average soon and more stable. To appreciate the relevance of this generalization process, the right image of Fig. 2 contains the final modeling provided by the best model after the DREAM process that, as it can be seen, contains a complete representation of the Gaussian bell.

One could question whether there is any advantage in performing this generalization using the models as seeds in the evolving population, or whether it would be better to perform a new search process over the combined EB. In the right graph of Fig. 4 we have represented the evolution of the absolute error in this generalized evolution for three cases: no models are introduced as seeds in the population (light greay), one model of each stage is introduced (dark grey) and the two models are introduced until they constitute half of the population (black). What is relevant in this figure is that the two cases where the models are injected as seeds obtain the final stable error level (around 0.03) in a lot less iterations than the other approach.

5   Procedural Memory

With regards to procedural memory, we are going to consider a process of behavior discovery during the sleeping time scale. We have a robot (Pioneer 2DX simulated model) that during its on-line operation has learnt a behavior that allows it to catch a moving light (cylindrical) by means of two light sensors. In this case, the satisfaction was directly the average light intensity detected after applying the actions selected by the behavior. It is used as the fitness function for the behavior evolution. A light model and the behavior were obtained within the MDB with an EB of 40 samples concurrently, as explained in section 3. Every time the robot reached the light (maximum intensity level), it was placed in a different position near the robot. The characteristics of the networks that implemented the model and the behavior were:

- *Light model*: a multilayer perceptron ANN with 4 inputs (2 corresponding to the intensity of light and 2 actions, the rotational speed of each wheel), one hidden layer of 12 neurons and 2 outputs (the predicted intensity of light).
- *Behavior*: a multilayer perceptron ANN with 2 inputs (intensity of light), one hidden layer of 7 neurons and 2 outputs (the rotational speed of each wheel).

The left plot of Fig. 4 shows, using black dots, (left vertical axis) the iteration the robot reached the light. As it can be seen, from iteration 400 onwards, the light model was successful and the behavior started to reach the light properly. Whenever the MDB is in operation, it is learning models for all of its sensors, whether they are being used in the current behavior or not. In this case, during the process of learning the behavior related to the light sensors, the MDB also obtained a world model corresponding to the sonar sensors, which detect the cylinder. In this case, the sonar model was a 10-16-8 neuron multilayer perceptron ANN with 8 inputs corresponding to the frontal sensors and 2 to actions, the outputs are the predicted sonar values.

Consequently, during the sleep time scale, the MDB can use this sonar model as a simulator in order to complete the acquisition of behaviors corresponding to a sensing modality not used in real time operation. To do it, a new behavior is defined using an 8-8-2 multilayer perceptron ANN that inputs sonar values and outputs the rotational speed of each wheel. This new behavior is evolved in the DREAM time scale using the previously obtained sonar model to provide the predicted sonar values, being the satisfaction the average intensity value of the two frontal sensors (equivalent to the light sensor experiment). The grey points shown in the right plot of Fig. 4 (right vertical axis) correspond to the iteration where the robot reached the light (average intensity above a threshold). They are displayed in order to show that in this case only 66 iterations where required to obtain a successful behavior because in DREAM scale the models need not be obtained.

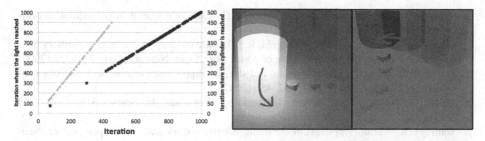

Fig. 4. Left: iterations where the light is reached using the light behavior (black) and the sonar one (grey). Right: sequences of actions for a Pioneer robot with both behaviors (light and sonar based).

The new behavior is stored in the LTM. When the robot starts interacting with the world again and requires this type of object catching behavior, it is selected very fast due to the fact that the behaviors in the LTM seed the population used during evolution. The right images of Fig. 4 display a typical sequence of actions of the Pioneer robot reaching the light in the learning stage and the execution of the behavior obtained during DREAM that uses the sonar sensors. As it can be seen, now the robot is able to catch a moving object with no light. It is important to note here that this behavior is complementary to the one it developed online and provides ways to perform the same task using different sensing modalities.

6 Conclusions

Sleeping seems to involve a series of cognitive processes that are of great importance for the adequate operation of the cognitive structures of humans when awake. These processes deal with the consolidation, generalization and overall preparation of the knowledge and experience acquired during the day for its more efficient use in subsequent learning and, in general, cognitive processes. In this paper, we have carried out an initial exploration of how sleep related processes could be used to an advantage in artificial cognitive architectures. In particular, we have proposed and tested two of sleep related mechanisms within the Multilevel Darwinist Brain cognitive architecture and shown how these mechanisms can lead to more efficient and adaptive behaviors in robots. This approach has been called DREAM, that is, Deferred Restructuring of Experience in Autonomous Machines. We are still in the first stages of exploring how DREAM like mechanisms can contribute to better and more efficient cognitive architectures, but we do believe that they can have an important impact on how memories are consolidated in these systems.

References

1. Walker, M.P., Stickgold, R.: Sleep, memory and plasticity. Annu. Rev. Psychol. 10, 139–166 (2006)
2. Paller, K.A., Wagner, A.D.: Observing the transformation of experience into memory. Trends Cogn. Sci. 6, 93–102 (2002)

3. Robertson, E.M., Pascual-Leone, A., Miall, R.C.: Current concepts in procedural consolidation. Nat. Rev. Neurosci. 5, 576–582 (2004)
4. Ellenbogen, J.M., Payne, J.D., Stickgold, R.: The role of sleep in declarative memory consolidation: Passive, permissive, active or none? Curr. Opin. Neurobiol. 16, 716–722 (2006)
5. Marshall, L., Born, J.: The contribution of sleep to hippocampus-dependent memory consolidation. Trends Cogn. Sci. 11, 442–450 (2007)
6. Miller, G.: Neuroscience. Hunting for meaning after midnight. Science 315, 1360–1363 (2007)
7. Squire, L.R.: Memory systems of the brain: A brief history and current perspective. Neurobiol. Learn Mem. 82, 171–177 (2004)
8. Moscovitch, M., Nadel, L.: Consolidation and the hippocampal complex revisited: In defense of the multiple-trace model. Curr. Opin. Neurobiol. 8, 297–300 (1998)
9. Walker, M.: The role of sleep in cognition and emotion. Ann. N. Y. Acad. Sci. 1156, 168–197 (2009)
10. Dumay, N., Gaskell, M.G.: Sleep-associated changes in the mental representation of spoken words. Psychol. Sci. 18, 35–39 (2007)
11. Ellenbogen, J., Hu, P., Payne, J.D., Titone, D., Walker, M.P.: Human relational memory requires time and sleep. Proc. Natl. Acad. Sci. 104, 7723–7728 (2007)
12. Tse, D., Langston, R.F., Kakeyama, M., Bethus, I., Spooner, P.A., et al.: Schemas and memory consolidation. Science 316, 76–82 (2007)
13. Hesslow, G.: The current status of the simulation theory of cognition. Brain Research 1428, 71–79 (2012)
14. Svensson, H., Thill, S., Ziemke, T.: Dreaming of electric sheep? Exploring the functions of dream-like mechanisms in the development of mental imagery simulations. Adaptive Behavior 21(4), 222–238 (2013)
15. Mel, B.W.: A connectionist model shed light on neural mechanisms for visually guided reaching. Journal of Cognitive Neuroscience 3, 273–292 (1991)
16. Nolfi, S., Tani, J.: Extracting regularities in space and time through a cascade of prediction networks: The case of a mobile robot navigating in a structured environment. Connection Science 11, 125–148 (1999)
17. Bellas, F., Duro, R.J., Faina, A., Souto, D.: Multilevel Darwinist Brain (MDB): Artificial Evolution in a Cognitive Architecture for Real Robots. IEEE Trans. on Autonomous Mental Development. 2(4), 340–354 (2010)
18. Kawamura, K., Dodd, W., Ratanaswasd, P., Gutierrez, R.A.: Development of a Robot with a Sense of Self. In: 6th IEEE CIRA, Espoo, Finland, June 27-30 (2005)
19. Bellas, F., Caamaño, P., Faiña, A., Duro, R.J.: Dynamic learning in cognitive robotics through a procedural long term memory. Evolving Systems 5(1), 49–63

Time in Consciousness, Memory and Human-Robot Interaction

Michail Maniadakis and Panos Trahanias

Computational Vision and Robotics Laboratory,
Institute of Computer Science,
Foundation for Research and Technology Helloas (FORTH)
Heraklion, Crete, Greece
{mmaniada,trahania}@ics.forth.gr

Abstract. Contemporary research endeavors aim at equipping autonomous robots with human-like cognitive skills, in an attempt to promote robotic intelligence and make artificial agents more natural and more human-friendly. However, despite the crucial role that sense of time has in our daily activities, the capacity of artificial agents to experience the flow of time remains largely unexplored. The inability of existing systems to perceive time acts as an obstacle in implementing conscious artificial agents that put their experiences on the past-present-future timeline and develop durable symbiotic relationships with humans. The present paper elaborates on time-cognition coupling suggesting that the equipment of artificial agents with human-like time perception and time processing capacities is a prerequisite for bringing robotic cognition close to human intelligence.

1 Introduction

Time perception is a fundamental component of cognition that structures the way we interpret procedures and events. As both perception and action evolve over time, timing is necessary to appreciate environmental contingencies, estimate relations between events and predict the effects of our actions. Since the day we are born, everyone's clock begins to run and our ability to perceive time links what we are to the past and the future, to our experiences and prospects.

Despite the fundamental role of time in human cognition it remains largely unexplored in the field of robotics. Surprisingly, there are not yet robotic systems equipped with temporal cognition, that is, which are aware of the notion of time as a unique entity that can be processed on its own right. Early works such as considering the integration of sensory-motor information over time [1], or turn taking [2], have not focused on sense of time and how artificial agents will acknowledge time as separate dimension of the world. A more explicit focus on the notion of time has self-organized in robotic agents solving a two-rule switching task, where duration is used to drive agent's decision in following either the one rule or the other [3,4]. In the last years we have developed a strong interest on temporal cognition investigating possible time representations

A.P. del Pobil et al. (Eds.): SAB 2014, LNAI 8575, pp. 11–20, 2014.

and duration processing mechanisms by considering some of the most widely used tasks by interval timing community, namely duration reproduction and duration comparison [5,6].

The current paper aims to present at the interdisciplinary audience of the SAB conference the key role of time perception in steering and improving the adaptivity of biological and artificial systems. More specifically, our intention is to make explicit that an animal or animat may exploit temporal information (e.g. how much time is required to accomplish a task) to better adapt its strategy towards a long-term goal. At the same time, considering the short-term aspects of life, time perception is necessary to make a system feel rush and accordingly adapt to emergency situations.

The present review elaborates on mind-time interactions, considering particularly the role of time in (i) developing consciousness and the sense of self, (ii) encoding, managing and processing past and future events, (iii) enhancing fluency in human-robot interaction. Additionally we discuss recent neurophysiological findings on time perception and we outline computational models addressing the interaction of time perception with other cognitive modalities, providing hints on equipping artificial agents with temporal cognition.

2   Time and Consciousness

Time perception is directly linked to consciousness because it makes us aware of change, movement, and succession across brief temporal intervals. By remaining conscious in the long-term we are able to experience the temporal framework and the evolution of events in the world. Sense of time supply us with access to our own past structuring our personality and the notion of self.

Traditional explanations on how the sense of self links to time perception make a division between the Moving-Time and Moving-Ego metaphors [7]. In the former, "time events" move with respect to a fixed observer from front (future) to back (past) (e.g. the winter went by), while in the latter the "observer" moves forward on the past-present-future timeline (e.g we are approaching the end of the year). In both cases there is a uni-directional flow of time relative to the observer. Directionality is a critical property that differentiates time from other senses (i.e. we can never experience a moment twice, but we can hear the very same tone as many time we want) suggesting that cognitive models should not consider time as one more typical system parameter.

According to Damasio, there are three levels of consciousness, namely protoself, core consciousness and extended consciousness [8]. Humans are assigned to the higher level, which assumes that the sense of self exceeds bodily states and is linked to historical times, enabling present to be associated with the past and the future. Animals are typically assigned to lower levels of consciousness, because they live their life being largely stuck in the present moment (i.e. be aware of only a short permanent present). In contrast, humans see the world from numerous time perspectives. It is our ability to travel backward and forward in subjective time, to recall or imagine events, that enables strong personal awareness [9]. Therefore time perception makes the difference.

By making artificial agents aware of and sensitive to the passage of time, we pave the way for enabling robots to recall/predict events and properly adapt to the heavily time structured human social life.

3   Time in Knowledge and Memory

Time plays a key role in the encoding of human memories and thus it is very surprising that, so far, knowledge has been encoded in artificial systems using flat, time-less representations that consider what and where, but not when. Even state of the art robots are not aware of the ordering of their experiences and cannot understand that what they perceive now might have been in a different state in the past. Only recently the EU funded project STRANDS has promised to initiate the 4D rather than 3D mapping of the world.

For humans, the ability to travel in the past is a highly integrative and constructive procedure that is based on the incremental synthesis of past events [10]. Interestingly, almost the same neural mechanisms are also employed when we try to predict future [11]. This suggests that robotic cognition may gain significantly by acquiring a mental time travel capacity that could subsequently support many other cognitive skills (mind reading, causal inferencing, etc.).

To accumulate knowledge over time, learning algorithms describe sequential changes in memory, triggered by the appearance of certain stimulus [12]. Temporal properties play a key role in improving the ability of artificial agents to encode new knowledge and be able to recall it based on either temporal (which city hosted SAB 2008?) or spatial (when SAB was in Osaka, Japan?) criteria.

In the opposite direction, our ability to forget over time enables the reorganization and better management of knowledge. The typical explanation of forgetting assumes information to decay over time making information held in short-term memory to be quickly forgotten unless it is constantly rehearsed or refreshed [13]. This is an issue that has recently attracted research interest in the field of robotics, with experimental works showing that robotic performance may significantly improve by means of forgetting unnecessary, erroneous, and expired data [14,15].

Given that knowledge sets the framework in which robots perceive, understand and act in the world, by considering the temporal aspects of knowledge and memories robots, will be capable to exploit the past in order to decide how to achieve certain goals in the future.

4   Symbiotic Human Robot Interaction

The core idea behind symbiotic human-robot interaction (HRI) regards the close and long-term coupling between humans and artificial agents. However, the majority of existing works assume interaction to evolve isolated from the ongoing and long lasting real world procedures. In order to develop robots that are actively integrated into the time-structured human life, artificial agents must be equipped with time processing skills, being capable to link their actions to the past and the future of the world. Broadly speaking, we can identify two dimensions in which time affects human-robot interaction.

- in dialogue management, where turn taking, action synchronization, and other short-term issues of multi-agent interaction are processed,
- in collaborative information processing, where the accumulated experiences of human-robot interaction lead to gradually more productive synergies between the two sides.

While an adequate number of works has explored the first dimension of human-robot interaction [16,17], the latter remains largely unexplored.

To highlight the role of time in synergetic HRI, we may consider a robotic assistant that helps its owner to prepare a dinner. The robot must recall past dinners with the participation of the visitors, bringing on its mind the type of wine they are fun of. To successfully recall the past, the robot is necessary to shift attention not in space (as usual) but in time, being able to recall information from a specific past period. The information gathered must be projected to the present, therefore affecting important aspects of the dinner preparation. The human mind is particularly efficient in jumping back and forth from one time period to the other, and our ability to perceive the interdependencies of asynchronous events enables their integration into a meaningful story that unfolds over time. Such a capacity is also crucial for artificial agents. By shifting attention to the past, the agent accomplishes time-based or context-based memory search, and by shifting attention to the future, the agent accomplishes action planning, targeting specific goals at specific moments in time.

Sense of time is also important for the here and now aspects of the interaction. Even if during an interaction session robot's attention may be focused on a past time period, a part of its mind must remain situated to the present dealing with real-time environment interaction issues. For example, time pressure significantly affects the way we choose and express actions. Therefore, in an emergency situation (e.g., barbecue meat is almost burned) the robot must not go for the more smooth or energy efficient solution, but for the faster solution.

Naturalistic multi-agent interaction involves a broad set of skills (e.g. perception, attention, memory storage and recall, future prediction, planning) with a strong temporal dimension that, if considered in computational implementations, has the potential to significantly improve human-robot synergies.

5   Time Perception Mechanisms in the Brain

Understanding the time processing mechanisms in the brain of animals and humans is a timely and very challenging issue that has attracted rapidly increasing interest in the neuroscience and cognitive science communities. Contemporary review papers and special journal issues have summarized and are testament to the new and burgeoning scientific findings in the field [18,19,20,21].

Over the past decade, a number of different brain areas have been implicated as key parts of a neural time-keeping mechanism, notably (among many others), event timing in the cerebellum [22], generalized magnitude processing for time, space and number in the right posterior parietal cortex [23,24], working memory related integration in the right prefrontal cortex [25,26], a right fronto-parietal network [27], coincidence detection mechanisms using oscillatory signals in fronto-striatal circuits [28], hippocampal time-cells focused on the relation of time and distance [29], as well as integration of ascending interoceptive (that is, body) signals in the insular cortex [30,31]. The participation of many brain areas in the processing of temporal information attest the key role of time in a broad range of cognitive capacities.

6   Computational Models of Time Perception

The following paragraphs summarize existing computational models dealing with the sense of time. The first part considers models of time perception that operate largely isolated from other cognitive skills, while the second addresses cognitive skills that have been extended in a temporal dimension.

Time/Duration Perception. In an attempt to explain where and how time is processed in the brain, a large number of neurocomputational models have been implemented, most of them concentrating on duration perception. Broadly speaking, two main approaches have been proposed in the literature to describe how our brain represents time [32,33]. The first is the dedicated approach (also known as extrinsic, or centralized) that assumes an explicit metric of time. The models included in this category employ mechanisms that are designed specifically to represent duration. Traditionally such models follow an information processing perspective in which pulses that are emitted regularly by a pacemaker are temporally stored in an accumulator, similar to a clock [34,35,36]. This has inspired the subsequent pacemaker approach that uses oscillations to represent clock ticks [37,38]. Other dedicated models assume monotonous increasing or decreasing processes to encode elapsed time [39,40]. The second approach includes intrinsic explanations (also known as distributed) that describe time as a general and inherent property of neural dynamics [41,42,43]. According to this approach, time is intrinsically encoded in the activity of general purpose networks of neurons. Therefore, rather than using a time-dedicated neural circuit, time coexists with the representation and processing of other external stimuli. However, besides the key assumption of multi-modal neural activity, the existing computational implementations of intrinsic interval timing models are not yet coupled with other cognitive or behavioral capacities within a broader functional context, and in that sense, the internal clock remains unaffected by outside processes. Only the Behavioral Theory of Timing [44] and the Learning to Time [45] make explicit coupling between time perception and behavior, assuming that the behavioral vocabulary of subjects and their current behavioral state support duration perception.

An attempt to combine dedicated and intrinsic approaches is provided by the Striatal Beat Frequency (SBF) model which assumes that timing is based on the coincidental activation of basal ganglia neurons by cortical neural oscillators [46,47]. The SBF model assumes a dedicated timing mechanism in the basal ganglia that is based on monitoring distributed neural activity in the cortex. Recently, SBF has been integrated into a generalized model of temporal cognition that subserves different aspects of perceptual timing, either duration based or beat-based [48]. In the same line, our recent work with simulated robotic agents has suggested a new biologically plausible mechanism for duration processing that incorporates both dedicated and intrinsic characteristics [49].

Cognitive Models Exploiting Sense of Time. Recently, an increasing number of computational cognitive models aim at integrating sense of time. The following list provides an outline of the existing approaches which accomplish early steps towards integrating time perception in intelligent artificial systems research:

- Time in decision making [3]. Artificial agents self-organize time perception capacity to support decision making.
- A grounded temporal lexicon [50]. Lingodroids (language learning robots) are employed to learn terms linking space and time.
- Interval timing grounded in motor activity [51]. Explore how body and arm movement serve as a rough temporal yardstick for time perception.
- Representation of duration [6]. Multimodal duration processing by artificial agents.
- Time perception as a secondary task [52]. Explore the coupling of interval timing, attention, perception and learning in the accomplishment of dual tasks.
- Past, Future Perception [53]. Predictable internal state dynamics result in significantly more robust systems, compared to equally performing memoryless systems which develop much more fragile internal mechanisms.
- Mental Time Travel [54]. Explore the ability to recall and potentially re-experience a previously experienced motion trajectory, by associating specific stimuli with specific memories.
- Learning Through Time [12]. Explore the temporal properties of learning by considering how the memory representation of stimulus changes over time.
- Forgetting [13]. Explaining how working memory evolves and reshapes through time.
- Memory Reconsolidation [55]. Episodic encoding based on the binding of events to their temporal context and learning-based memory reinstantiation.

As discussed above, time plays a key role in consciousness, memory and human-robot interaction. The integration of the above mentioned temporally extended cognitive capacities into a fully entimed system will pave the way for the next generation of robotic systems that will be actively integrated into human daily activities.

7   Implementing Temporal Cognition in Robotic Systems

The integration of the cognitive models summarized above is certainly not a straight forward procedure, given the heterogeneous computational approaches and the diverse assumptions adopted. However, there are directly applicable approaches that rely on conventional artificial intelligence methods e.g., temporal logic, or event calculus [56,57] that can significantly facilitate accomplishing time processing in robotic systems. It is surprising that despite the extensive experience that exists with such systems, the latter are rarely employed in robot implementations. However, it is noted that the use of time-stamps or other clock measures do not guarantee temporal cognition for artificial agents [58]. In fact, humans develop temporal cognition before being capable to use clocks, while animals that also perceive and process time cannot of course use clocks at all! Similar to robot vision, grabbing an image of RGB pixels, does not mean that thesystem is able to see and understand the world.

A crucial decision towards implementing artificial temporal cognition regards how time will be represented in the artificial mind. For example time-stamping and storing events in the level of milliseconds, implies that the robot will be aware of every single moment of its past (e.g. 6-months ago). Such an approach would render looking back in time computationally infeasible for artificial systems. Following a more biologically plausible approach, the perception of the past-present-future timeline assumes finer temporal granularity close to the present and a gradually coarser granularity when traveling backward and forward in time. This is the approachthat we follow in our ongoing work.

Overall, to proceed effectively towards equipping artificial agents with the ability to perceive and process time, we may consider the natural, developmental procedure of the human brain that enables time processing capacities to develop and gradually integrate with other cognitive skills. While primary sense of time matures very early in the human developmental procedure, our temporal cognition continuously improve until adolescence [59,60]. Following a similar procedure, computational implementations should first focus on basic skills such as duration processing or synchrony, then consider the wider timeline that spans over past present and future to explore time in memory, attention, learning, and action planning, proceed with time language interactions and finally consider how time integrates into complex cognitive capacities such as mind reading, or imagination.

8   Conclusions

Sense of time is without doubt not an optional extra but a necessity towards the development of truly autonomous and intelligent machines that are seamlessly and actively integrated into human societies. Evidently, if we are going to ever implement intelligent robots that live next to us and operate in a way comparable to humans, then these robots will be definitely equipped with advanced time perception and processing capacities. Systematic research efforts enabling artificial agents to consider the heavily time-structured human life are expected to provide new impetus in the way we study and implement intelligent systems, closing the gap between human and artificial cognition.

References

1. Nolfi, S., Marocco, D.: Evolving Robots Able To Integrate Sensory-Motor Information Over Time. Theory in Biosciences 120, 1–24 (2001)
2. Iizuka, H., Ikegami, T.: Adaptability and Diversity in Simulated Turn-taking Behavior. Artificial Life 10, 361–378 (2004)
3. Maniadakis, M., Trahanias, P., Tani, J.: Explorations on artificial time perception. Neural Networks 22, 509–517 (2009)
4. Maniadakis, M., Wittmann, M., Trahanias, P.: Time experiencing by robotic agents. In: Proc. 11th European Symposium on Artificial Neural Networks, pp. 429–434 (2011)
5. Maniadakis, M., Trahanias, P.: Experiencing and processing time with neural networks. In: Proc. 4th Int. Conf. on Advanced Cogn. Tech. and App. (2012)
6. Maniadakis, M., Trahanias, P.: Self-organized neural representation of time. In: Lee, M., Hirose, A., Hou, Z.-G., Kil, R.M. (eds.) ICONIP 2013. LNCS, vol. 8226, pp. 74–81. Springer, Heidelberg (2013)
7. Evans, V.: The Structure of Time. Language, meaning and temporal cognition. John Benjamins Publishing Company, Amsterdam (2004)
8. Damasio, A.: The feeling of what happens: Body and emotion in the making of consciousness. Vintage, London (2000)
9. Roberts, W.: Are animals stuck in time? Psychological Bulletin 128(3), 473–489 (2002)
10. Roberts, W., Feeney, M.: The comparative study of mental time travel. Trends in Cognitive Science 13(6), 271–277 (2009)
11. Hassabis, D., Kumaran, D., Vann, S., Maguire, E.: Patients with hippocampal amnesia cannot imagine new experiences. Proc. Natl. Acad. Sci. U.S.A. 104, 1726–1731 (2007)
12. Howard, M.: Mathematical learning theory through time. Journal of Mathematical Psychology (2014)
13. Oberauer, K., Lewandowsky, S.: Modeling working memory: A computational implementation of the time-based resource-sharing theory. Psychonomic Bulletin & Review 18(1), 10–45 (2011)
14. Freedman, S., Adams, J.: Filtering data based on human-inspired forgetting. IEEE Transactions on Systems, Man and Cybernetics: Part B - Cybernetics 41(6), 1544–1555
15. Gurrin, C., Lee, H., Hayes, J.: iforgot: A model of forgetting in robotic memories. In: 5th ACM/IEEE International Conference on Human-Robot Interaction, HRI 2010 (2010)
16. Holroyd, A., Rich, C., Sidner, C., Ponsler, B.: Generating connection events for human-robot collaboration. In: Proc. IEEE Int. Symp. on Robot and Human Interactive Communication, RO-MAN (2011)
17. Nikolaidis, S., Shah, J.: Human-robot teaming using shared mental models. In: IEEE/ACM International Conference on Human-Robot Interaction, Workshop on Human-Agent-Robot Teamwork (2012)
18. Szelag, E., Wittmann, M.: Time, cognition, thinking. Acta Neurobiologiae Experimentalis 64(3) (2004)
19. Meck, W.: Neuropsychology of timing and time perception. Brain & Cognition 58(1) (2005)
20. Crystal, J.: The psychology of time: A tribute to the contributions of russell m. church. Behavioural Processes 74(2) (2007)

21. Wittmann, M., van Wassenhove, V.: The experience of time: Neural mechanisms and the interplay of emotion, cognition and embodiment. Phil. Trans. Royal Society B 364, 1809–1813 (2009)
22. Ivry, R., Spencer, R.: The neural representation of time. Current Opinion in Neurobiology 14, 225–232 (2004)
23. Bueti, D., Bahrami, B., Walsh, V.: The sensory and association cortex in time perception. Journal Cognitive Neuroscience 20, 1054–1062 (2008)
24. Oliveri, M., Koch, G., Caltagirone, C.: Spatial temporal interactions in the human brain. Experimental Brain Research 195(4), 489–497 (2009)
25. Lewis, P., Miall, R.: Brain activation patterns during measurements of sub- and supra-second intervals. Neuropsychologia 41, 1583–1592 (2003)
26. Smith, A., Taylor, E., Lidzba, K., Rubia, K.: A right hemispheric frontocerebellar network for time discrimination of several hundreds of milliseconds. Neuroimage 20, 344–350 (2003)
27. Harrington, D., Haaland, K., Knight, R.: Cortical networks underlying mechanisms of time perception. Journal of Neuroscience 18, 1085–1095 (1998)
28. Hinton, S., Meck, H.: Frontal-striatal circuitry activated by human peak-interval timing in the supra-seconds range. Cognitive Brain Research 21, 171–182 (2004)
29. Kraus, B., Robinson, R., White, J., Eichenbaum, H., Hasselmo, M.: Hippocampal "time cells": Time versus path integration. Neuron 78(6), 1090–1101 (2013)
30. Craig, A.: Emotional moments across time: A possible neural basis for time perception in the interior insula. Phil. Trans. Royal Society B 364, 1933–1942 (2009)
31. Wittmann, M.: The inner experience of time. Phil. Tran. Royal Soc. B 364, 1955–1967 (2009)
32. Bueti, D.: The sensory representation of time. Frontiers in Integrative Neuroscience 5(34) (2011)
33. Ivry, R., Schlerf, J.: Dedicated and intrinsic models of time perception. Tr. in Cognitive Sciences 12(7), 273–280 (2008)
34. Woodrow, H.: The reproduction of temporal intervals. Journal of Experimental Psychology 13, 473–499 (1930)
35. Gibbon, J., Church, R., Meck, W.: Scalar timing in memory. In: Gibbon, J., Allan, L.G. (eds.) Timing and Time Perception, pp. 52–77. New York Academy of Sciences (1984)
36. Droit-Volet, S., Meck, W., Penney, T.: Sensory modality and time perception in children and adults. Behav. Process 74, 244–250 (2007)
37. Miall, C.: The storage of time intervals using oscillating neurons. Neural Computation 1, 359–371 (1989)
38. Large, E.: Resonating to musical rhythm: Theory and experiment. In: Grondin, S. (ed.) Psychology of Time, pp. 189–232 (2008)
39. Staddon, J., Higa, J.: Time and memory: Towards a pacemaker-free theory of interval timing. J. Exp. Anal. Behav. 71(2), 215–251 (1999)
40. Simen, P., Balci, F., de Souza, L., Cohen, J., Holmes, P.: A model of interval timing by neural integration. J. Neuroscience 31, 9238–9253 (2011)
41. Dragoi, V., Staddon, J., Palmer, R., Buhusi, C.: Interval timing as an emergent learning property. Psychol. Review 110(1), 126–144 (2003)
42. Karmarkar, U.R., Buonomano, D.V.: Timing in the absence of clocks: Encoding time in neural network states. Neuron 53(3), 427–438 (2007)
43. Wackermann, J., Ehm, W.: The dual klepsydra model of internal time representation and time reproduction. Journal of Theoretical Biology 239(4), 482–493 (2006)

44. Killeen, P., Fetterman, J.G.: A behavioral theory of timing. Psychological Review 95(2), 274–295 (1988)
45. Machado, A.: Learning the temporal dynamics of behavior. Psychological Review 104, 241–265 (1997)
46. Matell, M., Meck, W.: Cortico-striatal circuits and interval timing: Coincidence detection of oscillatory processes. Cogn. Brain Res. 21, 139–170 (2004)
47. Meck, W., Penney, T., Pouthas, V.: Cortico-striatal representation of time in animals and humans. Current Opinion in Neurobiology 18(2), 145–152 (2008)
48. Teki, S., Grube, M., Griffiths, T.: A unified model of time perception accounts for duration-based and beat-based timing mechanisms. Frontiers in Integrative Neuroscience 5(90) (2012)
49. Maniadakis, M., Hourakis, E., Trahanias, P.: Robotic interval timing based on active oscillations. In: Proc. International Conference on Timing and Time Perception, pp. 72–81 (2014)
50. Schulz, R., Wyeth, G., Wiles, J.: Are we there yet? grounding temporal concepts in shared journeys. IEEE Transactions on Autonomous Mental Development 3(2), 163–175 (2011)
51. Addyman, C., French, R., Mareschal, D., Thomas, E.: Learning to perceive time: A connectionist, memory-decay model of the development of interval timing in infants. In: Proc. 33rd Annual Conference of the Cognitive Science Society, COGSCI (2011)
52. Taatgen, N., van Rijn, H., Anderson, J.: An integrated theory of prospective time interval estimation: The role of cognition, attention and learning. Psychological Review 114(3), 577–598 (2007)
53. Choe, Y., Kwon, J., Chung, J.: Time, consciousness, and mind uploading. International Journal of Machine Consciousness 4(1), 257–274 (2012)
54. Hasselmo, M.E.: A model of episodic memory: Mental time travel along encoded trajectories using grid cells. Neurobiology of Learning and Memory 92(4), 559–573 (2009)
55. Sederberg, P., Gershman, S., Polyn, S., Norman, K.: Human memory reconsolidation can be explained using the temporal context model. Psychon Bull. Rev. 18(3), 455–468 (2011)
56. Brandano, S.: The event calculus assessed. In. In: Proc. Eighth International Symposium on Temporal Representation and Reasoning (2001)
57. Fisher, M., Gabbay, D., Vila, L.: Handbook of Temporal Reasoning in Articial Intelligence. Elsevier, Amsterdam (2005)
58. Pouthas, V., Perbal, S.: Time perception does not only depend on accurate clock mechanisms but also on unimpaired attention and memory processes. Acta Neurobiol. Exp. 64, 367–385 (2004)
59. Droit-Volet, S.: Child and time. In: Vatakis, A., Esposito, A., Giagkou, M., Cummins, F., Papadelis, G. (eds.) Time and Time Perception 2010. LNCS, vol. 6789, pp. 151–172. Springer, Heidelberg (2011)
60. Tucholska, K., Gulla, B.: Children's time experience and childhood memories legal aspects. In: First International Conference on Time Perspective (2012)

Non-representational Sensorimotor Knowledge

Thomas Buhrmann[1] and Ezequiel Di Paolo[1,2]

[1] IAS Research Centre, University of the Basque Country, Spain
thomas.buehrmann@google.com
[2] Ikerbasque, Basque Foundation for Science, Spain

Abstract. The sensorimotor approach argues that in order to perceive one needs to first "master" the relevant sensorimotor contingencies, and then exercise the acquired practical know-how to become "attuned" to the actual and potential contingencies a particular situation entails. But the approach provides no further detail about how this mastery is achieved or what precisely it means to become attuned to a situation. We here present an agent-based model to show how sensorimotor attunement can be understood as a dynamic and non-representational process in which a particular sensorimotor coordination is enacted as a response to a given environmental context, without requiring deliberative action selection.

Keywords: Sensorimotor contingencies, know-how, mastery, attunement.

1 Introduction

The sensorimotor approach to perception argues that in order to perceive one must have "mastered" the relevant sensorimotor contingencies (SMCs), i.e. one must acquire a kind of practical know-how, or implicit knowledge, of the laws governing the co-relation between bodily movement and associated sensory stimulation [1]. Moreover, to perceive here and now one has to exercise or deploy the mastered know-how and "tune into" the actual and potential contingencies of the current situation (ibid.). But the primary literature on the subject is mostly silent on the how this mastery is achieved, what form the practical know-how might take, or what kind of process the notion of attunement refers to. The purpose of this paper is to illustrate with a model what it might mean to exercise one's practical know-how in order to became attuned to a situation and enact the appropriate SMCs. But since the notion of attunement is tightly linked to that of mastery we have to first discuss the relation between the two concepts. In order to develop some intuition as to how they are to be understood, we can take a look at how they are used:

> "Over the course of life, a person will have encountered myriad visual attributes and visual stimuli, and each of these will have particular sets of sensorimotor contingencies associated with it. Each such set will have been recorded and will be latent, potentially available for recall: the brain thus has mastery of all these sensorimotor sets. But when a particular attribute is currently being seen, then the particular sensorimotor contingencies associated with it are no longer latent, but are actualized, or being currently made use of. [...] among all

A.P. del Pobil et al. (Eds.): SAB 2014, LNAI 8575, pp. 21–31, 2014.

previously memorized action recipes that allow you to make lawful changes in sensory stimulation, only some are applicable at the present moment. The sets that are applicable now are characteristic of the visual attributes of the object you are looking at, and their being currently exercised constitutes the fact of your visually perceiving that object." (ibid., p. 945)

"[...] seeing is constituted by the brain's present attunement to the changes that *would* occur as a consequence of an action on the part of the perceiver" (ibid., p. 968, italics added)

It is clear that "mastery" is supposed to refer to the "accommodation" of certain regularities in the environment, and attunement to the exploitation of these regularities. But "accommodation" in this context does not necessarily mean that the contingent aspects of the environmental regularities are stored internally by the agent, but simply that the agent has undergone some changes such that whenever the regularities present themselves in a new situation, the agent is able to re-enact sensorimotor engagements that have previously been adequate in similar sensorimotor situations. It is also implied that the act of exercising one's SM knowledge is not a deliberative process of consciously weighing different possible SM coordinations to engage in. It rather seems to be an automatic process in which the right coordination is solicited as a response to a particular situation, in other words a kind of "resonance" between environment and agent. Moreover, from the second quote it follows that the exercise of my know-how can be counterfactual, i.e. my perception of possibilities for interaction with an object depends not only on my current engagement with it, but also on my practical knowledge of properties of the object that are not directly available.

Before describing a dynamic model that we think captures the essence of the process of attunement, we draw on Merleau-Ponty's account of skill acquisition [2–4] to further elucidate some of these notions. Three aspects characterise the learning of sensorimotor skills according to Merleau-Ponty. Firstly, in the acquisition of everyday skills, the accumulation of experience serves to discriminate situations that solicit a particular response with increasing specificity. Secondly, experience also allows a person to incrementally refine her dispositions to respond to these solicitations. And thirdly, behavioural responses to a situation take the form of movement towards the completion of a Gestalt, or equilibrium, to which the body tends without the need to mentally represent it. Though still a rather abstract account of skill acquisition, translating these three elements into dynamical systems terminology allows us to arrive at a description that will be useful in the analysis and interpretation of models addressing the issues of mastery and attunement.

In correspondence to the three aspects, firstly, if we consider an agent as a dynamical system coupled to its environment, then different environmental conditions, reflected in different sensory inputs, can result in the divergence of initially identical agent states. At a future point in time, therefore, the agent can react to the same sensory stimulus in different ways, as the accumulated history of its coupling with the environment has left the agent in different parts of its state space. In other words, the accumulation of experience allows the agent to discriminate between different contexts when exposed to identical sensory perturbations. Secondly, the behaviour of the agent as a dynamical system depends on its limit sets. Since through continued environment interaction the agent is able to reach different areas of state space, from these different initial conditions the agent may then follow different behavioural tendencies as determined by its attracting and repelling sets. Experience therefore can also serve to tune those limit sets such that the agent's movement through state space corresponds to the desired response that a given situation solicits. And thirdly, the agent's movements are fully determined by the relaxation of its dynamics towards the limit set in whose basin it finds itself at any given time. And the agent can not in any meaningful way be said to represent what the final state is that it is tending towards.

In short, the learning of a SM skill, in this view, corresponds to the tuning of the agent's dynamical landscape such that different environmental contexts leave the agent in different parts of state space, and such that the appropriate response corresponds to a particular trajectory of the dynamics when relaxing towards equilibrium. We would like to suggest here then, that in the process of mastery an agent's dynamical landscape is shaped over time to incrementally refine the discrimination of and response to different environmental situations; and that attunement is a process of interaction with the environment, such that a particular situation solicits the appropriate sensorimotor coordination.

We next describe a model to illustrate this latter interpretation of attunement in more detail.

2   Materials and Methods

The model presented here consists of an agent artificially evolved to identify only through touch the properties of a planar surface presented at different relative orientations and positions. After a period of unconstrained interaction with the surface, the agent has to demonstrate that is has retained something about its properties by producing movements following the orientation of the surface without the surface being present any longer (i.e. without the corresponding sensory stimulation). In other words, the agent has to re-enact the now invisible surface, or act as if it was still present. Note that we consider the evolved agent as already having mastered the required skill. The analysis of the agent's behaviour focuses on how the acquired know-how is exercised.

The model is summarised in panel A of Figure 1. The agent's body is a two-joint arm controlled by a continuous-time recurrent neural network [5] and equipped with a touch sensor (pink, dotted line). The environment consists of a planar surface (green line) whose position and orientation relative to the arm can vary. The agent's touch sensor can register the distance to the surface when in close proximity, but the arm can freely pass through it. The agent's neural network has a fully connected hidden layer receiving three inputs: the arm's two joint angles $\theta_{1,2}$ and the distance D between end-effector and surface as measured by the sensor. Two output neurons are fully connected to the hidden layer and control the desired joint angles $\theta^d_{1,2}$. These are transformed by PD controllers into joint torques that are applied to the arm (blue arrows) to produce the required movement. The arm dynamics are given by a common model derived from Newton-Euler equations and d'Alembert's Principle (for details see [6]). The parameters of the PD controllers were tuned by hand to achieve a somewhat underdamped response.

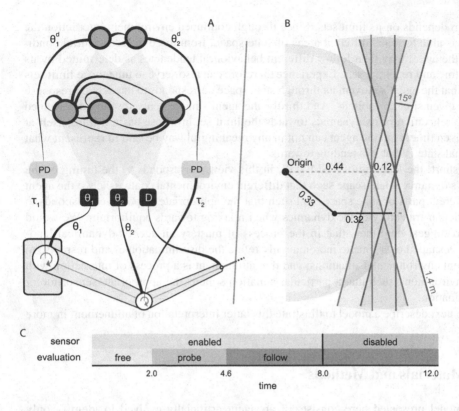

Fig. 1. Experimental setup. A: two-joint planar robot arm controlled by PDs whose set points (desired joint angles $\theta^d_{1,2}$) are determined by the outputs of a recurrent neural network. B: Dimensions of the arm and range of surface positions and orientations. Surfaces are presented at two positions and orientations covering a range of 30 degrees. C: time course of each trial showing the progression of evaluation phases and the state of the sensor.

All nodes in the agent's neural network are modelled as leaky integrators:

$$\tau_i \dot{y}_i = -y_i + \sum_{j=1}^{n} w_{ji} \sigma(y_j + \theta_j)$$

where y_i is the activation of neuron i, $\tau_i \in [0.01, 4]$ its time constant, $w_{ji} \in [-10, 10]$ the strength of the connection from neuron j to i, $\theta_j \in [-10, 10]$ a bias term, and $\sigma(x) = 1/(1 + e^{-x})$ a sigmoidal activation function. Both arm and neural dynamics are Euler integrated with a step size of 0.05.

The surface can vary in position and angle, and a unique combination is tested in each experimental trial. The range of surfaces evaluated is shown in panel B of Figure 1. The arm (shown in black) at maximum extension has a length of 0.65 units (indicated by the light grey half-disk). The distance sensor is attached at the end of the arm and can sense objects up to 0.05 units ahead (dark grey half-disk). Its response signal is inversely proportional to the sensed distance and scaled to the range [0, 1]. Surfaces are presented at two different positions (0.44 and 0.56 units from the arm's origin) and are 1.4 units in length. The angular range covered by the surfaces is $30°$ ($0 \pm 15°$). Two more surfaces per position are used in the experiment (at $\pm 7.5°$) but not shown here for clarity.

The task is to move the agent's end effector along the particular surface presented in each trial, even after its touch sensor is disabled. A version of the microbial genetic algorithm [7] is used to search for neural network parameters that allow the agent to solve this task. Each candidate solution is evaluated on 10 trials, in each of which the agent is presented with a different surface (2 positions x 5 orientations). The time course of fitness evaluation in each trial is shown in panel C of Figure 1. During the first 2 seconds the agent's movements are unconstrained, i.e. its behaviour does not contribute to its measured fitness. During the "probe" phase (2.6 s), the agent is rewarded for proximity to the surface but is otherwise free to move in an arbitrary manner. Its fitness in this period is equal to the end effector's average proximity to the surface (measured using the shortest distance). In the "follow" phase (last 4 seconds), the agent's fitness is determined by the combination of average proximity and the end effector's average velocity parallel to the surface (measured as the absolute length of the projection of the velocity vector onto the surface). After blackout, the agent can no longer sense the surface, yet has to keep moving along it (e.g. unidirectional or by oscillating back and forth in the corresponding plane). The total fitness of the agent in a single trial is the average of the fitness achieved in the probe and follow periods, and the overall fitness across all trials is equal to the minimum of individual trial fitnesses.

Given this experimental setup, there are two types of solutions to the task. After blackout, i.e. when the agent is "touch-blind" and has to re-enact the previously encountered surface orientation, the only sensory inputs available are the agent's current joint angles. Hence, if the agent were to rely on sensory inputs only to discriminate the different surfaces and produce a different SM coordination in response, this would imply that the joint configurations at the time of blackout would have to be unique for all surfaces encountered. If, in contrast, the joint configurations at blackout are not unique, then a successful agent must have used the initial exploration phase to reach different parts of its state space, such that different behaviours can be produced in response to identical sensory states. Such a process of state differentiation in covariation with relevant environmental variables we would then be happy to label "attunement".

3 Results

Successful agents evolved reliably with as few as 3 hidden neurons, but better performance could be achieved with a larger number. In the following we present results for an agent with 8 hidden neurons, which achieved a fitness of 82%.

3.1 Evolved Behaviour

In panels A-D of Figure 2 we show typical examples of the agent's end effector trajectories (grey, darker shades indicating greater touch response) overlaid on top of each corresponding environmental surface (red). The data is shown in joint space (θ_2 vs. θ_1), i.e. the red lines correspond to those joint configurations the arm would have to adopt to reach points on the surface. The left and right column show data for the two extremal surface orientations. The first and second row correspond to surfaces at the closer and farther distance respectively. Note that the simple planar environmental surfaces are in fact complex curves in motor space; and that surface orientation and position in Cartesian space seem to become surface position and scale in motor space respectively.

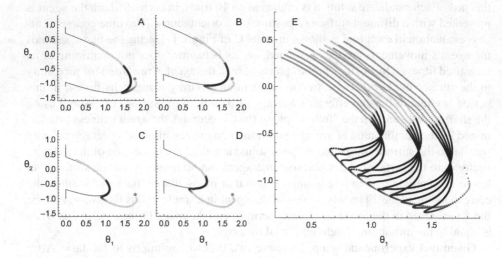

Fig. 2. Joint space trajectories of successfully evolved agent. A-D: Shown in red are those joint configurations that the agent would have to adopt to reach points on the surface, i.e. the planar surface translated into joint space. Overlayed in grey are the performed trajectories, with darker shades indicating greater touch sensor activity. Green markers indicate the initial position. A and B correspond to surfaces at different orientations (+- 15 degrees). C and D correspond to the same orientations as A and B respectively, but at a greater surface distance (+ 0.12). E: Trajectories for three surface positions (in red, green and blue) and five orientations, darker shades again indicating greater touch response.

Inspecting the trajectories we observe that the agent initially performs a stereotypical transient that eventually makes contact with each surface at a point that depends on the configuration of the surface (the trajectories turn from grey to black here). All points of first contact occur at the "lower" end of the area of highest curvature. After contact has been established, the agent uses its sensor to move the end effector along the surface in a single direction. Finally, when the sensor is disabled (trajectories turn grey again), the agent continues to move along the opposing side of the surface. While towards the end of the trial the agent begins to deviate from the surface, for a significant time after blackout the agent manages to follow it well.

At first glance the observed behaviour might not seem remarkable. However, the agent has control only over the position of the arm in joint space. Hence to follow the curvature of the surface, the neural network has to produce a complex time-series of joint angles such that the corresponding end-effector positions lie on that same curve.

In other words, after blackout the agent cannot rely on some form of inertia to keep it moving along the required curve. Nor can the agent simply hold certain variables fixed in order to keep moving in the same direction, as would be the case for a wheeled robot following a straight line for example.

The most important aspect of the observed behaviour is the fact that for each surface the agent produces a different trajectory after blackout, even though the touch sensor returns the same signal in all cases. This difference in SM behaviour in response to different surfaces becomes more salient when we draw all trajectories in a single figure, as shown in panel E for three different surface positions and five orientations each. We observe that some end effector trajectories cross each other in motor space but subsequently follow different paths. Since during this phase in the trial the same joint angles also serve as the only inputs to the agent's neural network (motor and sensory space are the same), it is already clear that the behaviour cannot be determined by instantaneous sensory input alone (since the same sensory input here leads to different behavioural responses). Instead, the differentiation of identical sensory configurations must be based on the history of the agent's engagement with the surface, as accumulated in the agent's state.

3.2   Generalization

Before identifying what sort of mechanism underlies the agent's unique behavioural response to identical sensory stimulations, we will demonstrate how the agent's performance generalises to a larger range of surface configurations than encountered during evolution, and identify the kind of features the agent might use to achieve this.

In panel A of Figure 3 we plot a heatmap of the agent's fitness as a function of surface orientation (horizontal axis) and position (vertical axis) at 30 different values each. The surface configurations used during evolution are located at the intersections of the red lines. It is clear that the agent establishes successful interactions with the surface over a wide range of surface configurations.

This task would be relatively simple if there existed a simple, instantaneous sensory feature that uniquely identifies each of the 900 tested surfaces. For example, since the agent initially performs a stereotypical transient, one could imagine that the time of first contact with the surface might be unique, or equivalently the joint configuration at this point in time; or, perhaps, the joint angles at the point when the sensor is disabled.

To see whether this is the case, in panel B of Figure 3 we plot for each of the 900 surface configurations a point whose coordinates are the time of first contact (t_c), as well as the state of the two joint angles when the sensor is disabled (denoted by $\theta'_{1,2}$). One can observe that the resulting points lie on a curved surface that folds back on itself in the t_c dimension. From the curvature of this manifold two implications can be derived. Firstly, there is no unique time of first contact across all surfaces (e.g. the top part of the manifold is curved such that points in closer and farther regions relative to the plane of the screen can have identical t_c coordinates). This can in fact be seen already in panel E of Figure 2, where trajectories for different surfaces split from the initial transient at the same time. It follows that the state of the proprioceptive joint sensors at this time cannot be unique. Secondly, because of the fold, the joint angle configuration $\theta'_{1,2}$ when the sensor is disabled does not uniquely identify each surface either.

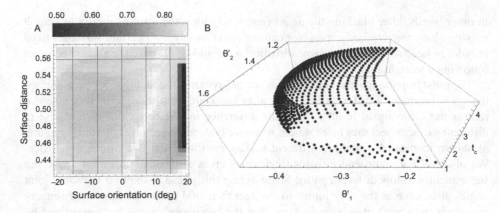

Fig. 3. Performance for 900 different surface configurations (30 orientations x 30 positions). A: heatmap of fitness achieved for each surface (for fitness scale see colour bar shown above, theoretical maximum = 1.0). The intersections of red lines indicate the 10 surfaces encountered during evolution. The dark area on the right corresponds to surfaces that the agent failed to re-enact. B: Scatter plot showing for each of the 900 surfaces a 3d point whose coordinates are the time of first contact between end effector and surface (t_C), and the joint configuration of the arm when the touch sensor is disabled ($\theta'_{1,2}$).

What is unique, however, is the combination of these two features, as there are no two points that coincide in both t_c and $\theta'_{1,2}$. It is clear that there must be some combination of features that can be used to distinguish all surfaces, as otherwise the agent would not be able to solve the task. The question is how the agent manages to retain information about the initial contact such as to respond appropriately later on when the sensor is disabled. In other words, how does the agent integrate sensory signals over time such that it can respond uniquely to ambiguous sensory information at the time of sensor blackout?

3.3 Neural Mechanism Underlying Surface Disambiguation

To better understand how the agent differentiates between surfaces even when instantaneous sensory feedback is not unique we look at the agent's dynamics in higher dimensions. Figure 4.A shows a projection of the agent's state that consists of the two joint angle sensors ($\theta_{1,2}$) and the output of a hidden neuron (h_1). Lines of the same colour correspond to trials where surfaces are positioned at the same distance but oriented differently. Colour shade varies with orientation, and different colours correspond to different surface positions. Black dots mark the time when the sensor is disabled.

Starting from a common initial position, the combination of all initial transients forms an arc that traces the stereotypical movement pattern exhibited by the agent if no surface was present. For different surfaces, then, the trajectories separate from this arc at different points, namely the point at which contact is made with the surface. One can observe that trajectories belonging to surfaces of different orientations but identical

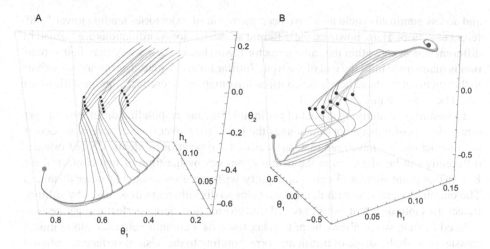

Fig. 4. Three-dimensional projection of the agent's neural state onto the two proprioceptive input neurons ($\theta_{1,2}$) and a hidden neuron (h_1). A: trajectories for three different surface positions (blue, green and red) and five different orientations each (shading of colour changes with surface angle). Black markers indicate the point of touch sensor deactivation and a grey marker the common initial state. B: Trajectories for two surface positions over a period of 50 s. A red marker indicates the common attractor position.

distances (i.e. those of the same colour) are already ordered at this time. In other words, the time of first contact correlates with surface orientations.

However, there are also trajectories that start diverging at the same point, even though the corresponding surfaces are located in different positions (differently coloured lines); i.e. trajectories belonging to different surface positions are still partly "entangled". During the period of sensor-based surface interaction, however, these trajectories eventually become disentangled, forming clearly separated bundles. For each surface position corresponding trajectories now form curved manifolds that lie parallel to each other, and in each of which trajectories are ordered by surface orientation. Thus when viewed from certain angles or in certain projections, trajectories belonging to different manifolds might seem to cross (like in Figure 2), while in fact being well separated in higher dimensions. Finally, just before the sensor is disabled, each manifold is being twisted. This preserves the established ordering, but ensures that subsequent parts of the trajectories are shaped such that their projections into Cartesian space are approximately straight (like the corresponding surface).

What keeps the trajectories separate after the sensor is disabled? Do they relax into different steady-states? To answer this question we observe the dynamics beyond the duration of the trial with the sensor remaining off. This makes the agent an autonomous system, which should eventually reach a steady state. The result can be seen in panel B of Figure 4, which shows the same projection as panel A, but from a different angle and for clarity only two surface positions. One can see that within the plotted duration of time, the agent approximately reaches steady-state, and in particular the same stable attractor for all trajectories. In principle the meticulous ordering of trajectories within and across manifolds could also have been the result of trajectories tending towards different attractors. Here, however, the different sensorimotor coordinations are formed by different transients within the same attractor basin, but in such a way that their separation is maintained until the end of the trial. Similar forms of state-determined sensitivity to the environment have been studied using information-theoretic techniques [8], which could be of use in this case as well.

In summary, underlying the act of distinguishing and responding differently to various surface positions and orientations is the integration over time of several aspects of the interaction. We have seen that surfaces that are positioned identically but oriented differently can be identified in the neural dynamics by the time of first contact alone. But at this point there still exists ambiguity with surfaces located at other distances. The ongoing interaction with the surface helps to disambiguate these cases by splitting trajectories into different manifolds. All trajectories now being perfectly separated and ordered in state space allows them to relax towards a common attractor along unique transients, with the shape of transients corresponding to the desired surface orientation.

4   Discussion

Our purpose has been to illustrate via a minimal model what it means to become attuned to a situation and enact the appropriate SMCs. We have shown that attunement can be interpreted as a continuous process of agent-environment interaction such that different situations are discriminated via the separation of the agent's dynamics. As a result, unique behavioural responses can be enacted in the form of particular transients during the relaxation towards equilibrium. Mastery of SMCs, then, corresponds to the process that shapes the dynamical landscapes of an agent such that attunement is possible.

As noted in the introduction, the dynamical process can be interpreted as a minimal example of Merleau-Ponty's motor intentionality, and thereby illustrate how agents exhibit embodied "purposeful" behaviours, without representing environmental features or explicit goals. Just like, for example, a tennis player who performs his serve or return without having to contemplate each required step, nor the details of the ideal posture to adopt when hitting the ball, the performance of a SM skill is more like a habitual relaxation towards an optimal movement "gestalt" that is only implicit in agent-environment dynamics, and which is solicited by a certain situation in the world.

Our model does not introduce new dynamical phenomena that we suppose to underlie the process of attunement. State retention and differentiation are well-known aspects of dynamical systems. We also do not advocate the particular methodology adopted here over other alternatives for investigating SMCs, such as information-theoretic analysis [8]. Nor did we aim to add to the already extensive catalogue of minimally cognitive behaviours that even simple dynamical agents can exhibit. The purpose, rather, was to clarify a core concept of the sensorimotor approach to perception, namely that of attunement. We believe that the methodology has been adequate, and the results sufficient, to show that the selection and exercise of SMCs can be understood as a dynamical process that does not require a dedicated mechanism or organisational level at which SMCs are "represented" (in any non-trivial sense of the term), nor the invocation of levels of explanation other than that of sensorimotor relations. Though the different

SMCs enacted by our agent were solutions to variants of the same task, this does not limit the applicability of our interpretation (for enactment of radically different SMCs see e.g. [9]). Equally, while for the investigated task successful agents' dynamics transiently separated into different manifolds depending on the environment, other manners of separating and organizing dynamics (e.g. by attractor basin) are also compatible with our account of attunement.

We have not here provided a model of how SM skills are mastered, i.e., how the dynamical landscape of the agent is altered through experience (the evolutionary search employed here to identify an appropriate agent is not meant to model the process of mastery). Yet we believe that simple models of the kind presented can contribute to filling in the gaps in sensorimotor theory. Not only by making more explicit what we mean when we talk about notions such as "mastery" or "attunement", but also by deriving implications that only become clear when these notions are operationalised [10]. One such implication is that sensorimotor theory does not have to evoke explicit representational vehicles, nor deliberative processes of action selection to account for the acquisition and exercise of SMCs. This lends further evidence to a radical reading of sensorimotor theory [11], which rejects the role of contentful representations.

Acknowledgements: Thanks to Randall Beer and Eduardo Izquierdo for their comments on an early draft of this work. This work is funded by the eSMCs: Extending Sensorimotor Contingencies to Cognition project, FP7-ICT-2009-6 no: 270212.

References

1. O'Regan, J., Noë, A.: A sensorimotor account of vision and visual consciousness. Behavioral and Brain Sciences 24, 939–1031 (2001)
2. Merleau-Ponty, M.: Phenomenology of Perception, 2nd edn. Routledge (2002)
3. Dreyfus, H.L.: Intelligence without representation. Merleau-Ponty's Critique of Mental Representation. Phenomenology and the Cognitive Sciences 1(4), 367–383 (2002)
4. Kelly, S.D.: Merleau-Ponty on the body. Ratio 15(4), 376–391 (2002)
5. Beer, R.D.: On the dynamics of small continuous-time recurrent neural networks. Adapt. Behav. 3(4), 469–509 (1995)
6. Hollerbach, M.J., Flash, T.: Dynamic interactions between limb segments during planar arm movement. Biological Cybernetics 44(1), 67–77 (1982)
7. Harvey, I.: The microbial genetic algorithm. In: Kampis, G., Karsai, I., Szathmáry, E. (eds.) ECAL 2009, Part II. LNCS, vol. 5778, pp. 126–133. Springer, Heidelberg (2011)
8. Beer, R., Williams, P.: Information processing and dynamics in minimally cognitive agents. Cognitive Science (in press, 2014)
9. Izquierdo, E., Buhrmann, T.: Analysis of a dynamical recurrent neural network evolved for two qualitatively different tasks: Walking and chemotaxis. In: Bullock, S., et al. (eds.) Artificial Life XI: Proceedings of the Eleventh International Conference on the Simulation and Synthesis of Living Systems, pp. 257–264. MIT Press, Cambridge (2008)
10. Buhrmann, T., Di Paolo, E.A., Barandiaran, X.E.: A dynamical systems account of sensorimotor contingencies. Frontiers in Cognition 4(285) (2013)
11. Hutto, D.D., Myin, E.: Radicalizing enactivism: Basic minds without content. MIT Press, Cambridge (2013)

Self-exploration of the Stumpy Robot with Predictive Information Maximization

Georg Martius[1,*], Luisa Jahn[2,3], Helmut Hauser[3], and Verena V. Hafner[2]

[1] Max Planck Institute for Mathematics in the Sciences, Leipzig, Germany
martius@mis.mpg.de
[2] Humboldt-Universität zu Berlin, Institut für Informatik, Berlin, Germany
[3] University of Zurich, Artificial Intelligence Lab, Zurich, Switzerland

Abstract. One of the long-term goals of artificial life research is to create autonomous, self-motivated, and intelligent animats. We study an intrinsic motivation system for behavioral self-exploration based on the maximization of the predictive information using the Stumpy robot, which is the first evaluation of the algorithm on a real robot. The control is organized in a closed-loop fashion with a reactive controller that is subject to fast synaptic dynamics. Even though the available sensors of the robot produce very noisy and peaky signals, the self-exploration algorithm was successful and various emerging behaviors were observed.

Keywords: Self-exploration, intrinsic motivation, robot control, information theory, dynamical systems, learning.

1 Introduction

One of the long term goals of artificial life research is to create autonomous, self-motivated, and intelligent animats. It has been repeatedly argued, e.g., in [19], that one of the prerequisites for a successful interaction of such complex agents with their environments is the exploitation of their embodiment. In other words, the agent has to acquire knowledge on the impact of its actions on its sensory information and the environment. Developmental robotics, aiming at mechanisms for creating a mind in an embodied agent through a development process, formulates the following additional requirements [11] for the learning system: not task specific, environmental openness, raw information processing, online learning and a continual learning ring/hierarchy.

In this context different artificial intrinsic motivation approaches have been proposed. For example, there exist frameworks based on learning progress [10, 18, 21] and novelty [9], on the reinforcement learning framework, or based on homeokinesis [4], predictive information maximization [12] and empowerment [8] as gradient methods on information theoretic or dynamical systems quantities.

This paper uses predictive information maximization (PIMAX) [12], which has been previously successfully applied in simulation, but is here, for the first time,

---

* GM was supported by a grant of the DFG (SPP 1527).

A.P. del Pobil et al. (Eds.): SAB 2014, LNAI 8575, pp. 32–42, 2014.

applied to a real robot, more specifically to the robot Stumpy [7]. Predictive information is the past-future mutual information and measures how much information (in Shannon sense) can be used from the past of a time-series to predict the future. It is different from the bare prediction quality as it also requires the information content itself to be high. This avoids the "dark room problem" [6], i.e., doing nothing in a dark room is best predictable. Consequently, if one would optimize the prediction quality, the agent would not depart from this situation. The PIMAX approach, however, differs by yielding active and coordinated behaviors from scratch in a short amount of time (a few minutes of interaction) and is thus particularly suitable for real robots where the possible interaction time is very limited. In order to estimate the predictive information locally, an internal model is required. This technique is widely used in robotics, e.g. to perform mental simulation [3, 20], and it is also believed to play an important role in human motor planning [22].

In terms of the above mentioned requirements for a developmental program our approach satisfies all but the learning hierarchy by being not task specific, environmentally open, operating on raw sensor information in an online learning fashion. Challenges we address are the from-scratch formation of sensorimotor coordinations leading to smooth behavior, the autonomous selection of sensor information for a particular behavioral mode and the coping with morphological changes.

The Stumpy robot used for the experiments was designed to comply with the principles of cheap design and ecological balance as described in Iida et al. [7], also see Pfeifer and Bongard [19] for a comprehensive overview. The basic design idea was to demonstrate the concept of embodiment, i.e., to show that complex behavior can emerge even from a simple structure due to its physical interaction with the environment. In its original form, the robot was controlled in an open-loop manner by an operator using a joystick. Despite its remarkably simple design, a range of interesting stable locomotion behaviors were demonstrated.

For our experiments we equipped Stumpy with additional sensors and created an adaptive closed-loop system enabling the robot to self-explore its behavior space. The added acceleration sensors provide signals that are very noisy and dominated by shock events. Nevertheless, the implemented approach was successful and was able to generate a variety of smooth locomotion behaviors. Section 2 will give an overview on the Stumpy robot followed by the description of the control algorithm in Section 3. In Section 4, the experimental results are presented.

2   Stumpy, the Pendulum Driven Rocking Robot

The robot Stumpy was first introduced in Iida et al. [7]. The mechanical design of the latest version of Stumpy (developed at the AI-Lab in Zurich [1]) is depicted in Fig 1(a). It has only two joints, which are actuated by servo motors.

The robot is a simple metallic beam structure. Note that due to its design the robot exhibits compliance to a certain extent by the torsion of the beams, which

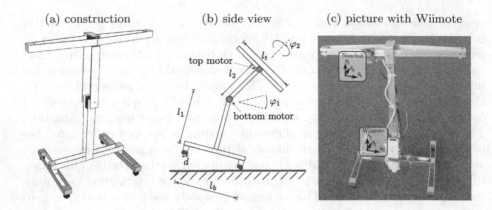

Fig. 1. The Stumpy. **(a,b)** Schematic construction: $d = 25\,\text{cm}$, $l_b = 30\,\text{cm}$, $l_1 = 25\,\text{cm}$, $l_2 = 20\,\text{cm}$, $l_t = 42\,\text{cm}$, $\varphi_1 = \pm 90°$, $\varphi_2 = \pm 35°$. **(c)** Picture of the robot.

allows for the emergence of dynamic behavior. In addition, rubber blocks are attached to the feet to absorb impact shock. While originally the robot was controlled by a human via a joystick in an open-loop fashion, for this work, Stumpy has been equipped with sensors in order to obtain a closed feedback loop that is autonomously driven by the PIMAX algorithm. For simplicity, we use the commercially available controllers of the gaming console Wii by Nintendo [17] called Wiimote and Nunchuk. Both measure the acceleration in all three dimensions in the range of $\pm 3\,\text{g}$ and $\pm 2\,\text{g}$, respectively. The placement of the sensors is depicted in Fig 1(c). The Wiimote can send the data via a Bluetooth connection to the controlling computer [5] at a frequency of approximately 13–25 Hz. The control signals are also sent to the robot via Bluetooth.

The locomotion of Stumpy is achieved by exploiting its inverse pendulum dynamics. By rotating the whole upper part of the body (using the bottom motor) left and right, enough momentum is eventually created to lift one side from the floor, to alternate between left and right on the spot. If the upper horizontal beam is moved as well (rotation of the top motor), it can perform forward and backward movements or turns. Human operators have been exploring many different modes by varying the parameter of the open-loop controller, which are frequency and amplitude of a sinus wave for both DoFs and a phase-shift between them. In contrast to that, in our case the robot is controlled by a reactive controller that uses only the available noisy sensors and it explores the robot's behavioral capabilities in an autonomous, intrinsically driven process.

3 Predictive Information Maximizing Controller

The controller we use for our experiments is the predictive information (PI) maximizing controller (PIMAX) introduced in Martius et al. [12].

We consider the sensor values as a stochastic process S_t with real-valued realizations $s_t \in \mathbb{R}^n$. The PI [2] measures the mutual information between past and future of a time series. Intuitively, the PI corresponds to how much information can be used from the past to predict the future. The rational to use the PI of the sensor stream as intrinsic motivation is that its maximization leads to a high variance in the sensor values, while keeping a temporal structure. We consider the simplified one-step PI

$$I(S_t; S_{t-1}) = \left\langle \ln \frac{p(s_t, s_{t-1})}{p(s_{t-1})p(s_t)} \right\rangle = H(S_t) - H(S_t|S_{t-1}) \qquad (1)$$

where $H(\cdot)$ denotes the Shannon entropy. In order to work with non-stationary processes, which is characteristic for this case, we consider a time-local version called TiPI. Furthermore, to turn this formula into an operational algorithm, we formulate it in the form of a dynamical system.

The stochastic process S can be decomposed as

$$s_t = \phi(s_{t-1}) + \xi_t = VK(s_{t-1}) + b + \xi_t \qquad (2)$$

into the deterministic model ϕ and a stochastic component ξ_t, also called prediction error. The matrix V and the vector b represent the parametrization of the predictor, which are adapted online by a supervised gradient procedure to minimize the prediction error $\xi^\top \xi$ as $\Delta V = \eta_\phi \xi a^\top$ and $\Delta b = \eta_\phi \xi$. The learning rate has been set to $\eta_\phi = 0.05$, which allows a fast adaptation process. The reactive controller K producing the actions (motor values) is realized as a neural network

$$a_t = K(s_t) = \tanh(Cs_t + h) \qquad (3)$$

with weight matrix C and bias vector h (tanh is understood component-wise). The entire setup is illustrated in Fig 2.

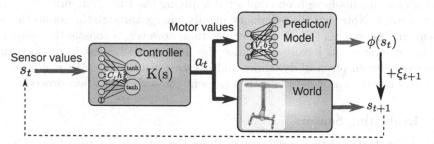

Fig. 2. Sensorimotor loop with controller, predictor and world

Let us now return to information theory. The TiPI is given by the mutual information conditioned on a fixed sensor state experienced at the beginning of a moving time window of τ steps $I^\tau(S_t; S_{t-1}) := I(S_t; S_{t-1}|S_{t-\tau} = s_{t-\tau})$, here we use the simplest case $\tau = 2$. With a coordinate transformation relative to the start of the time window $\delta s_{t'} = s_{t'} - s_{t-\tau}$ for $t - \tau \le t' < t$ we can approximate the TiPI assuming Gaussian noise by

$$I^\tau(S_t : S_{t-1}) = \frac{1}{2}\ln|\Sigma_t| - \frac{1}{2}\ln|D_t| \qquad (4)$$

where $\Sigma = \langle \delta s \delta s^\top \rangle$ is the covariance matrix of δS and $D = \langle \xi \xi^\top \rangle$ is the covariance matrix of the noise. Sampled covariance matrices tend to be very noisy. However, for calculating the gradient below we can make use of an explicit expression for the Σ using the model ϕ. This is done by approximating $\delta s_{t'}$ in terms of the Jacobian L (state dependent) as $\delta s_{t'} = L\,(s_{t'-1})\,\delta s_{t'-1} + \xi_{t'}$ where $\delta s_{t-\tau} = 0$. In our case the Jacobian matrix is given by $L = V G'\,(z)\,C$, where $z = Cs + h$ and $G'(z) = \mathrm{diag}[\tanh'(z_1), \ldots, \tanh'(z_m)]$.

The controller parameters (C,h) are adapted to increase the TiPI using gradient ascent, i.e. $\Delta C \propto \frac{\partial I^\tau}{\partial C}$, which yields the following simple update rules:

$$\frac{1}{\varepsilon}\Delta C_{ij} = \delta\mu_i \delta s_j - \gamma_i a_i s_j\,, \quad \text{and} \quad \frac{1}{\varepsilon}\Delta h_i = -\gamma_i a_i\,, \tag{5}$$

where all variables are time dependent and are at time t, except δs, which is at time $t-1$. The vector $\delta\mu \in \mathbb{R}^m$ is defined as

$$\delta\mu_t = G'V^\top \Sigma^{-1}\delta s_t \tag{6}$$

and the channel specific learning rates are given by $\gamma_i = 2\,(C\delta s_{t-1})_i\,\delta\mu_i$. The learning rate was set to $\varepsilon = 0.1$. It is interesting to note that the covariance matrix of the noise (D) cancels and does not enter the update formulas. The inverse of the covariance matrix Σ in Eq (6) is sampled with an exponential moving average with 100 timesteps. In practice, we found that it may even be replaced by the identity matrix (which is not done here). For the derivation and more details we refer to [12].

4   Experiments

Several experiments have been conducted applying the PIMAX algorithm to the Stumpy robot. Note that the behavior can only emerge through the connection of sensors and motors via (Eq 3). This connection, however, is constantly changing during exploration to locally maximize the TiPI. This results in an intricate interplay between physical dynamics and parameter dynamics. We will proceed by analyzing the sensor data and then present the self-exploration process.

4.1   Evaluating Sensors

First, we evaluated the sensors by controlling the robot in an open-loop fashion as described in [7] in a forward locomotion. Both motor signals followed a sine wave at 1.7 Hz with a certain phase-shift between the bottom and top motor. The corresponding sensor readings, however, are very noisy and, on first glance, do not seem to reflect the harmonic control signal (see Fig 3).

However, performing a wavelet transformation of the sensor time series allows us to identify two sensors (s_3, s_4) that show a major oscillatory component at 1.7 Hz (see Fig 4). However, to demonstrate that the algorithm is able to find its most valid sensor information on its own, we provided all sensors $(s_1, \ldots, s_6)$ to the controller. Although this seems to be a very challenging task, as we will see, our self-organizing control approach is able to overcome these difficulties.

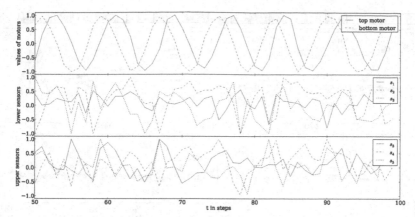

Fig. 3. Motor and sensor values for a forward motion. Top: motor values following a sine wave of 1.7 Hz (nominal angle normalized to [-1,1]). Center and bottom: sensor values from lower and upper acceleration sensors, see Fig 1(c). The harmonic control signal cannot be identified from the very noisy sensor readings. Update frequency was 14 Hz.

4.2   Behavioral Self-exploration

For the rest of the paper the robot is controlled by the reactive controller (Eq 3) with the learning dynamics given in Eq (5). Initialized with a "do nothing" controller (i.e., all synaptic weights set to 0) and a randomly initialized forward model, the robot starts to gently move after some initial time. The entropy term in the PI (Eq 1) drives the system to activity, which initially leads to a progressive noise amplification. As soon as the movements becomes large enough to cause a definite effect on the sensor values, the forward model is able to capture these correspondences and the movements become more coherent and related to the body/environment. A rocking behavior quickly emerges, which develops into different types of locomotion and swinging behavior. The evolution

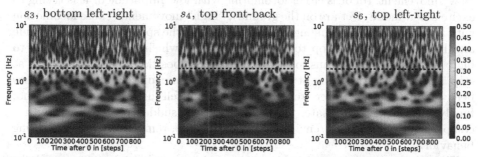

Fig. 4. Wavelet transform of sensor values for forward motion with open loop control. The prominent frequencies are clearly visible at 1.7 Hz for the sensors s_3 and s_4. Even though the robot is making periodical movements, the other sensors do not show a clear major frequency (s_1,s_2,s_5 are less pronounced than s_6). Update frequency: 14 Hz.

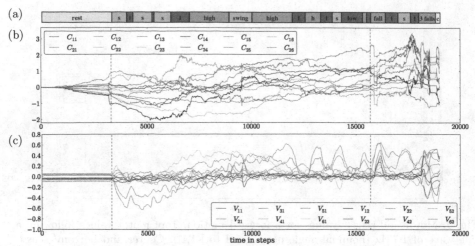

Fig. 5. Time evolution of the weights of the controller and the forward model.
(a) Movements classified visually into: rest, swinging, low, high, falling, and crawling
see text. (b) Entries of the controller matrix C over time. The weights adapt constantly without making big jumps. In this way the controller is able to produce various
motions, see (a). At about 15700 and 18000 the robot tips over. (c) Weights of the
forward model (matrix V). Update frequency was 23 Hz.

of the controller parameters during an typical run is displayed in Fig 5(b). The
elements of the matrix C (Eq 3) change constantly, which is expected from the
algorithm. The gradient on the TiPI is never zero as long as there is a non-
zero prediction error. This is counter-intuitive, but can be understood by the
fact that the landscape (the TiPI) changes with the behavior. Thus, all values
change during the whole experiment in a more or less smooth fashion. The
robot starts to move at approximatelly step 3000. Then it rather quickly enters a
swinging motion followed by a slow, but steady sweep through several behaviors,
see Fig 5(a). For simplicity the behaviors are grouped into the following types:
"low" movement: robot is either locomoting with low amplitude or it is trying to
excite a new mode (feet are on the ground); "high" movements: cause locomotion
with high amplitude; "swinging" means rocking at the spot with high amplitude
and balancing with the top to not fall; "falling": which is due to swinging to
high; and "crawling" means locomotion in laying position. The disturbance at
step 15700 is introduced by Stumpy falling over. Immediately afterwards it has
been manually lifted. After step 18000, the robot fell another three times and,
finally, was left in this state, where it produced, suddenly confronted with a
completely different body/environment relationship, remarkably fast a crawling
behavior.

There is no obvious relationship between the controller parameters and the
observed behavior (Fig 5(a,b)). Apparently, different parameter configurations
can lead to similar behavior. The forward model has a more defined structure, at
least later in the experiment, see Fig 5(c). During the swinging and high motions,

high rocking, slow locomotion   swinging, moving in place

Fig. 6. Different behaviors emerged from the control of the Stumpy with the PIMAX. During the swinging motion, the robot swings to either side and then, just before falling, moves the upper body towards the center. Further behaviors include fast locomotion with low amplitude, and swinging and turning to either side. Videos are available [16].

the values V_{32} and V_{62} (reflecting the correspondence between motor actions and left-right accelerations) raise in value. For low movements, the model collapses, because of no or little defined responses in the sensors.

In order to give an impression of the behavior, Fig 6 shows a series of frames for different movements. To get a quantitative characterization of the behavior, wavelet transformations of the motor and sensor values have been carried out and are presented in Fig 7. It can be seen how the main frequency changes with the behavior being lower for high and swinging movements and higher for low movements. Note that these frequencies are still lower than the ones induced by the forward movement in the open-loop setup (operator and joystick). It remains for future work to evaluate whether these movements are closer to the Eigenfrequency of the system and, thus, more energy efficient.

A variety of different behaviors have been generated including transitions between them. So far we have analyzed a single run to identify some key features of the behavioral self-exploration process. In order to see which effect the initialization has on the performance, we ran multiple runs and found consistently similar results. The exact order and timing of individual movements were different, but typically all types of movements have been generated.

4.3   Changing the Morphology

Since the PIMAX algorithm does not have any information about the robot under control (except the number of sensors and motors), changing the morphology of the robot should make no difference to the algorithm. It explores and exploits its given embodiment. In order to demonstrate this remarkable capability, we first put the Stumpy robot intentionally horizontally on the ground, as it already happened accidentally at the end of the exemplary run. The PIMAX algorithm achieves a crawling movement after a few seconds. The result can be seen in a video [16].

A modification of the morphology of the robot was carried out by putting Stumpy into a Chinese cooking pot, also called wok. The wok was modified on the bottom to make a smooth rotating movement possible and it was equipped with a heavy weight to prevent the construction from falling over. When the algorithm started to work, an emerging rotation motion of the wok was observed, see Fig 8.

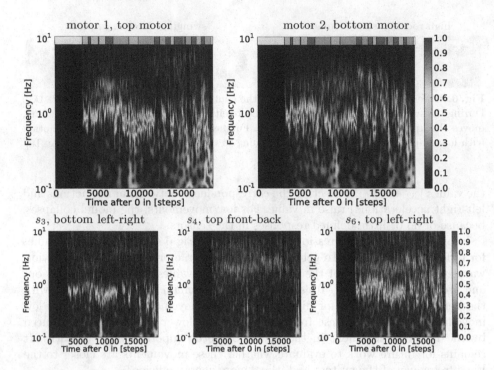

Fig. 7. Wavelet transform of the sensor and motor values for the exemplary experiment. It is clearly visible that the prominent frequency fluctuates around 0.5 to 1.5 Hz which corresponds to various motions. Also both motors behave in an individual way which leads to a high variance in motions and transitions between motions. Only the sensors s_3, s_4, and s_6 show a characteristic footprint of the motions (s_1, s_2, s_5 not shown). The sensor s_4 (top front-back) shows a faint trace typically at twice the frequency.

The motion was very steady and smooth, also due to the fact that the sensor readings were much smoother than compared to the previous experiments, where the robot had to deal with strong impacts. This can also be observed in the collected sensory data and the corresponding wavelet transformation in Fig 8. In this experiment the robot started to rotate already after about 70 seconds (step 1600). After 150 seconds (step 3250) the robot was manually stopped. It took the algorithm only a short amount of time to reenter the rotating motion (25 sec).

5   Discussion

We report on the control of the robot Stumpy with the PIMAX algorithm to obtain a self-organized behavioral exploration. Even though there is no specific goal, just the generic drive to locally maximize the predictive information of the sensor stream, the algorithm generates a variety of active behaviors that exploit the given embodiment. When the robot is upright, different movements emerge

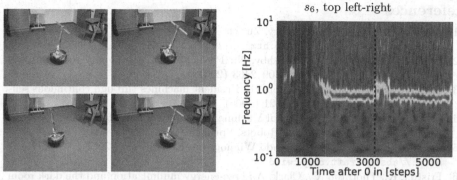

Fig. 8. Stumpy rotating with an attached wok. Left: frames from the behavior. Right: wavelet transform of the sensor s_6, ($s_{1,3,4}$ have a similar spectrum). The behavior is very smooth and steady at a frequency of $\approx 0.8\,\mathrm{Hz}$. The robot was stopped manually at step 3250 (black dashed line) and recovered itself, for videos see Martius et al. [16].

including various types of locomotion, turning, and swinging. When the robot lays on the ground, a crawling behavior is generated, and when the robot is placed in a wok (Chinese cooking pot) it starts to excite a stable rotation movement. The performance of the system is even more astonishing given the available sensor quality. The control of the robot is based on two 3-axis acceleration sensors in a reactive manner (no pattern generator nor recurrent connections, but fast synaptic dynamics). The acceleration sensor values are dominated by shock events and seem to be unusable for a smooth control at first glance. However, as it was demonstrated, the PIMAX algorithm organizes the sensorimotor loop in such a way that smooth behaviors are generated. Due to its fast adaptation mechanism, it can quickly react to changing responses of the physical system, e. g. due to a different behaviors mode. In this way it amplifies latent modes, such as swinging at intrinsic frequencies or the rotation of the robot with the wok. At the same time it can cope with drastically different situations, e.g. when the robot tips over.

On a higher level of learning, the found behaviors can be potentially memorized as primitives [14] such that they do not need to be rediscovered every time. As demonstrated (see Fig 5) the algorithm generates different behavioral modes that are persistent for some time and then transition to other modes. Each of these can be captured as a primitive behavior either by storing the controller parameters or by training a separate control module [14]. If goal directed behaviors are to be achieved then these primitives can be used as actions in a reinforcement learning setup. Alternatively, the self-organization process itself can be guided with various methods, see [13] for an overview, which have been shown to be particularly powerful in high-dimensional systems [15].

Acknowledgments. The authors thank Ralf Der for helpful discussions and the idea with the wok and Fumiya Iida for providing material on the Stumpy. LJ thanks Rolf Pfeifer and the AI-Lab team for their hospitality during her stay in Zurich and in particular Max Lungarella for helping with the robot.

References

[1] Artificial Intelligence Laboratory, Zurich (2013),
http://www.ifi.uzh.ch/ailab.html

[2] Bialek, W., Nemenman, I., Tishby, N.: Predictability, complexity and learning. Neural Computation 13(11), 2409–2463 (2001)

[3] Bongard, J.C., Zykov, V., Lipson, H.: Resilient machines through continuous self-modeling. Science 314, 1118–1121 (2006)

[4] Der, R., Martius, G.: The Playful Machine - Theoretical Foundation and Practical Realization of Self-Organizing Robots. Springer (2012)

[5] Smith, D.: Cwiid: Linux Nintendo Wiimote interface library (2014),
http://abstrakraft.org/cwiid

[6] Friston, K., Thornton, C., Clark, A.: Free-energy minimization and the dark room problem. Frontiers in Psychology 3(130) (2012)

[7] Iida, F., Dravid, R., Paul, C.: Design and control of a pendulum driven hopping robot. In: IEEE/RSJ International Conference on Intelligent Robots and Systems, vol. 3, pp. 2141–2146 (2002)

[8] Klyubin, A.S., Polani, D., Nehaniv, C.L.: Empowerment: A universal agent-centric measure of control. In: Evolutionary Computation. pp. 128–135 (2005)

[9] Lehman, J., Stanley, K.O.: Exploiting open-endedness to solve problems through the search for novelty. In: Proc. Intl. Conf. on Artificial Life (ALIFE XI), p. 329. MIT Press, Cambridge (2008)

[10] Luciw, M., Kompella, V., Kazerounian, S., Schmidhuber, J.: An intrinsic value system for developing multiple invariant representations with incremental slowness learning. Frontiers in Neurorobotics 7(9) (2013)

[11] Lungarella, M., Metta, G., Pfeifer, R., Sandini, G.: Developmental robotics: A survey. Connection Science 15(4), 151–190 (2003)

[12] Martius, G., Der, R., Ay, N.: Information driven self-organization of complex robotic behaviors. PLoS ONE 8(5), e63400 (2013)

[13] Martius, G., Der, R., Herrmann, J.M.: Robot learning by guided self-organization. In: Prokopenko, M. (ed.) Guided Self-Organization: Inception. Springer (2014)

[14] Martius, G., Fiedler, K., Herrmann, J.M.: Structure from Behavior in Autonomous Agents. In: Proc. IEEE IROS 2008, pp. 858–862 (2008)

[15] Martius, G., Herrmann, J.M.: Tipping the scales: Guidance and intrinsically motivated behavior. In: Advances in Artificial Life, pp. 506–513. MIT Press (2011)

[16] Martius, G., Jahn, L., Hauser, H., Hafner, V.V.: Supplementary materials (2014),
http://playfulmachines.com/Stumpy2014

[17] Nintendo: Wii official website (released 2006), http://www.nintendo.com/wii

[18] Oudeyer, P.Y., Kaplan, F., Hafner, V.V.: Intrinsic motivation systems for autonomous mental development. IEEE Transactions on Evolutionary Computation 11(2), 265–286 (2007)

[19] Pfeifer, R., Bongard, J.C.: How the Body Shapes the Way We Think: A New View of Intelligence (Bradford Books). The MIT Press (2006)

[20] Schillaci, G., Hafner, V.V., Lara, B.: Coupled inverse-forward models for action execution leading to tool-use in a humanoid robot. In: Proc. of 7th Intl. Conf. on Human-Robot Interaction (HRI 2012), pp. 231–232. ACM (2012)

[21] Schmidhuber, J.: Curious model-building control systems. In: Proc. Intl. Joint Conf. on Neural Networks, Singapore, pp. 1458–1463. IEEE (1991)

[22] Wolpert, D.M., Miall, R.C., Kawato, M.: Internal models in the cerebellum. Trends in Cognitive Sciences 2, 338–347 (1998)

Detecting the Vibration in the Artificial Web Inspired by the Spider

Eunseok Jeong and DaeEun Kim

Biological Cybernetics Lab
School of Electrical and Electronic Engineering
Yonsei University
Shinchon, Seoul, 120-749, South Korea
daeeun@yonsei.ac.kr
http://cog.yonsei.ac.kr/

Abstract. Most of the spiders can hunt a prey and avoid the threat of predators by sensing web vibration. Spiders have eight legs, and it has the sense organs to detect vibrations. These vibration sensing organs can be observed at the slit sensilla on each leg. A distribution of the web string tension effectivelytransfer the vibration of a spider web into another place. In order to investigate the characteristics of the spider web, we test various sensors in the artificial web. We apply a population coding approach to detect the orientation of the web vibration source. We demonstrate the result in the vibration experiments.

Keywords: Vibration sensing, web vibration, spider web.

1 Introduction

Spiders are one of the animals that can hunt prey and avoid the threat of predators by sensing vibration. Spiders have eight legs, and they have the sense organs to detect web vibrations. The vibration source is from preys or predators. Many scholars have studied the characteristics of vibrations from preys or predators and the behavior of spiders responding to the vibrations.

The spiders have the most complex system of vibration detectors embedded in their exoskeletons. They consist of lyriform organs, and the majority of the lyriform organs of the spider are located in the leg joints. These lyriform organs for sensing the vibration is formed by the two, called the HS-8, HS-10. The Hs-8 is positioned between the metatarsus and the tibia, and the Hs-10 is positioned between the tarsus and metatarsus. HS-8 is a proprioreceptor stimulated effectively by backward deflections of leg's joint. HS-8 is involved in kinaesthetic orientation and elicits muscle reflexes when stimulated [1,2,3,4]. HS-10 is a exteroreceptor stimulated effectively when the tarsus moves upwards and presses against the metatarsus where the organ is located. HS-10 is a highly sensitive vibration sensor which the spider uses to detect vibrations generated by prey, mates or predators[5,6,7,8].

A.P. del Pobil et al. (Eds.): SAB 2014, LNAI 8575, pp. 43–52, 2014.

Nerve signals generated through the compression and decompression of each slit of a spider are transmitted to the brain through the neuron signals. The spider can be recognize the vibration delivered by each foot, and it estimates the direction of the vibration source [9].

There are four types of vibrations in web threads. Longitudinal vibrations occur within the thread long axis and along the vibration propagation direction. Transverse and lateral vibrations are perpendicular to the long thread axis, as in the visible and audible vibration of a struck tennis racket. Transverse vibration is a kind of oscillation signals perpendicular to the web plane, whereas lateral vibration oscillations are within the web plane. These three vibration types are most relevant to the spider[10].

The longitudinal and transverse vibrations generated by insects are detected by the spider. The longitudinal and transverse vibration shows the maximum peak near 300Hz. The longitudinal transmission is attenuated by 0.3dB/cm in the range 10-2000Hz, and the transverse vibration transmission is more attenuated than the longitudinal vibration by -1.7dB/cm. The lateral vibrations transmission is less attenuated than the transverse vibration by -0.8dB/cm. But the lateral vibration has low magnitude than other vibrations [11].

2 Method

2.1 Angle Detection

We use a population coding method to detect the angle of vibration source. When the vibration is transmitted, each sensor detect the vibration. The time of vibration arrival is observed by each sensor, and a collection of the information can estimate the angle of vibration source (ϕ_s). Through each sensor angle (γ_l) , (γ_k) from the center of sensors, the diameter R of the circle inscribed in each sensor, and the velocity of propagation of vibration (v_R) in the sand, the angle of vibration source (ϕ_s) can be obtained according to the following the equation(1)[12].

$$\Delta t(\gamma_k, \gamma_l | \phi_s) = R/v_R[cos(\phi_s - \gamma_l) - cos(\phi_s - \gamma_k)] \tag{1}$$

If the velocity of propagation of vibration under the ground is constant, the angle of vibration source (ϕ_s) can be calculated using the time difference of vibration arrivals to each sensor and also the angle of each leg. The neuron activation is related to the time difference of vibration arrivals It is shown in the following equation(2~4).

$$ze^{i\phi} = \sum_{k=1}^{m} z_k e^{i\phi_k} = x + yi \tag{2}$$

$$x = \sum_{k=1}^{m} z_k cos(\phi_k), y = \sum_{k=1}^{m} z_k sin(\phi_k) \tag{3}$$

$$\phi = arctan(y/x), z = \sqrt{x^2 + y^2} \tag{4}$$

If ϕ is the angle of vibration source, equation (2) is represented by the weight of each sensor (z_k) and the angle of each sensor (ϕ_k). In the equation (2), $ze^{i\phi}$ is represented by a complex number through the Euler equation. Then the weight and angle of each sensor are represented in the equation (3). We can get the x and y in the equation (3), so the angle of vibration source (ϕ) is determined in the equation (4). Furthermore, it is possible, in addition to weight calculations using the time differences, to find the orientation of the vibration source by utilizing the difference in the magnitude of the vibration signal.

2.2   Piezoelectric Film Sensor

We use the piezoelectric film sensor to detect vibrations. It is a low-cost cantilever-type vibration sensor loaded by a mass to offer high sensitivity(1V/g) at low frequency. The flexible PVDF sensing element withstands high shock overload. The sensor has excellent linearity(¡1percents) and dynamic range, and can be used for detecting either continuous vibration or impacts.

The sensitivity of the piezoelectric film sensor follows a cosine law, when rotated horizontally around its axis, or vertically around its mid-point. At 90 degrees rotation in either plane, both baseline sensitivity and sensitivity at resonance are at a minimum. In theory, sensitivity should be zero in this condition. It is likely that some sensitivity around the resonance frequency will still be observed, but this may be unpredictable and is likely to be at least -16 dB with reference to the on-axis response.

We use the piezoelectric film sensor for vibration sensing. It can mimic the sensing organ of the spider. We designed a leg sensor consisting of the piezoelectric film sensor and the supporting rods.

3   Experiments

3.1   Materials of the Leg

We designed a vibration sensor system between the piezoelectric film sensor and the artificial web, which has a form of legs. The leg system transfers the string vibration to the piezoelectric sensor. We take the four material of the legs (nylon, optic fiber, thin optic fiber, stainless steel alloy). At first, we test the nylon string for the legs. The nylon string is also used for the artificial web. However, at the our sensor test, the magnitude of the vibration is not so good to transfer the vibration as shown in Fig. 1 (a). At second, We test the optic fiber string. The optic fiber string has a great vibration transmission characteristic, but it is easily bent to be used as legs with the piezoelectric sensor. This problem again appears in the thin optic fiber. At the last, we test the stainless steel alloy materials. It has tensile strength (psi - 100,000), and it has hardness (B85). So we

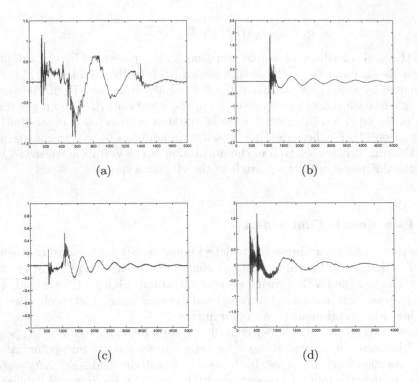

Fig. 1. The sensor test result depending on the material of the leg. (a) nylon (b) optical fiber (2mm) (c) thin optical fiber (1mm) (d) stainless steel alloy

take the stainless steel alloy for our experiment, and it has been used for the legs with the vibration sensor, as shown in Fig.1.

3.2 Experiments in the Artificial Web

The vibration sensor circuit design is shown in Fig.3. The whole circuit is powered by the power supply with 5V voltage. The four piezoelectric film sensors are mounted at the sides of body. The piezoelectric film sensor is effective to measure the vibrations. The piezoelectric film sensor's outputs are connected to instrumentation amplifier AD620. Their connection receives differential input. Two sensors are positioned symmetrically, and two signals made by a pair of sensors are compared to produce the sensor difference. The noise of signals is removed with a low pass filter. The amplified sensor signal is connected to DAQ board. The sampling rate of the DAQ is set on 10kHz because the string vibration sensor need not high frequency sensing. Depending on the magnet direction, the whole system can measure transverse or lateral vibrations.

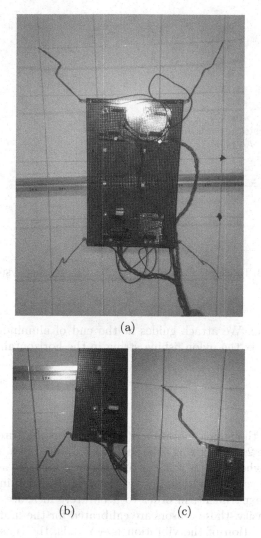

(a)

(b)   (c)

Fig. 2. The picture of artificial web and experiment circuit. (a) The entire circuit (b,c) The stainless steel leg and piezoelectric sensor.

For artificial web design, we have considered two materials, optic fiber, and nylon fishing string for vibration propagation. The optic fiber is made of plastic, thin and light, can endure strong tension. It looks like spider's string. However, the optic fiber is too fragile for the artificial web. Instead of the optic fiber, we take the nylon fishing string. The nylon fishing string can also be used instead of animal's whisker in before experiments. Therefore, in this experiment, nylon fishing string(1mm) is used instead of spider's string. It is heavy enough to be used in the experiment. Aluminum bars that have 2m length are used for

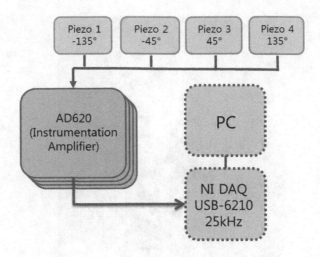

Fig. 3. Block diagram of string vibration sensing system

a rectangular frame. We attach guides at the end of aluminum bars, and the guides are used to fix the nylon fishing string in the horizontal direction.

4   Results

At first, we tested the string vibration at 20 touch points, three times. At this experiment, we use 2 meter string. The sensor is mounted in a direction perpendicular to a circle whose radius is 35cm. The touch is given as a forced vibration by hand during 10 seconds. Originally, we give the vibration in the form of impulse. Before the experiment, in order to accurately measure the difference of the vibration intensity, those sensors are calibrated for the uniform level.

When the orientation of the vibration is +Y axis, the sensor inputs at the angle of 45 deg and 135 deg arrives about 5 msec before the sensor inputs at the angle of -45 deg and -135 deg, and their magnitudes are also larger than the others. When the orientation of the vibration is -Y axis, the sensor inputs at the angle of -45 deg and -135 deg arrive before the other pair of sensor inputs. When the orientation of the vibration is -X axis, the sensor inputs at the angle of 135 deg and -135 deg arrive 5 mses before the sensor inputs at the angle of 45 deg and -45 deg. When the orientation of the vibration is +X axis, the reverse situation occurs.

The result of the estimation of vibration source is shown in Fig.5 when the magnitude of the vibration is used. The total experiments are performed 60 times, and the errors larger than 20 degrees occur only 16 times. The mean and standard deviation of errors are 12.6558 deg and 31.2276 deg, respectively. The result of the estimation of vibration source is shown in Fig.6 when the time

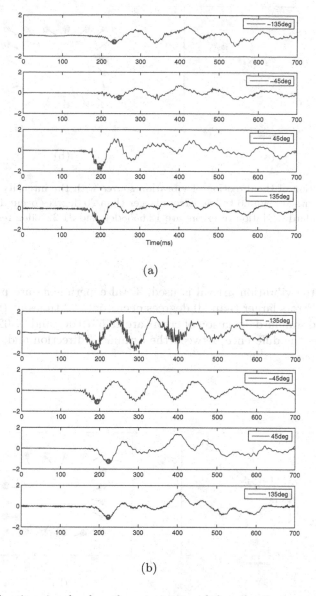

(a)

(b)

Fig. 4. The vibration signal; when the orientation of the vibration source is +Y axis (a) or -Y axis (b). (a) The sensor inputs at the angle of 45 deg and 135 deg arrive 5 msec before the sensor inputs at the angle of -45 deg and -135 deg, and their magnitude is larger than the others. (b) The sensor inputs at the angle of -45 deg and -135 deg arrive 5 msec before the sensor inputs at the angle of +45 deg and +135 deg, and the magnitudes are larger than the others.

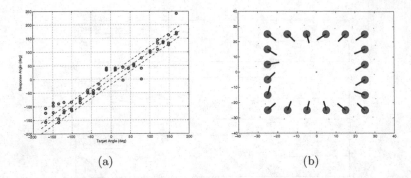

(a)   (b)

Fig. 5. Estimation of the direction of vibration source with the intensity of vibration. Total experiments are run 60 times. Errors larger than 20 degrees occur 16 times. The mean and standard deviation of errors are 12.6558deg and 31.2276deg respectively.

difference of the vibration arrival is used. Total experiments are performed 60 times again. Errors larger than 20 degrees occur only 22 times at this moment. The mean and standard deviation of errors are 23.5379 deg and 57.0200 deg. The error indicates the difference between the estimated direction and the accurate target direction.

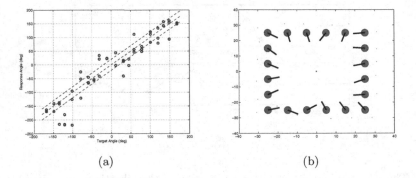

(a)   (b)

Fig. 6. Estimation of the direction of vibration source with the arrival time difference of vibration. Total experiments are run 60 times. Errors larger than 20 degrees occur 22 times. The mean and standard deviation of errors are 23.5379deg and 57.0200deg respectively.

5 Conclusion

We designed a system to detect the orientation of the vibration source in the artificial web. To localize a vibration source, we observe the arrival time difference of the vibration, and the magnitude difference of the vibration. Using piezoelectric sensors on a leg-like structure, the system can detect the vibrations transmitted through the leg, and a population coding approach has been applied to estimate the orientation of the vibration source.

Spiders can sense the vibration and track the vibration source by using silt sensila organs. We mimic the sensory system, using the piezoelectric film sensors on a leg-like structure. The piezoelectric film sensor generates electric voltage difference by a mechanical movement. From these characteristics, we make a bio-inspired system to track the vibration source by mimicking sensory structure of spiders.

We test the vibrations in a grid web. For future work, the spiral web can be tested. The spiral web consists of radii and spiral strings. We believe that the spiral web has better transfer characteristic than the grid web. Because the circular structure delivers vibrations between the outer web and inner web. The string in a circular form has large tension, and it is important to amplify the vibration signals and attenuate the noise signals. If we test the vibration detection system in the spiral web, it would be more accurate to estimate the location of the vibration source.

Acknowledgement. This work was supported by the National Research Foundation of Korea(NRF) grant funded by the Korea government(MEST) (No. 2012R1A2A4A01005677

References

1. Barth, F.G., Seyfarth, E.: Slit sense organs and kinesthetic orientation. Zeitschrift Fr Vergleichende Physiologie 74, 326–328 (1971)
2. Seyfarth, E., Barth, F.G.: Compound slit sense organs on the spider leg: Mechanoreceptors involved in kinesthetic orientation. Journal of Comparative Physiology 78, 176–191 (1972)
3. Seyfarth, E.: Lyriform slit sense organs and muscle reflexes in the spider leg. Journal of Comparative Physiology 125, 45–57 (1978)
4. Seyfarth, E., Pflger, H.: Proprioceptor distribution and control of a muscle reflex in the tibia of spider legs. Journal of Neurobiology 15, 365–374 (1984)
5. Barth, F.G.: Spider vibration receptors: Threshold curves of individual slits in the metatarsal lyriform organ. Journal of Comparative Physiology 148, 175–185 (1982)
6. Hergenrder, R., Barth, F.G.: The release of attack and escape behavior by vibratory stimuli in a wandering spider (Cupiennim salei keys). Journal of Comparative Physiology 152, 347–359 (1983)
7. Gingl, E., Burger, A., Barth, F.G.: Intracellular recording from a spider vibration receptor. Journal of Comparative Physiology A 192, 551–558 (2006)

8. Molina, J., Schaber, C.F., Barth, F.G.: In search of differences between the two types of sensory cells innervating spider slit sensilla (Cupiennius salei Keys). Journal of Comparative Physiology A 195, 1031–1041 (2009)
9. Schaber, C.F., Gorb, S.N., Barth, F.G.: Force transformation in spider strain sensors: White light interferometry. Journal of the Royal Society Interface 9, 1254–1264 (2012)
10. Masters, W.M., Markl, H.: Vibration signal transmission in spider orb webs. Science 213, 363–365 (1981)
11. Landolfa, M.A., Barth, F.G.: Vibrations in the orb web of the spider Nephila clavipes: Cues for discrimination and orientation. Journal of Comparative Physiology A 179, 493–508 (1996)
12. Brownell, P.H., van Hemmen, J.L.: Vibration sensitivity and a computational theory for prey-localizing behavior in sand scorpions. American Zoologist 41, 1229–1240 (2001)

Modelling Reaction Times in Non-linear Classification Tasks

Martha Lewis[1],*, Anna Fedor[2], Michael Öllinger[2],
Eörs Szathmáry[2], and Chrisantha Fernando[1]

[1] EECS, Queen Mary University of London
[2] Parmenides Foundation, Munich

Abstract. We investigate reaction times for classification of visual stimuli composed of combinations of shapes, to distinguish between parallel and serial processing of stimuli. Reaction times in a visual XOR task are slower than in AND/OR tasks in which pairs of shapes are categorised. This behaviour is explained by the time needed to perceive shapes in the various tasks, using a parallel drift diffusion model. The parallel model explains reaction times in an extension of the XOR task, up to 7 shapes. Subsequently, the behaviour is explained by a combined model that assumes perceptual chunking, processing shapes within chunks in parallel, and chunks themselves in serial. The pure parallel model also explains reaction times for ALL and EXISTS tasks. An extension to the perceptual chunking model adds time taken to apply a logical rule. We are able to improve the fit to the data by including this extra parameter, but using model selection the extra parameter is not supported. We further simulate the behaviour exhibited using an echo state network, successfully recreating the behaviour seen in humans.

1 Introduction

The theory of evolutionary neurodynamics [3] claims that population based parallel search takes place in the brain. This paper lays the foundations for further experiments to model the time complexity of human insight problem solving. It does so by fitting serial vs. parallel search models to cognitive tasks that go beyond the standard visual search paradigm, namely tasks involving linear and non-linear classifications. We are interested in the mechanisms the brain uses to do non-linear classification, and whether we can disambiguate hypotheses about these mechanisms by comparing reaction times (RT) in such tasks. An experiment into RTs in a linear classification task was conducted by Little et al using an experimental paradigm promoting serial processing of stimulus elements (elements were spatially separated and differences very small), and where subjects were explicitly instructed to implement logical rules [6]. We investigate RTs in a task in which the complexity of the task is minimised, to elucidate the mechanisms underlying non-linear classification.

---

* Corresponding author.

A.P. del Pobil et al. (Eds.): SAB 2014, LNAI 8575, pp. 53–64, 2014.

We examine whether the differences in RT may be explained solely by reference to the information needed for categorisation or alternatively, whether RT is a function of both the information needed for categorisation and also the time it takes to apply a logical rule to this information. To compare these two hypotheses, we firstly gather RT data in two experiments, briefly described below and detailed in section 2. We model the data thus obtained using firstly a drift-diffusion model of decision making, similar to that used in [6], and secondly using an echo state network [5]. Again, we describe these briefly below and give details in section 3. We find that the slower RTs in non-linearly separable tasks are best modelled as a function solely of the extra information needed to make the categorisation, and that the time taken to apply a logical rule does not need to be included.

We gathered data in two experiments. In the first, participants were presented with stimuli consisting of pairs of shapes, each shape a circle or a square, and were asked to classify stimuli according to either conjunction (AND), disjunction (OR) or exclusive-or (XOR). The second experiment extends the first and allows us to investigate time taken to apply a logical rule. One participant was presented with stimuli consisting of a number of shapes in an horizontal row. Stimuli were classified according to EXISTS, ALL and ODD. These are respectively extensions of the OR, AND, and XOR tasks. To see this, consider variables $A_1, A_2, ..., A_n$ that can take values True or False. To implement the category ALL, we can form the conjunction $\bigwedge_{i=1}^{n} A_i$. To implement the category EXISTS, we can form the disjunction $\bigvee_{i=1}^{n} A_i$. If we form the logical combination $\bigoplus_{i=1}^{n} A_i$, where $\oplus$ stands for XOR, we obtain the non-linearly separable category that can be characterised as having an odd number of variables with the value True.

To model the data thus collected, we use two different approaches. Firstly, an abstract model based on a random process, and secondly a more biologically plausible model that uses an echo state network [5]. The abstract model used is based on the idea that the decision as to the class to which a single shape belongs can be modelled as an accumulation of perceptual evidence. This has been used by, for example, [1,6,7,8] and a thorough review of this type of model is given in [13]. However we summarise the main ideas here for clarity. In our experiment, one variable, A, would be accumulating evidence that the shape is a circle, and another, B, would be accumulating evidence that the shape is a square. The decision as to whether the shape is indeed a square can then be implemented in (at least) two ways. Either the first out of A and B to reach a given threshold determines the decision made. This is called the *race* model. Alternatively, the evidence for circle and square can be integrated into one variable in which evidence for square increases the total and evidence for circle decreases the total. The decision is then made when the total either exceeds the threshold for square or falls below the threshold for circle. This is termed the *drift-diffusion* model (DDM), since the behaviour of the total may be modelled as a one-dimensional diffusion process with drift, in which the direction of the drift is determined by whether the shape actually is a circle or a square. The RT is modelled as the time at which either the upper or lower threshold is first hit. As [13] report, these models are argued to have neural correlates, so that the evidence totals referred to correspond to firing rates of single neurons or populations of neurons. It has also been shown that the DDM implements an optimal decision process, and further, that many variants of these two models may be reduced to the DDM [2]. We have therefore used a DDM to model reaction times to a single shape.

The experimental stimuli are, however, comprised of at least two shapes. In order to model the way in which multiple shapes are combined we use a rule-based model as in [6]. This type of model is described in detail in [4]. Briefly, suppose we are categorising a stimulus consisting of a pair of shapes, and that the stimulus should be classed in one category if both the shapes are squares, and in the other category otherwise. The decision about the whole stimulus is simply based on a logical combination of the decisions about the two shapes. The RT to the whole stimulus may then be derived as a combination of the RT to each shape. There are various ways in which this combination may be made, which we now enumerate. Firstly, suppose that the two shapes actually are squares. Then, if the two shapes are perceived in *serial*, the RT to the whole stimulus is modelled as the sum of the RTs to each shape. Alternatively, if the two shapes are perceived in *parallel*, the RT to the whole stimulus is modelled as the maximum of the RTs to each shape. Secondly, the combination process may be *exhaustive* or *self-terminating*. If exhaustive, a decision must be made about every shape before a decision may be made about the whole stimulus. If self-terminating, then if one of the shapes is sufficient to determine the state of the whole stimulus, the decision about the whole stimulus may be made early, without having come to a decision about the second shape. For example, suppose the stimulus consists of a circle on the left, square on the right. In the parallel case, the RT to the whole stimulus is then simply the RT to the left-hand shape, assuming that the shape is correctly perceived. In the serial case, the RT to the whole stimulus is either the RT to the left-hand shape, if the left-hand shape is looked at first, or the sum of the RTs if the right-hand shape is looked at first. Thirdly, the application of the logical rule may be instantaneous or may take a finite time. Lastly, the cases above assume that RT to each individual shape is independent of RT to other shapes. [14,15] have developed measures of interactivity between elements of a stimulus which can take account of the fact that perception of different elements of a stimulus may not be independent of one another. However, the data we have collected is insufficient to apply these measures and we therefore make the assumption of independence.

Within the current paper we use the DDM to model RTs to individual shapes, together with a rule based model to model RT to the entire stimulus, with the assumption that RT to shapes are independent. We will show that given these assumptions, a parallel, self-terminating model with instantaneous rule application best fits our data.

In contrast to these abstract models, the echo state network approach consists of a highly interconnected and non-independent network of artificial neurons. We simulate the first experiment, and find that the qualitative behaviour is reproduced, i.e. that categorization in the XOR condition takes longer than in the OR and AND conditions under a broad range of parameters. This supports the idea that the difference in RT can be explained purely by the time taken to perceive the shapes in the stimulus, since within the echo state network no logical rule is being applied.

We describe experiments and data in section 2. Section 3 models data from the two experiments using the DDM, and trains an echo state network to simulate data from experiment 1. Section 4 discusses results, proposing further work.

2   Methods and Results

2.1   Experiment 1: Reaction Times to Pairs of Shapes

Methods. Six male and six female participants (Ps) aged between 25 and 40 completed Experiment 1. Ps were colleagues of the authors and did not receive compensation. Each stimulus was made of pairs of shapes, each either a square (width 39 mm) or a circle (diameter 39mm), either side of a focus point which was a small red square. Centres of stimuli were 118 mm apart, 59 mm from the centre of the focus point. P was seated $\sim$ 60 cm from the screen and responded by pressing D or K on the keyboard. In each task, the stimuli were put into two classes and P instructed to respond D or K as summarized in table 1. Each P

Table 1. Numbers of stimuli types and correct responses

Stimulus type	OR	AND	XOR
Square Square	10, D	30, D	15, D
Square Circle	10, D	10, K	15, D
Circle Square	10, D	10, K	15, D
Circle Circle	30, K	10, K	15, K

completed each of three tasks: OR, AND and XOR in one go with instructions:

OR: "If one, or the other, or both the shapes are squares, please press D, and press K otherwise."

AND: "If both the shapes are squares, please press D, and press K otherwise."

XOR: "If one, or the other, but not both the shapes are squares, please press D, and press K otherwise."

To ensure that the P understood instructions, they were asked whether they understood and repeated the instructions back in their own words. Each task consisted of 60 presentations randomised for each P. The P pressed space to show a stimulus. The focal point was shown immediately and after a delay of 0.5-1.5s the stimulus shown. Equal numbers of D and K responses were elicited (table 1). Two Ps underwent each of six orderings of the tasks.

Results. RTs in the XOR task were slower than in the OR or AND task, with significant differences in distribution between OR and XOR, and AND and XOR, and no significant difference between OR and AND. Mean error rates were higher in XOR than in AND or OR, at 4%, 2.5% and 2.6% respectively.

Before analysis, we removed RTs below 200ms and above 5s as per [9]. This removed 2 RT in total. As RT are non-normally distributed and heavy tailed, we use median rather than mean, as recommended in [9]. Across all participants, median RT in OR was 0.547s, in AND 0.535s, and in XOR 0.597s. A repeated measures ANOVA across participants confirmed significant differences between the medians with $p < 0.01$. Tukey-Kramer post-hoc tests confirmed significant difference between median RT for AND and XOR ($p < 0.01$) and OR and XOR ($p < 0.01$), but no significant difference between OR and AND. A boxplot of the data is given in figure 1. The increased RT in the XOR condition could be explained by the fact that both shapes must be perceived before the stimulus may be categorised. The equal RT in the OR and AND conditions may be explained by the fact that they are equaivalent in terms of which shapes must be perceived in order to categorise the stimulus. This is further discussed in section 3.1.

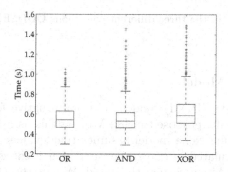

Fig. 1. Boxplot of RT data across all participants

2.2 Experiment 2: RT to Increased Numbers of Shapes

Methods. One of the authors underwent an extension to the OR/AND/XOR paradigm. The stimuli consisted of an horizontal row of n shapes, each either a square (width 20mm) or a circle (diameter 20mm). The row was centred around a focus point which was a small red square. Centres of the stimuli were 60 mm apart. The P was seated ~ 60 cm from the screen. Three tasks (EXISTS,ALL and ODD) were undertaken for each n. In each task, the stimuli were classified into two classes. The EXISTS task extended the OR task with D pressed if the stimulus had at least one square, K otherwise. The ALL task extended the AND task. The P pressed D if all shapes were squares, K otherwise. The ODD condition extended XOR. In this task, the P pressed D if an odd number of the shapes were squares, and K otherwise. For each task, for each $n = 1...18$ the P responded to 64 stimulus presentations, taking 6 hours in total. Breaks were taken after every three sets of trials. Stimuli were chosen for equal numbers of D and K responses and to ensure representation of stimuli with a specific number of squares in accordance with the distribution of such stimuli in the set of all stimuli of a particular length n.

Results. RT in the EXISTS and ALL conditions do not increase with n. RT in the ODD condition increase slowly from $n = 1...7$ and then increases more quickly (Figure 2).

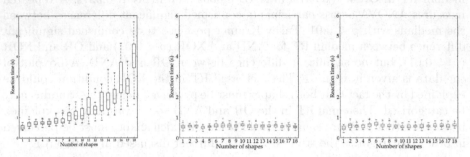

Fig. 2. Boxplots of RT in the three different conditions ODD, EXISTS and ALL

3   Modelling

3.1   Drift Diffusion Model

The drift diffusion model (DDM) models a two-alternative forced choice as a Wiener process with drift, proposed in [8]. We use this as a basis for RT to a single shape in a stimulus. The model assumes that evidence for or against a categorisation is accumulated in one stream and that a categorisation is made when the evidence first hits a certain threshold. We use the DDM in modelling because it implements an optimal decision-making procedure [2]. It should be noted that the white noise in the Wiener process has Fourier components at arbitrary high and low frequencies, since its correlation length is zero. Whilst the low frequencies are improbable, the high frequencies are completely unrealistic, since these imply arbitrary fast change in the drive. As a simplification, however, we use the DDM as it stands.

OR/AND/XOR Task Model

Modelling. We compare independent, instantaneous, exhaustive parallel and serial models with independent, instantaneous self-terminating parallel and serial models, in line with [6]. We fit the parallel and serial self-terminating models and conclude that the parallel self-terminating model provides the best fit.

In the exhaustive models each shape must be perceived before the stimulus as a whole can be categorised. In a serial exhaustive model, the RT to the whole stimulus is the sum of the RTs to each shape. In a parallel exhaustive model, it is the maximum of the RT to each shape. In a self-terminating model, RT

Table 2. Expressions for response times for serial self-terminating responses. $T_{SL}, T_{SR}, T_{CL}, T_{CR}$ stand for time to respond to a square on the left, square on the right, circle on the left, circle on the right respectively.

Stimulus (Serial)	OR	AND	XOR
Square-Square	$(T_{SL} + T_{SR})/2$	$T_{SL} + T_{SR}$	$T_{SL} + T_{SR}$
Square-Circle	$(T_{SL} + T_{CR} + T_{SL})/2$	$(T_{SL} + T_{CR} + T_{CR})/2$	$T_{SL} + T_{CR}$
Circle-Square	$(T_{CL} + T_{SR} + T_{SR})/2$	$(T_{CL} + T_{SR} + T_{CL})/2$	$T_{CL} + T_{SR}$
Circle-Circle	$T_{CL} + T_{CR}$	$(T_{CL} + T_{CR})/2$	$T_{CL} + T_{CR}$
Stimulus (Parallel)	OR	AND	XOR
Square-Square	$\min(T_{SL}, T_{SR})$	$\max(T_{SL}, T_{SR})$	$\max(T_{SL}, T_{SR})$
Square-Circle	T_{SL}	T_{CR}	$\max(T_{SL}, T_{CR})$
Circle-Square	T_{SR}	T_{CL}	$\max(T_{CL}, T_{SR})$
Circle-Circle	$\max(T_{CL}, T_{CR})$	$\min(T_{CL}, T_{CR})$	$\max(T_{CL}, T_{CR})$

to the whole stimulus can be terminated early if one of the shapes perceived is sufficient to determine the class of the stimulus. The times for each type of stimulus in self-terminating models are given in table 2.

Exhaustive and self-terminating models make qualitatively different predictions about RT in each condition: the exhaustive model predicts that OR/AND/XOR conditions will have equal mean RT whereas the self-terminating model predicts that mean RT in the OR and AND models will be equal and that mean RT in the XOR condition will be slower. Mean RT observed in the data follows the predictions of the self-terminating models so we reject the exhaustive model.

To generate RT to individual shapes, we simulate DDM trajectories using the Euler-Maruyama method. Each trajectory terminates when a threshold is hit, giving simulated RT for one shape. We assume that RT to shapes are i.i.d. Overall RT are calculated by combining individual RT using expressions in table 2 and the frequencies of stimuli given in table 1, giving a predicted distribution of RT to the whole stimulus. To fit the distribution, we used weighted sum of squares over the 0.1, 0.3, 0.5, 0.7 and 0.9 quantiles of the data and the error rate, as in [10]. The sum squared error (SSE) is minimised using mesh adaptive direct search as implemented in the MATLAB function `patternsearch`. The parameters we fit are the threshold z, the variance coefficient c^2, k a parameter to add noise to the starting point of the process, and σ to add noise to the drift rate. To compare, we also fit each of the OR, AND and XOR data as separate DDM processes with separate parameters, giving 12 in total.

Results. The parallel self-terminating model provides the best fit, evidenced in table 3. The separately fitted curves have lowest SSE. The parallel model has the highest adjusted R^2, indicating better fit when extra parameters are penalised.

Table 3. SSE for each model, with adjusted R^2 in brackets

Model	Parallel	Serial	Separate
OR	0.0303	0.182	0.0133
AND	0.0187	0.126	0.0176
XOR	0.0170	0.208	0.0229
Total	0.0669 (0.915)	0.539 (0.600)	0.0537 (0.796)

EXISTS/ALL/ODD Task

Modelling. We find the parallel model fits the EXISTS/ALL task, a parallel model fits the ODD task to 7 shapes, and a perceptual chunking model fits the ODD task for 7 or more shapes.

We fit four models to the data: parallel self-terminating; serial self-terminating; a mixed parallel and serial perceptual chunking model; and a perceptual chunking plus logical rule model. Our approach to modelling the EXISTS/ALL/ODD task extends that of the OR/AND/XOR task. In this case we model only mean RT. We develop expressions for mean RT to the stimulus as a function of RT to individual shapes, and fit these predicted means. We assume again that RT to shapes are i.i.d and that decision making is instantaneous (except in the perceptual chunking plus logical rule model). Expressions for mean RT are created via a similar procedure to that in section 3.1. For the ODD task, the parallel self-terminating model predicts $T_{odd,n}^{par} = \max(T_1, ..., T_n)$, where n is the number of shapes in the stimulus, T_i is the time taken to to perceive the ith shape and $T_{odd,n}^{par}$ indicates the mean RT predicted by the parallel self-terminating model in the ODD task for a stimulus of n shapes. The serial self-terminating model predicts $T_{odd,n}^{ser} = \sum_{i=1}^{n} T_i$. The EXISTS and ALL tasks are equivalent, and the time taken is dependent on n and on the number of squares in the stimulus k. The parallel self-terminating model predicts $T_{all,n}^{par} = \max(T_1, ..., T_n)/2 + \sum_{k=1}^{n} \binom{n}{n-k} \min(T_1...T_{n-k})/(2^n - 2)$. The serial self-terminating model predicts $T_{all,n}^{ser} = (\sum_{i=1}^{n} T_i)/2 + (\sum_{k=1}^{n} 2^{n-k} \sum_{i=1}^{k} T_i)/(2^n - 2)$. These expressions have been averaged over stimulus types and frequencies and order of processing.

To create a chunking model, we suppose that shapes are perceived in parallel up to a certain number m and then these chunks are perceived in serial. For the ODD task, this gives $T_{odd,n}^{chunk} = T_{odd,m}^{par} \times \max(1, n/m)$, where n/m is a smoothed expression for the number of chunks which has minimum 1. For the ALL task, the expression used is $T_{all,n}^{chunk} = T_{all,m}^{par} \times \max(1, 2 - 2^{-(n/m-1)})$. Here, the multiplier is obtained by solving the sum over k in $T_{all,n}^{ser}$.

To add the time taken to apply a logical rule linearly, a constant, multiplied by the number of shapes in the stimulus, is added to the chunking model. To model hierarchical application of a logical rule, a constant multiplied by the log of the number of shapes in the stimulus is added.

To fit the parallel and serial self-terminating model for the EXISTS/ALL conditions we simulate and combine $n = 1...18$ Euler-Maruyama drift diffusion trajectories according to the expressions for mean RT. Parameters and fitting procedures are as in experiment 1. To fit the chunking model, we follow a similar procedure, but fit the data for each different size of chunk and pick the best fit. To fit the chunking + logical rule models, we follow the same fitting procedure as for chunking, but with the additional parameter for the time taken to apply the logical rule.

Results. A parallel model of processing fits the data for EXISTS and ALL better than does the serial. (table 4). The best fit for the chunking model was obtained when chunk size was 18, i.e. all shapes were being processed in parallel. The perceptual chunking model fits the data in the ODD better than either the parallel or serial models. (table 4, figure 3). The perceptual chunking + logical rule model provides slightly lower SSE than the perceptual chunking model (table 4), but higher adjusted R^2, indicating that the extra parameter is not supported. In each of the perceptual chunking models applied to the ODD data, the best fit was obtained when the chunk size was 6.

Table 4. Weighted SSE, with adjusted R^2 in brackets. Parallel best fits EXISTS/ALL, Chunking best fits the ODD data when extra parameters penalised.

Model	Parallel	Serial	Chunking	Chunking + lin. rule	Chunking + log. rule
EXISTS	0.033	2.16	0.034	n/a	n/a
ALL	0.017	2.27	0.017	n/a	n/a
ODD	6.55	3.16 (0.750)	2.41 (0.795)	2.39 (0.769)	2.34 (0.785)

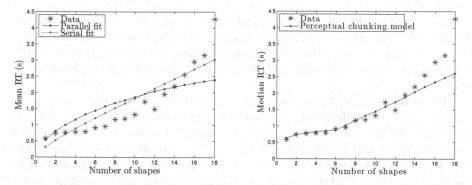

Fig. 3. Fitted RT in the ODD condition. The perceptual chunking model (right hand side) fits better than the serial or parallel models (left hand side).

3.2 Echo State Network Modelling

We further model experiment 1 using an echo state network approach. Rather than modelling RT as a function of shapes, we see how an interconnected reservoir of neurons can perform the task. We find that the qualitative results from experiment 1 are reproduced. This lends support to the thesis that the increased RT can be explained solely by perception time.

Detailed in [5], ESNs consist of a 'reservoir' of N sparsely connected recurrent artificial neurons which take K inputs and output to L nodes. The model used consisted of a fully connected reservoir of 500 leaky integrate and fire neurons, leak rate 0.1, spectral radius 0.96, input scaling 0.3, with three separate readouts with a tanh activation function, trained by gradient descent on the least mean square error function to approximate the target output 1 for class 1 and -1 for class 0. The reservoir was implemented using the Oger `LeakyReservoirNode` class [12] and the readout node was implemented using Pybrain [11]. The training data for the readouts were sampled from the time of stimulus presentation to 50 time-steps after stimulus presentation. The training phase of the logistic regression readout involved 20000 stimulus presentations. Online mini-batches of 1000 data points were applied for one epoch with a learning rate of 0.0001. The final trained readout was assessed in a test phase by presenting 1000 stimuli for each task. Noise of mean 0 and standard deviation 0.1 was applied to each input dimension.

The observed RT distribution (OR $\simeq$ AND < XOR) occurred naturally when the same random stimulus sequences provided to the human subjects was fed into the network. Stimuli were encoded as: Square-Square = [1,0, 1, 0], Square-Circle = [1,0, 0,1], Circle-Square = [0,1,1,0], Circle-Circle = [0,1,0,1]. Between stimuli input was [0,0,0,0]. During the test phase consisting of 1000 stimulus presentations per condition, but not the training phase, D was pressed if the readout value was greater than 0.7, and K was pressed if less than -0.7. The stimulus was removed when the button was pressed. Each presentation lasted 400 timesteps, with a 295 timestep rest period at the start to allow the reservoir to settle down.

Figure 4 shows the RT distribution of the coupled ESN/readout system for the OR, AND and XOR tasks. Blue shows correct button presses, and red shows incorrect button presses. Incorrect button presses predominate at shorter RT as in human subjects. OR and AND have similar distributions, whilst XOR is slower.

What is the cause of the slower RT in the XOR task compared to the AND and OR tasks? We believe the non-linear features in the ESN take some time to develop, whilst the linear features that can be used to solve the OR and AND problems exist in a form detectable by the readout right from stimulus presentation. The explanation for slower performance in the XOR than the OR and AND tasks given by this model is that extra time is needed for nonlinear features to be produced in the randomly connected ESN in order for the instantaneous readout to classify stimuli into their non-linear classes. In effect, more interactions must take place in the ESN.

4   Discussion

We have investigated RT to visual stimuli composed of combinations of shapes. We find that RT in visual XOR tasks are slower than RT in visual AND/OR tasks (section 2.1). Secondly, we find that in an extension of these tasks to increased numbers of shapes, RT in EXISTS/ALL tasks do not increase with the number of shapes n, but that RT in parity tasks increase and that the gradient

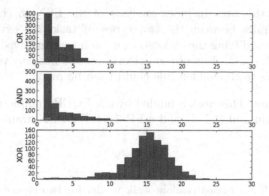

Fig. 4. Readouts for one ESN

of increase changes at about $n = 7$ (section 2.2). We model this behaviour using a drift diffusion model of RT to individual stimuli, comparing exhaustive and self-terminating stopping rules, and parallel and serial models of processing. The difference in RT in visual XOR tasks compared to visual AND/OR tasks is explained by the time needed to perceive the shapes in the various tasks, using a parallel drift diffusion model (section 3.1).

In the extended tasks, a parallel model fits the EXIST/ALL tasks. The increase in RT in the ODD task is explained by a combined parallel and serial model that assumes perceptual chunking, processing dimensions within the chunks in parallel, and the chunks themselves in serial. This fits better than either a pure parallel or a pure serial model. We contrast our models, which fit the RT to a function of the time taken to perceive each shape in the stimulus only, with a model in which RT is a function of time taken to perceive each shape in the stimulus plus a time taken to apply a logical rule. We find that adding a constant that scales linearly with the number of shapes improves the fit of the data, but using model selection, the use of the additional parameter is not supported (section 3.1).

The ESN model shows that the qualitative behaviour, i.e., an increase in RT for the XOR task, can arise purely out of the dynamics of a system of connected recurrent neurons. This supports the idea that the slower RT in the XOR task is a function purely of the time to gain the relevant information from the stimulus, rather than due to additional logical rule processing (section 3.2).

The perceptual chunking model we have developed does not account for the fast reaction times in the EXISTS/ALL tasks, or the much slower reaction times for larger numbers of shapes in the ODD task. This latter aspect might be explained by task ordering, and a further experiment in which, for example, the tasks are ordered from large numbers of stimuli to low numbers of stimuli might give different results. Further development of the model to include, for example, interactivity between the chunks might enable us to integrate the purely parallel model for the EXISTS/ALL task and the perceptual chunking model for the ODD task.

Further work in this area includes analysis of the ESN to characterise the differences in dynamics between the two types of task. An extension of this work could include modifying the tasks so that each task involved the finding of some hidden rule. A comparison of the performance of humans versus the ESN network on adapting to the hidden rule could then be made.

Acknowledgements. This work is funded by the FQEB Templeton Foundation Grant "Bayes Darwin and Hebb", and a FP-7 FET OPEN grant INSIGHT.

References

1. Gregory Ashby, F.: A biased random walk model for two choice reaction times. Journal of Mathematical Psychology 27(3), 277–297 (1983)
2. Bogacz, R., Brown, E., Moehlis, J., Holmes, P., Cohen, J.D.: The physics of optimal decision making: A formal analysis of models of performance in two-alternative forced-choice tasks. Psychological Review 113(4), 700 (2006)
3. Fernando, C.T., Szathmary, E., Husbands, P.: Selectionist and evolutionary approaches to brain function: A critical appraisal. Frontiers in Computational Neuroscience 6, 24 (2012)
4. Fific, M., Little, D.R., Nosofsky, R.M.: Logical-rule models of classification response times: A synthesis of mental-architecture, random-walk, and decision-bound approaches. Psychological Review 117(2), 309 (2010)
5. Jaeger, H.: The" echo state" approach to analysing and training recurrent neural networks-with an erratum note'. Bonn, Germany: German National Research Center for Information Technology GMD Technical Report, 148 (2001)
6. Little, D.R., Nosofsky, R.M., Denton, S.E.: Response-time tests of logical-rule models of categorization. Journal of Experimental Psychology: Learning, Memory, and Cognition 37(1), 1 (2011)
7. Nosofsky, R.M., Palmeri, T.J.: An exemplar-based random walk model of speeded classification. Psychological Review; Psychological Review 104(2), 266 (1997)
8. Ratcliff, R.: A theory of memory retrieval. Psychological Review 85(2), 59 (1978)
9. Ratcliff, R.: Methods for dealing with reaction time outliers. Psychological Bulletin 114(3), 510 (1993)
10. Ratcliff, R., Tuerlinckx, F.: Estimating parameters of the diffusion model: Approaches to dealing with contaminant reaction times and parameter variability. Psychonomic Bulletin & Review 9(3), 438–481 (2002)
11. Schaul, T., Bayer, J., Wierstra, D., Sun, Y., Felder, M., Sehnke, F., Rückstieß, T., Schmidhuber, J.: PyBrain. Journal of Machine Learning Research (2010)
12. Schrauen, B.: Organic environment for reservoir computing (oger) toolbox, http://organic.elis.ugent.be/organic/engine (accessed: January 05, 2014)
13. Smith, P.L., Ratcliff, R.: Psychology and neurobiology of simple decisions. Trends in Neurosciences 27(3), 161–168 (2004)
14. Townsend, J.T., Nozawa, G.: Spatio-temporal properties of elementary perception: An investigation of parallel, serial, and coactive theories. Journal of Mathematical Psychology 39(4), 321–359 (1995)
15. Townsend, J.T., Wenger, M.J.: A theory of interactive parallel processing: New capacity measures and predictions for a response time inequality series. Psychological Review 111(4), 1003 (2004)

Multiple Decoupled CPGs with Local Sensory Feedback for Adaptive Locomotion Behaviors of Bio-inspired Walking Robots

Subhi Shaker Barikhan[1,2], Florentin Wörgötter[1],

and Poramate Manoonpong[1,3],[*]

[1] Bernstein Center for Computational Neuroscience (BCCN), The Third Institute of Physics, University of Göttingen, 37077 Göttingen, Germany
[2] Institute of Computer Science, University of Göttingen, 37077 Göttingen, Germany
[3] Maersk Mc-Kinney Moller Institute, University of Southern Denmark, 5230 Odense M, Denmark
{s.shaker.barikhan,worgott}@dpi.physik.uni-goettingen.de, poma@mmmi.sdu.dk

Abstract. Walking animals show versatile locomotion. They can also adapt their movement according to the changes of their morphology and the environmental conditions. These emergent properties are realized by biomechanics, distributed central pattern generators (CPGs), local sensory feedback, and their interactions during body and leg movements through the environment. Based on this concept, we present here an artificial bio-inspired walking system. Its intralimb coordination is formed by multiple decoupled CPGs while its interlimb coordination is attained by the interactions between body dynamics and the environment through local sensory feedback of each leg. Simulation results show that this bio-inspired approach generates self-organizing emergent locomotion allowing the robot to adaptively form regular patterns, to stably walk while pushing an object with its front legs or performing multiple stepping of the front legs, to deal with morphological change, and to synchronize its movement with another robot during a collaborative task.

Keywords: Adaptive behavior, Hexapod locomotion, Brain-body-environment interaction, Autonomous robots, Neural networks.

1 Introduction

Legged animals show various locomotion behaviors (e.g., walk, trot, and gallop for quadruped, and metachronal, tetrapod, and tripod for insects) which are used for particular situations like walking on different terrains and/or morphological change. They also show impressive flexibility and adaptivity of their movements generated by a combination of biomechanics, neural control (e.g., central pattern generators (CPGs)), local sensory feedback, and their interactions during body

---

[*] Corresponding author.

A.P. del Pobil et al. (Eds.): SAB 2014, LNAI 8575, pp. 65–75, 2014.
© Springer International Publishing Switzerland 2014

and leg movements through the environment [5]. While all these key ingredients are important for the complex achievement, they have not been fully applied to artificial legged systems. Several works utilize multiple distributed nonlinear oscillators with predefined phase relationships among them as coupled CPGs for interlimb and intralimb coordinations as well as locomotion generation [3], [4], [10]. However, this control technique fails to adaptivity due to the lack of sensory feedback and the consideration of body-environment interactions.

A few works use sensory feedback to utilize the dynamic interactions to generate adaptive locomotion [13]. One of the sensory feedback techniques is a phase reset scheme which resets the phase of a CPG at the same time the foot of the robot touches the ground. It has been employed for locomotion control of quadruped and hexapod robots [2], [6]. Aoi et al. [2] have used the phase reset scheme to allow the quadruped robot to perform various gait patterns and to exhibit a hysteresis in gait transition similarly to humans and animals. Ambe et al. [1] have extended the phase reset scheme by including a phase inhibition mechanism. This results in the improvement of gait stability. However, the phase reset and inhibition mechanisms require the predefined phase relationships among CPGs (i.e., predefined interlimb coordination); thereby lacking in flexibility and independency. According to this, another sensory feedback approach which does not require predefined interlimb coordination has been introduced [12]. This approach is based on the alteration of CPG's phase with respect to the magnitude of local sensory feedback. This results in flexibility and adaptability to deal with the changes of weight distribution and locomotion speed of a quadruped robot.

Inspired by [12], we present here our hexapod walking system where its intralimb coordination is formed by six decoupled CPGs while its interlimb coordination is not predefined but achieved by the interactions between body dynamics and the environment through local sensory feedback of each leg. This results in self-organizing gaits allowing the robot to adaptively form regular patterns, to stably walk while pushing an object with its front legs or performing multiple stepping of the front legs, to deal with morphological change (handicap), and to synchronize its locomotion with another robot during a collaborative task. We emphasize that the novelty of this work is the resulting complex self-organizing behaviors which, to our knowledge, have not been so far presented.

2   Multiple CPGs with Local Sensory Feedback for Adaptive Locomotion Behaviors

Our neural locomotion control system (Fig. 1a) is composed of six identical decoupled control components. Each one of them consists mainly of four elements: 1) CPG mechanism with neuromodulation and local sensory feedback for generating adaptive locomotion, 2) CPG post processing unit (PCPG) for shaping CPGs' output signals, 3) phase switching network (PSN) and velocity regulating network (VRN) for walking directional control, 4) motor neurons for transmitting motor commands to the specific leg joints of a hexapod robot (Fig.

1b). Note that the PSN can switch the phase of the CPG outputs to lead or lag behind each other by $\pi/2$ in phase with respect to a given input for walking sideways. The VRN functions qualitatively like a multiplication function, having capability to increase or decrease the amplitude of the TC-joint signals and even to reverse them with respect to their control inputs. This results in various walking directions, like forward/backward, turning left/right, turning in different radians, or curve walking in forward and backward directions [11]. All neurons of our neural locomotion control system are modeled as discrete time non-spiking neurons. The activity of each neuron is developed as follows:

$$a_i(t+1) = \sum_{j=1}^{n} W_{ij}o_j(t) + B_i; i = 1, ..., n, \tag{1}$$

where n denotes the number of units, a_i their activity, B_i represents a fixed internal bias term together with a stationary input to neuron i, W_{ij} the synaptic strength of the connection from neuron j to neuron i, and o_i the neuron output. The output of neurons is calculated by using the hyperbolic tangent (tanh) transfer function, i.e., $o_i(t) = \tanh(a_i(t))$, where $o_i(t) \in [-1, 1]$, except CPG post-processing neurons, whose outputs are calculated by deploying a step function with a threshold value of 0.85 and integrator units, thus the CPG outputs are translated into ascending and descending slopes. Moreover, the motor neurons deploy piecewise linear transfer functions to calculate their outputs, where the upper and lower bounds are $+1$ and -1 respectively. For more details on all neural components except the CPG one, we refer to our previous work [11].

3   A CPG Mechanism with Local Sensory Feedback

In our locomotion control system, CPGs serve as rhythmic pattern generators producing asymmetrical periodic signals to control leg joints. Each of them consists of two fully connected neurons and an extrinsic modulatory input S which is projected to the synaptic connections of the neurons. This enables the frequency change of the CPGs by modifying the synaptic weights W (not shown here, but see [11]). To adapt the CPGs' signals for dealing with external perturbations and self-organizing interlimb coordination, we use a local sensory feedback mechanism inspired by [12]. Here, the ground reaction force at each leg is used as feedback to modulate the phase of its target CPG (see Fig. 1d). The neural activities of each CPG are given by:

$$a_1(t+1) = \sum_{j=1}^{2} W_{1j}o_j(t) + B_1 - \gamma_1 F(t)\cos(a_1(t)), \tag{2}$$

$$a_2(t+1) = \sum_{j=1}^{2} W_{2j}o_j(t) + B_2 - \gamma_2 F(t)\sin(a_2(t)), \tag{3}$$

$$o_i(t) = \tanh(a_i(t)); \; i \in \{1, 2\}, \tag{4}$$

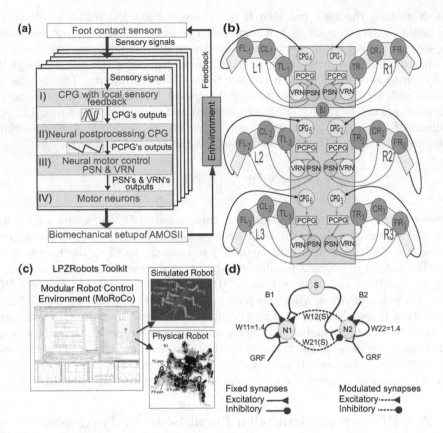

Fig. 1. (a) The diagram of an artificial bio-inspired walking system which consists of the biomechanical setup of the hexapod robot AMOSII (i.e., six 3-jointed legs, a segmented body structure with one active backbone joint (BJ), actuators, and passive compliant components [11]), sensors (i.e., proprioceptive and exteroceptive sensors), and neural mechanisms (I,II,III,VI). As we mentioned previously, our controller comprises six identical decoupled control components controlling six legs of AMOSII. **(b)** Multiple decoupled CPGs system applied to AMOSII for adaptive locomotion. CPG's outputs are modulated by local sensory feedback (black arrows). CPG outputs are projected to PCPGs (orange arrows) which translate them into ascending and descending slopes. These slopes will be fed to the PSN components (purple arrows). The outputs of the PSN are projected to the F(R,L), and C(R,L) motor neurons, as well as to the VRN (green arrows). The VRN's output is projected to the T(R,L) motor neuron (red arrows). **(c)** Modular Robot Control Environment embedded in the LPZRobots toolkit [9]. It is used for developing a controller, testing it on the simulated hexapod robot, and transferring it to the physical one. FC1, FC2, FC3, FC4, FC5, and FC6 are foot contact sensors. Each of them is installed at each leg. Each leg has three joints: the thoraco-coxal (TC-) joint enables forward and backward movements, the coxa-trochanteral (CTr-) joint enables elevation and depression of the leg, and the femur-tibia (FTi-) joint enables extension and flexion of the tibia. The morphology of these multi-jointed legs based on a cockroach leg [14]. **(d)** Wiring diagram of the CPG circuit. GRF represents the afferent feedback to modulate the CPG's outputs.

where γ_1 and γ_2 are positive constants. Here, γ_1 and γ_2 of the front legs are 0.04 and 0.03 respectively, γ_1 and γ_2 of the middle legs are 0.03 , and γ_1 and γ_2 of the hind legs are 0.035 and 0.03 respectively. $F(t)$ represents the continuous ground reaction force (GRF) detected by the foot contact sensor (FC), $F(t) \approx 0$ if a foot does not touch the ground.

The modulated CPG's output signals respond to the changes of the ground reaction force received from the foot contact sensor (FC). As local force feedback informs about the gait pattern, the robot state, and the terrain, the hexapod robot AMOSII will autonomously adapt its walking pattern. The effect of local sensory feedback on the CPG's outputs is not the same for all CPGs, but rather corresponds to the magnitude of the ground reaction force (GRF) and the activity of neurons. This variation of the influence on the CPGs will automatically yield phase differences among them, which will, in turn, be translated into proper interlimb coordination. As a result, the robot will perform an adaptive walking pattern. In this case, we do not have a fixed interlimb coordination, but rather a flexible one, since the walking pattern is subject to local sensory feedback, neural activities, and the body-environment interaction.

4   Intralimb and Interlimb Coordinations

Locomotion is achieved by proper interlimb and intralimb coordinations. The conventional way to design a gait is by defining the interlimb and intralimb neural connections. While the intralimb neural connections determine the coordination between joint movements within the leg, the predefined phase relationships among oscillators (CPGs) will fulfill interlimb coordination and enforce the planned gait. For example, a tripod gait is generated when the phase difference between each two adjacent CPGs is maintained to π. However, Owaki et al. [12] have proposed another hypothesis that interlimb coordination could rely on the physical interactions during walking rather than on explicit interlimb neural connections. Based on this assumption, the interlimb coordination of our system is realized by the body-environment interaction through local sensory information, whereas the intralimb coordination in each leg is achieved by the prewired neural connections from the PSN and VRN components to the motor neurons of each leg. Fig. 1b shows our decoupled CPGs model.

5   Experimental Results

We tested the performance of our artificial bio-inspired walking system on the simulated hexapod robot AMOSII in different cases. In all cases, we initiated AMOSII with an irregular gait, where the lateral legs move in phase, and the contralateral legs move antiphase. The CPG's frequency for all legs was 0.4 Hz except the CPG's frequency for the front legs (R1 and L1) in a multiple stepping experiment. Note that the amplitude of swing and stance phases is in a range of 45 and 75 degrees.

5.1   Transition from Irregular to Regular Gaits

As we have already mentioned, we initiated AMOSII with an irregular gait; therefore there is no leg elevation during swing phases. As soon as we enabled the local force feedback mechanism, AMOSII started to properly perform swing movement, i.e. no ground contact during the swing phase. A few steps later, AMOSII automatically adopted its walking pattern similar to a metachronal gait, where at least four legs are in the stance phase, and two legs are in the swing phase (see Fig. 2). The average walking speed of AMOSII after enabling the local force feedback mechanism was $\approx$ 5.01477 [cm/s].

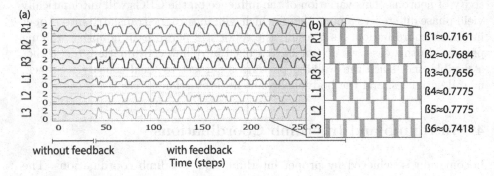

Fig. 2. (a) Experimental result of transition from irregular to regular gaits. Shown are the ground reaction forces (GRFs) detected by foot contact sensors. The yellow highlight area demonstrates that the robot could not lift up its legs during swing phase. **(b)** Gait diagram and the duty factors (βi where $i = 1, ..., 6$) matching the blue highlight area in (a). The blue bars refer to no ground contact during swing phase. Note that one time step is $\approx$ 0.037 s. It should be also noted that the foot contact sensors (FCs) in the simulated AMOSII calculate the ground reaction forces (GRFs) by measuring collision forces (penetration depth). We encourage readers to also see the video of this experiment at http://www.manoonpong.com/SAB2014/S1.mpg.

5.2   Adaptability to Different Functionalities of the Front Legs

Multiple Stepping of the Front Legs. Grabowska et al. [7] have referred to the special functionality of the stick insect front legs. It has been shown that the front legs perform multiple stepping and probing behavior during walking. This behavior is partially responsible for irregular gait occurrences. However, when prothoracic legs are ignored in the analysis of irregular gaits which are caused by the multiple stepping behavior, regular stereotypic gaits of the other legs can be observed. Inspired by this, in this experiment we tested our proposed walking system when the front legs were performing multiple stepping. We changed the default frequency of the two CPGs controlling the two front legs; thus both legs perform more steps than the other legs. The magnitude of the frequency change was arbitrary set as $f_1 = 1.3 * f_2$ and $f_4 = 1.6 * f_2$, and $f_2 = f_3 = f_5 = f_6 = 0.4$ Hz, where f_i is the frequency of the ith CPG. Fig. 3b exhibits that the mesothoracic and metathoracic legs performed a regular pattern. This walking pattern (two single leg swing phases follow synchronous swing of a diagonal pair of legs) is similar to a pattern of adult stick insects walking on a horizontal surface and their front legs performing multiple stepping [7]. The average walking speed in this situation was $\approx$ 5.29808 [cm/s]. Fig. 3a shows the locomotor behavior described as ground contact forces.

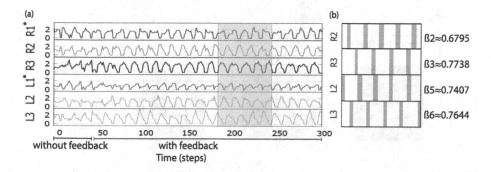

Fig. 3. Experimental result of multiple stepping of the front legs (R1 and L1). **(a)** The ground reaction forces (GRFs) exerted by the ground on the legs during multiple stepping. **(b).** Gait diagram of AMOSII and the duty factors (βi) matching the state in the highlight district in (a) after ignoring the ground reaction forces exerted on the front legs. The blue areas indicate no ground contact during swing phase. The video clip of this experiment can be seen at http://www.manoonpong.com/SAB2014/S2.mpg.

Pushing an Object. Another instance of the special duty of the front legs is for pushing an object. In this experiment, we modified the joint angles of the front legs to be suitable for the pushing mission. AMOSII revealed two different gaits based on the position of the pushed object related to AMOSII. The first gait was noticed when the mesothoracic legs were moving in phase to lift up the front part of the body. This pattern happened when AMOSII was trying to put the front legs above the pushed object (the average walking speed was $\approx$ 2.4178 [cm/s]). The second gait was tetrapod, which occurred when the front legs were already above of the pushed object (the average walking speed was $\approx$ 3.902 [cm/s]). The previously observed behavior plainly demonstrates the self-organizing locomotor behavior of our control system. However, different factors such as the shape of the object and its position related to AMOSII facilitated the occurrence of this locomotor behavior. Fig. 4 shows this behavior illustrated as the ground contact force signals, gait diagrams, and duty factors.

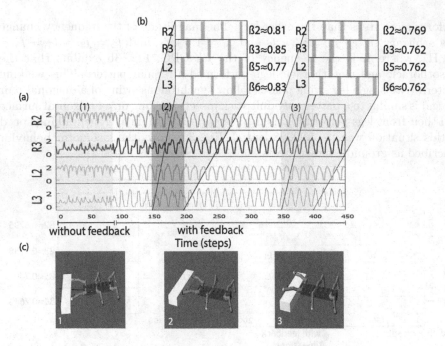

Fig. 4. Experimental result during pushing process. **(a)** The ground reaction forces (GRFs) exerted by the ground on the legs. State (1) presents the ground reaction force signals before introducing the feedback. State (2) presents the ground contact signals after activating the local sensory feedback mechanism. These signals indicate the middle legs were moving in phase. State (3) presents the ground contact signals where the front legs were on the top of the pushed object. **(b)** Gait diagrams and duty factors (βi) matching the states mentioned by (2) and (3) in (a). The blue areas indicate no ground contact during swing phase. **(c)** Snapshots of AMOSII while pushing the object. These snapshots match the states mentioned by (1), (2), and (3) in (a). Note that the weight of the object is 100 g. The video clip of this experiment can be seen at http://www.manoonpong.com/SAB2014/S3.mpg.

5.3   Adaptability to Morphological Change

Insects show a good ability to deal with different circumstances. They can overcome the problems arising from amputation of one or two legs. Graham [8] has investigated the impact of the leg amputation on locomotion. His observations indicate that insects can adapt their gaits after a leg amputation. In this experiment, we focused on the influence of the middle leg amputation on the locomotor behavior of AMOSII and assessed the efficiency of the proposed walking system to deal with a handicap situation. Therefore, we disabled the mesothoracic legs temporarily during the movement by lifting them up. In this way, they did not play any role in the walking process. The experimental result, illustrated by Fig. 5, indicates that AMOSII adopted a new gait (diagonal stepping) and was able to continue walking properly. This behavior provides a clue to the importance of sensory feedback to adapt gaits in response to morphological changes. The average walking speed of AMOSII while the middle legs were disabled was $\approx$ 4.7455 [cm/s], while the average walking speed before disabling the middle legs and after enabling them were 5.0075 [cm/s] and 5.1498 [cm/s] respectively.

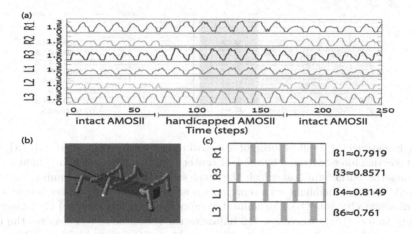

Fig. 5. Experimental result of our controller applied to the temporarily handicapped AMOSII. **(a)** The ground reaction forces during the movement of AMOSII whose middle legs were disabled temporarily. **(b)** Picture of AMOSII with the deactivated middle legs. **(c)** Gait diagram and duty factors (βi) corresponding to the highlight district in (a) after ignoring the middle legs. The blue bars refer to no ground contact during swing phase. We encourage readers to also see the video of this experiment at http://www.manoonpong.com/SAB2014/S4.mpg.

5.4   Coordinated Locomotion for a Collaborative Task

Coordinated locomotion between legged robots through local sensory feedback is an interesting aspect. This mission is difficult for a conventional nonadaptive locomotion control system. The is because the synchronization and coordination between the robots need to be achieved in order to generate combined locomotion. In addition, even if the locomotion is fulfilled, any minor perturbation can yield irregular gaits. According to this, an adaptive locomotion control system is required. Fig. 6 illustrates the ability of our adaptive control system for coordinating the locomotion of the two connected robots holding a sphere weighted 200 g (Fig. 6b). The coordinated locomotion is fulfilled by deploying only the physical interactions during the movement. Note that we implemented the same controller on these two robots and the two legs of each robot are fixed together. The average walking speed of these two robots was approximately 4.495 [cm/s].

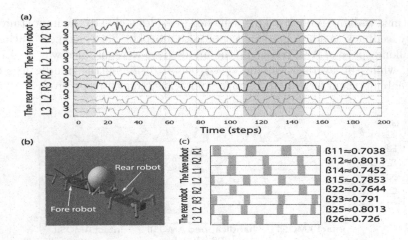

Fig. 6. Experimental result of locomotor coordination between two AMOSII. (a) The ground reaction forces detected by the foot contact sensors. The orange highlight sector represents the initial state, at which the local sensory feedback mechanism was not activated. The blue highlight area represents a sample of the GRFs after introducing the feedback mechanism. (b) Two connected robots holding a sphere. (c) Gait diagram and duty factors ((βij) where $i = 1, 2$ indicates the robot, i.e., $i = 1$ denotes the fore robot, $i = 2$ denotes the rear robot, and $j = 1, ..., 6$ refers to the legs). The gait diagram and duty factors match the blue highlight area in (a). The blue bars indicate no ground contact during swing phase. The video clip of this experiment can be seen at http://www.manoonpong.com/SAB2014/S5.mpg.

6 Conclusion

We presented an artificial bio-inspired walking system which is controlled by multiple decoupled CPGs. Besides, deploying the ground reaction forces (GRFs) as local sensory feedback allows for: 1) the modulation of CPGs' output signals, 2) the modification of the phase differences among CPGs. Due to a combination of biomechanics (body and leg structures), neural control (multiple decoupled CPGs), local sensory feedback, and their dynamical interactions through the environment, AMOSII can autonomously adapt its gait from irregular to regular gaits after a few steps. It is also able to perform suitable gaits corresponding to biological findings in the case of multiple stepping of the front legs, and to deal with morphological change as well. In addition, this approach can also coordinate locomotion between two connected robots for a collaborative task and realize a special functionality of the front legs such as pushing an object. While this approach can generate adaptive locomotion, it cannot achieve specific gaits due to the lack of neural connections among CPGs. In the future, we will further introduce the proper connections for specific gait generation. We will also apply this approach to our real hexapod robot AMOSII and test it in a real environment.

Acknowledgments. This research was supported by Emmy Noether grant MA4464/3-1 and BCCNII grant 01GQ1005A (project D1).

References

1. Ambe, Y., Nachstedt, T., Manoonpong, P., Wörgötter, F., Aoi, S., Matsuno, F.: Stability analysis of a hexapod robot driven by distributed nonlinear oscillators with a phase modulation mechanism. In: IEEE/RSJ International Conference on Intelligent Robots and Systems, pp. 5087–5092 (2013)
2. Aoi, S., Yamashita, T., Tsuchiya, K.: Hysteresis in the gait transition of a quadruped investigated using simple body mechanical and oscillator network models. Physical Review E 83(6), 061909 (2011)
3. Campos, R., Matos, V., Santos, C.: Hexapod locomotion: A nonlinear dynamical systems approach. In: IECON 2010-36th Annual Conference on IEEE Industrial Electronics Society, pp. 1546–1551 (2010)
4. Canavier, C.C., Butera, R.J., Dror, R.O., Baxter, D.A., Clark, J.W., Byrne, J.H.: Phase response characteristics of model neurons determine which patterns are expressed in a ring circuit model of gait generation. Biological Cybernetics 77(6), 367–380 (1997)
5. Dickinson, M.H., Farley, C.T., Full, R.J., Koehl, M.A.R., Kram, R., Lehman, S.: How animals move: An integrative view. Science 288(5463), 100–106 (2000)
6. Fujiki, S., Aoi, S., Kohda, T., Senda, K., Tsuchiya, K.: Emergence of hysteresis in gait transition of a hexapod robot driven by nonlinear oscillators with phase resetting. In: 2012 4th IEEE RAS & EMBS International Conference on Biomedical Robotics and Biomechatronics (BioRob), pp. 1638–1643 (2012)
7. Grabowska, M., Godlewska, E., Schmidt, J., Daun-Gruhn, S.: Quadrupedal gaits in hexapod animals-inter-leg coordination in free-walking adult stick insects. The Journal of Experimental Biology 215(24), 4255–4266 (2012)
8. Graham, D.: The effect of amputation and leg restraint on the free walking coordination of the stick insectCarausius morosus. Journal of Comparative Physiology 116(1), 91–116 (1977)
9. Hesse, F., Martius, G., Manoonpong, P., Biehl, M., Wörgötter, F.: Modular Robot Control Environment Testing Neural Control on Simulated and Real Robots. In: Frontiers in Computational Neuroscience, Conference Abstract: Bernstein Conference (2012), doi:10.3389/conf.fncom.2012.55.00179
10. Ijspeert, A.J., Crespi, A., Ryczko, D., Cabelguen, J.M.: From swimming to walking with a salamander robot driven by a spinal cord model. Science 315(5817), 1416–1420 (2007)
11. Manoonpong, P., Parlitz, U., Wörgötter, F.: Neural control and adaptive neural forward models for insect-like, energy-efficient, and adaptable locomotion of walking machines. Frontiers in Neural Circuits 7, 12 (2013)
12. Owaki, D., Kano, T., Nagasawa, K., Tero, A., Ishiguro, A.: Simple robot suggests physical interlimb communication is essential for quadruped walking. Journal of the Royal Society Interface 10(78) (2013)
13. Shim, Y., Husbands, P.: Chaotic exploration and learning of locomotion behaviors. Neural Computation 24(8), 2185–2222 (2012)
14. Zill, S., Schmitz, J., Büschges, A.: Load Sensing and Control of Posture and Locomotion. Arthropod Structure & Development 33, 273–286 (2004)

The Role of a Cerebellum-Driven Perceptual Prediction within a Robotic Postural Task

Giovanni Maffei[1], Marti Sanchez-Fibla[1],
Ivan Herreros[1], and Paul F.M.J. Verschure[1,2]

[1] SPECS, Technology Department, Universitat Pompeu Fabra, Carrer de Roc
Boronat 138, 08018 Barcelona, Spain
[2] ICREA, Institucio Catalana de Recerca i Estudis Avancats, Passeig Lluis
Companys 23, 08010 Barcelona
{giovanni.maffei,marti.sanchez,ivan.herreros,paul.verschure}@upf.edu

Abstract. Postural adjustments are acquired compensatory and anticipatory motor responses maintaining balance and equilibrium against
self-induced or external perturbations. It has been proposed that the
cerebellum could be involved in issuing such predictive motor actions.
However, it remains unclear what strategy is adopted by the brain in
order to make such prediction and how anticipatory and compensatory
components are integrated into a single response. Within this study we
are interested in the computational mechanisms underlying the acquisition of anticipatory responses in a postural task. We compare two alternative architectures representing two different hypotheses: anticipation
either as sensory-to-motor association or as sensory-to-sensory association. We propose to use a cerebellar model to control the acquisition of
an adaptive motor response in a simulated robotic setup. We devise a
scenario where a cart-pole robot is trained to predict a perturbation and
issue an anticipatory action to minimize the disturbance on its state of
equilibrium. Our results show that a cerebellum based architecture can
efficiently learn to reduce errors through anticipation. We also suggest
that a sensory-to-sensory prediction could be less expensive in terms of
energy cost and more robust when events violate the acquired prediction.

Keywords: Postural adjustments, cerebellum, sensory prediction, biomimetic, robotics, simulation.

1 Introduction

When learning to perform a skillful motor task such as skiing, one has to be able
to resist perturbations issuing appropriate motor actions in order to maintain
constant balance and equilibrium and avoid falls. The novice skier would tend to
correct a disturbance, due to wind or irregularity of the slope, at the time it is
experienced. However with practice and exercise, he would be able to recognize
an incoming disturbance and to trigger a preparatory motor action in order to
minimize the effect of the perturbation on his body configuration, his balance
and ultimately on his performance. Postural adjustments are described within

A.P. del Pobil et al. (Eds.): SAB 2014, LNAI 8575, pp. 76–87, 2014.

the realm of motor control as small muscular responses which constantly adjust the body configuration to maintain barycenter position and equilibrium while walking, lifting objects or during collisions with obstacles [1,2].

Experimental studies found that healthy subjects involved in motor tasks, such as catching a ball [3], or lifting objects of different weights [4], rely on progressively acquired motor patterns that enhance performance. Electromyographic recordings show that compensatory muscular activity posterior to the experienced perturbation is increasingly coupled with preparatory responses, possibly driven by the adaptation to the disturbance. Such results suggest that a preparatory action can be learnt and initiated in advance, and that postural adjustments can be decomposed in two elements: compensation and anticipation. Similar studies conducted on cerebellar patients show that they lack predictive anticipatory actions and correct response magnitude scaling when tested in postural tasks, such as standing still on a sliding platform [5,6] or minimizing the arm vertical shift while catching a falling object [7,8]. These findings would make the cerebellum an ideal candidate as neural substrate involved in the acquisition of adaptive postural motor responses.

Despite several mechanisms underlying postural control have been widely studied, it remains unclear what strategy is adopted by the brain in order to issue predictive motor responses. Moreover, it is poorly understood how anticipatory and compensatory components are integrated into a single response. A possible explanation is that these responses are both the result of an association between a sensory signal and a motor response. The former would be triggered by a sensory signal co-occurring with the perturbation, while the latter would be initiated by a sensory signal preceding the perturbation. The total motor response would therefore be the sum of the two components separately acquired and combined in more peripheral areas such as the spinal cord [9]. However results on the topographic organization of sensory and motor representations of the hand in the human cerebellum show that, unlike the neocortex, sensory and motor patches for the same finger do not overlap systematically, but are closely interdigitated in a nearly unrelated fashion [10]. The suggested close interaction between sensory and motor cerebellar circuits leads to an alternative explanation. It is indeed possible that compensatory and anticipatory responses are the result of the interaction of two predictions of different nature. Compensation could be achieved by mapping a sensory input into an adaptive motor response. Differently, anticipation could be achieved by associating a sensory signal anticipating the perturbation with the sensory signal perceived at the moment of the perturbation. This sensory prediction would then trigger the compensatory action in an anticipatory way.

With these hypotheses in mind we propose an adaptive control architecture formed by a compensatory and an anticipatory layer. The former acts as a fast feed-forward controller that corrects the effect of a perturbation after it has been experienced. The latter is responsible for anticipating the incoming perturbation and initiating an action in advance. We compare two alternative hypotheses to test the nature of anticipation: 1) a sensory to motor prediction, which associates a sensory event preceding the perturbation with an adaptive motor response, and 2) a sensory to sensory prediction, which associates a sensory signal with the expected sensory outcome of the perturbing event and, in turn, triggers a motor response. In addition we explore the role of cerebellar adaptive properties, proposing a learning strategy based on a model of the cerebellum where both compensatory and anticipatory components can be acquired by two independent instances of the same cerebellar controller [11,12,13] .

Coherently with human equilibrium tasks [6], we devise a simulated cart-pole setup in which a robot has to minimize the error provoked by a perturbation directed to the pole. Similarly to [13], where a real robot had to maintain constant speed anticipating the effect of the collision with an obstacle, the agent is equipped with sensors that allow to measure impact force and proximity. The former provides a sensory signal at the moment of the impact with an object allowing fast compensation. The latter perceives the distance from the object allowing anticipation. We propose an experimental procedure to compare the two architectures in terms of learning curve, error minimization and motor cost. Results suggest that an agent relying on an anticipatory sensory prediction can remarkably reduce the error with less effort. Moreover, this architecture appears to be more robust in case of ambiguity of the stimulus, as shown in trials where a sensory signal previously associated with a perturbation is no more reliable. Finally we discuss the obtained results in the light of recent physiological and behavioral evidences supporting the versatility of the cerebellum in learning associations outside the scope of motor control. Implications for bio-mimetic robot control are also taken into account.

2   Methods

Setup. In order to study the possible role of cerebellum in anticipatory responses to postural perturbations we devise a simulated physics based setup implementing the cart-pole dynamics (Fig. 1, *left*). A simulated agent has to resist a postural perturbation through anticipation in order to minimize error and energy cost. The agent is able to slide on a horizontal surface controlling one degree of freedom with the goal of maintaining the pendulum in a constant vertical equilibrium performing control against force of gravity and external perturbing forces. The agent is equipped with a proximity sensor and a pressure sensor detecting the distance to external bodies and eventually the magnitude of the force produced by the collision with them. A colliding object is directed to the extremity of the pendulum with a given constant velocity and force, therefore provoking a perturbation that affects the pendulum position and the state of equilibrium of the agent. The goal of the agent is to learn to associate sensory inputs to finely tuned motor responses in order to firstly compensate and secondly anticipate the perturbing event both in terms of magnitude and timing, therefore minimizing the pendulum deviation from the state of equilibrium with the minimum effort.

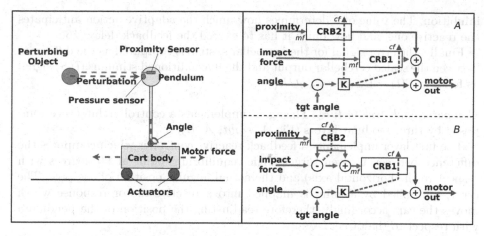

Fig. 1. *Left.* Cart-pole setup. Cart represented in equilibrium position (pendulum at 90 degrees) and incoming perturbation. Sensors are represented in green, actuators in red. *Right.* Computational Architectures. A. Sensory-to-motor and B. Sensory-to-sensory hypotheses. Sensory signals are represented in green. Motor signals are represented in red. Adaptive components are represented by two cerebellar modules ($CRB1$ and $CRB2$ respectively). Note the different input-output configuration for $CRB2$ in A, where the proximity signal is associated to a motor response and B, where the proximity signal is associated to the impact force. Mossy fibers (mf) represent the microcircuit input stage, while Climbing fibers (cf) provide the teaching signal (dashed line) via Inferior Olive (not displayed). K represents the gain of the reactive proportional controller that converts the sensory input into motor output.

Learning Algorithm. The bio-mimetic learning algorithm at the core of the behavior of the agent is based on an analysis-synthesis adaptive filter implementation mimicking the learning strategy of the cerebellar microcircuit [14,12]. The cue signal, representing the input conveyed by mossy fibers, is decomposed into several signals mimicking the expansion of information into cortical basis occurring within the cerebellar granular layer. The signal of the cortical basis is generated producing a fast excitatory component and a slow inhibitory one. Each component consists of a double exponential convolution with time constants randomly drawn from two flat probability distributions (a fast time constant, ranging from 5 to 50 ms and a slow one ranging from 50 ms to 2.5 s controlling the raise and the decay of the basis respectively, coherently with the physiological range of the time constants of the slow currents in the granular layer [15]). The value obtained after the two convolutions is then thresholded and scaled for each basis.

The output of the cerebellar controller is given by: $CR(t) = [\mathbf{p}(t)^T \mathbf{w}(t)]$ where $\mathbf{w}(t)$ is the vector of weights and $\mathbf{p}(t)$, the vector of basis, both in column form.

The weights are updated using the de-correlation learning rule: $\Delta w_j(t) = \beta E(t) p_j(t - \delta)$ where β is the learning rate and $E(t)$ is the error signal, computed by the inferior olive output. δ provides the latency of the nucleo-olivary inhibition. The value of δ determines how much the adaptive action anticipates the reactive one, and how much it has to exceed the feedback delay [16].

Finally, the error signal for the cerebellar system is computed as the difference between the scaled cerebellar output and the unconditioned stimulus (US) signal as follows: $E(t) = US(t) - k_{noi}CR(t - \delta)$

Computational Architecture. The agent implements a control architecture composed by three modular layers (Fig. 1, *right*, A, B).

The first layer implements a feedback reactive controller which computes the difference between a given target angle (equilibrium point at 90 degrees with respect to the horizontal axis) and the actual angular position of the pole. The error, multiplied by a gain, is mapped into a reactive motor response which moves the cart accordingly, therefore readjusting the position of the pendulum with respect to the target.

The second layer implements an instance of the cerebellar microcircuit, and it is responsible for acquiring compensatory responses. The cue signal is given by the force input resulting from the collision with the perturbing object. The signal to be learned (*teaching signal*) is given by the output of the reactive controller, encoding the action necessary to compensate for the pendulum error. The output of the controller is an acquired compensatory motor response acting in a feed-forward manner and summing to the output of the reactive controller.

The third layer of control, implementing a second instance of the same cerebellar microcircuit, is responsible for anticipatory responses.

In order to study how anticipation is performed within the context of anticipatory postural responses we propose two possible configurations which reflect, at the implementation level, the alternative hypotheses on the nature of such responses.

On one hand we propose a sensory-to-motor $(S2M)$ configuration (Fig. 1, *right*, A) which takes the input from the proximity sensors as cue signal and the output of the reactive controller as error signal. The output is represented by a feed-forward anticipatory motor response which is summed to the motor response of the compensatory and reactive layer.

Alternatively we test a sensory-to-sensory $(S2S)$ configuration (Fig. 1, *right*, B). In this case the cue signal is given by the proximity sensor value while the teaching signal is given by the force input resulting from the collision with the perturbing object. This controller outputs a predicted sensory signal anticipating the sensory consequences of the collision. The prediction is subtracted with a small delay from the real incoming sensory signal coherently with neurophysiological data on sensory integration between cerebellar driven prediction and actual somatosensory feedback [17]. The net force signal finally inputs the compensatory controller, which in turn triggers an action preceding the perturbation, therefore producing both an anticipatory and a compensatory motor output.

Experimental Design. The experimental session proceeds on a trial by trial base, having the agent set at a given position in a state of equilibrium at the beginning of every trial.

During each trial (5 seconds duration), a colliding object (25 kg) is directed to the extremity of the pendulum with a velocity equals to 1 m/s, therefore provoking a perturbation of 25 N affecting the pendulum position and the state of equilibrium of the agent.

We run a set of experiments to primarily test the effectiveness of such layered architecture in associating sensory inputs to finely tuned motor responses. The goal is learning to predict the perturbing event both in terms of magnitude and timing, issuing a motor action that minimizes the pendulum deviation from the state of equilibrium with the minimum effort.

We therefore compare the learning performances of the two alternative antic-ipatory configurations both in terms of learning capabilities and robustness to events that violate the acquired associations. In the first experiment we run a session of 50 trial for each of the two proposed architectures with the goal of comparing the dynamics in the acquisition of the compensatory and anticipatory responses. We are particularly interested in error minimization and efficiency in motor action cost. In the second experiment we test the acquired responses un-der a condition in which the perturbing object is still activating the proximity signal but is not provoking a perturbation anymore. We test both architectures under this condition for 10 trials looking at the robustness and flexibility of the architecture when events violate the acquired prediction.

3   Results

Experiment 1. The goal of this experiment is to test the learning capabilities of the proposed computational architecture under $S2M$ and $S2S$ conditions.

We train the agent to co-acquire both a compensatory and an anticipatory response with the goal of minimizing the deviation of the pendulum from a given target angle. The training session lasts 50 trials for both S2M and S2S architectures, during which a perturbation of constant magnitude of 5 N is sent to the pendulum with a delay of 1 sec from the beginning of the trial.

This perturbation magnitude provokes the sole feedback controller to reac-tively adjust the position of the pendulum (Fig. 2, *left*) showing a prominent oscillatory pattern which reduces the error over time but never stabilizes the pendulum to the desired position during the whole duration of the trial.

Under both $S2M$ and $S2S$ conditions, at the end of the training the robot is able to issue both an anticipatory and a compensatory response that minimize the effect of the incoming perturbation on the position of the pendulum (Fig. 2, *left*). We notice that a small deviation from the target is introduced by the agent itself as a consequence of the anticipatory response approximately 0.3 seconds before the perturbation. This well timed response allows the minimization of the perturbing force provoked by the collision, and therefore stabilizes the normalized cumulative error around a value of 0.05 (Fig. 2, *right*). If compared with the early trials, the intervention of the reactive controller at the end of the session is greatly reduced (Fig. 4, *right*) minimizing therefore the amount of energy required to stabilize the pendulum in a correct position.

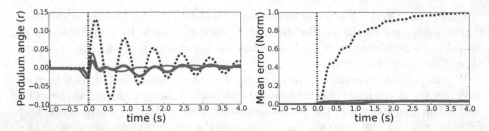

Fig. 2. *Left.* Pendulum Angle. *Right.* Normalized mean cumulative error. *Colorcode* : Blue dashed: reactive controller only (mean 10 trials). Red thick: S2M trained controller (mean 10 trials). Green thin: S2S trained controller (mean 10 trials). Black: perturbation onset.

The adaptive motor response at the end of the training experiment can be decomposed into two different elements.

Under the *S2M* (Fig. 3, *left*) condition we observe that a motor response triggered by the sensed impact with the colliding object is issued at the moment of the collision. It peaks before the response of the sole reactive controller, and allows a faster compensation. An additional motor response triggered by the proximity signal is issued before the perturbation onset, and it is added to the total motor response allowing anticipation.

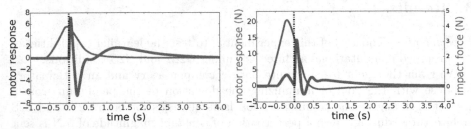

Fig. 3. *Left.* S2M adaptive responses. Magenta thin: anticipatory motor response. Red thick: compensatory motor response. Black dashed: perturbation onset. *Right.* S2S adaptive responses. Green thin: anticipatory sensory prediction. Red thick: anticipatory and compensatory motor response. Black dashed: perturbation onset.

Under the *S2S* condition we notice that a single adaptive motor response is issued accounting for both compensation and anticipation (Fig. 3, *right*). One single motor response is acquired at the level of the compensatory controller where, similarly to the *S2M* architecture, a force sensory input signaling the impact with the perturbing object triggers a fast motor response. However the anticipatory response is achieved by predicting the force sensory input from the proximity signal in a sensory to sensory fashion. The predicted signal then inputs the compensatory module which triggers a motor response in an anticipatory way.

Both architectures perform almost equally, with similar performance in terms of error minimization and learning curve slope (Fig. 4, *left*). However the total

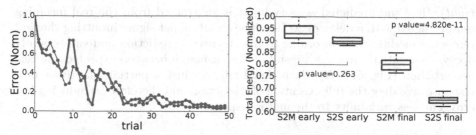

Fig. 4. *Left.* Learning curve during the training session (normalized cumulative error). Red thick: sensory-to-motor architecture. Green thin: sensory-to-sensory architecture *Right.* Total motor energy (sample of 10 trials per condition). We compare significance between S2M and S2S architectures at early learning stage and advanced learning stage.

adaptive energy produced by the *S2M* architecture is significantly higher than the one produced by the *S2S* architecture (Fig. 4, *right*).

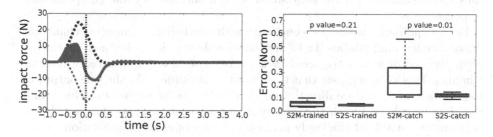

Fig. 5. *Left.* Sensory prediction - sensory input mismatch in catch trial. Blue dashed thick: sensory prediction output of $CRB2$. Red dashed thin: sensory prediction error. Green solid: net sensory input to $CRB1$. Filled green area: positive part of net sensory input triggering a partial motor response. *Right.* Normalized cumulative error (sample of 10 trials per condition). We compare significance between S2M and S2S architectures at advanced learning stage and during catch trials (experiment 2).

Experiment 2. The goal of the second experiment is to test the reliability and flexibility of the architecture in case of unexpected conditions, namely the amount of self induced error in the case that a cue signal previously anticipating the collision is providing no perturbation.

Once both anticipatory and compensatory responses are acquired we run a short session of 10 trials for each architecture setting the mass of the colliding object to 0g, and therefore producing a null perturbation.

Both controllers introduce an error triggered by an erroneous anticipatory response. However we observe that the self-induced error in the case of the S2M architecture is significantly higher and varying than the one introduced by the S2S architecture, which in turn appears to be more stable and more resistant to unexpected conditions (Fig. 5, *right*).

This difference could be due to the comparison between predicted sensory signal and real sensory signal found in the sensory to sensory architecture (Fig. 1, *right*). Here the predicted sensory input is subtracted from the real incoming sensory signal with a delay of 200 ms. The resulting net signal inputting the first cerebellar module rises according to the erroneous prediction and subsequently decays to negative values as a result of the mismatch between expected and real perturbation (Fig. 5, *left*). Such signal triggers just a partial adaptive motor response, avoiding the full execution of the action and therefore introducing less error and less variability to the motor response.

4   Discussion and Conclusion

Within this study we are interested in the computational mechanisms underlying the acquisition of anticipatory responses in a postural task. We compare two alternative architectures representing two different hypotheses: anticipation either as an acquired sensory-to-motor association or as an acquired sensory-to-sensory association. We also propose that cerebellum could be the neural substrate responsible for the acquisition of both anticipatory and compensatory responses.

Both hypotheses would be consistent with cerebellar learning mechanisms. Avoidance learning studies [18,19] indeed show how animals learn to produce a predictive motor action triggered by a sensory cue in order to avoid a noxious stimulus. This view suggests that the output of purkinje cells, the sole output of the cerebellum, would be directly contributing to motor responses. This would therefore be coherent with the sensory-motor association hypothesis which has been shown capable of efficiently perform in terms of error minimization within a postural task. According to this view the integration of two independent motor responses might take place at a peripheral stage, such as the spinal cord [9]. However the overall performance of the sensory-motor controller is not completely satisfying in terms of energy costs and robustness to unexpected conditions.

Postural control can be considered a complex task involving several sensory-motor interactions [1]. We suggest that with increasing complexity of the task, more sophisticated learning strategies might need to be applied by the brain. Interestingly, recent studies on the non-motor functions of the cerebellum [20] suggest that it would be capable of predictions outside the scope of adaptive motor control. Neuroimaging studies have shown that the human cerebellum is active during somatosensory processing [21] as well as visual and auditory perceptual tasks [22]. It has been also shown that cerebellar patients perform poorly in pure perceptual associative tasks where the prediction of a sensory signal is required to be learned from a second sensory signal [23,24]. Finally, anatomical studies show that the cerebellum has distinct projections to brain areas important for perception [25].

These findings could support the hypothesis which considers anticipatory responses in the brain as the result of the interaction among a pure sensory-to-sensory prediction and a sensory-to-motor prediction. This view would not contradict the well established findings on the cerebellar direct contribution to motor control, but would extend its adaptive properties to a more perceptual domain. We hypothesize that a possible advantage of relying on sensory predictions is the tendency to minimize the amount of action performed to achieve some motor goal. As we show in our results the sensory-to-sensory architecture achieves error minimization in a more efficient way compared with the sensory-to-motor one. Our assumption is that learning to produce one adaptive response driven by an expected sensory signal requires less energy than producing two, eventually antagonist, motor responses with different temporal profiles.

This may not be the only advantage. We show indeed that the sensory-to-sensory architecture is more stable and robust within conditions in which an ambiguous stimulus is suddenly provided. This result could be incongruous with findings from conditioning studies and avoidance learning. According to this paradigm a subject tested on catch trials would trigger a full motor response as result of a sensory-motor association, where diminished response would be gradually expected during the extinction phase. This view would therefore be more congruent with the sensory-motor hypothesis.

However behavioral results have suggested that healthy subjects trained to resist an expected perturbation tend to minimize self induced error in case of unexpected conditions, reducing the acquired motor response since the first trial [26]. This view is incongruous with the previous one, possibly requiring a more complex explanation. We propose that relying on a sensory prediction for anticipation could have an advantage in terms of performance, and eventually safety for an individual. As also proposed in [26], this could indeed be a mechanism that weights a sensory expectation with an actual sensory signal, partially preventing ambiguous stimuli to trigger inappropriate motor responses. The direct interaction between sensory and motor predictions in the cerebellum could be supported by physiological data showing a scattered an interdigitated topographic organization of sensory and motor areas in the cerebellar cortex [10]. As suggested by the authors such an arrangement may enable the cerebellum to quickly form new, and often context dependent, sensory-motor associations . This would ultimately be an important computational feature for learning new motor tasks, in which sensation and action might take on novel relationships.

The advantages above described could finally benefit robotic architectures. The proposed bio-mimetic approach would allow a more efficient adaptive control of posture in humanoid robots and, in general, a minimization of errors during navigation and manipulation tasks. The importance of learning to anticipate, as found in humans and animals, can therefore be directly applied to agents able to learn useful sensory-motor contingencies from the interaction with the environment. The proposed learning strategy represents indeed a model-free approach where physical properties of the environment are not assumed but progressively acquired. This could imply more flexibility and ability for an agent in adapting to its surroundings and learning appropriate motor responses from experience.

Acknowledgments. This work was supported by eSMC FP7-ICT- 270212.

References

1. Massion, J.: Postural control system. Current Opinion in Neurobiology 4(6), 877–887 (1994)
2. Peterka, R.J.: Sensorimotor Integration in Human Postural Control. J. Neurophysiol. 88(3), 1097–1118 (2002)
3. Shiratori, T., Latash, M.L.: Anticipatory postural adjustments during load catching by standing subjects. Clinical Neurophysiology 112(7), 1250–1265 (2001)
4. Flanagan, J.R., King, S., Wolpert, D.M., Johansson, R.S.: Sensorimotor prediction and memory in object manipulation. Canadian Journal of Experimental Psychology (22) (2001)
5. Timmann, D., Horak, F.B.: Perturbed step initiation in cerebellar subjects: 2. Modification of anticipatory postural adjustments. Experimental Brain Research. Experimentelle Hirnforschung. Expérimentation Cérébrale 141(1), 110–120 (2001)
6. Horak, F.B., Diener, H.C., Neurological, R.S.D.: Cerebellar control of postural scaling and central set in stance Cerebellar Control of Postural Scaling and Central Set in Stance. Journal of Neurophysiology 72(2), 479–493 (1994)
7. Lang, C., Bastian, A.: Cerebellar subjects show impaired adaptation of anticipatory EMG during catching. Journal of Neurophysiology, 2108–2119 (1999)
8. Serrien, D.J., Wiesendanger, M.: Role of the cerebellum in tuning anticipatory and reactive grip force responses. Journal of Cognitive Neuroscience 11(6), 672–681 (1999)
9. Bizzi, E., Cheung, V.C.K., D'Avella, A., Saltiel, P., Tresch, M.: Combining modules for movement. Brain Research Reviews 57(1), 125–133 (2008)
10. Wiestler, T., McGonigle, D.J., Diedrichsen, J.: Integration of sensory and motor representations of single fingers in the human cerebellum. Journal of Neurophysiology 105(6), 3042–3053 (2011)
11. Herreros, I., Maffei, G., Brandi, S., Sanchez-Fibla, M., Verschure, P.F.M.J.: Speed generalization capabilities of a cerebellar model on a rapid navigation task. In: 2013 IEEE/RSJ International Conference on Intelligent Robots and Systems, pp. 363–368. IEEE (November 2013)
12. Herreros, I., Verschure, P.F.: Nucleo-olivary inhibition balances the interaction between the reactive and adaptive layers in motor control. Neural Networks 47, 64–71 (2013)
13. Lepora, N.F., Mura, A., Krapp, H.G., Verschure, P.F.M.J., Prescott, T.J. (eds.): Living Machines 2013. LNCS (LNAI), vol. 8064. Springer, Heidelberg (2013)
14. Dean, P., Porrill, J., Ekerot, C.F., Jörntell, H.: The cerebellar microcircuit as an adaptive filter: experimental and computational evidence. Nature Reviews. Neuroscience 11(1), 30–43 (2010)
15. van Dorp, S., De Zeeuw, C.I.: Variable timing of synaptic transmission in cerebellar unipolar brush cells. Proceedings of the National Academy of Sciences of the United States of America, 1314219111 (March 2014)
16. Miall, R.C., Weir, D.J., Wolpert, D.M., Stein, J.F.: Is the cerebellum a smith predictor? Journal of Motor Behavior 25(3), 203–216 (1993)
17. Blakemore, S.J., Wolpert, D.M., Frith, C.D.: Central cancellation of self-produced tickle sensation. Nature Neuroscience 1(7), 635–640 (1998)
18. Jirenhed, D.A., Bengtsson, F., Hesslow, G.: Acquisition, extinction, and reacquisition of a cerebellar cortical memory trace. The Journal of Neuroscience: The Official Journal of the Society for Neuroscience 27(10), 2493–2502 (2007)

19. Hesslow, G.: Inhibition of classically conditioned eyeblink responses by stimulation of the cerebellar cortex in the decerebrate cat. J. Physiol. 476(2), 245–256 (1994)
20. Ramnani, N.: The primate cortico-cerebellar system: Anatomy and function. Nature Reviews. Neuroscience 7(7), 511–522 (2006)
21. Gao, J.H., Parsons, L.M., Bower, J.M., Xiong, J., Li, J., Fox, P.T.: Cerebellum Implicated in Sensory Acquisition and Discrimination Rather than Motor Control. Science 272(5261), 545–547 (1996)
22. Baumann, O., Mattingley, J.B.: Scaling of neural responses to visual and auditory motion in the human cerebellum. The Journal of Neuroscience: The Official Journal of the Society for Neuroscience 30(12), 4489–4495 (2010)
23. Roth, M.J., Synofzik, M., Lindner, A.: The cerebellum optimizes perceptual predictions about external sensory events. Current Biology: CB 23(10), 930–935 (2013)
24. O'Reilly, J.X., Mesulam, M.M., Nobre, A.C.: The cerebellum predicts the timing of perceptual events. The Journal of Neuroscience: The Official Journal of the Society for Neuroscience 28(9), 2252–2260 (2008)
25. Dum, R.P., Strick, P.L.: An unfolded map of the cerebellar dentate nucleus and its projections to the cerebral cortex. Journal of Neurophysiology 89, 634–639 (2003)
26. Crevecoeur, F., Scott, S.H.: Priors engaged in long-latency responses to mechanical perturbations suggest a rapid update in state estimation. PLoS Computational Biology 9(8), e1003177 (2013)

Biomimetic Agent Based Modelling Using Male Frog Calling Behaviour as a Case Study

Søren V. Jørgensen[1], Yves Demazeau[2],
Jakob Christensen-Dalsgaard[3], and John Hallam[4]

[1] Center for Biorobotics, Maersk McKinney Moeller Institute
University of Southern Denmark
svjo@mmmi.sdu.dk
[2] CNRS — LIG
38000 Grenoble
Yves.Demazeau@imag.fr
[3] Center for Sound Communication, Institute of Biology
University of Southern Denmark
jcd@biology.sdu.dk
[4] Center for Biorobotics, Maersk Mc-Kinney Moeller Institute
University of Southern Denmark
john@mmmi.sdu.dk

Abstract. A new agent-based modelling tool has been developed to allow the modelling of populations of individuals whose interactions are characterised by tightly timed dynamics. The tool was developed to model male frog calling dynamics, to facilitate research into what local rules may be employed by individuals to generate their observed population behaviour. A number of existing agent-modelling frameworks are considered, but none have the ability to handle large numbers of time-dependent event-generating agents; hence the construction of a new tool, RANA. The calling behaviour of the Puerto Rican Tree Frog, *E. coqui*, is implemented as a case study for the presentation and discussion of the tool, and results from this model are presented. RANA, in its present stage of development, is shown to be able to handle the problem of modelling calling frogs, and several fruitful extensions are proposed and motivated.

1 Introduction

In many cases, modelling interaction of agents in a population at the level of the agents themselves requires an ability to manage timing constraints. For example, calling frogs emit their calls at times which are influenced by what they hear, and the time at which they hear emitted calls from other frogs are determined by the physical process of sound propagation in their environment. In the current state of the art there is a lack of agent-based simulation tools able to support such precise time-based models of large populations of agents; we therefore describe RANA, a new tool we have built with that goal in mind.

A.P. del Pobil et al. (Eds.): SAB 2014, LNAI 8575, pp. 88–97, 2014.

Agent-based modelling offers an interesting way of performing biologically inspired simulations. Agent based social interaction models have been constructed[3], and biomimetic modelling is supported by various tools including the Netlogo framework[15], which contains a good number of ready-to-run biomimetic models. An example of biomimetic agent-based behaviour modelling has been published on Caribou herds in the Arctic[9]. However, simulating male frog calling behaviour dynamics has a different set of requirements from agent-based models such as these: male frog calling simulation requires the ability to perform simulation of high precision timing based emission and processing of events, taking physical constraints such as the speed of sound and neural processing time into account. What is proposed here is an agent modelling framework that is flexible and powerful enough to enable both advanced behavioural design and the precision required to achieve results from simulated agents consistent with observation of the natural creatures. Our solution offers flexible agent implementation using an existing high-performance scripting language[5], which interfaces with a user configurable event processing framework — events in this case being any external action taken by the agents in the simulation, such as calling out or moving.

The main purpose for the suggested agent modelling framework is to enable the design of agent behaviour that mimics observed behaviour in natural agents so as to further the understanding of the natural agents' interactions and how group behaviour might be affected by individual agent attributes. Taking physical constraints such as neural processing time and sound propagation into account.

2   Frogs as a Case Study for Agent Based Modelling

Male frog mating call dynamics is a complex subject. Frogs have through evolution been physically shaped to optimize their chance of survival and procreation through highly specialized calling behaviour. The evolution of each subspecies of frog is strongly influenced by the success of male frogs in attracting females while using minimal energy in the presence of competing calls from other males and interference from other environmental factors. It is not just a matter of optimizing the call strength, duration and frequency of the individual male frog. Different species employ different algorithms that take both physical and environmental constraints into account when choosing when to emit a call: for instance, a poorly timed call might alert predators and enable them to locate the unlucky individual.

It is worth mentioning that there are generally two types of calling behaviours, antiphonal (asynchronous) and chorusing (synchronous). E.g the Natterjack chorus while the *E. coqui* perform their calls asynchronous with two to three neigbouring callers.

It would be interesting to uncover what external attributes a male frog can consider for utilization in order to achieve optimal performance in the highly competitive environment during mating seasons, and how the choices of the individuals affect the dynamics of the whole frog population. To enable the simulation of male calling dynamics a high-performance agent-based modelling tool is warranted; A tool that allows for very high precision, optimized for event broadcasting rather than peer to peer interaction.

Simulating the Asynchronous Calling Behaviour of *E. coqui.* Simulations of the Puerto Rican Tree Frog *E. coqui* have been described in the literature[2]. In that project, simulations were constructed based on models of two or three frogs. The project also determined that each male *E. coqui* only reacts to a maximum of three neighbouring callers.

Only involving a couple of individuals in a simulation is questionable since *E. coqui* populations generally have a very high density of male individuals per acre (up to 133,000 [8]). It would be interesting to simulate a much larger population to check how population size and density might affect each individual's behaviour.

Population Wide Stochastic Modelling. Previous work modelling whole populations has taken the approach of stochastic modelling [10], which allows the setup of an efficient population-wide model that can take several attributes into account as well as the different states the male frog can be in during mating season. The model deals with the four different states listed below.

- **Calling**: the frog emits calls and expends energy doing so.
- **Foraging**: the frog does not call but charges up energy instead.
- **Satellite**: the frog does not call, but attempts to intercept females attracted by nearby male callers. This is typically a behaviour used by weaker males, where they attempt to save energy by using the call of another male frog to attract mates.
- **Hiding**: the frog can neither mate nor recharge energy.

The only stochastic variable in the model is the rate at which the frog's energy level replenishes.

Neural Network Decision Model. An alternative approach to the problem of modelling the frog's decision process is to use a neural network[11] where relevant attributes both dynamic and static — such as refractory period, energy level and neighbouring call strength — are presented as inputs to a network that determines the frog's actions.

A neural network approach has been successfully implemented a related case to determine female frog response biases to male frog calling[13], of the *Túngara*. The neural network managed, successfully, to recognize the males mating calls and with great degree of precision capable of determining how well females generalized to many novel calls.

3   Utilization of Agent-Based Simulation to Improve the State of the Art

The existing modelling techniques mentioned above allow the construction of rather advanced simulations; however the models are either limited in scope or do not take individualism directly into account. Agent-based modelling is flexible in that agents are modelled as individuals, and may all differ. Their decisions are based on locally available information, so can reflect rather more specific or sophisticated modelling assumptions than population-based models; for instance, multi-species interactions can easily be handled in an individual-based framework. It becomes possible to experiment with the relationship between locally available information, local descisions and emergent global behaviour of the agent population in a wider range of circumstances than population models typically allow. Agent-based modelling is, depending on the modelling language, very flexible and is agnostic about the implementation of the local decision model, enabling for instance neural network representations or state-based models that describe an agent's behavioural profile. Advanced swarm behaviour achieved through agent-based modelling has previously demonstrated in Reynolds graphic behavioural model[14].

3.1   State of the Art Modelling Frameworks

Several existing agent-based modelling frameworks were considered for frog calling behaviour simulation, to determine whether they were usable as-is, or with reasonable extension and modification. The following frameworks were reviewed.

- **NetLogo**: Even though there exist many examples of Netlogo models of biomimetic behaviour, the Nlogo modelling language is limited in scope, and Nlogo is not designed for high-precision time-based simulation.
- **Repast[12]**, in its various configurations, supports Nlogo, Java and C++ agents. However, modelling options such as C++ and Java, necessary for time-based event management, will require framework recompilation.
- **GAMA[4]**: The GAML modelling language is limited in scope, making the necessary modelling primitives hard to realise, and GAMA is tied to the heavy Eclipse development environment.
- **JADE[1]**, Java based agent design, requires sophisticated programming knowledge. It supports a very limited number of agents, and is not suited for high-precision simulations.

While it might have been possible to adapt one of the frameworks to suit the problem domain, none of them naturally or natively support the simulation of large numbers of agents interacting via events whose timing is critical and determined by environmental physics. We therefore decided to develop a new framework from scratch. This enables the creation of a platform independent framework specifically designed towards high-volume high-precision simulations, thereby offering good performance on agent handling without compromising agent design complexity or simulation integrity.

It also gives the opportunity to develop a lightweight framework, which at its core is independent of heavy components such as Eclipse and the Oracle Java Virtual Machine.

3.2 Agent Design Using Lua

The developed simulation framework, RANA[6] (Reproduction of Artificial and Natural Agents), uses Lua[5] as its principal agent modelling language, though models can also be coded in C++. Instead of inventing a new agent design language, Lua is chosen as the main modelling language. Lua is widely used as a scripting language for embedded systems, and is compact, efficient and easy to interface with lower level languages such as C or C++. Furthermore, it is a powerful modern language with a clean design, making it simple to learn. Using Lua makes it possible to offer several flexible template agents that regular users can utilize to design their own agents while allowing advanced users to design and implement complex agent behaviour. The only constraint on models is that they implement the predefined functions for event handling and processing through which the event-handling core of the simulation interacts with the models.

Advanced users can choose to implement their agent designs in C++, and compile the agents into the framework. Compilation time is not significant on modern platforms since RANA is a lightweight framework, and C++ agents carry a significant performance advantage, but the implementation complexity is significantly greater for a given behaviour complexity than constructing the model using Lua.

RANA offers an easy to learn agent modelling framework that comprises a powerful but efficient programming language, Lua. By providing a number of template agents the modelling threshold is set to a point where it should be possible for non-programmers to design complex biomimetic interactive behaviour simulations. There is no requirement to run a heavy duty development environment, or have knowledge of software development tools: a simple text editor is all that is needed. Nevertheless Lua enables the design of advanced agents with attributes and functions that can help the researcher uncover the underlying mechanics of the simulated agents through careful experimentation.

Lua was chosen as the design language as it provides a fast and easy to use API to the native language of RANA, C++. Futhermore it is possible to reach a very high level of abstraction through the development of species specific Lua libraries.

3.3 Agent Mechanics

The RANA agent has several functions available to it during a simulation run. Mainly there are two different event-handling functions, one for handling events issued by fellow agents and one that allows the agent to perform an internal action at a clearly defined time. The agent also has an init function that will be called on simulation start-up, were they can set up their behavioural attributes.

There is also a simulation-end function which allows the Agent one final action enabling agent-specific data-collection.

At the start of a simulation run each agent is initialized. The simulator then moves time forward until an agent decides that it is time to initiate an event. Fellow agents register the event and calculate when it will arrive locally, taking into account environmental physics, i.e. a call event will propagate with the speed of sound. The agent can also take neural processing time and other internal factors into account when responding to the event, and thus a group dynamic begins, where agents respond to each others' events depending on their internal and external state. The agents can then output the results of their individual behaviour to the console or write it to a binary data file which can be used for post processing.

4   Model Testing

Example models have been designed in an attempt to build agents that mimic behaviours described in the aforementioned literature on frog modelling.

4.1   The *E. coqui* Male Calling Behaviour

The modelled *E. coqui* has, aside from position and an ID provided by the simulator, the attributes listed in Table 1.

Table 1. Attributes of the template frog and their distribution

Attribute (value)	Description
intensityThr (0.8)	Minimum Sound intensity to trigger response, intensity level at source is 1.0
CallStrength (35–50)	How far a call travels before reaching intensity level 0.5
EnergyLvl (0.0–1.0)	Amount of energy a frog starts out with
EnergyRegenRate (0.01–0.0125)	Amount of energy a frog regenerates every second
CompelRegenRate (0.02–0.04)	If the frog has not registered any neighbouring calls for a while it will perform a spontaneous call once the Compellevel goes to 11. The regenrate determines how much the compel level regenerates every second, and any call made will reset the compel level. This attribute determines how bold the frog is.

The model will actively attempt to avoid call overlap with its two strongest neighbours, which is a normal *E. coqui* male behavioural pattern taking on an asynchronous behaviour. The duration of the *E. coqui* call is 375[ms]; the model takes this into account, as well as the frog's neural processing time of approx. 35[ms].

The frogs are placed in a grid, with equal distance to one another.

The distribution function for the call events sound intensity is defined as an exponential decreasing function, which outputs a sound intensity level between 0 and 1 as a function of distance from origin. The frogs in the simulation will ignore any intensity level below 0.8 (calls made more than 6 to 8[m] away).

The model registers, via a special data collector agent, how many calls it has made with no neighbouring overlap, with overlap from a single neighbour and how many calls it has attempted to make with no overlap.

The simulation area size is 10x10[m], and three simulations with increasing density is run, with 15, 35 and 63 frogs. Each simulation is run 5 times.

Results. In a sparse environment with 15 frogs, all frogs managed to expend their energy as fast as it regenerated. Thus they performed optimally from an energy point of view. 82–87% of all calls were made asynchronously with the chosen neighbouring callers the rest were performed with overlap. The frog managed to anticipate when neighbouring callers would call in more than 98% of the cases.

With 35 frogs, the average percentage of success rate is 80–82%, the call frequency falls as a consequence of the density increase, the anticipation rate remains as 98%.

At 63 frogs, the average success rate is 79–80%, again the call frequency falls slightly, anticipation rate stays above 98%.

Discussion. We observed that the proportion of calls overlapping with a chosen neighbour changes slightly with increasing density of frogs, for the range of densities tested. It was hoped that over time the model would cause the frogs to settle into a regular rhythm, and they did manage that reasonably well. The Model did not achieve complete antiphonal success though. The reason for this is probably that while one frog might consider another a neighbour, the vice versa is not necessarily true due to the variance in call strength.

Since agents were not able to move in this simulation, the individuals were forced to remain where initially placed, rather than being able to move to a more favourable position as a real frog might. The implementation of the states identified in the stochastic model could also give a more dynamic calling environment, and possibly decrease the overall call overlap.

It is worth noting the simulation results are heavily dependent on how likely the frogs are to initiate a call spontaneously and how advanced their call anticipation algorithm really is. Further observation into *E. coqui* calling behaviour could give a more precise view of how bold these frogs generally are.

4.2   Modelling Female Mating Call Response

For some species of frog females will perform courting calls[16]. These calls serve to entice nearby males to perform courting calls of their own. In this simulation we designed a female frog that move around the environment at random. Whenever she comes within the vicinity of a strong male caller, as determined by the sound intensity, she will begin responding with a courting call. This will cause every male in the females vicinity to increase their call frequency and intensity. After a couple of seconds of courting, the female then moves to another location, looking for another group of males to entice.

Results. The movement and calling of the frogs in this simulation is visualized via a separate piece of software developed to enable visualization of the agent event activity[7]. The visualizer showed that the model was successfull. The females courting call will incite nearby males and they will then increase their call frequency either until the female stops courting or they run out of energy. Once the female stops courting the courting males fall silent, while their energy replenishes. Once replenished the males resume with regular mating calls.

Discussion. Simulating movement and its effect on results, is something that still needs to be researched properly. This simulation merely demonstrates that it is something the simulation core will support. However more advanced models will need to be designed in order to achieve proper results that are applicable to real behaviour of the simulated animal.

5   Further Work

There are also many possibilities for further study of the simple frog model described above: a full investigation of the effects of the various parameters on the population behaviour is the most pressing. Extension of the decision model to improve its abilities to desynchronise with its neighbours is also indicated. For instance, one might include a random back-off interval after a call, as is used in algorithms for coordinating access to shared media such as ethernet links or wireless spectrum.

Performing biomimetic modelling has proven to be no simple task. The *E. coqui* model's relatively simple behaviour requires several hundred lines of script coding. If the tool is to be used more generally by non-programmers, a lot of the functionality needed to make a model must be implemented in a library of building blocks of some kind. Fortunately, Lua allows several straightforward ways to accomplishing this. Alternatively, a domain-specific modelling language could be devised, though by its very nature this restricts the freedom of the modeller while simplifying the expression of models that are supported by the language.

There are also many possibilities for expansion of framework, both in regards to model features and expansion of the simulation core. While the modelling capabilites meet our basic requirements of scalability to large numbers of agents (tests with thousands of agents and hundreds of thousands of events have been run), there are some extensions that would strengthen the behavioural modelling capabilites of RANA.

The frog taxonomy is very diverse, and the communication algorithms each sub-species employ varies greatly, due to environmental factors and the physiology of the animal. Unfortunately, documentation of frog communication *algorithms* is quite sparse, and to enable the modelling of individual agents it is important to perform species specific field work which entails setting up listening arrays to localise individual frogs while providing data on call timing and call characteristics. Furthermore, unobtrusive observation on the habitat may uncover movement patterns of males and females and general behaviour patterns. Other aspects such as mating success rate of satellites versus callers could also be uncovered better. This fieldwork will allow improvements to be made to the basic model frogs as further significant factors influencing calling are identified and taken into account.

The agent should also be able to query relevant factors of its local environment, such as temperature, humidity and lighting level. To enable this the simulator should include some environment simulation; as a minimum, a map of a habitat could be loaded into the simulator along with some known environmental parameters. Frog models could them employ movement to find ebvironmentally favourable spots from which to call.

6   Conclusion

A new modelling tool, RANA, has been presented which supports high-volume and high-precision agent-based modelling in which environmental physics plays a significant part in the interaction of agents. The simulation core handles the exchange of events with micro-second timing precision, while agents employ models coded as Lua scripts to initiate, receive and respond to events. The tool was developed to support agent-based modelling of calling frogs and is illustrated with a simple simulation of the ansynchronous calling behaviour of the Puerto Rican Tree Frog.

The simulator incorporates features that allow the modelling of individual decision processes dependent on local environmental factors and internal state as well as communication from other agents. As such, it can be used for other simuation tasks in addition to the frog-modelling which provided the primary motivation for the work. Multispecies simulations are straightforward, as each agent acts as an individual with its own decision model.

Several proof of concept simulations have been performed using RANA, such as doing a template frog simulation that include females traversing the environment inciting males with courting calls. As well as predation and elimination of species based on call performance.

References

1. Bellifemine, F.L., Caire, G., Greenwood, D.: Developing Multi-Agent Systems with JADE. Wiley (2007), http://www.amazon.ca/Developing-Multi-Agent-Systems-Fabio-Bellifemine/dp/0470057475/sr=8-1/qid=1170365284/ref=sr_1_1/702-0885532-1303250?ie=UTF8&s=books

2. Brush, J.S., Narins, P.M.: Chorus dynamics of a netropical amphipian assemblage: Comparison of computer simulation and natural behaviour. Animal Behaviour (1989)
3. Gilbert, N.: Computer simulation of social processes. Social Research Update 6 (1994)
4. Grignard, A., Taillandier, P., Gaudou, B., Vo, D.A., Huynh, N.Q., Drogoul, A.: GAMA 1.6: Advancing the art of complex agent-based modeling and simulation. In: Boella, G., Elkind, E., Savarimuthu, B.T.R., Dignum, F., Purvis, M.K. (eds.) PRIMA 2013. LNCS, vol. 8291, pp. 117–131. Springer, Heidelberg (2013)
5. Ierusalimschy, R.: Lua 5.2 reference manual (2011–2013), http://www.lua.org/manual/5.2/ (online; accessed February 1, 2014)
6. Joergensen, S.V., Demazeau, Y., Christensen-Dalsgaard, J., Hallam, J.: RANA, agent based real-time broadcasting simulation framework (2013-2014), https://github.com/sojoe02/RANA (online; accessed January 24, 2014)
7. Joergensen, S.V., Demazeau, Y., Christensen-Dalsgaard, J., Hallam, J.: RANA visualizer an agent event visualization framework (2013-2014), https://github.com/sojoe02/Kasterborous_Visualizer/ (online; accessed January 24, 2014)
8. Kaiser, B.A., Burnett, K.M.: Economic impacts of e. coqui frogs in hawaii. 2006 Annual meeting, July 23-26, Long Beach, CA 21313. American Agricultural Economics Association (New Name 2008: Agricultural and Applied Economics Association) (2006), http://ideas.repec.org/p/ags/aaea06/21313.html
9. Lesins, G., Higuclu, K.: Agent based modelling of caribou environmental interactions in the Canadian arctic. The International Environmental Modelling and Software Society (2010)
10. Lucas, J.R., Howard, R.D., Palmer, J.G.: Callers and satellites: Chorus behaviour in anurans as a stochastic dynamic game. Animal Behaviour (1993)
11. Phelps, S.M.: History's Lessons, A Neural Network Approach to Receiver Biases and the Evolution of Communication, pp. 67–78. Smithsonian Instituion Press, Washington (2001)
12. North, M.J., Nicholson, C.T., Ozik, J., Tatara, E.R., Macal, C.M., Bragen, M., Sydelko, P.: Complex adaptive systems modeling with Repast Simphony (2013), http://link.springer.com/article/10.1186/2194-3206-1-3/fulltext.html (online; accessed February 3, 2014)
13. Phelps, S.M., Ryan, M.J.: Neural networks predict response biases of female túngara frogs. Proceedings of the Biological Sciences / The Royal Society 265(1393), 279–285 (1998), http://dx.doi.org/10.1098/rspb.1998.0293
14. Reynolds, C.W.: Flocks, herds and schools: A distributed behavioural model, in computer graphics. SIGGRAPH, 25–34 (1987)
15. Tisue, S., Wilensky, U.: Netlogo: A simple environment for modeling complexity. In: International Conference on Complex Systems, pp. 16–21 (2004)
16. Wells, K.D., Swartz, J.J.: The Behavioral Ecology of Anuran Communication, pp. 44–89. Springer Handbook of Auditory Research (2006)

Snapshot Homing Navigation Based on Edge Features

SeungMin Baek and DaeEun Kim

Biological Cybernetics Lab.
School of Electrical and Electronic Engineering
Yonsei University
Shinchon, Seoul, 120-749, South Korea
{bsmin,daeeun}@yonsei.ac.kr
http://www.cog.yonsei.ac.kr

Abstract. The insect has a navigation ability to estimate the direction to their habitat using visual information after finding their food. It is known that many insects including ants can use visual snapshot around them for homing navigation. Inspired by this navigation ability of insect, many navigation algorithms have been suggested. One of the navigation algorithms is the average landmark vector (ALV) algorithm to calculate the direction to the target location relative to the current location. This algorithm is based on the observation of landmarks from visual information. Observing and identifying landmarks in real environment is a challenging problem. For the snapshot model, the feature extraction from the visual image plays an important role. Segmentation or clustering over color pixels may not provide a robust solution to find landmarks in the snapshot model. In this paper, we suggest that a vertical edge features with neighbor pixel colors can be a very efficient and effective solution to identify landmarks. These vertical edge features are not warped by the movement of camera, and they maintain the characteristic for the movement of a robot. We test a new algorithm of detecting these vertical edge features as landmarks and finding the correspondence between those landmarks at the nest and at the current location. As a result, the algorithm easily determines the homing direction.

1 Introduction

Collett et al. has studied the navigation capability of insects [1]. They mainly observe the navigation behavior of honeybees and ants. These insects use their visual information to find the direction to the target location. It is reported that the bees and ants not only use their visual information to navigate, but also can learn about the location of landmarks. Identifying landmarks is a key in the navigation algorithm[2].

From this navigation ability, the "snapshot hypothesis" has been suggested [9]. This hypothesis claims that the insect can find target direction by comparing scenes at the target location and at the current location. With this hypothesis,

A.P. del Pobil et al. (Eds.): SAB 2014, LNAI 8575, pp. 98–107, 2014.

many navigation algorithms have been suggested [8]. Lambrinos et al. apply this navigation method of insects to the real robot [13]. Their work provides an algorithm called the Average Landmark Vector (ALV) [3]. This algorithm is based on landmark vectors which are defined by unit vectors from its location to observed landmarks. The difference of average landmark vectors at the target and the current location directs the target direction relative to the current location. This algorithm needs identifying landmarks in the visual snapshots [15]. We suggest that detecting vertical edge features as landmarks and their ALV vectors can easily determine the homing direction.

Interestingly, the concrete line can be a landmark in the insect behavior [4]. From this idea, we use the vertical edge features as landmarks. To confirm the correspondence between the edge lines, we apply the histogram of oriented gradient (HOG) descriptor technique. The histogram of oriented gradient descriptor generates descriptors for lines. This feature has been used to detect human beings [5] [12], and it is a good candidate for landmark discrimination. In our approach, a set of the HOG feature over vertical edges can determine the signature of a landmark. The signature of landmarks in the home snapshot and compare to those in the snapshot taken at the current location, and then a set of valid landmarks can determine the homing direction using the ALV algorithm.

2 Method and Material

2.1 Experimental Environment

We construct an environment to obtain the image information. In this environment, there are many kinds of objects in the environment like cabinets, chairs. Front and rear view of the environment is in figure 1(c), (d). We set the testing area in the environment, and we divide the area into grid, and obtain the images from the points. The distance between adjacent grids is about 20 centimeter. We set a point at the center of grid as the target location. The top view of the environment is given in figure 1(b).

2.2 Image Processing

In the environment, we take images to find the target location relative to current location by comparing image from two locations. We use the omni-directional camera to obtain visual information around the camera. An example of omni-directional camera is in figure 1(a). This image is warped by spherical mirror. We warp this image into a panoramic image. We use the nearest interpolation rule to warp this image. The result image is in figure 1(e).

These panoramic images are still warped along the y-axis. This is the reason why we choose the vertical edges as landmarks. We can calibrate this warping effect, but this procedure may include loss of information by interpolation.

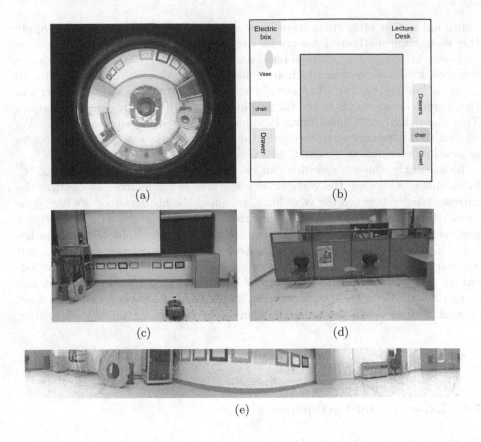

Fig. 1. (a) Omni directional image, (b) Overall environment, (c) Front view and a robot, (d) Rear view of the environment, (e) Converted panoramic image

2.3   Line Detection

First, we obtain the edge of image, and mapping this into the Hough coordinate. Example of this is in figure 2. We apply the canny edge detection, and the result image is in figure 2(a). This edge image can show the edge image well. This includes many line segments. With this image, we map this image into the Hough coordinate. The relationship of the Hough transform for an edge point is shown in the figure 2(b). In this figure, the distance from the origin and the tangential angle are the axis of the Hough coordinate. For this mapping relationship, an edge point is mapped into a curve on the Hough coordinate. The mapping result is in figure 2(c). Each curve implies one edge point. Crosses on the figure are representing the local maximum points of this graph. We can find many line segments in this graph. The result of line detection is in figure 2(d). This includes too many line segments to use landmarks. The landmarks need to have its own characteristic, but the many lines are much overlapped or are

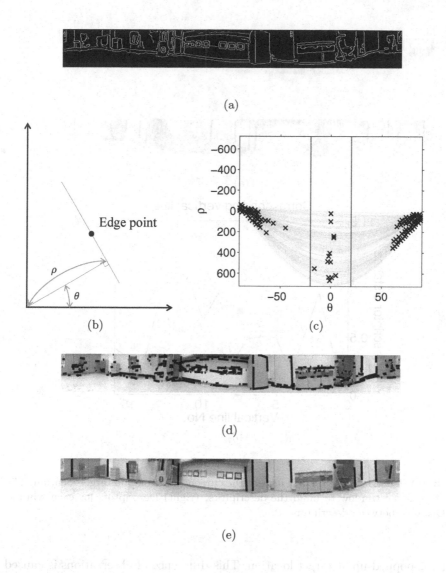

Fig. 2. (a) Edge detection of a panoramic image, (b) Mapping relationship (c) Mapping result and clustering, (d) Detected lines, (e) Detected vertical lines

not located in the right place. To refine this result, we filter those lines by choosing the appropriate angle θ ($-20°$ $20°$) degree as shown in figure 2(c). In the figure 2(e), we can obtain vertically oriented edges will be the candidate of landmarks.

In figure 3(a) (left), we detect vertical lines in the panoramic image at the current location and target location. For these the detected lines, we need to find the correspondence between lines. Some of lines at the current location disap-

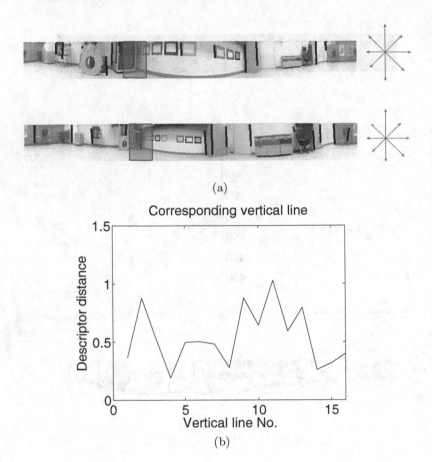

(a)

(b)

Fig. 3. (a) (left) Detected vertical lines at the current location and target location. The blue box is the window to build the descriptors, (right) Descriptors for each window (b) Distance between descriptors.

pears or popped up at target location. This difference of observations is caused by changed observing locations and different point of views towards objects. This observing location difference cause the difference of observing angle of objects. To find out the correspondence between landmarks at both locations, we apply the histogram of oriented gradient (HOG) technique. This technique generates the descriptors of each landmark. We set a window for each detected line. The width of window is 40 degree, and the height of this window is the same with the height of panoramic image. An example of this window is the blue box in figure 3(a). For this window, we apply the R-HOG filters to generate the descriptors for each vertical line. We calculate gradients for each pixel on window along x-axis, and y-axis. We also calculate an orientation from the gradients. Binning of these orientations on the window is the HOG descriptor. An example of the descriptors for the edge of line at edge features is shown in figure 3(a) (right). These descriptors at the corresponding line are similar. For one line edge at the current location, we compare the HOG feature to that for each candidate line at the target location. The distance between a pair of the HOG features for all candidate line edges is shown in figure 3(b). We can confirm the right corresponding line at target location has minimum distance.

2.4 Refining Processing

To improve the performance, there is a refining process available. The correct matching of edge features has no much change of angular position in the omni directional image while wrong matching has large displacement. We calculate the amount of landmark shift along the x-axis in the panoramic image for a matching, and filtering it. If there is a matching of edge features whose displacement along the x-axis is over than a threshold, no correspondence of matching is found. We use a window to build the HOG descriptor, but we can divide this window into many sub windows to expand the descriptor. We divide this window into 3 by 3 sub-windows. We have total 48 dimension descriptors for each edge. For a detected vertical edge at the current location, we compare this to all candidates in the target location, and find the edge feature which has the minimum difference of signatures.

This processing is weak to occlusion. This occlusion problem causes serious degrade of performance. We need to solve this problem with additional processing. After finding the corresponding edge feature at the target location, we compare this edge feature to those of all detected vertical edges at the current location. For the correspondence matching of edge features, we calculate the matching distance between the HOG descriptors and find the minimum distance to determine the correspondence of landmarks. Here, we only allow one-to-one correspondence. If there are multiple candidates over the target landmark, we take the best candidate with the minimum matching distance.

3 Result

In the experiments, a robot takes snapshot images at each location and determines homing direction. The robot extracts vertical edges by the Hough transform, and initially uses these as landmarks. We apply the HOG descriptors to find the correspondence between landmarks. With these landmarks, we apply the ALV method to estimate direction toward the target location at the center of test area in figure 1(b).

Figure 4(a) shows estimated homing direction toward the target location from the current location. This result shows the performance using a window with 40 degrees ($-20°$ $20°$) around the vertical edge. To find the optimal size of window, we tested the performance depending on the window size in figure 4(b). The performance is evaluated by the average angular error over all tested points, and its standard deviation. This result implies that a window of 60 degrees

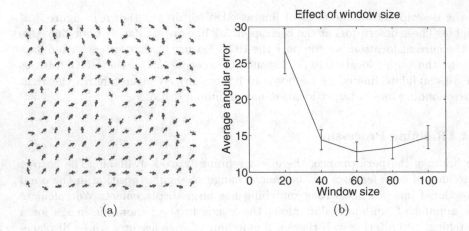

(a)   (b)

Fig. 4. (a) Estimated target(center of area) direction from current location(start point of vector) before refining process. (b) Average angular error by different size of window for the HOG descriptor.

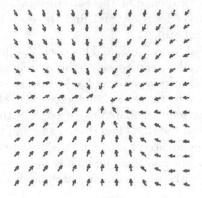

Fig. 5. Estimated target direction after refining process

$(-30°\ 30°)$ around the vertical edge is most suitable for the environment, but its computational cost is increased proportionally. For this reason, we use a window of 40 degrees with similar performance to find the target direction. We use the R-HOG filter to build the HOG descriptor of window around the vertical edge.

We apply the refining process, and its result is in figure 5. These processes are much complex than using just the HOG descriptor, but the performance is drastically improved. In this process we use a window of 40 degrees for the HOG descriptor, 9 sub-windows, and 50 degree cut-off threshold for correspondence matching. The average angular error of this algorithm is 12.58 degrees, and its standard deviation is 9.73 degrees for all the grid points in the testing area.

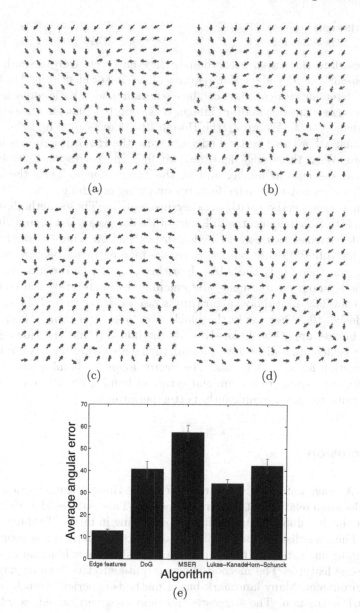

Fig. 6. Performance Comparison.(a) Using Difference of the Gaussian feature extraction, (b) Maximally stable extremal regions feature extraction. (c) Lukas-Kanade optical flow, (d) Horn-Schunk optical flow (e) Average angular error and standard deviation for each algorithm.

4   Discussion

Many insects find their way, even though they have relatively a small size of nervous system. The ALV algorithm requires observing or identifying landmarks. We suggest detecting vertical edges can be a solution to identify landmarks rather than extracting segmentation of an image. It is reported that ants use edges for landmark detection [4]. We apply the Hough line detection to find the vertical line in an image. For these vertical edges, we use the HOG descriptors for each edge feature. With these edge features, we find the correspondence between landmarks at the current image, and at the target image. Then the refining process helps filter out noisy edge features or wrong matching.

We compare our method with another method [7]. Those methods use the feature extraction techniques, the different of the Gaussian(DoG), and the maximally stable extremal regions(MSER) feature extraction. Those algorithms generally provide robust feature points. Here, we take extracted feature points as landmarks, and then apply the ALV algorithm over the landmarks. We tested those methods in our environment, and calculate estimated target direction for each grid point The optical flow algorithm is also available to find the landmark correspondence [10]. They apply the block matching algorithm to find the optical flow, but we apply the Lukas-Kanade method [11] and the Horn-Schunck algorithm to calculate optical flow. Similar to the above methods, we estimated homing direction for all test points. The vector maps for homing are shown in figure 6. When we compare the angular errors of homing direction, our method with edge features shows significantly better performance.

5   Conclusion

The ALV (Average Landmark Vector) algorithm estimates the direction toward the target location relative to the current location. This requires identifying landmarks, but this has difficulty in the image processing in terms of robustness and efficiency. Thus, a holistic approach like image distance method has been attractive for homing navigation. In this paper, we suggest a robust landmark detection based on edge features. The method shows a quite effective homing navigation in real environment. Many landmark-based methods experience much difficulty in landmark extraction. The suggested method uses vertical edges which are mostly invariant to warped images and the edge feature over neighbor pixels can be good candidates of landmarks. It is not known yet what kind of visual processing or landmark extraction process insects use. Our method may possibly provide a hint of understanding landmark-based navigation for insects.

Acknowledgments. This work was supported by the National Research Foundation of Korea(NRF) grant funded by the Korea government(MEST) (No. 2012R1A2A4A01005677).

References

1. Collett, M., Collett, T.S., Srinivasan, M.V.: Insect navigation: Measuring travel distance across ground and through air. Current Biology 16(20), R887 (2006)
2. Graham, P., Collett, T.S.: Bi-directional route learning in wood ants. Journal of Experimental Biology 209(18), 3677–3684 (2006)
3. Lambrinos, D., Moeller, R., Labhart, T., Pfeifer, R., Wehner, R.: A mobile robot employing insect strategies for navigation. Robotics and Autonomous Systems 30(1), 39–64 (2000)
4. Harris, R.A., Graham, P., Collett, T.S.: Visual cues for the retrieval of landmark memories by navigating wood ants. Current Biology 17(2), 93 (2007)
5. Dalal, N., Triggs, B.: Histograms of oriented gradients for human detection 1, 886–893 (2005)
6. Ballard, D.H.: Generalizing the Hough transform to detect arbitrary shapes. Pattern Recognition 13(2), 111–122 (1981)
7. Ramisa, A., et al.: Combining invariant features and the ALV homing method for autonomous robot navigation based on panoramas. Journal of Intelligent & Robotic Systems 64(3-4), 625–649 (2011)
8. Franz, M.O., Schlkopf, B., Mallot, H.A., Blthoff, H.H.: Where did I take that snapshot? Scene-based homing by image matching. Biological Cybernetics 79(3), 191–202 (1998)
9. Cartwright, B.A., Collett, T.S.: Landmark learning in bees. Journal of Comparative Physiology 151(4), 521–543 (1983)
10. Vardy, A., Moeller, R.: Biologically plausible visual homing methods based on optical flow techniques. Connection Science 17(1-2), 47–89 (2005)
11. Lucas, B.D., Kanade, T.: An iterative image registration technique with an application to stereo vision. In: IJCAI, vol. 81, pp. 674–679 (August 1981)
12. Corvee, E., Bremond, F.: Body parts detection for people tracking using trees of histogram of oriented gradient descriptors. In: 2010 Seventh IEEE International Conference on Advanced Video and Signal Based Surveillance (AVSS), pp. 469–475. IEEE (August 2010)
13. Moeller, R., Lambrinos, D., Pfeifer, R., Labhart, T., Wehner, R.: Modeling ant navigation with an autonomous agent. From Animals to Animats 5, 185–194 (1998)
14. Deans, S.R.: Hough transform from the Radon transform. IEEE Transactions on Pattern Analysis and Machine Intelligence (2), 185–188 (1981)
15. Yu, S.E., Lee, C., Kim, D.: Analyzing the effect of landmark vectors in homing navigation. Adaptive Behavior 20(5), 337–359 (2012)

Ground-Nesting Insects Could Use Visual Tracking for Monitoring Nest Position during Learning Flights

Nermin Samet[1], Jochen Zeil[2], Elmar Mair[4],
Norbert Boeddeker[3], and Wolfgang Stürzl[4]

[1] Department of Computer Engineering, Bilkent University, Turkey
[2] Research School of Biology, The Australian National University
[3] Department of Cognitive Neuroscience, Bielefeld University, Germany
[4] Institute of Robotics and Mechatronics, German Aerospace Center (DLR)

Abstract. Ants, bees and wasps are central place foragers. They leave their nests to forage and routinely return to their home-base. Most are guided by memories of the visual panorama and the visual appearance of the local nest environment when pinpointing their nest. These memories are acquired during highly structured learning walks or flights that are performed when leaving the nest for the first time or whenever the insects had difficulties finding the nest during their previous return. Ground-nesting bees and wasps perform such learning flights daily when they depart for the first time. During these flights, the insects turn back to face the nest entrance and subsequently back away from the nest while flying along ever increasing arcs that are centred on the nest. Flying along these arcs, the insects counter-turn in such a way that the nest entrance is always seen in the frontal visual field at slightly lateral positions. Here we asked how the insects may achieve keeping track of the nest entrance location given that it is a small, inconspicuous hole in the ground, surrounded by complex natural structures that undergo unpredictable perspective transformations as the insect pivots around the area and gains distance from it. We reconstructed the natural visual scene experienced by wasps and bees during their learning flights and applied a number of template-based tracking methods to these image sequences. We find that tracking with a fixed template fails very quickly in the course of a learning flight, but that continuously updating the template allowed us to reliably estimate nest direction in reconstructed image sequences. This is true even for later sections of learning flights when the insects are so far away from the nest that they cannot resolve the nest entrance as a visual feature. We discuss why visual goal-anchoring is likely to be important during the acquisition of visual-spatial memories and describe experiments to test whether insects indeed update nest-related templates during their learning flights.

Keywords: Insect navigation, visual tracking, learning flights, homing.

A.P. del Pobil et al. (Eds.): SAB 2014, LNAI 8575, pp. 108–120, 2014.

1   Introduction

Many insects, in particular ants, bees and wasps, are competent navigators and are known to heavily rely on vision to memorize places and routes (reviewed in [1,2]). The landmark panorama [3,4], the sun, the pattern of polarized skylight [5] and even the Milky Way [6] provide them with an external compass reference. For visual homing, insects acquire scene memories at their nest or at newly discovered feeding sites during highly structured learning flights or learning walks [7,8]. There is evidence that insects acquire locale memory during this learning process, in particular visual information that allows them to subsequently return to the goal [9,10,1]. A common feature of learning flights and learning walks is the way, in which the insects carefully control where they see the nest entrance as they pivot around and back away from the nest (see references in [1]). This appears to be a crucial element of acquiring views for homing, most probably because it allows insects to memorize the visual panorama always in association with the goal direction. In ground-nesting wasps, the nest entrance position is clearly under visual control, because the insects track a small patterned disk when it is moved away from the nest entrance [10]. In contrast, ants use path integration information when they turn back and look across the nest during their learning walks [8].

For flying insects, there are several options to keep track of the nest entrance position: they may continuously update their position relative to the nest, based on estimates of their own movements, that is, use path integration information, like ants do [8]. However, it is not clear how accurately flying insects could employ path integration in this task, considering that they operate in three dimensions and at high speed. Learning flights have also been considered and modelled as a procedure akin to SLAM (simultaneous localization and mapping) [11], which, however, would appear to be quite computationally demanding.

Our aim here is to explore the possibility that insects visually track the nest entrance and its immediate visual environment (see [9,10,12]). We pay particular attention to the problem of tracking a location in the natural environment of ground-nesting wasps and bees that undergoes complex visual transformations as the insects pivot around it and gain distance from it. We will show that the nest direction can be estimated by means of a dynamic template update procedure, even in situations in which the nest entrance itself cannot be resolved due to the limited resolution of the insect eye.

We proceeded in two steps: First, we used an existing data bank of reconstructed views during the learning flights of bees and wasps (e.g. [13,14,15]) and remapped these images according to an equidistant fisheye projection. In the second step, we developed and tested seven different template tracking methods and analysed how well each kept track of the nest location in these image sequences. We find that tracking is robust, provided templates are dynamically updated and suggest that the comparison of nest-registered snapshots with what a homing insect currently sees can in principle be used to predict the movement direction required to reach the goal position.

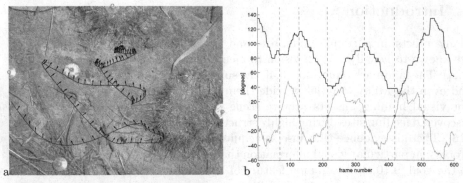

Fig. 1. a) The trajectory (blue curve) of a ground-nesting bee's learning flight, over-laid on a frame recorded with the downward looking high-speed camera. Black arrows indicate head orientation, plotted every 5th frame, i.e. every 20 ms; red dots highlight positions where the nest is "head-on", i.e. at 0° azimuth in the bee's visual field). The red cross indicates the nest position. The green dots highlight metal pins in the ground that were used to determine the transformation between the high-speed stereo system and the computer model of the environment. b) Head orientation (black curve) and azimuth angle of the nest in the visual field (green). The red dots (as in a) and the dashed vertical lines indicate 0° nest azimuth angle.

2   Reconstruction of the Visual Input Perceived by Insects

For this study we used existing learning flight data of three ground-nesting wasps (*Cerceris australis*) and of one ground-nesting bee (species not identified). In the following we describe briefly our approach for reconstructing the visual input the insects perceived during these flights, which forms the basis for the evaluation of our nest tracking hypothesis.

2.1   Recording and Path Reconstruction of Learning Flights

Wasps and bees were filmed with high-speed stereo cameras at 250 fps. The angle between the two cameras was about 90°: while one camera was viewing the recording area from above, the second camera was positioned close to the ground, viewing the scene from the side. The 3D flight path and the head yaw orientation were determined frame-by-frame using custom-made software (see [13,16] for details).

As example we show in figure 1 the flight path and the head orientation for the learning flight of a ground-nest bee. Interestingly, the nest is rarely seen directly in front (at 0° azimuth in the visual field) but is kept most of the time at 20°-50° in the lateral visual field. Furthermore, head orientation does not change smoothly but abruptly. Between these fast turns, which are called "saccades", the head orientation is kept virtually constant.

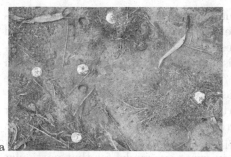

a   b

Fig. 2. a) Rendered image showing the part of scene that is seen by the downward looking high-speed camera (see figure 1 a). b) Panoramic image (covering 360° × 180° in equi-rectangular projection) rendered with 2 pixels/degree at a position of the learning flight (frame 216, see figure 1 b), where the bee faces the nest entrance, which is highlighted by a red arrow.

2.2   Generating Computer Models of the Local Environment

We generated 3D models of the environments in which we had recorded the learning flights of insects. For the bee environment (Mount Majura Nature Park, Canberra, Australia; flight recorded January 2012) we used a combination of 3D reconstruction tools [14]. An area around the nest entrance covering about $1\,m^2$ was reconstructed using bundle adjustment with sub-sequential dense pairwise stereo processing on a set of 40 photos that were taken with a 10 mega-pixel camera with "locked focus" setting. This high resolution local model was complemented with point clouds acquired with a laser-range finder colour camera combination (Z+F IMAGER 5006). The different parts of the model were aligned using a set of large metal pins (some of them are visible in figure 1 a). Examples of rendered images are shown in figure 2.

The wasp learning flights were recorded in 2006, when we had no reconstruction equipment available. We thus modified our approach for generating a 3D model of that environment. Local models covering the nest entrances and their neighborhood (in an area of about 35 cm×45 cm) were created by manually identifying about 270 corresponding points in stereo images and determining their 3D coordinates. The resulting 3D points were then triangulated and a video frame of the downward looking camera was mapped to the resulting wire-frame. In addition a 3D model of the surrounding scene was generated using the Z+F IMAGER 5006 in 2011. While the fine structure of the local scene had changed noticeably, the overall depth structure of scene remained, even after 5 years, basically the same. The model acquired with the laser-range finder and the local model were registered using nails hammered into the ground (which had remained there for more than 5 years).

2.3   Rendering Insect Views

After determining the transformation between the stereo camera system and the computer model by means of markers in the ground, images can be rendered along insect flight paths. We use six virtual cameras oriented along the six normal vectors of a cube to cover the large field of view of insect eyes. The rendered views were converted to grey-level images and then remapped to a single planar image according to an equidistant fisheye projection ("f-theta lens") with radial resolution of either 1°/pixel or 2°/pixel (see examples in figure 3). The optical axis of this virtual fisheye lens was pitched by −45° with respect to the horizontal, which helped to reduce distortions in the image regions relevant for tracking. For the learning flight of the ground-nesting bee we used in addition also a pixel mapping that resembles the spatial sampling of the eyes of a worker honeybee [17]. Although not necessarily an exact eye model for that particular species, this representation allowed us to study the "hand-over" of the tracked region between the two eyes (see figure 6).

3   Methods for Nest Tracking

In this section we introduce our methods for testing the nest tracking hypothesis. We use a comparatively simple template-based approach, which we consider biologically plausible because it shares similarities with current view-based models of insect navigation [2,18].

Suppose that we have the image sequence of a learning flight $\{I_n\}$ where $n = 1, 2, 3, ...$ is the frame number. We attempt to track the nest through the learning flight sequence by extracting an initial square template T from the first frame I_1 with the nest in the centre. We then search for the region in the following frame(s) that matches the current template best. Assuming a reasonably high frame rate, the nest cannot change its location much from frame to frame and the search can be restricted to an area centred around the best matching region in the previous frame.

We used two different similarity functions for determining the best match between the template and image regions within the search area. We select the position $(x_n^{\mathrm{opt}}, y_n^{\mathrm{opt}})$ either of the minimum of the *Sum of Squared Differences* (SSD),

$$\mathrm{SSD}_n(x, y) = \sum_{x', y'} (T_n(x', y') - I_n(x + x', y + y'))^2 \ ,$$

or of the maximum of the *Normalized Correlation Coefficient* (NCC),

$$\mathrm{NCC}_n(x, y) = \frac{\sum_{x', y'} (T_n(x', y') - \bar{T}_n) \cdot (I_n(x + x', y + y') - \bar{I}_n(x, y))}{\sqrt{\sum_{x', y'} (T_n(x', y') - \bar{T}_n)^2 \cdot \sum_{x', y'} (I_n(x + x', y + y') - \bar{I}_n(x, y))^2}} .$$

With n indicating the frame number and $\bar{T}_n$, $\bar{I}_n(x, y)$ the mean pixel value of template and image region.

We tested seven variants of template-based methods (M1-M7) for nest tracking that differ in the way the template is updated:

M1: No Template Update. We use the template extracted from the first frame of the learning flight to find matches in all the subsequent frames: $T_{n+1} = T_1$ for all $n \geq 1$.

M2: Template Update (in each frame). M1 is likely to fail when the insect's distance to the nest entrance increases. As a simple solution to this problem we update the template continuously in order to keep the similarity high between the template and the current nest region: $T_{n+1} = \text{crop}(I_n, x_n^{\text{opt}}, y_n^{\text{opt}})$ for all $n \geq 1$, where '$\text{crop}(I, x, y)$' describes the extraction of the template from image I at position (x, y).

M3: Template Update on Rotated Image. Due to the rapid changes in head orientation (see figure 1 b), even a template that is updated in each frame can give a poor match after a saccade and can cause significant deviation of the best matching image region from the image part containing the nest. However, saccadic head movements are initiated by the insects themselves and pure rotations, so that the image shifts they generate are predictable and can be accounted for by, for instance, an efference copy command. M3 is an extension of M2: It compensates for turns by counter-rotating both the previously updated template (as described for M2) and the centre of the search region.

M4: Template Update on Rotated Image with Contour Detection. A problem with M2 and M3 is that the area of best match tends to drift away from the nest region due to the accumulation of small errors with each update. In order to remove this template drift, at least as long as the nest is visible in the image, we added, as an extension of M3, a contour detection stage. Contours are determined around the position of the best match. Then, assuming that the contour closest to the position of the best match belongs to the nest, the template is updated with the image region centred at this contour.

M5: Template Update on Rotated Image with Rotation Angle Threshold. An alternative approach, in particular in case the nest entrance is not detectable at later stages of the learning flight, is to try to limit the number of template updates. M5 is a variation of M3: we compensate for rotations but keep the current template unless the rotation angle is larger than a defined threshold value.

M6: Template Update on Rotated Image with Cumulative Angle Threshold. Instead of considering just the turn angle between consecutive frames as in M5, we now update the template only if the cumulative turning angle, i.e. the change of head orientation since the last update, exceeds a certain threshold.

M7: Template Update on Rotated Image with Matching Score Threshold. This method is similar to M5 and M6. However, instead of the rotation angle we consider the matching score. The template is updated only if the similarity between the current template and the current best match falls below a certain threshold (for the dis-similarity measure SSD we update the template only if the matching score raises above a certain threshold).

Each of these tracking algorithms was implemented in C++ using the template matching methods provided by the OpenCV library (http://opencv.org). The implementation uses 40 by 40 pixel templates and the search area was restricted to a 70×70 pixel region. For M5 and M6, threshold angles for head rotation were fixed to 5° and 10° (cumulative angle), respectively. The matching

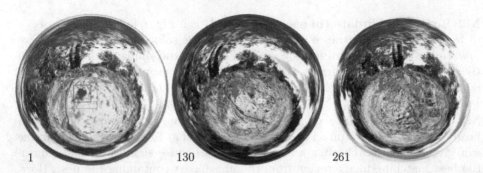

Fig. 3. The first, an intermediate and the last frame of *wasp learning flight 1*. The dashed rectangle overlaid on frame 1 depicts the central part of the image used to display the tracking sequences in figure 4. Red arrows point to the nest position.

score threshold of M7 was set empirically to 3×10^6 for SSD and to 0.70 for NCC.

4   Experiments and Results

In this section, we will first show detailed results for the different tracking methods focusing on *wasp learning flight 1*. We will then present results of the tracking methods for different learning flights and investigate the effects caused by reducing the resolution of the images and the precision with which the rotation angle is known.

Figure 3 shows three example frames from *wasp learning flight 1* which consists of 261 frames reconstructed at 50 fps (i.e. at every 5th position of the recorded flight path that was filmed at 250 fps). The red box in the first frame highlights the image region centred around the nest entrance that is used as initial template. The green square depicts the search area for the next frame. As can be seen from figure 3, apparent size of the nest entrance becomes smaller and eventually invisible. Images were rendered with 1°/pixel, which is still higher than the resolution of most insect eyes, including those of wasps and bees [19].

As illustrated in figure 4, the performance of individual tracking methods is quite different. We defined a tracking method to fail when the true nest position is located outside the best matching image region (depicted by the red box). The frames where this happened first are marked by a red cross in the lower right corner. For the results presented in figure 4 SSD was used as similarity measure. M1 has no template update and fails, as expected earlier than all other methods, at frame 56. The continuously updating template method M2 can track the nest region more than twice as long as M1, but fails at frame 138 due to drifts because of rotation induced template mismatches. M3 and M4, which both compensate for rotations, are successfully tracking the nest region for the entire learning flight. M4 has almost perfect tracking performance until about frame 150 after which the nest entrance is too small to be detected by the contour

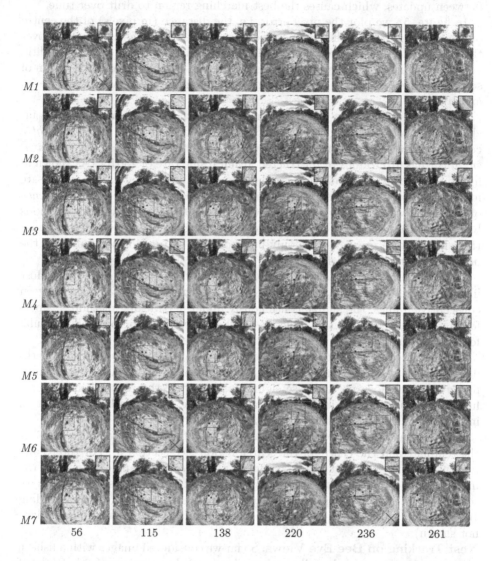

Fig. 4. Frames were some tracking methods fail while others succeed for *wasp learning flight 1*. Each row shows results for a different method, indicated by labels M1-M7 on the left. Frame numbers are given below. Insets in the upper right corner of each frame show the respective template. Red crosses in the lower right corners mark frames were individual tracking methods failed first. Blue dots mark the true nest position. Red boxes with a red dot in their centre show the best matching image regions. The green rectangle defines the search area.

finding algorithm. M5, M6 and M7 fail earlier because of the accumulating error between updates, which causes the best matching region to drift over time.

In figure 5 a we plot the pixel error, i.e. the distance (in pixels) of the centre of the best match from the true nest position in the image, for all methods over the full duration of the recorded flight. On average, tracking can be slightly enhanced by using the normalized cross correlation (NCC) instead of the sum of squared differences (SSD) for calculating the matching score (compare figure 5 a and b).

The proposed tracking methods were tested with 3 more learning flights including a bee learning flight. *Wasp learning flight 2* and *wasp learning flight 3* consist of 164 and 220 frames, respectively, reconstructed at 50 fps. The *bee learning flight* has 610 frames reconstructed at full frame rate of 250 fps. As shown in figure 5 c, tracking methods that regularly update the template and compensate for rotations performed also best for *wasp learning flight 2* due to the presence of structures with high contrast close to the nest. On average, tracking methods had the smallest error for *wasp learning flight 3* (figure 5 d), most likely because the entrance hole presented the only high contrast feature in the vicinity of the nest (see inset in upper left corner).

Tracking results for the *bee learning flight* are shown in figure 5 e,f. Most likely due to the higher frame rate, which reduces the amount of change between consecutive frames, the simple continuously updating tracking method 2 is performing much better for this flight (see yellow curve and compare with results for wasp learning flights in figure 5 a-d that were reconstructed with 50 fps).

In order to see the *effect of image resolution* we also tested the tracking methods with half resolution images, i.e. $2°$/pixel instead of $1°$/pixel. As shown in figure 5 f, error does not increase significantly despite the reduced image resolution. The same conclusion can be drawn from the results with half resolution images for wasp learning flights (data not shown).

Tracking methods M3-M7 compensate for head rotations by counter-rotating the template and the centre of the search region (see section 3). For the results presented so far we used the exact value of the turning angle. However, the insects may not be able to predict saccade-induced image shifts accurately. We confirmed that turning angles do not have to be known exactly, because adding 10% noise to the turning angles did not significantly affect performance (data not shown).

Nest Tracking on Bee Eye Views. So far we considered images with a fisheye projection that covered the full viewing sphere and thus the large field of view of both insect eyes combined without the discontinuity introduced by having two eyes. For modeling visual tracking of the nest in a more realistic way we created views according to a model that resembles the spatial sampling of the eyes of a worker honeybee [17]. Due to the binocular overlap, the nest, when located in the frontal visual field, will be visible in both eyes (see left side of figure 6), which may facilitate switching the tracking of the nest from one eye to the other.[1] For

---

[1] Interestingly, the binocular overlap is larger in the lower visual field (the region onto which the image of the nest will be projected) than in the frontal visual field.

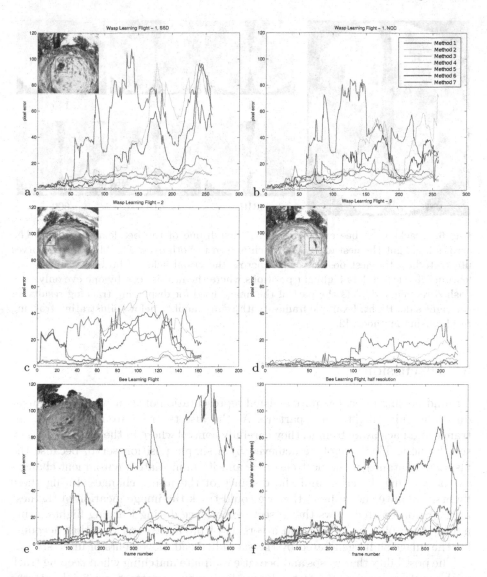

Fig. 5. Performance of different template tracking methods for three wasp learning flights (a-d) and one bee learning flight (e,f). SSD was used as similarity with the exception of b) which shows results for NCC. Insets in the upper left corners show the central part of the first frame of the respective learning flight; red boxes highlight the initial tracking template. f) Angular error for half image resolution.

implementing tracking on bee eye views we extended the search area to both eyes whenever the best match region found in the previous frames is close to the inner border of an eye. The right side of figure 6 shows six example frames from tracking method M2. The true nest location is kept within the region of the best match for the whole sequence of 610 frames.

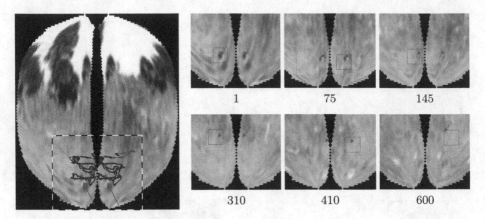

Fig. 6. Tracking on bee eye views. Left: First frame of the bee learning flight. The arrows highlight the nest entrance, which is seen in both eyes. The blue dotted curves illustrate how the nest position moves across the visual fields of both eyes during the learning flight, red dots highlight positions where the nest is seen by one eye only. The dashed rectangle depicts the part of the image used for displaying tracking results on the right side. Right: Example frames (with frame number below) illustrating tracking results using method M2.

5 Discussion

Ground-nesting insects acquire a visual representation of their nest environment during learning flights on departure. As the insects pivot around the nest entrance and back away from it, they carefully control where in the visual field they see the nest. This cannot be achieved by a simple position servo, because the visual appearance of the nest entrance and its immediate environment changes as the viewing direction and the distance of the insect changes during these flights. We have shown here, that we could track the image location of the nest in the reconstructed views that insects experience during learning flights, using updated template matching and a version of predictive tracking that accounts for the image shifts generated by the saccadic head movements of insects.

The possibility that wasps and bees use template matching when keeping track of the nest location can be tested by modifying high-contrast, artificial patterns around the nest entrance during learning flights. It is already known that the insects track such patterns when they are shifted [10] and a break-down of nest position control in the visual field in the presence of rapid pattern changes (not shifts) would indicate that the insects do employ template matching during their learning flights.

Why is visual goal-anchoring so important during the acquisition of visual-spatial memories? We suggest that it allows the insects to continuously form a strong association between changing views and the direction to the nest. After all, the purpose of this learning process is to ensure that sufficient information has been acquired to allow the insect to pinpoint its nest on subsequent returns. The systematic, periodic structure of learning flights (in terms of the temporal sequence of bearing and orientation changes) indicates that the insects have several opportunities during these flights to check and re-check what they have learnt for consistency.

References

1. Zeil, J., Boeddeker, N., Stürzl, W.: Visual homing in insects and robots. In: Floreano, D., Zufferey, J.C., Srinivasan, M.V., Ellington, C. (eds.) Flying Insects and Robots, pp. 87–100. Springer, Heidelberg (2009)
2. Zeil, J.: Visual homing – an insect perspective. Current Opinion in Neurobiology 22, 285–293 (2012)
3. Zeil, J., Hofmann, M., Chahl, J.: Catchment areas of panoramic snapshots in outdoor scenes. Journal of the Optical Society of America A 20(3), 450–469 (2003)
4. Graham, P., Cheng, K.: Ants use the panoramic skyline as a visual cue during navigation. Current Biology 19, R935–R937 (2009)
5. Evangelista, C., Kraft, P., Dacke, M., Labhart, T., Srinivasan, M.V.: Honeybee navigation: Critically examining the role of the polarization compass. Phil. Trans. R Soc. B 369, 20130037 (2014), doi:10.1098/rstb.2013.0037
6. Dacke, M., Baird, E., Byrne, M., Scholtz, C., Warrant, E.: Dung beetles use the milky way for orientation. Current Biology 23(4), 298–300 (2013)
7. Zeil, J., Kelber, A., Voss, R.: Structure and function of learning flights in bees and wasps. Journal of Experimental Biology 199, 245–252 (1996)
8. Müller, M., Wehner, R.: Path integration provides a scaffold for landmark learning in desert ants. Current Biology 20, 1368–1371 (2010)
9. Zeil, J.: Orientation flights of solitary wasps (Cerceris; Sphecidae; Hymenoptera). I. Description of flight. Journal of Comparative Physiology A 172, 189–205 (1993)
10. Zeil, J.: Orientation flights of solitary wasps (Cerceris; Sphecidae; Hymenoptera). II. Similarities between orientation and return flights and the use of motion parallax. Journal of Comparative Physiology A 172, 207–222 (1993)
11. Baddeley, B., Philippides, A., Graham, P., Hempel de Ibarra, N., Collett, T.S., Husbands, P.: What can be learnt from analysing insect orientation flights using probabilistic SLAM? Biol. Cybern. 101, 169–182 (2009)
12. Zeil, J.: The control of optic flow during learning flights. Journal of Comparative Physiology A 180, 25–37 (1997)
13. Zeil, J., Boeddeker, N., Hemmi, J., Stürzl, W.: Going wild: Toward an ecology of visual information processing. In: North, G., Greenspan, R. (eds.) Invertebrate Neurobiology. Cold Spring Harbor (2007)
14. Stürzl, W., Mair, E., Hirschmüller, H., Zeil, J.: Mapping the navigational information content of insect habitats. In: Front. Physiol. Conference Abstract: International Conference on Invertebrate Vision (2013), doi:10.3389/conf.fphys.2013.25.00085
15. Mair, E., Stürzl, W., Zeil, J.: Benchmark 3D models of natural navigation environments @ www.insectvision.org. In: Front. Physiol. Conference Abstract: International Conference on Invertebrate Vision (2013), doi:10.3389/conf.fphys.2013.25.00084

16. Zeil, J., Narendra, A., Stürzl, W.: Looking and homing: How displaced ants decide where to go. Philosophical Transactions B 369(1636), 20130034 (2014), doi:10.1098/rstb.2013.0034
17. Stürzl, W., Boeddeker, N., Dittmar, L., Egelhaaf, M.: Mimicking honeybee eyes with a 280° field of view catadioptric imaging system. Bioinspiration & Biomimetics 5, 36002 (2010)
18. Wystrach, A., Graham, P.: What can we learn from studies of insect navigation? Animal Behaviour 84, 13–20 (2012), doi:10.1016/j.anbehav.2012.04.017
19. Land, M.F.: Visual acuity in insects. Annual Review of Entomology 42, 147–177 (1997)

Adaptive Landmark-Based Navigation System Using Learning Techniques

Bassel Zeidan[1], Sakyasingha Dasgupta[2], Florentin Wörgötter[2],
and Poramate Manoonpong[2,3]

[1] Faculty of Mathematics and Computer Science, Institute of Computer Science,
University of Göttingen, D-37077 Göttingen, Germany
[2] Bernstein Center for Computational Neuroscience (BCCN) University of
Göttingen, D-37077 Göttingen, Germany
[3] The Mærsk Mc-Kinney Møller Institute, University of Southern Denmark, 5230
Odense M, Denmark
bassel.zeidan@gmail.com,{dasgupta,worgott}@gwdg.de,poma@mmmi.sdu.dk

Abstract. The goal-directed navigational ability of animals is an essential prerequisite for them to survive. They can learn to navigate to a distal goal in a complex environment. During this long-distance navigation, they exploit environmental features, like landmarks, to guide them towards their goal. Inspired by this, we develop an adaptive landmark-based navigation system based on sequential reinforcement learning. In addition, correlation-based learning is also integrated into the system to improve learning performance. The proposed system has been applied to simulated simple wheeled and more complex hexapod robots. As a result, it allows the robots to successfully learn to navigate to distal goals in complex environments.

Keywords: Goal-directed behavior, Sequential reinforcement learning, Correlation based learning, Neural networks, Walking robots.

1 Introduction

Attempts to create autonomous robots that can move around and navigate toward a (distal) goal have been ongoing for over 20 years [12]. A lot of effective robotic navigation systems have been proposed. Some of them use internal representations (e.g. generalized voronoi diagrams [9], place cells [10], etc). Others use potential fields [11]. Reinforcement learning (RL) has been widely used for navigation learning [2,10]. The learning process of RL systems is guided by reward signals and based on a trial and error mechanism. This mechanism gives the system an adaptive property to cope with different situations and unexpected scenarios. However, RL systems require many learning trials to solve problems that have large state spaces.

In this paper we present an adaptive navigation system based on sequential reinforcement learning. It is inspired by animal navigation behavior where animals including gerbils [13] and ants exploit environmental features (landmarks) to find the right direction. The presented system treats environmental

A.P. del Pobil et al. (Eds.): SAB 2014, LNAI 8575, pp. 121–131, 2014.
© Springer International Publishing Switzerland 2014

landmarks as subgoals that guide the navigation process. In contrast to other subgoal-based navigation systems [7,8], the presented system relies on exploiting the local property of radial basis function networks to solve subgoal-based tasks. These networks enable the system to perform such tasks efficiently in large continuous spaces while keeping the system structure simple. Furthermore, the special feature of our approach is the integration of correlation-based learning (ICO learning) into the system. ICO learning acts here as adaptive exploration which improves learning performance. The proposed system is tested on a simple wheeled robot and a more complex hexapod robot. It allows the robots to effectively navigate to distal goals in complex environments.

2   Sequential Learning Strategy

The presented navigation system operates based on a sequential learning algorithm which treats environmental landmarks as subgoals. By learning to reach these subgoals in the right order, the system learns an entire trajectory which leads to the final goal. This is done by performing a sequence of RL learning phases. The term "learning phase" is given to a learning process that enables a robot to move from one subgoal to the next. The robot receives a positive reward each time it reaches a subgoal in the correct order. This order is defined by the system designer. The system's behavior is checked after a fixed number of trials in a special test trial in which no exploration signals are produced to test the learned policy. The policy improvements stop and the exploration signals are turned off after a test trial for each learning phase that its related subgoal was reached in the right order during the test trial (see Algorithm 3.3).

Using a normal RL system is insufficient for sequential learning. This is because it uses the same representation of the state space for different learning phases. This causes the system during a learning phase to overwrite what has been learned in other learning phases. Our approach to overcome this problem is to feed the index of the current targeted subgoal as an additional input called the Subgoal Definer (SD) input to the RL system. This enables the system to become aware of the change that happens after reaching a subgoal. One dimension in the input space is sufficient to enable the system to cope with any number of subgoals. Using this additional input gives a better representation of the state space where the same state of the robot in the environment is represented differently for different learning phases.

3   Adaptive Landmark-Based Navigation System

The learning process of the presented navigation system is an actor-critic method [1], a special type of temporal difference (TD) RL. This method has an ability to produce a smooth control signal because of its ability to handle continuous action spaces. In addition, it is based on a biological learning model [6].

The proposed system consists of the following four units: 1) the actor 2) the critic 3) the exploration unit 4) the final output policy unit. (see Fig. 1a).

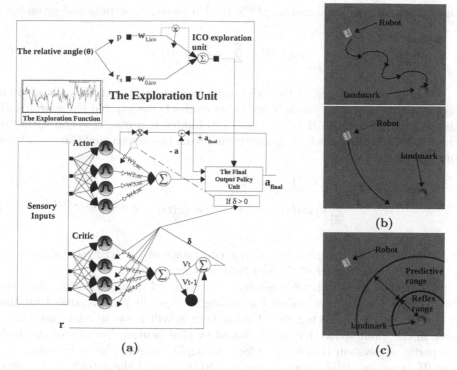

Fig. 1. (a) The proposed system's structure and units. The TD error effect on the system's structure. (b) The upper/lower picture shows the effect of using an insufficient big/small value respectively for the exploration unit's parameter ($w_{0,ico}$). (c) The input signals' ranges of the ICO exploration system.

3.1   The Actor and Critic

The actor is responsible for the policy. The critic estimates the expected total payoff (V) value. During learning, the TD error drives the learning process by guiding the actor's policy and improving the critic's estimation. The TD error is calculated by:

$$\delta_t = r_t + (\gamma V_t) - V_{t-1}, \tag{1}$$

where δ is the TD error. γ is the discount factor $\in [0, 1]$. V is the expected total payoff value (V value). r_t is the received reward at time step t.

Radial basis function (RBF) networks are used as function approximators to give the system the ability to handle continuous spaces and to produce a smooth control signal. Each RBF network consists of two layers. The first layer consists of hidden neurons that have radial basis activation functions. The second layer consists of output neurons. The output of each output neuron is calculated as the weighted linear combination of the hidden neurons' outputs and given by:

$$y_j(x(t)) = \sum_{i=1}^{H} w_{i,j} v_i(x(t)),$$ (2)

where y_j is the output of the j-th output neuron. $x(t)$ is the presented input signal at time step t. $w_{i,j}$ is the weight that connects the i-th hidden neuron with the j-th output neuron. H is the number of hidden neurons. v_i is the output of the i-th hidden neuron which is constructed from the normalized Gaussian basis functions as:

$$v_i(x(t)) = \frac{a_i(x(t))}{\sum_{j=1}^{H} a_j(x(t))},$$ (3)

$$a_i(x(t)) = e^{-||S_i^T(x(t)-C_i)||^2}.$$ (4)

S_i is the diagonal matrix of the inverse covariance of the RBF neural network. C_i is the function center of the i-th hidden neuron.

The RBF centers and variances don't get modified during learning. However, the network's weights get updated according to a specific learning rule. Updating a certain weight connected to a hidden neuron will have an effect on a local area in the input space that is dominated by that neuron. Because of this local property, our system is able to perform multiple learning phases by using only one RL structure. RBF networks are used to implement the actor and the critic. Using nonlinear approximators for both enables the system to cope with any environment configurations. The weights of the critic RBF network are updated by [1]:

$$\frac{dw_{i,cr}(t)}{dt} = \lambda \delta v_{i,cr}(x(t)), i = 1, 2, 3, ..M$$ (5)

where λ is the critic learning rate. $v_{i,cr}(x(t))$ is the output of the critic network's i-th hidden neuron. M is the number of hidden neurons in the network.

The actor improves the policy by learning previous taken actions that yielded good outcomes. A class of algorithms called CACLA is used to update the actor [3]. CACLA helps RL systems to perform stable learning in continuous action spaces with a good convergence property. It exhibits better performance in comparison to other update rules. The actor network's weights are updated by:

$$\frac{dw_{i,ac}(t)}{dt} = \eta(a_{final,t} - a_t) v_{i,ac}(x(t)), i = 1, 2, 3, ..N$$ (6)

where η is the actor learning rate $\in [0,1]$. $a_{final,t}$ is the actual (final) action value of the system at time step t. a_t is the actor's output (action value) at time step t. $v_{i,ac}(x(t))$ is the output of the actor network's i-th hidden neuron. N is the number of hidden neurons in the actor RBF network.

The goodness of a taken action can be assessed by checking the TD error sign at the next time step. Here, a positive TD error indicates that the previously taken action was good while a negative TD error indicates that it was bad. This way, the actor learns towards a taken action only if the TD error is positive. On the other hand, the previously taken action is ignored if the TD error is negative.

3.2   The Exploration Unit

This unit is responsible for producing an exploration signal. This signal is combined with the actor's output during learning to produce the system's final output (action value). It allows the system to discover new areas in the state space. The function shown in Eq. 7 is used to produce the exploration signal [1].

$$\epsilon_t(v) = \zeta \Phi_t min[1, max[0, \frac{V_{max} - V_t}{V_{max} - V_{min}}]], \tag{7}$$

where $\epsilon_t(v)$ is the exploration signal at time step t. ζ is a scale factor. Φ_t is a Gaussian distribution noise with the mean of zero and the standard deviation of one. V_t is the V value at time step t. V_{max} and V_{min} are the maximum and minimum observed V values and they are assigned dynamically during learning.

A new exploration unit is integrated into the system to improve the performance. This unit is added based on the idea of using landmarks as attraction locations since they lead to the right direction. It produces a continuous signal which pulls the robot towards a nearby landmark if it is located within a certain range. Correlation-based learning, called input correlation learning (ICO learning) [4], is used to implement this unit. ICO exploration unit takes two input signals: a predictive signal and a reflex signal and both are the relative angle between the robot and the nearby landmark. However, they are received at different times. The predictive signal is received first then the reflex signal comes later (see Fig. 1c). The output of the ICO exploration unit is given by:

$$\epsilon_{ico} = pw_{1,ico} + r_0 w_{0,ico}, \tag{8}$$

where p is the predictive input. $w_{1,ico}$ is the plastic synapse of the predictive input. r_0 is the reflex input. $w_{0,ico}$ is the synaptic strength of the reflex input.

ICO learning correlates between these two input signals which gives the system after learning the ability to predict the reflex signal before it happens and to prevent it from happening. $w_{1,ico}$ changes according to the ICO learning rule:

$$\frac{dw_{1,ico}(t)}{dt} = \mu p \frac{dr_0(t)}{dt}, \tag{9}$$

where μ is the learning rate $\in [0, 1]$. The learning stops when the system is able to pose the robot directly towards a nearby landmark within the predictive range. The robot enters the reflex range after learning with the relative angle of zero degree from the landmark to the robot (no learning occurs).

The reflex signal represented by $r_0 w_{0,ico}$ in Eq. 8 is able by itself to produce this behavior. However, this is possible only if $w_{0,ico}$ is tuned carefully. The tuning should enable the system to produce an output which is suitable for the range of the input control signal and also for the frequency with which it is fed to the robot. Choosing a bad value for $w_{0,ico}$ causes undesirable behaviors (see

Fig. 1b). Tuning this parameter requires detailed information about the robot's structure. In addition, fixing it causes the loss of the adaptivity property and the lack of flexibility against changes. ICO learning provides a powerful mechanism to tune the system. $w_{0,ico}$ is fixed to a constant value[1] and $w_{1,ico}$ is modified by ICO learning until it converges to an optimal value which generates the desired behavior while avoiding bad situations.

This unit could pull the robot blindly towards a wrong landmark because it is not able to assess the quality of performing this behavior [2]. On the other hand, the RL system assesses each action before it gets learned by the actor. The assessment process is done using the received TD error. Based on that and since the ICO system learns faster than the RL system, the unit's output signal is used as an additional exploration signal which aids the system during learning. However, it doesn't contribute in the final output of the system after learning.

3.3   The Final Output Policy Unit

The way the exploration signal is being used has a profound impact on the performance. This unit combines other units' outputs to produce the final output (action value) of the system. The final output is determined as shown in Algorithm 1. The algorithm produces the final output during learning. However, after learning the actor's output is the only one considered as a final output.

Algorithm 1: Determine the final output of the system

---

if *a landmark is in the predictive or reflex range* **then** $a_{final,t} \leftarrow \epsilon_{ico,t}$
else if *the trial number mod 2 = 0* **then** $a_{final,t} \leftarrow \epsilon_t(v) + a_t$
else $a_{final,t} \leftarrow \epsilon_t(v)$
return $a_{final,t}$

---

4   Experimental Results

The proposed system has been applied to two simulated robots: the wheeled robot NIMM [2] and the hexapod robot AMOS [5].

4.1   Experiment 1: NIMM in an Environment with Three Subgoals

The goal of this experiment is to investigate the system's efficiency and to assess the benefit of using the ICO exploration unit. The robot should learn to reach two subgoals (1 and 2) and the goal (3) in the right order sequentially (see Fig. 2a). The robot receives +1 reward at each subgoal if it is reached in the correct order. The robot receives four input signals: the relative angle from the three

---

[1] Based on the range of the input control signal, the system designer specifies a reasonable value for $w_{0,ico}$. Even if this value is not optimal and causes undesirable reflex behavior, this will not affect the ICO system final output after learning. This is because this reflex signal will be eliminated when the ICO learning process ends.

Algorithm 2: Sequential reinforcement learning algorithm

Initialization: the exploration is ON for all learning phases.
set $w_{i,ac}$, $w_{i,cr}$ and $w_{1,ico}$ to 0.0
repeat
     $SD \leftarrow 0$
     repeat
         $x(t) \leftarrow$ *sensory inputs* & SD
         if *a test trial OR*
             the exploration is OFF for the current learning phase **then**
$$a_{final,t} \leftarrow a_t \leftarrow \sum_{i=1}^{N} w_{i,ac} v_{i,ac}(x(t))$$
         else
$$a_t \leftarrow \sum_{i=1}^{N} w_{i,ac} v_{i,ac}(x(t)), \; V_t \leftarrow \sum_{i=1}^{M} w_{i,cr} v_{i,cr}(x(t))$$
$$\epsilon_t(v) \leftarrow \zeta \Phi_t min[1, max[0, \tfrac{V_{max}-V_t}{V_{max}-V_{min}}]], \; \epsilon_{ico,t} \leftarrow p w_{1,ico} + r_0 w_{0,ico}$$
            if *a landmark is in the reflex range* **then**
$$w_{1,ico} \leftarrow w_{1,ico} + \mu p(r_{0,t} - r_{0,t-1})$$
            $a_{final,t} =$ determine the final output of the system (Algorithm **??**)
            $\delta_t = r_t + (\gamma V_t) - V_{t-1}$
            $w_{i,cr} = w_{i,cr} + \lambda \delta_t v_{i,cr}(x(t-1))$
            if $\delta_t > 0$ **then** $w_{i,ac} = w_{i,ac} + \eta(a_{final,t-1} - a_{t-1})v_{i,ac}(x(t-1))$
         if *the next subgoal is reached* **then** $SD \leftarrow SD + 1$
     until *the termination of the current trial*
     if *a test trial* **then** turn the exploration off for all achieved learning phases
until *the actor's policy converges to an optimal one (i.e. the exploration is off
for all learning phases)*

(sub)goals to the robot and the SD input. The system produces one control
signal to control the robot. The sign and the amplitude of the control signal
determine the steering direction (left or right) and the steering angle of the
robot, respectively. The number of hidden neurons in the actor and critic RBF
networks is set to 625. The number of bases on each input dimension of the actor
and critic is set to 5. The width of the Gaussian basis functions is set to twice
the distance between its center and the center of its nearest neighbor. The actor
learning rate η is set to 0.02 and the critic learning rate λ to 0.05. The discount
factor γ is set to 0.9999. For the ICO learning parameters, the ICO learning
rate μ, the predictive range and the reflex range are set to 0.4, 0.06 and 0.023,
respectively. For the exploration function parameters, the scale factor ζ is set to
0.5. V_{min} is set to 0 and V_{max} is assigned dynamically during learning.

The results shown in Figs. 2b *and* 2c show that the system is reliable and
effective to allow the robot to perform the sequential navigation task. It can be
observed in Fig. 2c that using the ICO unit has a significant impact on the system
performance. Based on this result, this unit will be integrated into the system
and used as an essential element of the system for any further experiments. The

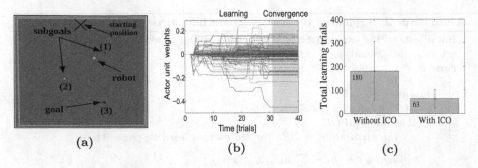

Fig. 2. (a) The set up of experiment 1. (b) The actor RBF network's weights during learning until the policy converges to an optimal one after 32 trials. (c) The average number of trials needed until an optimal policy is obtained. The experiment was performed 60 times. In 30 of them, the system operates without the ICO exploration unit and 30 of them with it.

speedup factor of using the ICO exploration unit is calculated as follows:

$$The\ speedup\ factor = \frac{learning\ time\ (trials)\ without\ ICO}{learning\ time\ (trials)\ with\ ICO} = \frac{180}{63} = 2.85$$

4.2   Experiment 2: NIMM Robot in a Complex Environment

In this experiment a more complex environment is used where the subgoals are placed far from each other. In addition, obstacles are installed between them to make them harder to be reached. The robot should learn to reach all subgoals (1, 2 and 3) and the goal (4) in the right order (see Fig. 3a). The robot gets rewarded with +1 at each subgoal if it is reached in the correct order and with -1 if it hits an obstacle. The robot detects obstacles using its infrared sensors. The sensors' signals are not used as inputs to the system. However, when the sensors are activated, a negative reward signal is sent to the system. This usage of the sensors' signals is sufficient to enable the system to achieve the task. The system produces one control signal to control the robot and it receives four input signals: two inputs as the distance between the robot and the two transmitters T1 and T2. One input as the relative angle from T3 to the robot and the SD input. Determining the type of the input signals and the locations of the signal transmitters is not arbitrary. These signals provide for the system a representation of the robot's states in the environment. To perform a successful learning process, this representation must be sufficient to cover all states and it must be unique for different states. In the presented experiments, these conditions are fulfilled. The number of hidden neurons in the actor and critic RBF networks is set to 875. The number of bases on each input dimension of the actor and critic is set to 5, 5, 5 and 7, respectively. The width of the Gaussian basis functions is set to twice the distance between its center and the center of its nearest neighbor. The actor learning rate η is set to 0.025 and the critic learning rate λ to

0.06. The discount factor γ is set to 0.9999. For the ICO learning parameters, the ICO learning rate μ, the predictive range and the reflex range are set to 0.6, 0.055 and 0.025, respectively. The exploration function is modified to produce more curvy exploration trajectories as follows:

$$\epsilon_t(v) = \zeta \Phi_t(min[1, max[0, \frac{V_{max} - V_t}{V_{max} - V_{min}}]])^2, \tag{10}$$

The scale factor ζ is set to 23. V_{min} and V_{max} are assigned during learning. As observed from Figs. 3b *and* 3c the system successfully enabled the robot to perform the navigation task even in a complex environment.

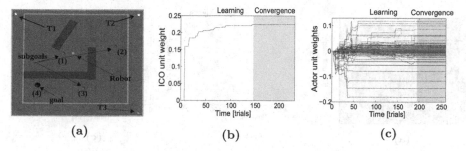

(a)   (b)   (c)

Fig. 3. (a) The set up of experiment 2. (b) The ICO exploration unit weight during learning. It converges to an optimal value after 144 trials. (c) The actor RBF network's weights during learning until the policy converges to an optimal one after 183 trials. The average number of trials that are needed until an optimal policy is obtained is 258±161. A video of this experiment can be seen at [http://www.manoonpong.com/SAB2014/SVideo1.mpg]. In addition, another experiment for long-distance navigation learning can be also seen at [http://www.manoonpong.com/SAB2014/SVideo2.mpg].

4.3   Experiment 3: AMOS in a Multiple-Goal Environment

The proposed system is used to control the simulated hexapod robot AMOS [5]. AMOS's walking ability relies on the movements of its six legs which are controlled by signals received at the legs' joints and produced by a two neurons oscillator (CPG)[5]. The presented system produces one output signal. The sign and the amplitude of this signal determine the steering direction (left or right) and the steering angle of the robot, respectively. This signal is used to modify the amplitude of the oscillator's signals and thus it enables AMOS to turn left or right. The robot should learn to reach all subgoal and the goal in the right order which is 1, 2, 3, 4, 5 (see Fig. 4a). The robot receives four input signals: two inputs as the distance between the robot and the two transmitters T1 and T2. One input as the relative angle from T3 to the robot and the SD input. The robot receives +1 reward at each subgoal if it is reached in the correct order and with -1 if the robot hits an obstacle. The robot detects obstacles using its ultrasonic sensors. The number of hidden neurons in the actor and critic RBF networks is set to 1512. The number of bases on each input dimension of the actor and critic is set to 6, 6, 6 and 7 respectively. The width of the Gaussian basis functions is set to twice the distance between its center and the center of its nearest neighbor. The actor learning rate η is set to 0.03 and the critic learning rate λ to 0.05. The discount factor γ is set to 0.9999. For the ICO learning parameters, the learning rate μ, the predictive range and the reflex range are set to 0.6, 0.13 and 0.07, respectively. For the exploration function parameters, the scale factor ζ is set to 0.04. V_{min} and V_{max} are assigned dynamically during learning. Figs. 4b *and* 4c demonstrate that the system successfully enabled the hexapod robot to perform the navigation task.

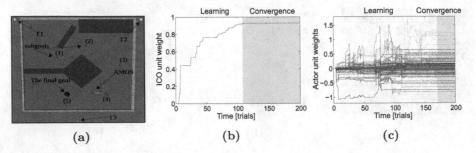

(a)   (b)   (c)

Fig. 4. (a) The set up of experiment 3. (b) The ICO exploration unit weight during learning until it converges to an optimal value after 109 trials. (c) The weights of the actor RBF network during learning until the policy converges to an optimal one after 172 trials. The average number of trials that are needed until an optimal policy is obtained is 346 ±265. A video of this experiment can be seen at [http://www.manoonpong.com/SAB2014/SVideo3.mpg]

5   Conclusions

In this paper a powerful landmark-based navigation system is proposed. It is based on sequential reinforcement learning. The experimental results show that the system enables robots to successfully learn to navigate in complex scenarios with high performance and a 100% success rate. The system is flexible to cope with different environments as well as transferable to different robots. The integration of the ICO exploration unit into the system shows an impressive and profound impact on the system performance.

In fact, using sequential RL provides a proof of concept template to solve tasks that have a sequential nature (e.g. teaching a robot arm to make a cup of coffee). A sequential task is a task that can be divided into smaller assignments that should be performed in a specific order. In the future work, we will test the navigation system on our real wheeled and legged robots. Furthermore, we will look into the possibility of extending the system to give it the ability to determine an optimal sequence of subgoals among different valid sequences. In addition, we will investigate using new methods that enable the system to overcome partially observable MDP cases (e.g. using recurrent neural networks[14]).

Acknowledgements. This research was supported by Emmy Noether grant MA4464/3-1 and BCCNII grant 01GQ1005A (project D1).

References

1. Doya, K.: Reinforcement Learning in Continuous Time and Space. Neural Comput. 12(1), 219–245 (2000)
2. Manoonpong, P., Kolodziejski, C., Woergoetter, F., Morimoto, J.: Combining Correlation-based and Reward-based Learning in Neural Control for Policy Improvement. Advances in Complex Systems 16(02-03) (2013), doi:10.1142/S021952591350015X
3. Hasselt, H., Wiering, M.: Reinforcement Learning in Continuous Action Spaces. In: Proceedings of the 2007 IEEE Symposium on Approximate Dynamic Programming and Reinforcement Learning, ADPRL (2007)
4. Porr, B., Woergoetter, F.: Strongly Improved Stability and Faster Convergence of Temporal Sequence Learning by Utilising Input Correlations Only. Neural Comput. 18, 1380–1412 (2006)
5. Manoonpong, P., Pasemann, F., Woergoetter, F.: Sensor-driven Neural Control for Omnidirectional Locomotion and Versatile Reactive Behaviors of Walking Machines. Robotics and Autonomous Systems 56(3), 265–288 (2008)
6. Woergoetter, F., Porr, B.: Temporal Sequence Learning, Prediction, and Control - A Review of Different Models and their Relation to Biological Mechanisms. Neural Comp. 17, 245–319 (2005)
7. Bakker, B., Schmidhuber, J.: Hierarchical Reinforcement Learning with Subpolicies Specializing for Learned Subgoals. In: Proceedings of the 2nd IASTED International Conference on Neural Networks and Computational Intelligence, pp. 125–130 (2004)
8. Botvinick, M.M., Niv, Y., Barto, A.C.: Hierarchically Organized Behavior and its Neural Foundations: A Reinforcement Learning Perspective. Cognition 113(3), 262–280 (2009), doi:10.1016/j.cognition.2008.08.011
9. Masehian, E., Naseri, A.: Mobile Robot Online Motion Planning Using Generalized Voronoi Graphs. Journal of Industrial Engineering 5, 1–15 (2010)
10. Sheynikhovich, D., Chavarriaga, R., Strösslin, T., Gerstner, W.: Spatial Representation and Navigation in Bio-inspired Robot. In: Wermter, S., Palm, G., Elshaw, M. (eds.) Biomimetic Neural Learning. LNCS (LNAI), vol. 3575, pp. 245–264. Springer, Heidelberg (2005)
11. Ge, S.S., Cui, Y.J.: Dynamic Motion Planning for Mobile Robots Using Potential Field Method. Autonomous Robots 13(3), 207–222 (2002)
12. Arkin, R.C.: Behavior-based Robotics. MIT Press, Cambridge (1998)
13. Collett, T.S.: The Use of Visual Landmarks by Gerbils: Reaching a Goal When Landmarks are Displaced. Journal of Comparative Physiology A 160(1), 109–113 (1987)
14. Dasgupta, S., Woergoetter, F., Morimoto, J., Manoonpong, P.: Neural Combinatorial Learning of Goal-directed Behavior with Reservoir Critic and Reward Modulated Hebbian Plasticity. In: 2013 IEEE International Conference on Systems, Man, and Cybernetics (SMC), pp. 993–1000 (2013)

Robustness Study of a Multimodal Compass Inspired from HD-Cells and Dynamic Neural Fields

Pierre Delarboulas[1,2], Philippe Gaussier[1],
Ramesh Caussy[2,3], and Mathias Quoy[1]

[1] Neurocybernetic team, ETIS, CNRS UMR 805
[2] Partnering Robotics
[3] PREG-CRG École Polytechnique, Institut de l'Économie Numérique

Abstract. In this paper, we study a robust multi modal compass for a vision based navigation system. The model mimics several aspects of the head direction cells found in the postsubiculum of the rat. Idiothetic information is recalibrated according to the learning of visual stimuli associated to robust landmarks. The model is based on dynamic neural fields allowing building attractors associated to the compass direction. The novelty of the model relies in the way the decision of the sensor fusion is re-injected in the visual compass allowing a robust decision-making. Robotics experiments show the capability of the model to merge different sources of information when their predictions are coherent. When the information become incoherent because the inputs propose quite different directions, the system is able to bifurcate on one coherent solution in order to maintain the temporal coherency of its behavior.

Keywords: Autonomous and bio-inspired robotics, Navigation and mapping, multimodal sensors, action selection.

1 Introduction

One of the central problem, shared by most algorithms for autonomous mobile robot navigation, is to obtain an estimate of the robot orientation. Except for a few cases [21], [9], almost all the algorithms (SLAM, GPS algorithms, snapshot model derivations [5], appearance-based approaches ...) have to solve this problem. Idiothethic information such as odometry, accelerometers, or inertial systems can be used to estimate a homing vector but they are subject to cumulative error. Hence, mobile robot navigation have been guided by the need to introduce allothetic cues (occupancy grid, SLAM algorithm, appearance-based approaches). SLAM approaches generally try to jointly estimate the position and the orientation by means of EKF (Extended Kalman Filter) [26][4][17] or PF (Particle Filter) [26]. The estimation of the orientation can even be derived from the estimation of the position (two successive positions provide an estimation of the orientation) but then the direction accuracy is directly linked with the precision of the position estimation. In visual SLAM approaches, the position of

A.P. del Pobil et al. (Eds.): SAB 2014, LNAI 8575, pp. 132–143, 2014.
© Springer International Publishing Switzerland 2014

the visual cues are generally considered as some variables of the state vector but can also be used during a correction phase [18].

Neuro-ethological studies have highlighted that the capability of path integration in animals relies on allothetic (vision, audition, touch, smell) and idiothetic information (proprioception of the actuator and vestibular information) [8]. These two sources are supposed to be merged in a global path integration system. In parallel, neurobiologists have also shown the existence of head direction cells (HD-cells) in different areas of the brain [19]. Cells in the postsubiculum area (PoS) seem to provide an allothetic estimation of the head direction based on visual cues extracted by visual cortex, whereas cells in the anterodorsal thalamic nucleus (ATN) rely on idiothetic information from lateral mammillary nuclei (LMN) which merges HD-Cells with angular head velocity (AHV) Cells. [23] proposes a complete review of the biological models of HD-cells until [20] & [2]. Merging several allothetic and idiothetic modalities seems to be a good strategy to obtain a reliable estimate of the robot orientation and develop robust exploratory behaviour [22]. Inspired by neuro-ethological data, [2] proposed a hippocampal model of the place cell in which the vision (of a distant light for example) enables to reset the idiothetic integrator. More recently, [3] showed optical flow is also used to build HD-Cells. Head movements provoke optic field flow signals affected the directional firing of HD neurons. However, the problem of the integration of idiothetic information with allothetic cues has in fact rarely been highlighted ([20] is a rare example). [12] proposes a generic architecture called the PerAc architecture can learn a sensory motor dynamics approximating a given behaviour and has been used in many navigation tasks [11], [7]. [16] proposed to use a parallel PerAc loop in order to center the gaze on a particular object by associating visual features with their angular distance from the center of the object. [13] proposed a model of visual compass derived from this system by associating landmarks with their angular distance from a given local reference. This paper also investigated how the visual compass can be used as a calibrator for a vestibular/proprioceptive integration. However, the system remained at the level of the proof of concept.

In the general frame of a neurobiologically plausible model [12]we propose here to study an architecture, inspired by the functionning of HD-Cells, merging several allothetic and idiothetic modalities to provide a reliable and resilient orientation system. The interest of our approach relies in the feedback of past information in a dynamic neural field allowing averaging different sources of information or bifurcating on one source of information according to their angular distance and their temporal stability.

2   Our Model to Tackle Navigation Tasks

We propose a model based on the PerAc architecture [12]. It uses a place cells recognition model described in [6] to learn place-action associations. This model is based on a bio-inspired visual processing system extracting the "What" (landmark) and "Where" (azimuth) signals from images provided by an active camera mimicking the head. Fig 1 summarizes the processing implemented on our robot. Focus point are computed as the local maximal of a difference of Gaussian filter (DOG) applied on the gradient image. Local views are extracted around each focus point [10]. A log-polar mapping is used to transform the local-view, providing some robustness to scale and rotation variations. The global *"Where"* information is provided by adding the horizontal position of the landmark in the image to the agent orientation. *"What"* and *"Where"* information are then merged in a 2-dimensional map of neurons corresponding to the perirhinal and parahippocampal cortex (PrPh). To avoid computational explosion the matrix is not explicit, only the encountered products are learned on the Pi units representing PrPh. These neurons are activated if their inputs from *"What"* and *"Where"* pathways are co-activated. A place is completely characterized by the activity in this matrix. This activity is learned in a last neuronal group modeling EC (Enthorinal Cortex). A winner take all (WTA) mechanism is used in EC to select the most active "Place Cell".

The association of a given Place Cell and an action is performed by linking the Place Cell with the direction of movement that has been performed. This simple associative learning between places and actions enables to generate a sensory-motor dynamics approximating a homing or a route following behaviour [12].

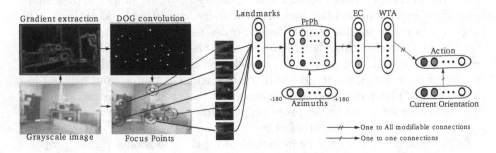

Fig. 1. Block diagram of the global navigation architecture for visual navigation. It is composed of a visual system that focuses on points of interest by extracting small images in log-polar coordinates (landmarks), then a layer merging *"What"* (landmarks) and *"Where"* (azimuth) information, a place recognition layer (EC followed by WTA) and finally a sensory-motor layer (action) which associates the place cell with the direction performed.

The complete architecture requires measuring angles either according to an absolute direction or one reliable landmark. Next section proposes a model inspired by HD-Cells allowing the merging of visual cues with proprioceptive information, to create a resilient and reliable orientation system.

3   Multimodal Compass

The model presented in fig.2 is inspired by the interaction loop between the post-subiculum (PoS) and the anterodorsal thalamic nucleus (ADN) studied in rats. PoS maintains HD-Cells activity using visual cues from the visual cortex while ADN uses idiothetic information from the lateral mammillary nuclei (LMN). LMN merges activity of HD-Cells with angular head velocity (AVH) Cells before discharging to ADN. The absolute orientation of the head of the animal would be obtained thanks to recurrent activity between PoS and ADN [23]. In our model, a "Visual Compass" (VC) learns to predict the head orientation $\hat{\theta}_H$ by associating the landmarks and their angular position θ_L in the visual field to the head angular position θ_H. Predictions of $\hat{\theta}_H$ are used to feed a Fusion Sensor model (FS). Using a dynamic neural field, FS merges Allothetic (visual compass $\hat{\theta}_H$ and magnetic compass θ_M) and Idiothetic (proprioceptive orientation θ_P) information and constructs the absolute orientation of the head of the robot θ_H. The robustness of the system comes from the interaction loop between VC and FS. The proprioceptive orientation θ_P is constructed using the robot odometry and the position of the head relative to its body. A magnetic compass is used to improve the system robustness. From the viewpoint of the biological system, the magnetic compass could be a real magnetic compass (as found in the mole brain for instance) or a distant landmark more stable than the landmarks in the foreground. Moreover the magnetic compass gives a simple way to test our architecture (it can be disturbed by a simple magnet simulating strong landmark shift in the visual fields).

The previously introduced place recognition architecture provides a robust gradient of localization (an activity level which decreases monotonically with the distance to the learned location). We deduce from this result that the features extracted by the visual system are really pertinent to characterize the location. Figure 3 presents the model of "Visual Compass". For a landmark L, a reference $\theta_{L/H}$ is computed by shifting the current orientation θ_H of the robot head with the position of the landmark θ_L in the visual field. A LMS algorithm following Widrow & Hoff learning [27] is used to learn $\hat{\theta}_{L/H}$ when a landmark is visible :

$$w_{ij}(t + dt) = w_{ij}(t) + \epsilon \cdot (S_j(t) - \hat{S}_j(t)) \cdot S_i^L(t) \tag{1}$$

With w_{ij} the synaptic weight between the jth neuron of the group $\hat{\theta}_{L/H}$ and i^{th} landmark. $S_j(t)$ is the activity of the jth neuron of the group $\theta_{L/H}$ and $\hat{S}_j(t)$ is the activity of the jth neuron of the group $\hat{\theta}_{L/H}$. $S_i^L(t) = 1$ if the landmark i is the winner and 0 otherwise. The prediction of the shifted $\hat{\theta}_{L/H}(j)$ is simply computed as :

$$\hat{\theta}_{L/H}(j) = \sum_i^{N_L} w_{ij} \cdot L_i \tag{2}$$

where w_{ij} is the synaptic weight learned in eq. 1, L_i is the activity of the ith neuron landmark and N_L the number of landmarks. The construction of the

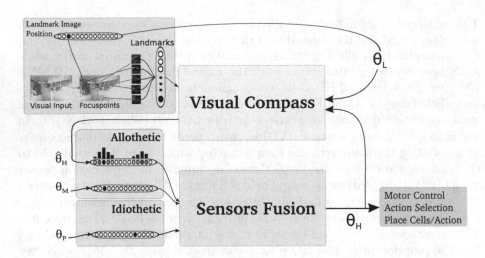

Fig. 2. Block diagram of the orientation system. 1) "Visual Compass" learns to predict $\hat{\theta}_H$ the head orientation of the robot by associating the landmarks and their positions θ_L in the visual field with the head position θ_H. 2) "Sensors fusion" merges allothetic (Visual and Magnetic compass) and idiothetic information to compute the orientation of the head θ_H. θ_H is propagated to Visual Compass and the rest of the system.

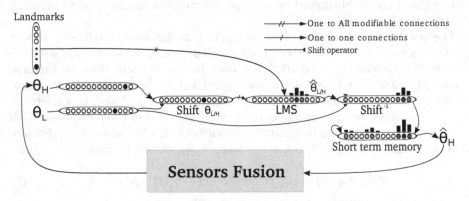

Fig. 3. Diagram of the Visual Compass. Visual Compass receives Landmarks and their position θ_L in the visual field. For landmark L, a reference $\theta_{L/H}$ is computed by shifting the current orientation θ_H of the robot head with the position θ_L. A classical conditioning following the LMS algorithm of Widrow & Hoff is used to learn $\hat{\theta}_{L/H}$ when a landmark is visible. Shifting this prediction with the position θ_L enable to build a prediction $\hat{\theta}_H$ of the head orientation of the robot. The prediction of landmarks from a given image are summed in a short term memory before being sent to the sensors fusion model.

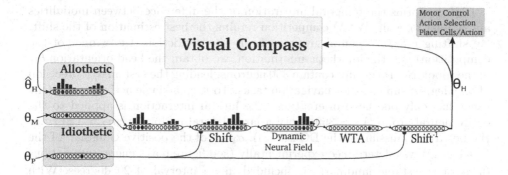

Fig. 4. Block diagram of the Sensors fusion model. Sensors fusion merge allothetic information with idiothetic to compute a reliable $\hat{\theta}_H$. The shift between Allothetic and Idiothetic modalities is sent as input to a Dynamic Neural field driven by the amari equation. Properties of the DNF allow to keep a consistent measure of this shift. A winner takes all (WTA) competition retains the best estimation which is shifted by the idiothetic modality to construct the head orientation θ_H of the robot.

prediction $\hat{\theta}_H$ of the global orientation does not use $\theta_{L/H}$ or θ_H. After learning, the system predicts the head orientation $\hat{\theta}_H$ by adding the prediction of the shift $\hat{\theta}_{L/H}(j)$ to the landmark position θ_L. The learning rate ϵ controls the speed at which the system learns to predict $\hat{\theta}_{L/H}$. We want a model able to predict reliable orientations just after learning new place cells and also able to adapt the recognition to changes of the environment. We set ϵ to a high value ($\epsilon = 1$ or 0.5) when learning the landmark and let it adapt slowly otherwise, with a small value ($\epsilon = 0.1$ or 0.05) to adjust the recognition. The system proceeds image by image with 5 landmarks per image. Prediction $\hat{\theta}_H$ of landmarks from a given image are stored in a short term memory before discharge to the fusion model, then the memory is reset ready to treat a new image.

The figure 4 describes in details the different operations performed by the "Sensors Fusion" model. Allothetic information are first summed in a neural group. Then the network computes the shift between the allothetic and idiothetic information which is sent as input to a Dynamic Neural field (DNF) driven by the Amari equation [1] :

$$\tau \cdot \frac{u(x, T)}{dT} = -u(x, T) + I(x, T) + h + \int_{z \in V_x} w(z) \cdot g(u(x - z, T))dz \quad (3)$$

where $I(x, T)$ are the inputs to the system from main behaviour. τ is the relaxation rate of the system. $w(z)$ is the interaction kernel in the neural field activation. These interactions are modeled by a difference of Gaussian (DOG) on-center [1] V_x is the lateral interaction interval. $g(u(x - z, T))$ is the activity of neuron x according to the potential $u(x, T)$.

---

[1] DOG equation : $w(z; \mu, \sigma_1, \sigma_2) = \frac{1}{\sigma_1\sqrt{2\pi}} \exp(-\frac{(z-\mu)^2}{2\sigma_1}) - \frac{1}{\sigma_2\sqrt{2\pi}} \exp(-\frac{(z-\mu)^2}{2\sigma_2})$.

DNF performs the temporal integration of the difference between modalities and winner take all (WTA) competition retains the best estimation of the shift. By shifting ($shift^{-1}$ neural group in fig.4) the prediction (the winner of the competition) and the idiothetic information, we obtain the head orientation θ_H of the robot. Neural groups contain 360 neurons, leading the system to a precision of one degree, sufficient for navigation tasks. To keep a single activity peak (the robot has only one head orientation), the lateral interaction is applied to the entire neural group ($V_x = 360$), with a large lateral inhibition : $\sigma_2 = 120$ (σ of the negative Gaussian of the DOG $w(z)$). σ_1 (σ of the positive Gaussian of the DOG $w(z)$) was determined experimentally (see figure 6.a) : energy predictions $\hat{\theta}_{L/H}$ of the stable landmarks is included in an interval of 20 degrees. With $\sigma_1 = 10$, DNF averages inputs with an angular distance lower than 20 degrees ($2\sigma_1$)

4   Results

Figure 5 illustrates the dynamic properties of the multimodal compass. The robot learns a Place Cell with only two salient objects in the visual field (the coat racks on images 1 and 2). Figure 5.1 shows the location of the coat racks when learning the Place Cell. After a while, the coat racks are moved (Figure 5.2). The experiment was conducted two times, one with and one without the magnetic compass. Figures 5.a to 5.f show the evolution of the system during the experiment, each includes the following information : small blue curves represent orientation predicted by landmarks and the magnetic compass, red dashed curves show the DNF input (sum of the small blue curves) and large black curves are the DNF output. Figures 5.a, 5.b and 5.c show the results of the experiment with the magnetic compass, whereas figures 5.d, 5.e and 5.f show the results without. Figures 5.a and 5.d show the state of the system after learning the Place Cell. Modalities predict close orientations, driving DNF to converge to the average of activities. Figures 5.b and 5.e show the state of the system after moving the coat racks. The predictions of the landmarks are shifted, driving the DNF to select an new orientation. On figure 5.b, the magnetic compass is stable enough to maintain the orientation and inputs from VC are filtered. On figure 5.e, DNF selects one of the two predicted directions and filters the second. Figures 5.f and 5.c show the state of the system after VC updated $\hat{\theta}_{L/H}$ predictions. This experiment is similar to experiments conducted in rats with the cue card ([25], [24]), where a rotation of this salient visual landmark leads to a corresponding shift in the preferred firing direction of HD cells. Moreover in case of competition between two salient visual landmark, our model is able to bifurcate on one coherent solution in order to maintain the temporal coherency of its behavior.

A second experiment was performed showing the capabilities of the system during a route following task. Robot learns online a set of 8 place-action associations during the guidance of the robot by the human teacher (see figure 7.1). The robot navigates for 10 laps. Visual compass uses $\epsilon = 0.5$ during learning phase and

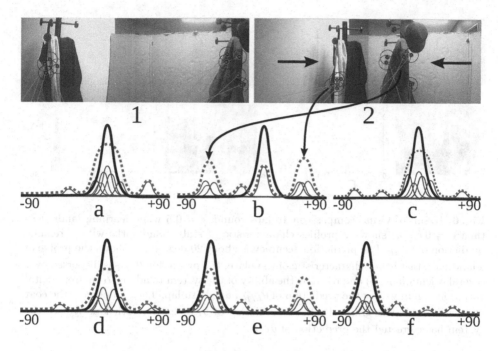

Fig. 5. Dynamic properties of the multimodal compass. Learning a Place Cell with only two salient objects in the visual field (the coat racks on images 1 and 2). 1) shows the location of the coat racks when learning the Place Cell. 2) After a while, the coat racks are moved. The experiment was conducted two times, one with and one without the magnetic compass. a) to f) show the evolution of the system during the experiment, each include the following information : small blue curves represent orientations predicted by landmarks and the magnetic compass, red dashed curves show the DNF input (sum of the small blue curves) and large black curves are the DNF output. a), b) and c) show the results of the experiment with the magnetic compass, whereas d), e) and f) show the results without it. a) and d) show the state of the system after the convergence of learning. Modalities predict close orientations, driving DNF to converge to the average of activities. b) and e) show the state of the system after moving the coat racks. The predictions of the landmarks are shifted, driving the DNF to select a new orientation. b) the magnetic compass is stable enough to maintain the orientation and inputs from VC are filtered. e) DNF selects one of the two predicted directions and filters the second. f) and c) show the state of the system after VC updated $\hat{\theta}_{L/H}$ predictions.

$\epsilon = 0.05$ when the robot is performing task. Figure 6.a shows 2 characteristic profiles of stable landmarks with a reliable prediction of $\hat{\theta}_{L/H}$. Energy predictions $\hat{\theta}_{L/H}$ is included in an interval of 20 degrees. Figure 6.c shows the profile of landmark that is not characteristic of the place. The prediction $\hat{\theta}_{L/H}$ is dispersed over several orientations. Figures 6.b and 6.d shows the ability of the system to adapt to environmental variations. On b we can see the prediction of $\hat{\theta}_{L/H}$ at the 5th lap. Then an object (the coat rack) is moved in the environment. The graph 6.d

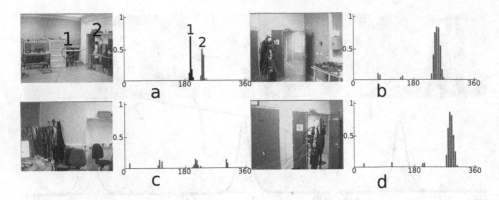

Fig. 6. Result of visual compass on 10 laps round. $\epsilon = 0.5$ when learning landmarks then $\epsilon = 0.05$. a) shows 2 profiles characteristic of stable landmarks with a reliable prediction of $\hat{\theta}_{L/H}$. The prediction accuracy is about 20 degrees. c) shows the profile of a landmark that is not characteristic of the place, the prediction $\hat{\theta}_{L/H}$ is dispersed over several orientations. b) and d) show the ability of the system to adapt to environmental variations. In b) we see the prediction of $\hat{\theta}_{L/H}$ at the 5th lap. Then an object (the coat rack) is moved. The graph d) shows prediction of $\hat{\theta}_{L/H}$ at the 10th lap. We see the system has corrected the prediction of $\hat{\theta}_{L/H}$.

shows prediction of $\hat{\theta}_{L/H}$ at the 10th lap. We see the system has corrected the prediction of $\hat{\theta}_{L/H}$. Figure 7 shows the response to various perturbations of the compass and the resulting behavior of the robot. We placed electromagnetic perturbations (blue circle on figure 7.a) in the environment (using a magnet when the robot enters into the area). Figure 7.b shows the trajectory performed by the robot using only a magnetic compass (multimodal compass turns off) : robot is not able to cross the perturbations areas. Figure 7.c shows the result with the multimodal compass turn on : the behavior of the robot is not affected by magnetic distortions, the path conforms to the expected trajectory. We see, on figure 7.e the perturbations on the magnetic compass (red curve), but θ_H (blue curve) remains consistent during the crossing of disturbed areas. On figure 7.d, the allothetic inputs are inhibited while navigating. Orientation is calculated only using odometry and DNF memory. After one lap, the orientation of the robot drifts due to odometry cumulative error, leading the robot to deviate from its path (the red dotted curve). We see, on figure 7.f, odometric (green curve) and θ_H (blue curve) signals remain consistent when VC is off. When VC is restarted, we see the gap between θ_H and VC signals corresponding to odometry cumulative error, then θ_H is quickly recalibrated by the VC.

5   Conclusion

We have presented a resilient and reliable orientation system inspired by Head Direction Cells. The network computes an absolute orientation of the head as a

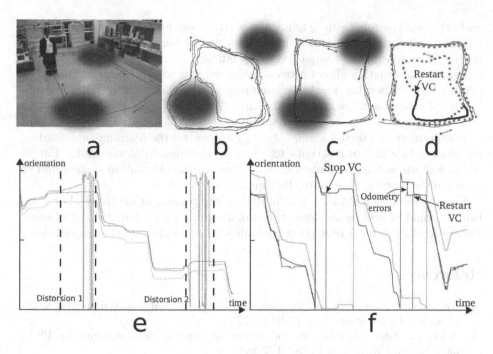

Fig. 7. a) Route following tasks performed by the robot. Blue circles represent perturbations area, Place Cells are represented by green arrows b) Trajectory performed by the robot using only a magnetic compass (multimodal compass turns off), robot is not able to cross perturbations area. c) Trajectory performed by the robot with multimodal compass, its behavior is not affected by magnetic distortions. e) Evolution of different signals during the navigation (Magnetic compass in red, Odometry in green and θ_H in blue), θ_H remains consistent during the crossing of disturbed areas despite of the perturbation on the magnetic compass. d) During the round, the allothetic inputs are inhibited. Orientation is calculated only using odometry and DNF memory. After one lap, the orientation of the robot drifts due to odometry cumulative error, leading the robot to deviate from its path (the red dotted line). Then the allothetic inputs are reactivated, the robot returns quickly on the learned trajectory (the thick black line). f) Evolution of different signals during the navigation (Visual compass in red, Odometry in green and θ_H in blue) Odometric and θ_H signals remain consistent when VC is off. When VC is restarted, we see the gap between θ_H and VC signals corresponding to odometry cumulative error. θ_H is quickly recalibrated by the VC.

result of modules inspired by the postsubiculum and the anterodorsal thalamic nucleus. The merging of allothetic and idiothetic information requires a shifting mechanism which is not detailed in this paper but which could be based on Ullman and Koch model [15] or on the attractor based solutions proposed by Redish [20] and other numerous authors. The visual information drives the system ([28], [24]). In the absence of visual information, our model continues working but errors are accumulated. The system can automatically recalibrate the integrated internal signal from the visual information as soon as they are present and reliable. The robot can dynamically learn to use new visual landmarks and automatically adapt its predictions to improve its long-term navigation capabilities. The multimodal compass is really efficient in already known areas. The integrated information allows generalization to new areas. However, the robot needs to recruit new landmarks for each new visited place, which could be problematic for scaling to large environments. A good solution would be to filter ineffective landmarks in order to maintain a reasonable number when scaling.

Furthermore, we used a simple strategy to control the learning rate, leading the system to a lack of reactivity to adapt to environmental variations. Future works will use self-assessment to detect failure in the orientation system and to regulate the learning rate more efficiently. [14].

Finally, the fusion model is not limited to the context of multimodal orientation. It could be seen as an elementary building block for intelligent data fusion. Future works will focus on testing its ability to generalize to other modalities.

References

1. Amari, S.: Dynamics of pattern formation in lateral-inhibition type neural fields. Biological Cybernetics 27(2), 77–87 (1977)
2. Arleo, A.: Spatial learning and navigation in neuro-mimetic systems. In: Ph.D. dissertation, Universit de Paris VI (2000)
3. Arleo, A., Déjean, C., Allegraud, P., Khamassi, M., Zugaro, M.B., Wiener, S.I.: Optic flow stimuli update anterodorsal thalamus head direction neuronal activity in rats. Journal of Neuroscience 33, 16790–16795 (2013)
4. Caltabiano, D., Muscato, G., Russo, F.: Localization and self-calibration of a robot for volcano exploration. In: Proceedings of the IEEE International Conference on Robotics and Automation, vol. 1, pp. 586–591 (2004)
5. Cartwright, B., Collett, T.: Landmark learning in bees 151, 521–543 (1983)
6. Cuperlier, N., Quoy, M., Gaussier, P.: Neurobiologically inspired mobile robot navigation and planning. Frontiers in NeuroRobotics, 1 (2007)
7. Cuperlier, N., Quoy, M., Giovannangeli, C., Gaussier, P., Laroque, P.: Transition cells for navigation in an unknown environment, 286–297 (2006)
8. Etienne, A., Jeffery, K.: Path integration in mammals. Hippocampus, 180–192 (2004)
9. Franz, M., Schölkopf, B., Bülthoff, H.: Homing by parametrized scene matching. In: Advances in Artificial Life: Proc. of the European Conference on Artificial Life (1997)
10. Gaussier, P., Joulain, C.: A model of visual navigation: How to explain "place cells" and "view cells" activities. In: European Conference of Visual Perception ECVP 1998 (1998)
11. Gaussier, P., Joulain, C., Banquet, J., Leprtre, S., Revel, A.: The visual homing problem: An example of robotics/biology cross fertilization. Robotics and Autonomous System 30, 155–180 (2000)
12. Gaussier, P., Zrehen, S.: Perac: A neural architecture to control artificial animals. Robotics and Autonomous Systems 16(2), 291–320 (1995)
13. Giovannangeli, C., Gaussier, P.: Orientation system in robots: Merging allothetic and idiothetic estimations. In: 13th International Conference on Advanced Robotics (ICAR 2007), pp. 349–354 (2012)

14. Jauffret, A., Cuperlier, N., Tarroux, P., Gaussier, P.: From self-assessment to frustration, a small step toward autonomy in robotic navigation. Frontier in Neurobotics (2013)
15. Koch, C., Ullman, S.: Shifts in selective visual attention: Towards the underlying neural circuitry. Human Neurobiology 4, 219–227 (1985)
16. Leprêtre, S., Gaussier, P., Cocquerez, J.: From navigation to active object recognition. In: The Sixth Int. Conf. on Simulation for Adaptive Behavior SAB 2000 (2000)
17. Martinelli, A., Tomatis, N., Siegwart, R.: Simultaneous localization and odometry self calibration for mobile robot. In: Autonomous Robots, vol. 22, pp. 75–85 (2006)
18. Panzieri, F.P.S., Ulivi, G.: Vision based navigation using kalman approach for slam. In: 11th. Int. Conf. on Advanced Robotics, Coimbra, Portugal (2003)
19. Redish, A., Elga, A., Touretzky, D.: Head direction cells in the deep cell layers of dorsal presubiculum in freely moving rats. Network, 10 (1984)
20. Redish, A., Elga, A., Touretzky, D.: A coupled attractor model of vision can sometimes predict a correct estimation, calibrating the rodent head direction system. Network, 7 (1996)
21. Röfer, T.: Controlling a wheelchair with image-based homing. In: AISB Symposium on Spatial Reasoning in Mobile Robots and Animals (1997)
22. Sheynikhovich, D., Grèzes, F., King, J.-R., Arleo, A.: Exploratory behaviour depends on multisensory integration during spatial learning. Artificial Neural Networks and Machine Learning 7552, 296–303 (2012)
23. Taube, J.S.: The head direction signal: Origins and sensory-motor integration. Annual Review of Neuroscience 30, 181–207 (2007)
24. Taube, J.S.: Head direction cells recorded in the anterior thalamic nuclei of freely moving rats. Journal of Neurosciences 15, 70–86 (1995)
25. Taube, J.S., Muller, R.U., Ranck Jr., J.B.: Head-direction cells recorded from the postsubiculum in freely moving rats. ii. effects of environmental manipulations. Journal of Neurosciences 10, 436–447 (1990)
26. Thrun, S.: Robotic mapping: A survey. In: Lakemeyer, G., Nebel, B. (eds.) Exploring Artificial Intelligence in the New Millenium, Morgan Kaufmann (2002)
27. Widrow, B., Hoff, M.E.: Adaptive switching circuits. IRE Wescon Convention Record 4, 96–104 (1960)
28. Zugaro, M.B., Arleo, A., Berthoz, A., Wiener, S.I.: Rapid spatial reorientation and head direction cells. Journal of Neurosciences 23, 3478–3482 (2003)

Developmental Dynamics of RNNPB:
New Insight about Infant Action Development

Jun-Cheol Park[1], Dae-Shik Kim[1], and Yukie Nagai[2]

[1] Department of Electrical Engineering, Korea Advanced Institute of Science and
Technology, Daejeon 305-701, Republic of Korea
{pakjce,daeshik}@kaist.ac.kr
[2] Department of Adaptive Machine Systems, Osaka University, Osaka 565-0871,
Japan
yukie@ams.eng.osaka-u.ac.jp

Abstract. Developmental studies have suggested that infants' action is
goal-directed. When imitating an action, younger infants tend to reproduce the goal while ignoring the means (i.e., the movement to achieve
the goal) whereas older infants can imitate both. We suggest that the
developmental dynamics of a Recurrent Neural Network with Parametric Bias (RNNPB) may explain the mechanism of infant development.
Our RNNPB model was trained to reproduce six types of actions (2 different goals x 3 different means), during which parametric biases were
self-organized to represent the difference with respect to both the goal
and means. Our analysis of the self-organizing process of the parametric
biases revealed an infant-like developmental change in action learning:
the RNNPB first adapted to the goal and then to the means. The different saliency of these two features caused this phased development. We
discuss the analogy of our result to infant action development.

Keywords: Cognitive developmental robotics,Infant action development,
Recurrent neural network, RNNPB.

1 Introduction

It is known that infants can understand and imitate adults' goal-directed actions
as reported in previous empirical studies [1, 2]. The study of Carpenter et al. [3]
compared an ability of imitation of a goal-directed behavior between 12-month-
old and 18-month-old infants when an adult demonstrated actions with two
different goals and two different motion styles. Their results demonstrated that,
younger infants achieved the goals of the actions while ignoring the motion styles
(i.e., the means). Older infants, however, reproduced the both without ignoring
them.

Why is there a difference in the ability between younger and older infants
in terms of two aspects of the goal-directed action? A perspective of cognitive
developmental robotics has suggested computational approaches to understanding the internal mechanisms of cognitive developmental process of humans [4,5].

A.P. del Pobil et al. (Eds.): SAB 2014, LNAI 8575, pp. 144–153, 2014.
© Springer International Publishing Switzerland 2014

Tani and Ito [6] suggested a neural network model called a Recurrent Neural Network with Parametric Bias (RNNPB). The key feature of an RNNPB is that it can encode multiple dynamic patterns into a static activity of the parametric bias (PB) units and the representation of the PB units is self-organized during learning process. It is also known that the RNNPB has biological plausibility such as mirror neuron property [6,7]. Hence, this architecture has been used in robotic experiments for goal-directed action imitation [6,8]. The study by Ito et al. [9] showed that a self-organized representation of the PB units exhibits a generalization capability in case of simple action learning.

Our study investigates how PB units are gradually self-organized during learning of an RNNPB in order to represent the two aspects of goal-directed actions (i.e., the goal and means). It can be expected that the PB units would be organized to be able to distinguish all trained actions, as previous studies have shown. The dynamical changes in learning process, however, cannot be predicted because there have not yet been any studies of that. If there are meaningful relation between the dynamic changes of the PB units and the two aspects of goal-directed actions, it would provide new insights into the mechanism of infant development of goal-directed behavior.

2   Goal-Directed Behavior

A virtual robot arm, which consists of two joints, is defined in a simulated environment as illustrated in Fig.1(a). In this environment, each joint ($\theta = [\theta_1, \theta_2]^T$) moves from 0 to 180 degrees in a two dimensional space. Inspired by the experiment of Carpenter et al. [3], goal-directed actions are designed to reveal two aspects of reaching behavior: the goal and the means. The goal of an action is moving the arm from the initial position to one of two goal positions (A, B). The means of an action is matching the trajectory of the movement.

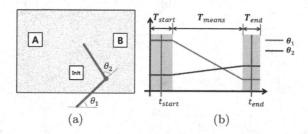

(a)   (b)

Fig. 1. (a) An overview of task and simulation environment. (b) The sequence of joint angles.

As shown in Fig. 1(b), the motor behavior consists of three parts. In the first part, the arm waits at the initial state for T_{start} time steps, and then moves to the goal state for T_{means}. Finally, it stays at the goal state for T_{end}. Hence, a

Table 1. Lists of reference behaviors

	Goal	Period	Amplitude		Goal	Period	Amplitude
A_0	A	-	-	B_0	B	-	-
A_1	A	T_{means}	α	B_1	B	T_{means}	α
A_2	A	$0.5T_{means}$	α	B_2	B	$0.5T_{means}$	α

reaching behavior appears in the form of time sequence of joint angles Θ whose length is $L = T_{start} + T_{means} + T_{end}$.

For each goal position (A, B), there are three different types of movements to achieve the goal (see Fig.2). Thus, there are totally six reference motor behaviors (2 simple movements + 4 hopping movements) as explained in Table 1. A_0 and B_0 are simple movements, which have straight trajectories of the joint angles from the initial posture to the goal posture (see Figs.2(a) and (d)). A_1, A_2, B_1 and B_2 are, in contrast, hopping movements, which add a sinusoidal perturbation with a different period (see Figs. 2(b), (c), (e) and(f)). In our experiment, the agent is supposed to experience a desired motor behavior $\Theta_{ref} \in \left\{ \Theta_{\{A_0, A_1, A_2\}}, \Theta_{\{B_0, B_1, B_2\}} \right\}$ through, for example, kinesthetic teaching.

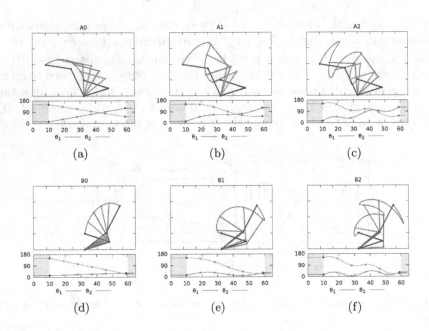

Fig. 2. Three different movements for two goal positions. (a) to (c) are reaching for the goal A, and (d) to (f) are for the goal B.

3   An RNNPB Model for Learning Agent

The main feature of an RNNPB [6] is that it can encode multiple dynamics of input/output relationships using static activation of PB units, where PB units are self-organized through learning process. The agent can be modeled to build its own internal memory for goal-directed actions based on its own experiences.

3.1   Architecture of the Model

As modified version of Jordan-type recurrent neural networks [10], an RNNPB basically consists of input/output units in a three-layered structure and context units with closed feedback. In addition, it has PB units in the input layer, which enable the network to learn multiple actions. (see Fig. 3(a)). The parameters of the network are $\Psi = \{\mathbf{W}_{21}, \mathbf{W}_{32}, \mathbf{b}_2, \mathbf{b}_3\}$, where $\mathbf{W}_{21}$ and $\mathbf{b}_2$ are the connecting weight and the bias between the first and hidden layers, and $\mathbf{W}_{32}$ and $\mathbf{b}_3$ are the same between the hidden and third layers.

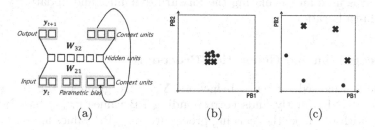

(a)   (b)   (c)

Fig. 3. (a) An RNNPB model consists of three layers: input layer, hidden layer, and output layer. (b) and (c) indicate the PB space before learning and after learning, respectively. The six goal-directed actions $\mathbf{Y}_{ref}$ are encoded as different PB values $\mathbf{x}_{recog}$, which are illustrated as markers in the space.

In our experiment, the activity of input/output units represent normalized joint angles of the virtual robotic arm $\boldsymbol{\theta}$. Hence the number of input/output units is 2, and the activity of input/output units is denoted by $\mathbf{y} = [y_1, y_2]^T$. PB units have two elements because it is easy to visualize and analyze them in a two-dimensional space. The number of the context and hidden units is empirically set to be able to represent all the reference behaviors.

3.2   Learning Procedure

The main rule of learning is to update the network parameters Ψ to enable the agent to generate desired motor behaviors. The agent initially has randomly initialized network parameters Ψ^0. When the agent experiences a desired motor behavior $\mathbf{Y}_{ref} \in \left\{\mathbf{Y}_{A_{\{0,1,2\}}}, \mathbf{Y}_{B_{\{0,1,2\}}}\right\}$ as a form of a normalized time sequence $\mathbf{Y} = [\hat{\mathbf{y}}_1, \cdots, \hat{\mathbf{y}}_L]$, the network parameters Ψ^n at the n-th iteration are updated to minimize errors $\mathbf{E}_t^{out}$ between the desired values $\hat{\mathbf{y}}_t$ and the outputs predicted by the network $\mathbf{y}_t$ for all time steps ($1 \leq t \leq L$). Back Propagation Through Time (BPTT) [11] is used for updating Ψ.

$$\mathbf{E}_t^{out} = \hat{\mathbf{y}}_t - \mathbf{y}_t \qquad (1)$$

During the BPTT process, the back-propagated delta values for the hidden units δ_{hid}, the input units δ_{in}, the output units δ_{out}, the context units δ_{cxt}, and the PB units δ_{PB} are calculated from the error of the outputs $\mathbf{E}_t^{out}$ from 1 to T time steps. Especially values of PB units ($\mathbf{x} = [x_1, x_2]^T$) are updated by Eq. (2).

$$\Delta\rho_{PB}^{(i)} = k_{bp} \sum_{t=1}^{T} \delta_{PB,t}^{(i)}$$

$$x^{(i)} = sigmoid(\rho_{PB}^{(i)}) \qquad (2)$$

After the value of the PB units $\mathbf{x}_i^{(n)}$ is determined for behavior i at the n-th iteration, it is used for calculating the forward dynamics and updating ψ^{n+1} in the $(n+1)$-th iteration.

3.3   Recognition and Generation Procedure

When the normalized reference behaviors $\mathbf{Y}_{ref}$ are given in the recognition phase, the RNNPB firstly finds corresponding PB values $\mathbf{x}_{recog}$ based on the BPTT algorithm. Unlike the learning procedure, only PB values are updated in the recognition phase.

In the generation phase, the RNNPB generates new motor behaviors $\mathbf{Y}_{gen}$ based on the PB values $\mathbf{x}_{recog}$ recognized in the previous phase. The activity of the output units at t time step is calculated using the network parameters Ψ. As the output is directly used as the values of the input units at $t+1$ time step, a sequence of motor behavior is generated step by step.

3.4   Role of PB Values

A set of static PB values represents a corresponding action as a characteristic of the RNNPB model. The PB values, which range from 0.0 to 1.0, are self-organized through learning so as to represent all the experienced actions. Thanks to linearity (not globally but locally) in the PB space, the RNNPB can also represent novel behaviors by combining experienced actions. Figs. 3(b) and (c) illustrate how the PB space is self-organized through learning. Before learning (see Fig. 3(b)), the six goal-directed actions are not separated from each other. The RNNPB at this stage would thus produces only one type of motion. The PB values for the six actions gradually change during learning. After learning (see Fig. 3(c)), the six actions will be discriminated as six different PB values, which can generate the desired actions.

4   Experimental Results

We trained an RNNPB model to reproduce the six goal-directed actions described in Section 2.

4.1   Learning Curve

The ability of an agent with the RNNPB model was assessed in terms of two viewpoints. The first point of view is whether the agent successfully reaches the desired goal posture from the initial posture. An error E_{goal} was calculated by taking the average of two error values at the initial posture E_{start} and the end posture E_{end}. The two error values (E_{start} and E_{end}) were obtained by calculating Euclidian distance between the reference motor behaviors $\mathbf{y}_t^{ref} \in \mathbf{Y}_{ref}$ and generated motor behaviors $\mathbf{y}_t^{gen} \in \mathbf{Y}_{gen}$ at t_{start} and t_{end}, respectively (see Fig. 1(b)).

$$E_{start} = \left\| \mathbf{y}_{t_{start}}^{ref} - \mathbf{y}_{t_{start}}^{gen} \right\|, \ E_{end} = \left\| \mathbf{y}_{t_{end}}^{ref} - \mathbf{y}_{t_{end}}^{gen} \right\|$$

$$E_{goal} = \frac{E_{start} + E_{end}}{2} \tag{3}$$

The second point of view is measuring how accurately the agent traces the style of movements. An error of the means E_{means} was defined as the averaged error over T_{means} time steps, where Euclidian distance between the reference motor behaviors $\mathbf{y}_t^{ref}$ and generated ones $\mathbf{y}_t^{gen}$ was applied.

$$E_{means} = \frac{1}{T_{means}} \sum_{t \in T_{means}} \left\| \mathbf{y}_t^{ref} - \mathbf{y}_t^{gen} \right\| \tag{4}$$

Fig. 4 shows the average value of E_{goal} and E_{means} for 100 RNNPBs with different initial parameters Ψ^0. As the RNNPB models have been trained, the error values also have decreased. The average error for the goal became smaller than the average error of the means when the networks had been trained enough.

4.2   Dynamics of PB Space and Generated Output

To investigate the developmental dynamics of the PB space and its relation to the action generation, E_{means} was examined for all possible PB values. Additionally a recognized PB value $\mathbf{x}_{ref}$ for each reference action $\mathbf{Y}_{ref}$ and generated output $\mathbf{Y}_{gen}$ were calculated. Three iteration points (0, 10,000 and 200,000) were picked up based on the error curves to show the dynamical self-organization of the PB space. Fig. 5 shows the result for an RNNPB among the 100 trained RNNPBs. On the left-side of this figure (see Figs. 5 (a), (c) and (e)), the direction and the

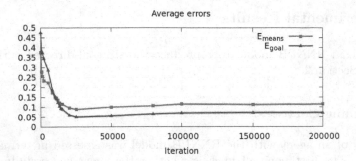

Fig. 4. The transition of errors in terms of the goal E_{goal} and the means E_{means}. The two curves plot the average of 100 networks with different initial parameters.

color of triangular markers indicate which types of actions ($\mathbf{S_x}$) have a minimum error value with the corresponding PB values.

$$\mathbf{S_x} = \underset{\mathbf{S} \in \{A_0, \cdots, B_2\}}{\operatorname{argmin}} \left\{ E_{means} \middle| \mathbf{Y}_{ref} = \mathbf{Y_S} \right\} \tag{5}$$

On the right-side of the figure (see Figs. 5 (b), (d) and (f)), the reference behaviors $\mathbf{Y}_{ref}$ (thick lines) and the generated outputs $\mathbf{Y}_{gen}$ (thin lines) are plotted for the six different actions. Recognized PB values for each reference behavior $\mathbf{x}_{recog}$ are painted as a circle with a triangular marker in (a), (c), and (e).

The result shows that the agent has gradually improved the ability to reproduce the reference actions as it increases experiences. Meanwhile, the PB space is gradually self-organized to represent the actions. When the agent has no experience of the reference behaviors (0 iteration), it cannot produce the desired actions due to the undifferentiated PB values (see Figs. 5 (a) and(b)). When the agent has been trained for 10,000 iterations, it generates simpler behaviors (i.e. A_0 and B_0) well, while producing larger errors for the hopping actions (i.e., A_1, A_2, B_1, and B_2) (see Figs. 5 (c) and (d)). The PB space separates only between A and B but not within A and B, indicating that the goal of the actions has been acquired but the means has not yet. When the agent is fully trained, it finally generates the six actions in terms of both the goal and the means. The well-organized PB values enable the agent to discriminate the actions (see Figs. 5 (e) and (f)). Taken all together, phased learning (i.e., first learning the goal of the actions and then the means) has been achieved through the development.

5   Discussion

Empirical studies of infant action development have shown that only older infants can imitate both of two aspects of the adults goal-directed actions. Our result of the self-organizing dynamics of the PB space also showed similar characteristic of the infant development. In terms of the trajectory of the reference behavior

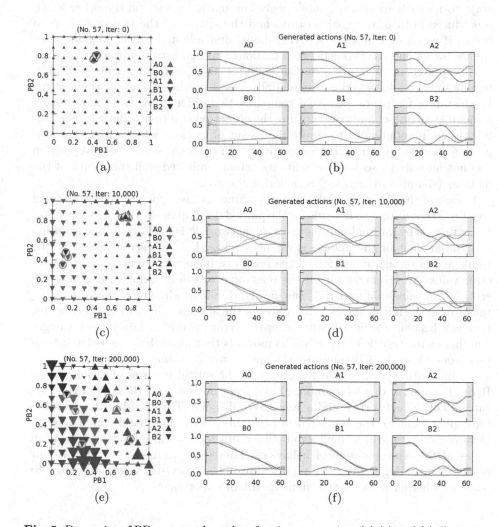

Fig. 5. Dynamics of PB space and results of action generation. (a) (c) and (e) illustrate which reference actions (from A_0 to B_2) have a minimum error in the PB space. The direction and the colors of triangular markers indicate the goal and the style of motion, respectively. The size of the markers indicates the amount of error E_{means}: The larger a marker is, the smaller the error is. Recognized PB values $\mathbf{x}_{recog}$ are illustrated as a circle with triangular markers inside. (b) (d) and (f) represent $\mathbf{Y_{gen}}$ (thin lines) for all reference actions $\mathbf{Y_{ref}}$ (thick lines) in the time domain. The red and green lines are the first and second joint angles, respectively.

Y_{ref} and the generated action Y_{gen} (see Fig. 5), the immature agent that was trained 10,000 iterations reproduced the goal position well and only the simple trajectories without sinusoid movement. The mature agent, on the other hand, reproduced both of the goal postures and the shapes of the trajectories. As a result, it was found that the RNNPB model first adapted to the goal and then the means among the two aspects of motions through learning process.

As reported in the studies by Carpenter et al. [3] and Bekkering et. al [12], infants imitate adults action differentially based on the salience of the actions. For instance, Carpenter et al. [3] compared two different types of movements: (a) sliding an object and (b) bouncing the object several times. Both 12- and 18-month-old infants tended to ignore the means of motions when a toy house was given as the goal position (House condition). In contrast, when the goal position was not indicated (No house condition), infants imitated well the means of the motions (sliding and hopping) as ignoring the goals.

In case of the RNNPB model, the error function used for the BPTT learning (see Eq. 2) seems to be a key rule for the phased development of the two aspects of the actions. The internal parameter of the network Ψ is updated at one iteration and the amount of the update is calculated based on the error values for the whole action sequence and for all the reference behaviors. Hence, the effects of error values are averaged for all the reference behaviors. That is, it makes the error of the transition part (i.e., the means) diminish while relatively enhancing the error in the initial and the goal states of the actions. The errors of the means, however, become a salient feature after the errors of the goal decreased enough. Another characteristic of the RNNPB model is that more than one behavior can be encoded into the PB values by the one network parameter.

An interesting point is that the change of the salient features of actions in the RNNPB model is due to its internal maturing procedure without changing the capacity of the network or giving any external signal. This could be one of possible explanations for the development of infants' ability for goal-directed actions. However, there is still a small gab between our model and infant mechanism in terms of the representation of behaviors. Therefore, we intend to improve our model by including multimodal representation such as visual information and to examine whether it can better simulate infant experiments.

6   Conclusion

In this study, we trained the RNNPB model to reproduce the six goal-directed actions using the virtual robot arm. The goal-directed actions were composed of the two different goal positions and the three different means of motions. While the network was gradually trained, the organization of the PB space and the generated actions were analyzed. As a result, the agent trained for 10,000 iterations could generate the simple actions well as fulfilling the goal but not the hopping actions. The agent trained for 200,000, in contrast, could generate both the simple and the hopping actions accurately. Taken together, our RNNPB model first adapted the goal and then the means during learning process. Finally, we discussed that these self-organized developmental changes in the RNNPB may explain the mechanism of infant development of goal-directed actions.

Acknowledgment. This study is partially supported by JSPS/MEXT Grants-in- Aid for Scientific Research (Research Project Number: 24000012, 24119003, 25700027), by the Research Center Program of IBS(Institute for Basic Science) in Korea(HQ1201) and by the Brain Research Program through the National Research Foundation of Korea funded by the Ministry of Science, ICT & Future Planing (NRF-2010-0018837).

References

1. Meltzoff, A.N.: Understanding the intentions of others: Re-enactment of intended acts by 18-month-old children. Developmental Psychology 31(5), 838 (1995)
2. Carpenter, M., Akhtar, N., Tomasello, M.: Fourteen-through 18-month-old infants differentially imitate intentional and accidental actions. Infant Behavior and Development 21(2), 315–330 (1998)
3. Carpenter, M., Call, J., Tomasello, M.: Twelve-and 18-month-olds copy actions in terms of goals. Developmental Science 8(1), F13–F20 (2005)
4. Asada, M., MacDorman, K.F., Ishiguro, H., Kuniyoshi, Y.: Cognitive developmental robotics as a new paradigm for the design of humanoid robots. Robotics and Autonomous Systems 37(2), 185–193 (2001)
5. Asada, M., Hosoda, K., Kuniyoshi, Y., Ishiguro, H., Inui, T., Yoshikawa, Y., Ogino, M., Yoshida, C.: Cognitive developmental robotics: A survey. IEEE Transactions on Autonomous Mental Development 1(1), 12–34 (2009)
6. Tani, J., Ito, M., Sugita, Y.: Self-organization of distributedly represented multiple behavior schemata in a mirror system: Reviews of robot experiments using rnnpb. Neural Networks 17, 1273–1289 (2004)
7. Cuijpers, R.H., Stuijt, F., Sprinkhuizen-Kuyper, I.G.: Generalisation of action sequences in rnnpb networks with mirror properties (2009)
8. Yokoya, R., Ogata, T., Tani, J., Komatani, K., Okuno, H.G.: Experience-based imitation using rnnpb. Advanced Robotics 21(12), 1351–1367 (2007)
9. Ito, M., Tani, J.: Generalization in learning multiple temporal patterns using rnnpb. In: Pal, N.R., Kasabov, N., Mudi, R.K., Pal, S., Parui, S.K. (eds.) ICONIP 2004. LNCS, vol. 3316, pp. 592–598. Springer, Heidelberg (2004)
10. Jordan, M.: Attractor dynamics and parallelism in a connectionist sequential network. In: Proceedings of the Eighth Annual Conference of the Cognitive Science Society (1986)
11. Werbos, P.J.: Backpropagation through time: What it does and how to do it. Proceedings of the IEEE 78(10), 1550–1560 (1990)
12. Bekkering, H., Wohlschlager, A., Gattis, M.: Imitation of gestures in children is goal-directed. The Quarterly Journal of Experimental Psychology: Section A 53(1), 153–164 (2000)

Simulating the Emergence of Early Physical and Social Interactions : A Developmental Route through Low Level Visuomotor Learning

Raphael Braud, Ghiles Mostafaoui, Ali Karaouzene, and Philippe Gaussier

Neurocybernetic team, ETIS
ENSEA, University of Cergy-Pontoise
95302 France
{raphael.braud,ghiles.mostafaoui,ali.karaouzene,gaussier}@ensea.fr
http://www-etis.ensea.fr/index.php/equipe-neurocybernetique.html

Abstract. In this paper, we propose a bio-inspired and developmental neural model that allows a robot, after learning its own dynamics during a babbling phase, to gain imitative and shape recognition abilities leading to early attempts for physical and social interactions. We use a motor controller based on oscillators. During the babbling step, the robot learns to associate its motor primitives (oscillators) to the visual optical flow induced by its own arm. It also statically learn to recognize its arm by selecting moving local view (feature points) in the visual field. In real indoor experiments we demonstrate that, using the same model, early physical (reaching objects) and social (immediate imitation) interactions can emerge through visual ambiguities induced by the external visual stimuli.

Keywords: Visuomotor learning, developmental learning, neural networks, human robot interaction.

1 Introduction

For future interactive robots, expected to cohabit with us in social environments, the ability to perceive, recognize and learn human actions remain a difficult but crucial question. These new artificial agents must be capable of detecting and of predicting human movements to adapt their behaviors in social contexts. Consequently, it seems important to understand the human development process that leads to early physical and social cognition in order to build bio-inspired robots permitting safe and intuitive human robot interactions.

One of the first rising issue is how to perceive biological motion which is an important primitive for communication, learning and imitation in human-human interactions. The human ability to perceive biological motion (movements of living beings) is remarkably robust. We can consider that the widespread recognition of biological movements are based on specific characteristics but the exact nature of these features remains not clearly defined, scientists being

A.P. del Pobil et al. (Eds.): SAB 2014, LNAI 8575, pp. 154–165, 2014.
© Springer International Publishing Switzerland 2014

divided between shape (ventral pathway in the brain) and kinematics (dorsal pathway in the brain) [1]. The roles of each pathway is still confused. A fairly complete neural model summarizing a possible integration of the two pathways for biological motion detection can be found in [2].

Additionally, this remarkable capacity to perceive biological motion seems to appear at early stages of infant development. In fact, psychological studies point out the neonate's capacities to imitate simple facial expressions as demonstrated by the studies conducted by Meltzoff and Moore [3]. Considering the very basic visual perception abilities of the newborns we may question the reason of this early emergence (or presence) in human development, of a particular sensibility or competence for human motion perception. In [4], Meltzoff suggested in his "Like Me" theory that humans tend to recognize cross-modal equivalence between perceived actions and self representation of their own movements. The author argued that this way of recognizing self in others could be a prime step for social cognition as it can be used to analyze, imitate and learn biological movements (other's actions). Consequently, biological motion detection can be defined as "resonance measurement " system that compares proprioception (perception of our own motor dynamics) and exteroception (perception of other's movements). The evidence of the motor controllers influence on learning and perceiving motion was described by numerous other psychological studies. In [5], Viviani and Stucchi showed the coupling between motor and perceptual processes while perceiving dotted points moving with trajectories respecting the *two third power low*. Recent studies point out the strong link between perceiving and executing movements [6]. This resonance between producing actions and perceiving others movements was also highlighted by the importance of synchrony during human social interactions. Developmental studies acknowledged synchrony as a prime requirement for interaction between a mother and her infant. An infant stops interacting with her mother when she stops synchronizing her movements [7]. These observations also imply the importance of a dynamical loop of treatment between motor production (proprioception) and visual perception.

Keeping in view the importance of motor resonance in social interaction, it has also been widely studied and used to improve human robot communications in particular through the notion of learning by imitation [8][9]. Numerous different works used motor babbling as a starting point to obtain imitative behaviors [10][11]. A possible bio-inspired approach is to rely on mirroring systems which constitute one of the main way to explain imitation behavior [12]. However, many of these works are based on internal models dedicated to specific behaviors. Furthermore, assessing whether there is imitation or not (goal directed imitation vs simple immediate movement imitation), and consequently guessing what should be the underlying mechanism still a challenging question for developmental studies. Our approach will tend to examine very early mechanisms leading to imitation and reaching behaviors without any use of a specific pre-defined internal model. We will demonstrate that these capacities could emerge through visual ambiguities as proposed in [13] or [14]. Additionally, we will question a possible use of a set of oscillators as motor primitives.

Inspired by the above state of the art, we will investigate in this paper the two main following questions: i) How can a robot gain, from a developmental learning, a cross-modal knowledge linking motor production and visual perception? ii) How the robot can use this self-expertise to acquire an early social cognition: emergence of imitative capacities and interaction possibilities with the surrounding physical word (humans, objects etc.)? The precise theoretical and experimental context of the presented work is defined in the next section.

2   Theoretical and Experimental Context

To answer the above theoretical questions, we wish to explore the recognition and the imitation of actions or gestures as a filter that could be built during early interaction (learning to recognize the motor dynamics of self in the perception of other's movements) and not as a pre-defined cascade of ad-hoc filters, leading to the building of the notion of self and others through actions. We defend the idea that intuitive interactions can be seen as an emergent function of sensori-motor dynamics.

To confirm our assumptions, we propose here to simulate, on a robotic platform, the behavior of infants aged approximatively from 0 to 3 months in the specific context of early simple gestures imitation and reaching trials triggered by a visual stimulus. Infants competences regarding the pre-cited context can be coarsely summarized by the following development schedule extracted from [15]:

- Pre-Natal: Grasp reflex on tactile feedback, Proprioceptive-motor mapping (Arm babbling)
- 1 month: Learning of saccade mapping (Moving Eyes and head to targets), Initial mapping of movements and vision (directed but unsuccessful hand movements), Initial goal directed reaching triggered by a visual stimulus without using visual feedbacks to mid-reach movement correction
- 3 months: Reach and miss (with contacts) triggered by visual stimulation, Initial learning of eye-hand mappings, Reaches are visually elicited but without continuous feedback (the gaze still focused on the target and not the hand)
- 4 months: Primitive hand-eye mapping : Successful visual goal directed reaching appears around 3-4 months after birth

We invite the reader to refer to [15] for a complete detailed and referenced development calendar.

We use a minimal setup including a Katana arm, a pan tilt camera, different objects (for reaching trials) and a human partner. Our objective here is to simulate the above behavioral development process by giving the robot the ability :

- to obtain a cross-modal visuomotor knowledge from a babbling step using a very coarse motor controller (oscillators) and low level visual features (optical flow)
- to imitate the human partner on the basis of visuomotor resonance
- to learn its arm shape and to focus its visual attention on it through statistical integrations of visual saccades during the babbling
- and finally to initiate an emerging reaching trial directed by an external visual stimuli (attractive objects) through visual ambiguities

We will experimentally show that all these early capabilities could emerge from very low level visuomotor learning. The developed neural model will be detailed bellow after presenting, in the next section, the considered motor and visual primitives.

3   Motor and Visual Primitives

3.1   The Motor Controller

Recent studies suggested that the motor cortex responses during reaching contain a brief but strong oscillatory component, even if the movement itself is not oscillatory [16]. Inspired by these recent neurobiological findings, in this study we will investigate the notion of rhythmic patterns and motor control using oscillators. The other underlying reason behind this choice is to avoid the use of complex motor controllers implying a substantial refined proprioceptive knowledge which is not expected to be found during the early stages of development.

Our motor controller is illustrated in figure 1. Each articulation of the Katana arm is fed by a set of oscillators. Each oscillator is based on a simple model made of two neurons $N1$ and $N2$ [17]. The frequency of the oscillator depends on the three parameters $\alpha 1$, $\alpha 2$ and β :

$$N_1(n+1) = N_1(n) - \beta N_2(n) + \alpha 1 \ and \ N_2(n+1) = N_1(n) + \beta N_2(n) + \alpha 2 \ (1)$$

The control signal feeding each articulation is then obtained by a weighted sum of the different oscillators :

$$\theta_j(t) = \sum_{i=1}^{n} w_i^j . O_i(t). \tag{2}$$

$O_i(t)$ is the output signal of the oscillator i and w_i^j is a weight representing the contribution of the oscillator i to the control signal $\theta_j(t)$ of the articulation j.

3.2   Motion Direction-Selective Neurons for Low Level Visual Features Extraction

Neurobiological records of cells from V1 and MT brain areas showed that the V1 neurons and most of the MT neurons are sensitive to preferred motion directions, these neurons were called *component direction-selective neurons* by Movshon [18]. A smaller part (20%) of the MT neurons respond best to pattern's directions, they are called *pattern direction-selective neurons*.

To simulate these motion selective neurons, we first estimate, for each pixel of the image, the velocity vectors induced by movements in the robot visual field. We used a hierarchical implementation of the classical Horn & Shunk optical flow algorithm [19] based on the works of Amiaz et al [20]. Using the extracted optical flow, we will now define the component direction-selective neurons. The firing of each of these neurons (A_i) is proportional to the angular distance between the visual stimulus (optical flow) and its preferred direction weighted by the motion intensity as : $A_i = \exp^{-(\frac{(\beta - \beta_i)^2}{2\tau_1^2})} \cdot (1 - \exp^{-(\frac{V^2}{2\tau_2^2})})$.

β is the direction of the computed optical flow,β_i is the preferred direction of the direction-selective neuron i, V is the motion intensity, τ_1 and τ_2 are the coefficients regulating the dynamic of the neuron activation respectively for the motion direction and the motion intensity. τ_1 and τ_2 are experimentally set to a value of 20 to optimize the neurons dynamics reacting to the observed range of motion intensities.

Further studies on selective-directional neurons showed that the reactivity range (around the preferred direction) of these neurons is about 40 to 60 degrees [21]. Consequently, we defined 6 different classes of selective neurons reacting for the given preferred motion direction : $0^0, 60^0, 120^0, 180^0, 240^0$ and 300^0. As we are using image coordinates, the Y axis is directed to the south (90^0). For high motion intensities, this type of neuron will respond with a value of 1 if the optical flow direction is equal to its preferred one, its firing will decrease gradually for lower motion intensities and optical flow directions far from the preferred one. Each velocity vector computed (for each pixel of the image) by the optical flow algorithm is then coded by 6 neurons sensitive to different motion directions. As a result, for an image of 640x480 pixels we will obtain 6x640x480 direction-selective neurons.

Pattern direction-selective neurons are then introduced to integrate the responses of the direction-selective neurons. For simplicity and to insure a real time interaction, we define only 6 pattern direction-selective neurons corresponding to the above preferred motion directions (see Figure 1). To obtain the response of a pattern direction-selective neuron sensitive to the motion direction i we integrate the activations of all the direction-selective neurons sensitive to the same motion direction i. A video illustrating the direction selective neurons responses to different movements can be found on our website [1].

4   Visuomotor Learning and Low Level Imitation

In previous studies, we have proposed that a low-level imitation (imitation of meaningless gestures) can be an emergent property of a simple perception-action

---

[1] http://www.etis.ensea.fr/ neurocyber/Videos/lowLevel_Reaching/video_
directionSelectiveNeurons.avi

homeostat based on perception ambiguity [13]. Based on this assumption, we present in this section a neural network model (see figure 1 A) that allows a robot to learn its own perceived motion and to imitate a human partner owing to visual ambiguities.

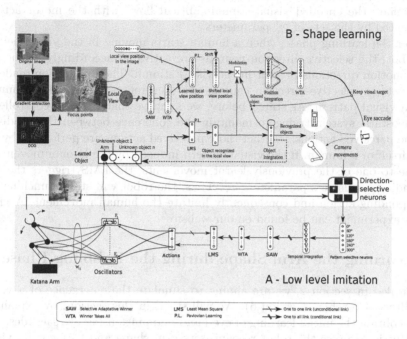

Fig. 1. Global Architecture, Part A : Neural model for motion learning and immediate imitation, Part B : Neural model for object and arm learning and recognition

Here, the motor controller is composed by 9 oscillators with 3 different frequencies and 3 different phase shifts. The control signal for each robot joint j is obtained by summing the different oscillators output modulated by the weights w_i^j (see equation 2). As a first trial, the weights w_i^j are randomly chosen, the robot starts to move according to this set of parameters. Unfortunately, even with this small number of oscillators, most of the obtained actions were difficult to analyze, and not really biologically plausible (in particular because of the mechanical characteristics of the Katana arm). For the sake of simplicity, in this experiment we decided to settle the weights w_i^j to obtain only 3 different rhythmic actions : a horizontal motion (A1) and two diagonal ones (A2 and A3).

The model illustrated figure 1-A works in two phases :

Firstly, during a very simple babbling step the robot learn its own dynamics. The robot starts moving by altering randomly the three actions A1,A2 and A3. A Selective Adaptive Winner (SAW, an ART-based neural networks) is fed by the time integration of the 6 pattern direction-selective neurons responses which react differently to the perceived robot's arm actions. Depending on the vigilance parameter of the SAW, if the new inputs are too different from the neurons encoding the previous ones, new encoding neurons are recruited. A Winner Takes All (WTA) is then used to select the relevant SAW neurons encoding at best the inputs from the pattern-directional neurons. These selected neurons represent the unconditional inputs of an LMS (Least Mean Square) network which learn to associate the encoded visual stimuli (optical flow) with the motor actions represented by the sets of w_i^j parameters.

After the learning phase, when a human starts moving in the visual field of the robot, the selective-direction neurons are activated accordingly to the different motion directions present in the visual stimuli. The integration made by the 6 pattern selective-direction neurons are then representative of the human motion visual pattern. As stated before, we suppose that the arm controller is a homeostatic system trying to maintain the coherence between the produced and the perceived actions, whether those perceived actions are performed by the robot itself or a human. If the visual pattern induced by the human movements is close to one of the previously learnt movements, the LMS triggers the corresponding oscillator's parameters w_i^j. Thus, the robot will start launching the corresponding action and consequently imitate the human movement. A video of this experiment can be found on our website[2].

5   Learning the Arm Shape during the Babbling Phases

As detailed in section 2, we are aiming to simulate the emergence of a visual goal directed reaching (section 6). We will start, in this section, by explaining how to obtain the initial learning of eye-hand mappings using eye saccades. Our objective is to make the robot recognize its arm shape and to focus its visual attention on it. For doing that, we will use and define a neural model for object recognition inspired by the works in [22] and [23]. The general principal of this model is to learn local views of the objects in the basis of point of interest detection (focus points simulating eye saccades). As illustrated Fig. 1-B, the spatial gradient information is first extracted from the grayscale images. The resulted image gradient is then convolved by a DOG (Difference Of Gaussian) filter. The output of this process is a saliency map which highlight regions in the image having a local structure shape like corners. Local maxima are then selected from this saliency map.

Local views collecting the pixel around each detected interest points (here on a radius of 20 pixels) are then extracted and filtered by a log polar transform in order to be robust to scale changing and rotational variations. The filtered local views feed the Selective Adaptive Winner (SAW), if the new inputs (local views) are too different from the previous ones, new encoding neurons are recruited. A Winer Take All (WTA) is then used to select the winning local views.

The model presented in (Fig. 1 B) can be divided into two parts. The recognition of what is the object, and the localization of "where" is the object. A first

---

[2] http://www.etis.ensea.fr/ neurocyber/Videos/lowLevel_Reaching/video_lowLevelImitation.avi

LMS (Least Mean Square) algorithm is used for the "what" pathway to learn the local views associated to each object. The number of neurons in the LMS is then corresponding to the number of possible objects to learn. In the where pathway, two LMS are used to associate the object center position respectively on the x and y axis relative to the local views belonging to it. As presented figure 2, after the learning phase, each selected local view (point of interest) has its own prediction of the object center. If most of them predict the same position, the object is well recognized. In the opposite case, several positions of the object center will be predicted without a majority vote permitting to identify a winner (see figure 2). If an object is learned at a given position and detected in another one, the output of the LMS shift the learn position relative to the actual position allowing to predict the object position.

The previous model is then used to learn the robot its own arm shape without any added a priori knowledge. To do so, during the babbling phase, the robot also starts to detect feature points in the visual field using the general model for object recognition previously described. Additionally, the saliency maps resulting from the DOG filtering is modulated by the motion intensities (optical flow). Thus, if we assume that the robot will be able to perceive its moving arm during the whole babbling step, statistically, the detected feature points (or focus points) will mostly belong to the arm of the robot. The robot will consequently "statistically" learn the shape of its arm rather than other objects from the background.

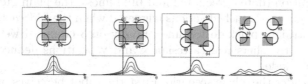

Fig. 2. Schematic example of object position estimations

6 Visual Ambiguities and Emergence of a Visual Directed Reaching

After the learning phases (babbling), our robot is able to recognize its arm and to locate its visual focus of attention on it. Lets now consider, besides the robot arm, the presence of an added visual stimulus attracting the robot's visual attention. To simulate that, we will first simply and similarly use the previous shape learning neural model to make the robot learn a new object. The considered object is then "shacked" in front of the robot while its arm is not moving, consequently the learned local views will statistically belong to this newly added object. As explained in the previous section, the model we used for object recognition can locate objects positions relative to the center of the image.

Thus, if an object (or the robot's arm) is located in the images, we can use its predicted position to shift the pan-tilt camera to center the recognized object in the image using a neural field. If two recognized objects are seen (shared visual attention) by the robot, its pan-tilt camera move alternatively from an object to another, this process simulate human eye saccades.

As a consequence, if the robot can perceive its arm and focuses its visual attention on it, and if simultaneously a human shows a learned object somewhere in the visual field, the camera starts moving alternatively from the arm to the object. An optical flow is then generated because of this shared visual attention. By using the neural model for imitating actions (see section VI and figure 1), this induced optical flow will be coded by the directional and pattern selective neurons leading the LMS to trigger the corresponding motor primitive which produces an oscillatory arm movement in the direction of the located object. An experimental example is illustrated in figure 3. After the learning steps, the robot can perform and imitate 3 different movements as described section VI. It also learned to perceive and focus its attention on its arm and another external object (here, an Aibo robot). 3-A represent three snapshots from the experiment; 3-B illustrates the activities of the LMS neurons dedicated to object recognition (green for the arm and red for Aibo), a threshold decids if an object is recognized or not is represented by the dotted straight line; 3-C and D shows the X and Y neural fields activities (blue line) and the Pan and Tilt camera movements (dotted green line); 3-E highlights the 6 pattern selective directional neurons firing; 3-F illustrate the activities of the LMS neurons dedicated to the 3 actions recognition (doted green, red and blue lines), the plain green, red and blue lines represent the launched actions triggered when the LMS activity is over the threshold (straight black dotted line); finally on 3-G and H we can see the evolution of the arm pliers real cartesian x and y positions deduced from the Katana physical model.

Lets now consider the whole scenario. First the robot perceives only its arm. The arm is recognized and located in the center of the image. The learned object (Aibo) is then presented by a human interactant on the left upper side of the image. Consequently, the arm and the object are simultaneously recognized and located (brown area of the figure 3 B). Because of this shared visual attention, the pan-tilt camera (controlled by the Neural Fields) starts moving toward the recognized object (figure 3 C and D) inducing an optical flow in the visual field. This optical flow is then encoded by the pattern direction selective neurons (figure 3 E). As the camera is moving from the right to the left upper side (toward Aibo), it generates an inverted optical flow directed to the right and down side (O^o and 60° because of the inversion of the Y axis). The directional neurons trigger the corresponding learned oscillatory arm movement (action 2 on figure 3 F). Consequently, as proved in figure 3 G and H, the robot's arm starts moving toward the detected learnt object (Aibo): left direction on the x axis and upward on the y axis.

This behavior simulates an emerging visual goal directed reaching trial induced by visual ambiguities. A video of this final experiment can be find on our web site[3]

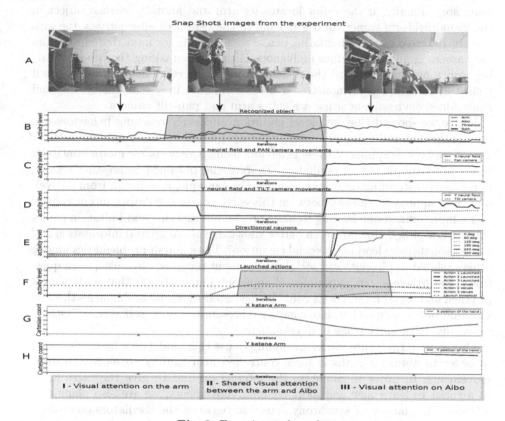

Fig. 3. Experimental results

7   Conclusion

We presented here a developmental approach for investigating the emergence of early physical and social interaction from a learning stage of visuomotor cross-modal knowledge by using a neural network model. We simulate, on a robotic platform, the developmental behavior of infants aged approximatively from 0 to 3 months in the specific context of initial simple gestures imitation and early reaching trials triggered by an external visual stimulus. First, during a babbling step, the robot learns to associate its motor primitives to the optical flow induced by its own arm. In parallel, the robot statistically learn its arm shape, by modulating the feature points detection and the local views learning with motion intensities (optical flow). Similarly, if the arm stops moving, the robot can learn new shacked external objects. After the learning phase if a human

---

[3] http://www.etis.ensea.fr/ neurocyber/Videos/lowLevel_Reaching/video_LowLevelReaching.avi

starts moving in the visual field, his movements induce visual ambiguities which make the robot starts imitating the human as it tries to maintain the balance between the visual stimuli and the motor controller as learned during the babbling step. Finally, if the robot locates its arm and another learned object in the visual field, its camera starts moving to the center of alternatively the arm and the detected object, simulating ocular saccades. As for immediate imitation, the camera oscillations induce ambiguous optical flow making the robot initiating arm movements toward the located object. The efficiency of the proposed neural architecture is demonstrated by experiments in a real indoor and non constrained environment using a Katana arm and pan-tilt camera.

Hence we showed that low level imitation and early reaching behaviors can emerge through ambiguous visuomotor perception. Additionally we demonstrated a possible bootstrapping of these behaviors using a very coarse motor controller based on a simple set of oscillators. Despite the obtained interesting results, numerous outstanding questions remains. For example, how to fill, from a developmental approach, the gap between this early coarse oscillatory motor control and a more refined one leading to more precise interactions and imitation games (object grasping)? How to gain a better knowledge about spatial information and peripersonal space leading to social cognition? These harsh problematics among others related to physical and social development remains, obviously, open questions. Nevertheless, our experimental approach demonstrates that early simple physical and social interactions could be mediated by visual ambiguities through visuomotor learning rather than complex representations of "self" versus "Other" especially at an early stage of development.

Our short-term future works are aiming to use this model on a hydraulic robot in order to obtain a realistic force controlled arm leading to more "natural" movements. In order to maintain the interaction and to give the capabilities to a robot to learn new and more complex movements, we are also planing to introduce the notion of synchrony detection between the oscillators controlling the arm and the visual stimuli as proposed in our previous work on simple oscillatory movements [24]. Thus, a refined interaction can be obtained during immediate and differed imitation games. More precisely, the weights modulating the influence of each oscillator on the arm joints (set to a fixed value in this article) must be learnt during bidirectional imitation games.

References

1. Lange, J., Lappe, M.: The role of spatial and temporal information in biological motion perception. Advances in Cognitive Psychology 3(4), 419 (2007)
2. Giese, M.A., Poggio, T.: Neural mechanisms for the recognition of biological movements. Nature Reviews Neuroscience 4(3), 179–192 (2003)
3. Meltzoff, A.N., Moore, M.K.: Imitation of facial and manual gestures by human neonates. Science 198(4312), 75–78 (1977)
4. Meltzoff, A.N.: 'Like me': A foundation for social cognition. Developmental Science 10(1), 126–134 (2007)

5. Viviani, P., Stucchi, N.: Biological movements look uniform: Evidence of motor-perceptual interactions. Journal of Experimental Psychology: Human Perception and Performance 18(3), 603 (1992)
6. Casile, A., Giese, M.A.: Possible influences of motor learning on perception of biological motion. J. Vis. 4, 221a (2004)
7. Nadel, J., Carchon, I., Kervella, C., Marcelli, D., Rserbat-Plantey, D.: Expectancies for social contingency in 2-month-olds. Developmental Science 2(2), 164–173 (1999)
8. Breazeal, C., Scassellati, B.: Robots that imitate humans. Trends in Cognitive Sciences 6(11), 481–487 (2002)
9. Lopes, M., Santos-Victor, J.: A developmental roadmap for learning by imitation in robots. IEEE Transactions on Systems, Man, and Cybernetics, Part B: Cybernetics 37(2), 308–321 (2007)
10. Rao, R.P., Shon, A.P., Meltzoff, A.N.: A Bayesian model of imitation in infants and robots. In: Imitation and Social Learning in Robots, Humans, and Animals, pp. 217–247 (2004)
11. Demiris, Y., Meltzoff, A.: The robot in the crib: A developmental analysis of imitation skills in infants and robots. Infant and Child Development 17(1), 43–53 (2008)
12. Oztop, E., Kawato, M., Arbib, M.: Mirror neurons and imitation: A computationally guided review. Neural Networks 19(3), 254–271 (2006)
13. Gaussier, P., Moga, S., Quoy, M., Banquet, J.P.: From perception-action loops to imitation processes: A bottom-up approach of learning by imitation. Applied Artificial Intelligence 12(7-8), 701–727 (1998)
14. Nagai, Y., Kawai, Y., Asada, M.: Emergence of mirror neuron system: Immature vision leads to self-other correspondence. In: 2011 IEEE International Conference on Development and Learning (ICDL), vol. 2, pp. 1–6. IEEE (August 2011)
15. Law, J., Shaw, P., Earland, K., Sheldon, M., Lee, M.H.: A psychology based approach for longitudinal development in cognitive robotics. Frontiers in Neurorobotics 8(1) (2014)
16. Churchland, M.M., Cunningham, J.P., Kaufman, M.T., Foster, J.D., Nuyujukian, P., Ryu, S.I., Shenoy, K.V.: Neural population dynamics during reaching. Nature (2012)
17. Revel, A., Andry, P.: Emergence of structured interactions: From a theoretical model to pragmatic robotics. Neural Networks 22(2), 116–125 (2009)
18. Movshon, J.A., Adelson, E.H., Gizzi, M.S., Newsome, W.T.: The analysis of moving visual patterns. Pattern Recognition 54, 117–151 (1985)
19. Horn, B.K., Schunck, B.G.: Determining optical flow. In: 1981 Technical Symposium East, pp. 319–331. International Society for Optics and Photonics (November 1981)
20. Amiaz, T., Lubetzky, E., Kiryati, N.: Coarse to over-fine optical flow estimation. Pattern Recognition 40(9), 2496–2503 (2007)
21. Hol, K., Treue, S.: Different populations of neurons contribute to the detection and discrimination of visual motion. Vision Research 41(6), 685–689 (2001)
22. Gaussier, P., Joulain, C., Zrehen, S., Banquet, J.P., Revel, A.: Visual navigation in an open environment without map. In: Proceedings of the 1997 IEEE/RSJ International Conference on Intelligent Robots and Systems, IROS 1997, vol. 2, pp. 545–550. IEEE (1997)
23. Lepretre, S., Gaussier, P., Cocquerez, J.P.: From navigation to active object recognition (2000)
24. Hasnain, S.K., Mostafaoui, G., Gaussier, P.: A synchrony-based perspective for partner selection and attentional mechanism in human-robot interaction. Paladyn 3(3), 156–171 (2012)

Intrinsically Motivated Decision Making for Situated, Goal-Driven Agents

Mohamed Oubbati, Christian Fischer, and Günther Palm

Institute of Neural Information Processing, University of Ulm, Germany

Abstract. Goal-driven agents are generally expected to be capable of pursuing simultaneously a variety of goals. As these goals may compete in certain circumstances, the agent must be able to constantly trade them off and shift their priorities in a rational way. One aspect of rationality is to evaluate its needs and make decisions accordingly. We endow the agent with a set of needs, or drives, that change over time as a function of external stimuli and internal consumption, and the decision making process hast to generate actions that maintain balance between these needs. The proposed framework pursues an approach in which decision making is considered as a multiobjective problem and approximately solved using a hierarchical reinforcement learning architecture. At a higher-level, a Q-learning learns to select the best learning strategy that improves the well-being of the agent. At a lower-level, an actor-critic design executes the selected strategy while interacting with a continuous, partially observable environment. We provide simulation results to demonstrate the efficiency of the approach.

1 Introduction

Goal-driven models of agency focus on how agents set several goals, make decisions about how to achieve those goals, and act on these decisions [1]. There have been several contributions on goal-driven models, including goal management in cognitive architectures [2], goal-driven autonomy [3], meta-reasoning [4], goal generation [5] and multi-strategy learning [6]. While these approaches may perform well in simple cases, they will face many difficulties in more complex real-world environments. Due to resource limitations (computation, energy), partial information of the environment and time-varying goal importance, the designer is required to anticipate what discrepancies can occur, define what goals should be pursued and constantly set new priorities for these goals. To increase autonomy of goal-driven agents, we are investigating the role of motivation in the decision making process. A typical motivational framework would possess an internal motivational system, a priority mechanism to adjust the relative urgency of the drives, and an efficient decision-making process [7]. Under this perspective, we introduce a biologically inspired learning architecture that takes into account internal needs and external stimuli to decide what should be learned in a particular situation. The concept is based on fundamental mechanisms of animal behavior. Animal research suggests that behaviors are governed by two distinct processes of decision making: a goal-directed and a habit process [8]. The goal-directed process often relies on anticipated outcomes, that are motivationally meaningful –i.e., pleasurable or important for survival. The habit process, on the other hand, entails association between

A.P. del Pobil et al. (Eds.): SAB 2014, LNAI 8575, pp. 166–175, 2014.

situations and actions that are learned from experience, for example through reinforcement learning. The interaction between these two systems has recently been argued to be hierarchical [9]. The goal-directed process selects a goal, and decides which habitual actions should be executed to reach that goal. Thus, in this paper, we aim to deliver a hierarchical reinforcement learning framework for intrinsically motivated goal-driven agents. The proposed learning system is depicted in Fig. 1. Similar to [10], we endow the agent with drive dynamics (motivational model) that are related to survival, such as eating, drinking, and avoiding harmful stimuli. According to the *options* framework [11], we predefine a set of fixed strategies (options) to form what we call the *repertoire of learning strategies*. Each strategy gives priority to one or more drives by changing their motivational weights. At a higher level, we design a goal-directed system as a Q-learning that iterates through all available strategies keeping a record of the expected outcome for each, and chooses the one that best improves the agent's *well-being*. As in [12], the well-being is considered as a weighted combination of the drives using the motivational weights. At a lower level, the habit system executes the selected strategy while interacting with a continuous, partially observable environment. Similar to [13], the habit system is implemented as an actor-critic design (ACD). The critic, in this implementation, is a reservoir computing (RC) network [14]. Since the current application requires the simultaneous satisfaction of multiple drives (objectives), the proposed RC-ACD has to be extended to the multiobjective case. A single reservoir estimates the value functions $J_{1,2,3}$ related to the drives, and provides their gradients to the actor.

The rest of the paper is organized as follows. After giving some background information about our motivational situated agent, we describe the multiobjective RC-ACD. Next, we introduce the motivational decision maker, and we provide some simulation results.

2 Motivational Situated Agent

2.1 Motivational Model

We endow the agent with three drives hunger,thirst, and safety. Each drive is characterized by the attributes D_i^s, D_i^g, D_i^t, D_i^l and D_i^p. The attribute D_i^s indicates the current strength/intensity and takes values between 0 (satisfied) and 1. At each time step D_i^l, this strength varies with a factor D_i^g until a total duration of D_i^t. The importance of each drive is D_i^p. The dynamics of a drive can be described as follows [12]:

$$D_i^s(k + 1) = \begin{cases} D_i^s(k) + D_i^g - \alpha_j \cdot U_j(k) & \text{if } D_i^l > D_i^t \\ 0 & \text{if } D_i^l \leq D_i^t \end{cases} \quad (1)$$

where α_j is a step factor.

2.2 Situatedness

The agent is situated, since it is completely dependent on online, simulated sensor data. We consider interaction between the agent and its environment as one dynamical system described by

$$s(k + 1) = F[s(k), a(k)] \quad (2)$$

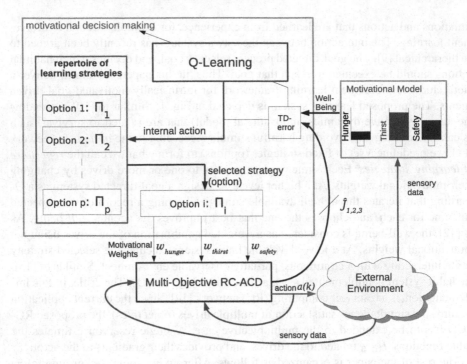

Fig. 1. Overview of the goal-driven hierarchical reinforcement learning

where $s(k)$ is the state, $a(k)$ denotes the action, i.e. the agent's heading φ, and F is a nonlinear function. The state estimation $\hat{s} \in R^3$ is performed using distances e_i to three stationary landmarks.

$$e_i(k) = d_l \cdot \|l_i\|, (i = 1, 2, 3). \tag{3}$$

where d_l is a scaling factor, and l_i is the distance between the agent and the landmark i.

3   Multiobjective RC-ACD

Suppose one associates with the coupled agent-environment (2) the performance index J_l for each drive l.

$$J_l[s(i)] = \sum_{k=i}^{\infty} \gamma^{k-i} U_l[s(k), a(k)], \tag{4}$$

where U_l is the utility function for objective l and γ is a discount factor with $0 < \gamma < 1$. According to Bellman [15], the optimal cost-to-go function for each objective l is

$$\hat{J}_l[s(k)] = \min_{a(k)} \left\{ U_l[s(k), a(k)] + \gamma \hat{J}_l[s(k+1)] \right\} \tag{5}$$

and the corresponding action $a(k)$ that achieves this optimal cost at time k is

$$a(k) = \arg\min_{a(k)} \left\{ U_l[s(k), a(k)] + \gamma \hat{J}_l[s(k+1)] \right\} \tag{6}$$

We consider a continuous environment containing two regions for resources (food and drink) with different values. These regions are to be acquired. The environment also has a dangerous region, which has to be avoided. These regions could be represented by any utility functions. In this paper, we create a three-objective optimization problem represented by three utilities U_1, U_2 and U_3, related to hunger, safety and thirst, respectively. The choice of these functions is inspired from the multiobjective objective problems analyzed in [16], and projected on the two dimensional environmental space (x,y). They are desined as

$$U_1(x, y) = 2 \cdot \exp\left(-\left(\frac{(x - 50)^2}{2 \cdot 25^2} + \frac{(y - 104)^2}{2 \cdot 25^2}\right)\right) \tag{7}$$

$$U_2(x, y) = -2 \cdot \exp\left(-\left(\frac{(x - 50)^2}{2 \cdot 13^2} + \frac{(y - 80)^2}{2 \cdot 13^2}\right)\right) \tag{8}$$

$$U_3(x, y) = 2 \cdot \exp\left(-\left(\frac{(x - 50)^2}{2 \cdot 25^2} + \frac{(y - 56)^2}{2 \cdot 25^2}\right)\right) \tag{9}$$

Due to the curse of dimensionality, i.e. computational complexity increases exponentially with dimensionality of the application or the size of the state space, obtaining $a(k)$ is a hard task. The framework of ACD addresses this porblem by using a system called "critic" that approximates $\hat{J}_l$ and adapts $a(k)$ such that U_l is optimized in the long run. In almost all efforts the critic's training uses feedforward networks [17]. A drawback here is that feedforward networks work well in problems that require computation of static functions. In real world however, one encounters many problems which cannot be solved by learning a static function because the function being computed changes with each input received. This situation can be rectified by the introduction of feedback (recurrent) connections in the network. In this paper, we implement a recurrent reservoir as a critic [14], but adapted to a multiobjective reinforcement learning problem. A single reservoir estimates the three utilities J_l simultaneously, and provides their gradients to the actor.

3.1 Multiobjective RC Critic

The core idea of RC consists of using a large recurrent network as a "reservoir" of excitable complex neural dynamics, from which readout neurons can learn to map the reservoir state to a target output. The activation of internal neurons of RC is updated according to

$$X(k + 1) = f(W_{in}U_{in}(k + 1) + WX(k)) \tag{10}$$

where the inputs $U_{in}(k) = (s(k), a(k))$, X is the reservoir state, and $f = tanh()$. The input and reservoir weights (W_{in}, W) are generate randomly such that the "echo state" property is met [18]. In this case, only weights connections from the reservoir to the outputs W_{out}^l are to be adjusted. According to (5), each output weight W_{out}^l will be trained forward in time by minimizing the quadratic error measures

$$\|E_l\| = \sum_k E_{lk} = \sum_k [\hat{J}_l(k) - U_l(k) - \gamma\hat{J}_l(k + 1)]^2, (l = 1, 2, 3) \tag{11}$$

One simple way to train W_{out}^l is to use the recursive least square method as following

$$W_{out}^l(k) = W_{out}^l(k-1) + L(k)E_{lk} \tag{12}$$

The gain vector $L(k)$ is updated as

$$L(k) = P(k)X(k) = P(k-1)X(k)\left(1 + X^t(k)P(k-1)X(k)\right)^{-1} \tag{13}$$

and

$$P(k) = \left(I - L(k)X^t(k)\right)P(k-1) \tag{14}$$

$P(k)$ is usually referred to as the covariance matrix.

After each adjustment of $W_{out}^l(k)$, the estimation output $\hat{J}_l$ is calculated as

$$\hat{J}_l(k) = W_{out}^l(k)X(k)). \tag{15}$$

3.2   Action Selection

As in [12], the well-being is considered as a weighted combination of the drives. Thus, the action control aims at maximizing the combination $\hat{J}$ of performance indexes J_l:

$$\hat{J}(k) = w_{hunger}(k) \cdot \hat{J}_1(k) + w_{thirst}(k) \cdot \hat{J}_2(k) + w_{safety}(k) \cdot \hat{J}_3(k) \tag{16}$$

where the motivational weights $\{w_{hunger}, w_{thirst}, w_{safety}\}$ represent the selected learning strategy by the goal-directed Q-learning (see paragraph 4).

The actor uses a simple gradient descent search that maximizes $\hat{J}$.

$$a(k+1) = a(k) + \delta\frac{\partial\hat{J}(k)}{\partial a(k)} \tag{17}$$

where δ is the learning rate. The gradient of $\hat{J}$ with respect to $a(k)$ can be computed using the chain rules

$$\frac{\partial\hat{J}(k)}{\partial a(k)} = \frac{\partial\hat{J}(k)}{\partial X(k)}\frac{\partial X(k)}{\partial a(k)} \tag{18}$$

where

$$\frac{\partial\hat{J}(k)}{\partial X(k)} = W^{out}(k) \tag{19}$$

and

$$W^{out}(k) = w_{hunger} \cdot W_{out}^1(k) + w_{thirst} \cdot W_{out}^2(k) + w_{safety} \cdot W_{out}^3(k) \tag{20}$$

Assuming that $W_{in} = [W_a W_s]$ concatenation of action and state input weights we obtain

$$\frac{\partial X(k)}{\partial a(k)} = (I - X^2(k))W_a^T \tag{21}$$

where I denotes the column vector of 1. Hence

$$\frac{\partial\hat{J}(k)}{\partial a(k)} = W^{out}(k)(I - X^2(k))W_a^T \tag{22}$$

Equation (22) shows that the partial derivative of $\hat{J}$ with respect to a depends only on the W_{out} update and on the current reservoir state. Thus, in contrast to a typical layered neural networks, RC structure offers a simple way to calculate the gradient of $\hat{J}$. From (17) and (22) we obtain

$$a(k+1) = a(k) + \delta W^{out}(k)(I - X^2(k))W_a^T. \tag{23}$$

4 Motivational Decision Making

We first performed a series of optimization runs of the Multiobjective RC-ACD for different motivational weights $\{w_{hunger}, w_{thirst}, w_{safety}\}$, and selected several strategies to form the repertoire of learning strategies. A strategy Π is represented through its motivational weights as

$$\Pi_i = [w^i_{hunger}, w^i_{thirst}, w^i_{safety}] \tag{24}$$

We design the goal-directed process as a Q-learner that iterates through all available strategies keeping a record of the expected outcome for each, and then chooses the strategie that best improves the *well-being*. The well-being $Wb(k)$ at time k is defined as

$$Wb(k) = Wb_{ideal} - \sum_i D_i^p \cdot D_i^s(k) \tag{25}$$

The ideal well-being Wb_{ideal} is the motivational state, where all drives are satisfied, i.e. when $D_i^s = 0$ for all i. In the simulation, we set $Wb_{ideal} = 3$. At each iteration, the Q-learner receives the levels of the drives D_i^s, and the expected utilities $\hat{J}_l$ from the external environment as the state, and Wb as the reward signal. The Q-value for each conrol strategy Π_i is formulated as follows

$$Q_{\Pi_i}(k) = R(k) + \gamma_Q \cdot \max_{\Pi_j \in \Pi}(Q_{\Pi_j}(k + t_{epi})) \tag{26}$$

where $R(k)$ is the well-being W_b, γ_Q is the discount factor and t_{epi} is the episode time steps. These values are adapted according to the following equation

$$Q_{\Pi_i}(k) = (1 - \beta) \cdot Q_{\Pi_i}(k) + \beta \cdot \left(R(k) + \gamma_Q \cdot \max_{\Pi_j \in \Pi}(Q_{\Pi_j}(k + t_{epi})) \right) \tag{27}$$

where $\beta \in [0, 1]$ is the learning rate, i.e the forgetting factor. To learn the Q-values, a one-hidden layer feed-forward neural network is utilized. Depending on the motivational state represented by the drives D_i and the external state represented by the learned utilities $\hat{J}_i$, the neural net approximates the Q-value for each control strategy Π_i.

5 Results

We set the parameters of RC critic as follows. The spectral radius $\alpha = 0.4$, the reservoir units $N = 40$ and the reservoir connectivity $c_{dr} = 20\%$. The training is performed

in a sequence of 500 episodes (max episode length: 100 iterations). The Q-learning
decision maker uses a feed-forward network with one hidden layer of 100 neurons, a
discount factor $\gamma_Q = 0.7$, a learning rate $\beta = 0.35$ and the time steps of an episode
$t_{episode} = 15$ iterations. The repertoire of learning strategies contains Five (5) control stragies (options): $\Pi_1 = [1.0, 0.0, 0.0]$, $\Pi_2 = [0.0, 0.0, 1.0]$, $\Pi_3 = [1.0, 0.5, 0.0]$,
$\Pi_4 = [0.0, 0.5, 1.0]$, $\Pi_5 = [1.0, 0.0, 1.0]$. We performed several experimental tests; two
of them are reported here. In each experiment, the learning process goes through two
phases. During the exploration phase, the Q-learner randomly selects strategies from
the repertoir of learning strategies, in order to train the feed-forward network. After this
phase, the Q-learner uses the well-being as a reward signal to select more systematically a desired strategy. Table 1 presents the dynamics parameters of the drives for each
experiment. In experiment 1, the hunger drive is characterized by a low growth factors
$D_i^g = 0.006$ comparing with that of thirst $D_i^g = 0.015$. This means that thirst needs
more attention than hunger. However, the drive of hunger will increase immediately
after satisfaction ($D_i^t = 0$). In contrast, the drive of thirst remains unsatisfied during
$D_i^t = 60$ time steps. Therefore, in the time interval $[0, 70]$ the Q-learner favorises more
the strategy Π_2 that gives more importance to the drive of thirst (Fig. 2(a)). After satisfying thirst, we can observe how the Q-learner mainly switches his decision between
the two strategies Π_4 and Π_1. These strategies give more importance to thirst, but also
to either to safety or to hunger. Thus, the type of motivational decision making, we
are advocating, is continuously reevaluated according to the motivational state of the
agent. Figures 2(c) and 3(a) show the temporal evolution of the drives and the global
well-being during the first 200 episodes, respectively. Fig. 3(a) illustrate the well-being
during the whole experiment. It should be noted that during exploration, the average
of the well-being is 1.5421, and during exploitation it is increased to 1.9520. In the
experiment 2, the growth factors D_i^g of hunger and thirst are almost similar (Table 1).
This may increase the conflict between these drives. During the first 80 episodes, the
Q-learning gives more importance to hunger and safety than thirst. We can observe how
it keeps his decision for Π_3 more than Π_4 (Fig. 2(b)). This explains why in that period
thirst was not well optimized (Fig. 2(d)). Due to the limited number of strategies, the
learning process has needed significantly longer time than in the previous experiment
to find a possible compromise between all drives (Fig. 3(b)). During exploration, the
average of the well-being is $0, 8453$, and during exploitation it it is increased to 1.8346.

Table 1. Dynamics parameters of the drives

| | Experiment 1 | | | Experiment 2 | | |
	D_i^s	D_i^g	D_i^t	D_i^s	D_i^g	D_i^t
Hunger	0.5	0.006	0	0.5	0.013	60
Safety	0.5	-0.005	0	0.5	-0.004	0
Thirst	0.5	0.015	60	0.5	0.012	150

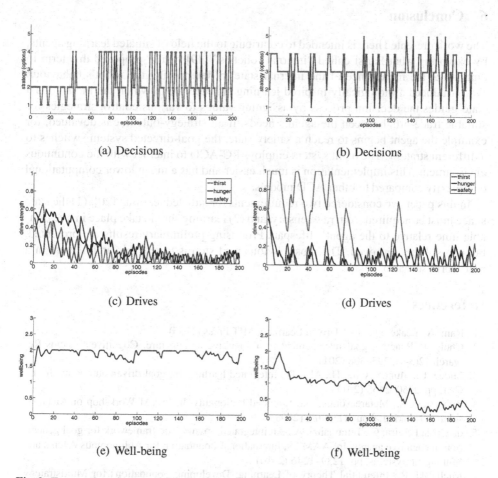

(a) Decisions

(b) Decisions

(c) Drives

(d) Drives

(e) Well-being

(f) Well-being

Fig. 2. Temporal evolution of the decision, the drives and the well-being during the first 200 episodes. Left pannels (experiment 1) and right pannels (experiment 2)

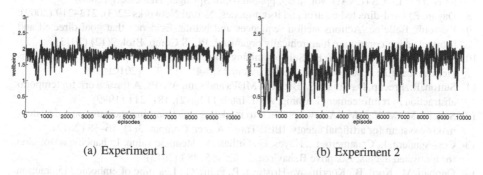

(a) Experiment 1

(b) Experiment 2

Fig. 3. The temporal evolution of the well-being during the whole experiments

6 Conclusion

The work presented here is intended to contribute to the field of situated learning agents, by exploring what Parisi called "internal robotics" [19]. Parisi proposed this term to emphasize the importance of the internal state in determining the robot's behaviour. We introduced a biologically inspired learning architecture in which the motivational state guides the decision process by assigning values to various control strategies for suitable trade-offs between the agent's needs. If an strategy-outcome is devalued, for example the agent begins to reach a satiety state, the goal-directed system switches to a different strategy. The habit system employs RC-ACD to interact with the continuous environment. This implementation is much easier and has a much lower computational complexity compared to other ACD models.

In this paper, we considered two requirements for situated learning [20]: (1) the state space must be acquired from raw sensory, and (2) learning should take place in a reasonable time relative to the agent's lifespan. Promising preliminary results are presented, but can still be improved. The most obvious next step is to test this architecture in a real-world scenario.

References

1. Ram, A., Leake, D.: Goal-Driven Learning. MIT Press (1995)
2. Choi, D.: Reactive goal management in a cognitive architecture. Cognitive Systems Research 12(3-4), 293–308 (2011)
3. Jaidee, U., Munoz-Avila, H., Aha, D.: Integrated learning for goal-driven autonomy. In: IJCAI, pp. 2450–2455 (2011)
4. Zilberstein, S.: Metareasoning and Bounded Rationality. In: AAAI Workshop on Metareasoning: Thinking about Thinking (2008)
5. da Costa Pereira, C., Tettamanzi, A.: An integrated possibilistic framework for goal generation in cognitive agents. In: AAMAS, International Foundation for Autonomous Agents and Multiagent Systems, pp. 1239–1246 (2010)
6. Michalski, R.: Inferential Theory of Learning: Developing Foundations for Multistrategy Learning. In: Machine Learning, A Multistrategy Approach. Morgan Kaufmann (1994)
7. Konidaris, G., Barto, A.: An adaptive robot motivational system. In: Nolfi, S., Baldassarre, G., Calabretta, R., Hallam, J.C.T., Marocco, D., Meyer, J.-A., Miglino, O., Parisi, D. (eds.) SAB 2006. LNCS (LNAI), vol. 4095, pp. 346–356. Springer, Heidelberg (2006)
8. Dayan, P.: Goal-directed control and its antipodes. Neural Networks 22(3), 213–219 (2009)
9. Dezfouli, Balleine: Actions, action sequences and habits: Evidence that goal-directed and habitual action control are hierarchically organized. PLoS Comp. Biol. 9(12) (2013)
10. Butz, M., Shirinov, E., Reif, K.: Self-organizing sensorimotor maps plus internal motivations yield animal-like behavior. Adaptive Behaviour 18(3-4), 315–337 (2010)
11. Sutton, R., Precup, D., Singh, S.: Between MDPs and semi-MDPs: A framework for temporal abstraction in reinforcement learning. Artif. Intel. 112(1-2), 181–211 (1999)
12. Salichs, M., Malfaz, M.: A new approach to modeling emotions and their use on a decision-making system for artificial agents. IEEE Trans. Affect. Comput. 3(1), 56–68 (2012)
13. Cos-Aguilera, I., Canamero, L., Hayes, G., Gillies, A.: Hedonic value: Enhancing adaptation for motivated agents. Adaptive Behaviour 21(6), 465–483 (2013)
14. Oubbati, M., Kord, B., Koprinkova-Hristova, P., Palm, G.: Learning of embodied interaction dynamics with recurrent neural networks: some exploratory experiments. Journal of Neural Engineering 11(2), 026019 (2014)

15. Bellman, R.E.: Dynamic Programming. Princeton Univ. Press, NJ (1957)
16. Deb, K.: Multi-objective genetic algorithms: Problem difficulties and construction of test problems. Evolutionary Computation 7(3), 205–230 (1999)
17. Prokhorov, D., Wunsch, D.: Adaptive critic designs. IEEE Transactions on Neural Networks 8, 997–1007 (1997)
18. Jaeger, H.: The 'echo state' approach to analysing and training recurrent neural networks. Technical Report 148, AIS Fraunhofer, St. Augustin, Germany (2001)
19. Parisi, D.: Internal robotics. Connection Science 16, 325–338 (2004)
20. Konidaris, G.D., Hayes, G.M.: An architecture for behavior-based reinforcement learning. Adaptive Behavior 13(1), 5–32 (2005)

An Anti-hebbian Learning Rule to Represent Drive Motivations for Reinforcement Learning

Varun Raj Kompella, Sohrob Kazerounian, and Jürgen Schmidhuber

IDSIA, Galleria 2, Manno-Lugano, Switzerland
{varun,sohrob,juergen}@idsia.ch

Abstract. We present a motivational system for an agent undergoing reinforcement learning (RL), which enables it to balance multiple drives, each of which is satiated by different types of stimuli. Inspired by drive reduction theory, it uses Minor Component Analysis (MCA) to model the agent's internal drive state, and modulates incoming stimuli on the basis of how strongly the stimulus satiates the currently active drive. The agent's dynamic policy continually changes through least-squares temporal difference updates. It automatically seeks stimuli that first satiate the most active internal drives, then the next most active drives, etc. We prove that our algorithm is stable under certain conditions. Experimental results illustrate its behavior.

Keywords: Motivational Drives, Reinforcement Learning, MCA, Animats.

1 Introduction

Reinforcement Learning (RL) methods [1] have proven quite powerful in endowing agents with the ability to learn to achieve goals across a wide variety of settings. Typically however, within any given setting, the agent lacks a motivational system that would allow it to differentially value various types of simultaneous (possibly conflicting) goals and actions [2,3]. We introduce a novel method inspired by drive theory [4,5,6], which enables an agent to learn from multiple types of rewarding stimuli [7,8], even as its preferences for those stimuli change over time. Importantly, this method achieves behavioral success under these conditions, while learning online.

Although definitions of drive and motivation abound across a number of interdisciplinary fields, including psychology, neuroscience, and artificial intelligence, we follow that of Woodworth [4], who suggested hunger and thirst as prototypical bodily drives. As the levels of hunger and thirst change in time, an agent is motivated to initiate behaviors that satisfy one or the other drive. There are two primary methods by which such drives are typically represented in the artificial intelligence literature: The first makes use of homeostatic drive regulation, wherein actions that push a physiological state variable towards its equilibrium are rewarded, while actions that push the state variable away from that equilibrium are punished [9,3]. The second, following Hull [10,2] makes use of drive states that vary from "fully satiated", to "fully unsatiated", with actions that satiate active drives being rewarded.

A.P. del Pobil et al. (Eds.): SAB 2014, LNAI 8575, pp. 176–187, 2014.

Hullian and homeostatic drive reduction are highly dependent on physiological parameters however, and are therefore not always ideal in modeling robotic agents. Rather than explicitly model time-varying drive states and the changes to those drive levels resulting from various types of rewarding behavior, our method instead attempts to *balance* the various types of rewarding stimuli an agent has received. Doing so allows an artificial or robotic agent to successfully modulate its behavior in response to active drives, without making its successful behavior dependent on careful parameter selection. In this system, an agent's drive towards a particular stimulus depends, in part, on how much of that stimulus it has acquired in its recent history, weighed against how much it desires alternative stimuli. When the agent receives one type of rewarding stimulus, its drive for that particular stimulus should decrease, while its drive for other types of stimuli should increase. One elegant method for modeling this input-dependent drive switching, is to note that as the agent experiences a changing distribution in its input stimuli, estimating the covariance of this distribution yields a minor component (MC; [11]) which points in the direction of the least received stimuli. In order to compute the minor component, we use Peng's Minor Component Analysis (MCA; [12]) algorithm, which uses a low-complexity, online, anti-hebbian updating rule, making it suitable for open-ended learning. Moreover, such a representation system, allows us to incorporate intrinsically rewarding behaviors as just another drive of the agent. As discussed by White [13], there is no simple way to reconcile curiosity driven behaviors, with drive reduction theory. As we show in simulations however, it is rather simple to do with an MCA based drive representation.

On its own, this enables an agent to represent drives. It does not however, explain how an agent can learn which actions bring about the desired types of input stimuli. To this end, we propose an online, model-based least-squares policy iteration technique, called MCA-PI, to combine our MCA based drive-representation and action selection for a simulated robotic agent. We prove that MCA-PI is stable under certain conditions and present experimental results to demonstrate its performance.

The rest of the paper is organized as follows: Sec. 2 presents details of representing drives using MCA. Sec. 3 discusses our MCA-PI algorithm and an analysis of its dynamical behavior. Sec. 4 presents experimental results and Sec. 6 concludes.

2   Representing Drives with MCA

We present a method to represent drive motivations using Minor Component Analysis (MCA):

(a) Input Stimuli Vector: The input stimulus is an n-dimensional real-valued vector $\xi = [\xi_1, ..., \xi_n]^T$, where each dimension represents a particular type of stimulus. For example, let food (ξ_1;) and water (ξ_2;) be two types of stimuli for an agent. When the agent receives only $\xi_1 = 2$ units of food, the corresponding input stimulus vector is $\xi = [2, 0]$.

(d) Stimulus Priority Vector: A stimulus priority vector $\rho = [\rho_1, ..., \rho_n]$, $\rho_i \in (0, 1]$ determines a priority weighting for each stimulus type. A high-value of ρ_i indicates that the agent takes longer time to satiate stimulus ξ_i.

(b) Drive Vector: The agent's drive at any time t is represented by an n-dimensional unit-vector $D(t) = [d_1(t), ..., d_n(t)]^T$, where each dimension $d_i(t) \in [0, 1]$ represents an individual drive component for the stimulus ξ_i. A high value of $d_i(t)$ indicates that the agent desires the corresponding stimulus ξ_i.

(c) Drive-Vector Update: The drive vector is updated incrementally using Peng's MCA learning rule:

$$D(t) = (1 - \eta)\ D(t-1)\ -\ \eta\ (D(t-1) \cdot \Lambda \boldsymbol{\xi}(t))\ \Lambda \boldsymbol{\xi}(t) \tag{1}$$

$$D(t) \leftarrow D(t)/\|D(t)\| \tag{2}$$

where η is a constant learning rate, Λ is a $n \times n$ diagonal matrix with ρ_i^{-1} as its entries. The normalization step in (2) is required to make it adaptive to non-stationary input data [14].

(e) Scalar Reward: The scalar reward $r(t)$ given to the agent is computed by projecting the input stimulus on to the current drive vector:

$$r(t) = D(t) \cdot \Lambda \boldsymbol{\xi}(t) \tag{3}$$

The agent gets higher scalar rewards if it receives a stimulus-vector $\boldsymbol{\xi}(t)$ whose direction-cosine (DC) w.r.t $D(t)$ is close to one. That is to say, the more closely the stimulus vector matches the drive vector, the more rewarding that stimulus will be. The agent, driven by higher rewards r, will be motivated to visit and then remain in the places where it is getting the currently rewarding stimuli. However, as the agent continues to remain in those places, the recent history of the MCA comes to be dominated by samples of the current stimulus distribution, which drives the minor component away from the current drive direction (see Figure 1). As a consequence, the longer an agent continues to receive the same stimulus, the less and less rewarding it becomes (i.e., the agent becomes *satiated*)

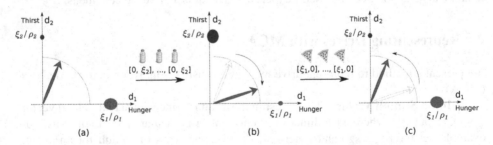

Fig. 1. The MCA drive-vector ($D(t)$, indicated by the bold arrow) points to the direction of stimuli that it received least in its recent history (anti-hebbian like behavior). (a) $D(t)$ at some arbitrary time t. (b) When the agent receives water stimulus (ξ_2), $d_2(t)$ decreases and $d_1(t)$ increases, therefore $D(t)$ slowly turns toward the "hunger" drive-direction. (c) Similarly, when the agent receives food, the vector slowly turns toward the "thirst" drive-direction.

Algorithm 1: MCA-PI $(\mathcal{S}, \mathcal{A}, \mathcal{P})$

```
// Ξ : Stimulus function (|S||A| × n) matrix
// R : Reward function (|S||A| × 1) vector
// φ^{S×A} : State-Action basis function
// D : MCA drive vector
// Λ : Diagonal matrix with {ρ_1^{-1}, ..., ρ_n^{-1}} entries
```

1 **for** $t \leftarrow 0$ to ∞ **do**
2      $s_t \leftarrow$ current state
3      $a_t \leftarrow$ action selected by policy π_t in state s_t
4   Take action a_t, observe next state s_{t+1} and stimulus $\boldsymbol{\xi}(t+1)$

    //Update Stimulus Function
5      $\Xi(s_t, a_t) \leftarrow \Xi(s_t, a_t) + \eta_{t+1}^{\text{stim}}(\boldsymbol{\xi}(t+1) - \Xi(s_t, a_t))$

    //Update MCA Drive Vector
6      $D \leftarrow (1 - \eta)\, D - \eta\,(D \cdot \Lambda \boldsymbol{\xi}(t+1))\, \Lambda \boldsymbol{\xi}(t+1)$
7      $D \leftarrow D/\|D\|$

    //Update Reward Function
8      $R \leftarrow |\Xi \Lambda D|$

    // Update Policy
9      $\pi_{t+1} \leftarrow$ LSTDq-Model-Update($\phi^{S×A}, \mathcal{P}, R, \gamma, \pi_t$)
10 **end**

3 Action Selection: MCA-Based Policy Iteration (MCA-PI)

Unlike previous implementations that represent drives independently in an RL framework [2,15], an MCA-based drive representation takes all drives into consideration and computes a resultant unit drive-vector $D(t)$. $D(t)$ does not necessarily indicate the level of satiation, instead it optimally points in the direction of stimuli that the agent received least in its recent history. Based on the drive at time t, the agent needs to shape its behavior to acquire the least received stimuli. However, to learn an optimal behavior (policy), in principle, one needs to take into account the internal drive vector components $(d_1, ..., d_n)$ as a part of the agent's state-space, along with the external world state. This makes the resultant state space large - exponential in the number of drive components. Konidaris and Barto [2] have used a multi-goal RL approach with SARSA(0) [16] instead, to learn a composite value function for action selection. In a similar way, the MCA drive vector can be combined with SARSA(0), where each drive-component $d_i(t)$ corresponds to a particular goal. However, a drawback of this approach is that since the internal drive-function changes quite quickly over time, the resulting decision process is *non-Markovian*. Therefore, single-step on-policy SARSA(0) algorithm that requires a decaying exploration rate for optimal performance [17], may not converge to an optimal policy. This problem can be overcome if a transition model of the external world environment is known.

Algorithm 1 shows the pseudocode of MCA-PI algorithm. Given a transition model for the external world $\mathcal{P} : \mathcal{S} \times \mathcal{A} \times \mathcal{S} \rightarrow [0, 1]$, for each time-step the algorithm incrementally updates its estimate of the stimulus function Ξ (a matrix of size $(|\mathcal{S}||\mathcal{A}| \times n)$), MCA-drive vector D, and the reward function R (a vector of size $|\mathcal{S}||\mathcal{A}| \times 1$). It then evaluates the current policy for the new reward function R using simulated samples (s, a) from $\mathcal{P}$, and generates a policy for the next time-step based on the updated value-function.

3.1 Dynamical Analysis

In this section, we study the dynamical behavior of MCA-PI algorithm. The main goal here is to show that the algorithm makes the agent balance between multiple drives in an uniform manner.

Outline: We first define *policy-sets*, such that for any arbitrary trajectory of policies within each set, the reward function converges to a unique fixed point (Definition 1). We then show that the policy-sets are non-empty in Theorem 1. Since MCA-PI is an approximate policy-iteration technique, we show in Theorem 2 that the error between the approximate value-function and the true-value function is bounded. Finally, in Theorem 3 we show that the sequence of policies generated by the MCA-PI algorithm, shifts between the policy-sets in a cyclical manner.

Conditions: The following conditions are necessary for the rest of the analysis:
(1) The learning rate of MCA satisfies: $\eta\lambda_1 < 0.5$, $0 < \eta \leq 0.5$, where λ_1 is the largest eigenvalue of the expected covariance matrix C $(=E[\boldsymbol{\xi\xi}^T])$ of the input stimulus data $(\boldsymbol{\xi} \in \mathbb{R}^n)$.
(2) C is a symmetric nonnegative definite matrix. This condition is initially met by the agent's exploration using Gaussian *optimistic-initialization* [18], and later by the algorithm switching dynamics.
(3) The columns of stimulus-function matrix Ξ are not all-ones or a constant multiple of all-ones vector[1]. This condition, which is trivial, says that the agent does not receive equal amounts (or zero) of a particular stimulus at all world states. In which case, there is no planning required for that stimulus and the drive-vector dimension can be reduced to $(n-1)$.

Using Condition (2), C can be factorized into VLV^{-1}, where V is the eigenvector matrix (columns representing unit-eigenvectors v_i) and L is a diagonal matrix with corresponding eigenvalues (λ_i). In addition, the eigenvectors $\{v_i | i = 1, 2, ..., n\}$ (sorted according to $\lambda_1 > \lambda_2 ... > \lambda_n$) form an orthonormal basis spanning $\mathbb{R}^n$, where v_1 is the principal-component and v_n is the minor-component. Therefore, the drive vector $D \in \mathbb{R}^n$ can be represented as a linear combination of the basis-vectors $D(t) = \sum_{i=1}^{n} w_i(t)v_i$, where $w_i(t)$ are some coefficients. Lemma 1 shows that the drive vector $D(t)$ converges to the component with the least-eigen value v_n (minor-component).

Lemma 1. *If Conditions (1)&(2) are satisfied, the following limits of the coefficients w_i hold true:*

$$\lim_{t \to \infty} w_i(t) = 0, \ \forall i \in 1, ..., n-1 \quad and \quad \lim_{t \to \infty} w_n(t) = 1$$

---

[1] All-ones vector is a vector where every element is 1.

Proof. The proof follows from Lemma 3 in [14].   □

Definition 1. *Let* $\Pi^i, \forall i \in \{1, ..., n\}$ *denote sets of stationary policies* ($\pi : S \times A \mapsto [0, 1]$) *defined over the underlying irreducible Markov chain, s.t., for any trajectory* $\zeta = \{\pi_t \in \Pi^i, \forall t > 0\}$,

$$\lim_{t \to \infty} R^\zeta(t) = \Xi \Lambda v_i \tag{4}$$

Theorem 1. *If condition (3) is satisfied,* $\Pi^i, \forall i \in \{1, ..., n\}$ *are non-empty disjoint sets.*

Proof. Since, Ξ does not contain scalar multiples of all-ones column vectors (Condition (3) and Lemma 1), there exists at least one trajectory ζ of policies where $\mathbb{E}[\boldsymbol{\xi}\boldsymbol{\xi}^T | \pi; \forall \pi \in \zeta]$ has the minor-component v_i. Since, each $v_i, \forall i \in \{1, ..., n\}$ are orthonormal, the policy-sets are disjoint.   □

Theorem 2. *At any time* t, *let* $\pi_t, \pi_{t+1}, ..., \pi_{t+m}$ *be any arbitrary sequence of policies, such that,* $\pi_m \in \Pi^i, \forall m = t, t+1, ...,$. *Let* $\widetilde{Q}^{\pi_t}, \widetilde{Q}^{\pi_{t+1}}, ..., \widetilde{Q}^{\pi_{t+m}}$ *be the corresponding sequence of approximate value functions as computed by LSTDQ. Then, there exists a positive scalar* δ *that bounds the errors between the approximate and the true value functions over all iterations:*

$$\|\widetilde{Q}^{\pi_m} - Q^{\pi_m}\|_\infty \leq \delta, \quad \pi_m \in \Pi^i, \forall m = t, t+1, ...,$$

Proof. The Least-Squares fixed-point approximation [19] of the value function for a stationary transition model P and reward function R can be written as $\widehat{Q}^\pi = A^\pi \phi^T R$, where $A^\pi = \phi \left(\phi^T (\phi - \gamma P^\pi \phi)\right)^{-1}$. For a given stationary reward function R, there exists a positive scalar ϵ that bounds the error between the least-squares fixed-point approximation and the true value function :

$$\|\widehat{Q}^{\pi_m} - Q^{\pi_m}\|_\infty \leq \epsilon, \quad \forall m = t, t+1, ...,\tag{5}$$

From Theorem 1, we have since $\pi_m \in \Pi^i, \forall m = t, t+1, ...,$, there exists a fixed point R^* to the sequence of reward functions. Therefore, $\|R_m - R^*\|_\infty \leq \nu \implies \|A^{\pi_m}\phi^T R_m - A^{\pi_m}\phi^T R^*\|_\infty \leq \nu \implies \|\widetilde{Q}^{\pi_m} - \widehat{Q}^{\pi_m}\|_\infty \leq \nu$. Using (5) and *triangle-inequality* we get, $\|\widetilde{Q}^{\pi_m} - Q^{\pi_m}\|_\infty \leq \epsilon + \nu \ (\equiv \delta), \quad \pi_m \in \Pi^i, \forall m = t, t+1, ...,$ □

Theorem 3. *Let* $\pi_t, \pi_{t+1}, \pi_{t+2}, ...$ *be a sequence of policies generated by the algorithm at any arbitrary time* t. *Then,* $\exists N \in \mathbb{N}^+$, *such that:*

$$\{\pi_t, \pi_{t+1}, ..., \pi_{t+N}\} \subseteq \Pi^i, \quad \{\pi_{t+N+1}, \pi_{t+N+2}, ...\} \subseteq \Pi^j, \quad j \neq i, i \in \{1, ..., n\}$$

Proof. Since, MCA-PI is an approximate policy iteration algorithm, it follows from Theorem 2 that the generic bound on policy iteration applies (See Theorem 7.1 [19]). Therefore, the value-function converges toward the true value function Q^* corresponding to the current reward function ($\Xi \Lambda v_n$). However, a policy $\pi_{v_n}^*$ based on Q^* maximises expected cumulative rewards, i.e. $\mathbb{E}[\gamma^t \Xi \Lambda v_n]$, which is maximal only when the principal component of $\mathbb{E}[\boldsymbol{\xi}\boldsymbol{\xi}^T | \pi_{v_n}^*]$ is equal to v_n. Since MCA by definition computes the minor component, it follows that $\pi_{v_n}^* \in \Pi^j, j \neq i$. This implies that there exists a positive integer N, where the policies $\{\pi_{t+N+1}, \pi_{t+N+2}, ...\} \in \Pi^j$.   □

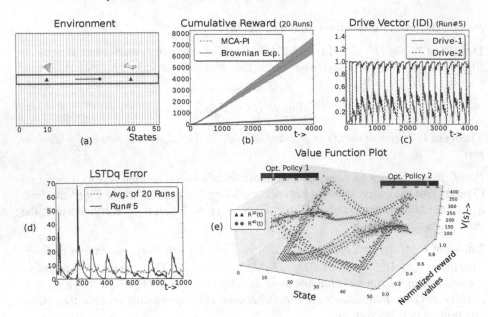

Fig. 2. Figure best viewed in color. See text for accompanying details.

Theorems 1, 2 and 3 explain the switching dynamics of the algorithm between multiple drives.

4   Experimental Results

4.1   Experiment 1: Hallway

We evaluate our algorithm here on a classic example of a 50 state closed Markov Chain (Fig. 2(a); [19]). The agent at each state can take three deterministic actions: *left*, *right* and *stay*, except for the boundary states 0 (*right* and *stay*) and 49 (*left* and *stay*). At state 10, the agent receives a stimulus (food) $\xi_1 = [6\ 0]^T + \mathcal{N}(\mu = 0, \sigma = 2)$ and at state 40, it receives a stimulus (rest) $\xi_2 = [0\ 6]^T + \mathcal{N}(\mu = 0, \sigma = 2)$. $\mathcal{N}(\mu, \sigma)$ represents an additive Gaussian noise with mean μ and standard deviation σ. The agent has equal priority towards both stimuli ($\rho = [1, 1]$).

We use a constant learning rate ($\eta = 0.01$) for the MCA update, a discount factor $\gamma = 0.95$, and indicator basis functions ($\phi^{S \times A}$) to represent each state. An initial policy (π_0) and a drive-vector (D) are set arbitrarily. The approximate stimulus function Ξ is *optimistically-initialized* [18] to $\mathcal{N}(\mu = 0, \sigma = 0.3)$ for all states and dimensions.

As a baseline comparison, we evaluate the performance of an agent carrying out brownian exploration vs. an agent carrying out MCA-PI. The agent using brownian exploration would also continually visit both the stimulus sources over time. Figure 2(b) shows the cumulative reward with respect to time, averaged over 20 trials for the two models (shaded region represents the standard deviation). It is clear from the figure that the MCA-PI approach results in a deliberative behavior in comparison with the standard brownian motion (with a mean velocity equal to 4 states/timestep). Figure 2(c) shows the changing MCA drive-vector over time for a single run. The drive-vector periodically switches between $v_2 \rightarrow v_1 \rightarrow v_2$, as derived in Theorem 3. The LSTDq error $\|\widetilde{Q}^{\pi^t} - \widehat{Q}^{\pi^{t+1}}\|$ peaks momentarily (see Fig. 2(d)) whenever the agent switches between the policy sets Π^i of one stimulus, to the other. However, the error drops down quickly thereby resulting in the next switch. The red dashed line indicates the average error for 20 different runs. Figure 2(e) shows the variation of the state-values (mean and the standard deviation over 20 runs) with the changing reward values at states 10 (blue triangles and cyan error bars) and 40 (red circles and yellow error bars). It is clear from the figure that the value of state 10 is higher whenever the projection $\|r\| = \|\Xi \cdot \Lambda v_2\|$ is higher, which makes the agent shift to state 10. It stays there until the drive reduces and the value of state 40 becomes higher. The constant switching between the sources balance both drives in an uniform manner. The video for the experiment can be found at URL: http://www.youtube.com/watch?v=Mk_wyJ8mQcU

4.2   Experiment 2: Three Room Maze

Here, we evaluate MCA-PI on a larger discrete-state three room maze environment. There are in total 200 reachable states and two door-ways as shown in Figure 3(a). The agent can take 5 deterministic actions: *left*, *right*, *north*, *south* and *stay*, except at the states next to the room boundary. Each room has a distinct stimulus source placed arbitrarily. The agent has equal priority towards all the stimuli ($\rho = [1, 1, 1]$).

We use a constant learning rate ($\eta = 0.01$) for the MCA update, a discount factor $\gamma = 0.85$, and 30 Laplacian eigen-map features (Proto Value Functions; [20]) as basis functions ($\phi^{\mathcal{S} \times \mathcal{A}}$) to represent each state. An initial policy (π_0) and a drive-vector (D) are set arbitrarily. The approximate stimulus function Ξ is optimistically initialized to $\mathcal{N}(\mu = 0, \sigma = 0.3)$ for all states and dimensions.

Figure 3(b) shows the cumulative stimulus over time for 20 runs of the experiment. We see that the agent accumulates each of the sources nearly equally. The drive vector D switches periodically between v_1, v_2 and v_3 (Fig. 3(c)), and is stable with a low LSTDq error over time (Fig. 3(d)). It can be seen in Figure 3(c) that the switching starts after a delay $t \gtrsim 1000$ time-steps. This is due to the updating estimate of the stimulus function (Ξ) upon exploring via optimistic initialization. Figure 3(e)-(g) shows three sets of value functions and corresponding policy plots at different time instants, directing the agent to each of the stimulus sources. The video for the experiment can be found at URL: http://www.youtube.com/watch?v=ZbvSSmZrOzc

4.3   Experiment 3: Extrinsically and Intrinsically Motivated Agent

In this experiment, we consider an agent that is both extrinsically and intrinsically motivated. Intrinsically motivated (curious) agents not only focus on potentially externally posed tasks, but also creatively invent self-generated tasks that have the property of currently being still unsolvable but easily learnable. The theory of Artificial Curiosity (AC; [21]) introduces a mathematical formalism for describing curiosity and creativity in artificial agents. A creative agent needs two learning components: an adaptive encoder of

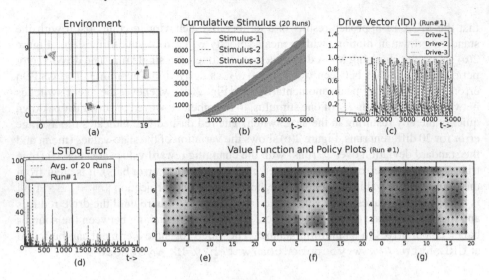

Fig. 3. Figure best viewed in color. See text for accompanying details.

the growing history of observations and a reinforcement learner. The *learning progress* of the encoder becomes a *curiosity* reward for the reinforcement learner. For the sake of consistency as well as simplicity, we use of another instance of the MCA algorithm coupled with Robust Online Clustering (ROC; [22]) an as an encoder[2]. We refer to it as intMCA for the rest of the paper.

The agent is in an environment with two extrinsic stimulus sources $\{\xi_1 = food,$ $\xi_2 = bed\}$ and two different learnable signal sources (represented by a *book* and *music* as shown in Figure 4(a)) that constitute two sources for curiosity-stimulus (ξ_3). When the agent is at the states corresponding to *book* and *music*, it receives a 2-dimensional input signal $\mathbf{x}^{book}$ (Figure 4(b)) and $\mathbf{x}^{music}$ (Figure 4(c)) given by:

$$\mathbf{x}^{book} : \begin{cases} x_1(t) = \sin(t) + \cos(11t)^2 \\ x_2(t) = \cos(11t) \end{cases}, \mathbf{x}^{music} : \begin{cases} x_1(t) = \sin(2t + \frac{\pi}{3}) - \cos(11t)^2 \\ x_2(t) = \cos(11t) \end{cases} \quad (6)$$

These signals are expanded into a five-dimensional polynomial space ($[x_1, x_2, x_1^2, x_2^2, x_1 x_2]$) and normalized (*whitened*) to have unit-variance. MCA when applied to the *derivative* of the normalized signals (approximated by backward-difference), learns the underlying slowly changing driving forces [23], which are $\sin(t)$ (Figure 4(d)) and $\sin(2t + \pi/3)$ (Figure 4(e)). When the intMCA feature outputs become stable, the intMCA-error (ε) decreases. This decrease results in a proportional curiosity stimulus:

$$\xi_3 = \text{Clip}(-\dot{\varepsilon}, 0, 12) \quad (7)$$

---

[2] Note that this implementation is not strictly limited to the MCA and can easily be replaced with any other adaptive learning machine.

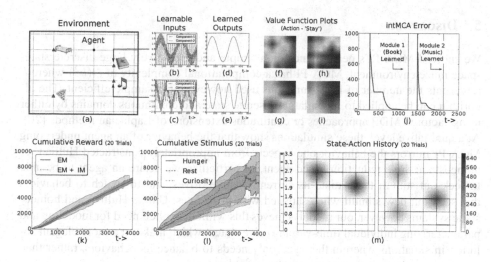

Fig. 4. Figure best viewed in color. See text for accompanying details.

ξ_3 is clipped to lie in the range $[0, 12]$ to keep it bounded and comparable with the other stimuli (ξ_1, ξ_2). The agent's drive-vector D is a 3-dimensional vector representing *hunger*, *rest* and *curiosity* drives. The agent has equal priority towards all the stimuli ($\rho = [1, 1, 1]$). The approximate stimulus function Ξ is optimistically initialized to $\mathcal{N}(\mu = 0, \sigma = 0.3)$ for all states and dimensions. The agent can take 5 deterministic actions: *left*, *right*, *north*, *south* and *stay*, except at the states next to the room boundary.

Similar to the earlier experiments, the agent quickly learns the model for the stimulus function Ξ. However, in this case it is non-stationary since ξ_3 vanishes when the learning of the intMCA completes (Eq. (7)). The initial behavior of the agent is similar to the extrinsically motivated agent, which sequentially switches between the states corresponding to the stimuli. However, since ξ_3 decreases, the agent continues to seek the stimulus ξ_3 further. This allows it to completely learn the signal. Once the error ε drops down close to zero, intMCA module is saved for future-use and a new intMCA is created. The agent is again initialized with optimistic values to allow it to explore. Now since, the agent no longer receives any curiosity stimulus ξ_3 at the state where the earlier intMCA module was learned, it goes to the other signal source to get ξ_3. Figures 4(f)-(i) show localized state-value functions learned for *stay* action. Figure 4(j) shows the estimation error plot over execution time showing two decaying peaks for each of the signal sources. Figure 4(k) shows cumulative reward averaged over 20 trials (shaded region represents the standard deviation) for the EM+IM agent and the EM-only agent from the earlier experiment. From the plot it is clear that the method works similarly to the EM-only experiment. Figure 4(l) shows individual cumulative stimulus components averaged over 20 trials. The curiosity stimulus is lower compared to the other stimuli. This is because of its vanishing nature. Figure 4(m) shows the state-action history for each module learned averaged over 20 Trials. The video for the experiment can be found at URL: http://www.youtube.com/watch?v=cqvw-MxZkOA

5 Discussion

We showed MCA-PI's performance on a simple and a relatively large discrete state-space maze environment. MCA-PI has a computational complexity of $O(k^2)$ where k represents the number of basis-functions used however, it is sample efficient. The algorithm can be applied to much larger discrete state and continuous domains by either using factored MDP approaches or continuous extensions of Laplacian methods [20]. At a qualitative level, these simulations show that the behavior of an agent undergoing MCA-PI mirrors the behavior one expects from appropriately constructed Hullian, or homeostatic drive reduction based agent. In particular, we desire an agent to be able to seek out stimuli that satiate its currently active drives, and to switch to behaviors that seek out new stimuli when satisfied with prior ones. Unlike Hullian and homeostatic systems however, our model achieves this without explicit need for modeling and parameterizing individual time-varying drive states, which makes it a more elegant solution in situations wherein the agent only needs to balance its behaviors, rather than maintain pre-defined physiological state variables.

6 Conclusions

The canonical RL literature tends to ignore that robotic agents and animats operating in real-time, complex, and changing environments typically have to monitor several continuous, time-varying reward types in an online fashion. While some methods have attempted to address this by developing motivational frameworks which make use of Hullian drives, or homeostatic drive theory, these methods tend to focus on physiological state variables as found in biological agents. Instead, we present a method that is motivated by drive theory, but which represents an agent's drive by means of Minor Component Analysis. Doing so enables an agent to balance between competing drives in a manner which doesn't depend on physiological parameters, but rather, the relative levels of the various rewarding stimuli it seeks.

Acknowledgments. This work was funded through SNF grant #138219 (Theory and Practice of Reinforcement Learning II) and #270247 (NeuralDynamics project).

References

1. Sutton, R.S., Barto, A.G.: Reinforcement learning: An introduction, vol. 1. Cambridge Univ Press (1998)
2. Konidaris, G., Barto, A.: An adaptive robot motivational system. In: Nolfi, S., Baldassarre, G., Calabretta, R., Hallam, J.C.T., Marocco, D., Meyer, J.-A., Miglino, O., Parisi, D. (eds.) SAB 2006. LNCS (LNAI), vol. 4095, pp. 346–356. Springer, Heidelberg (2006)
3. Cos, I., Cañamero, L., Hayes, G.M., Gillies, A.: Hedonic value: Enhancing adaptation for motivated agents. Adaptive Behavior 21(6), 465–483 (2013)
4. Woodworth, R.S.: Dynamic psychology, by Robert Sessions Woodworth. Columbia University Press (1918)

5. Hull, C.L.: Principles of behavior: An introduction to behavior theory. Century psychology series. D. Appleton-Century Company, Incorporated (1943)
6. Wolpe, J.: Need-reduction, drive-reduction, and reinforcement: A neurophysiological view. Psychological Review 57(1), 19 (1950)
7. Barrett, L., Narayanan, S.: Learning all optimal policies with multiple criteria. In: Proceedings of the 25th International Conference on Machine Learning, pp. 41–47. ACM (2008)
8. Vamplew, P., Dazeley, R., Berry, A., Issabekov, R., Dekker, E.: Empirical evaluation methods for multiobjective reinforcement learning algorithms. Machine Learning 84(1), 51–80 (2011)
9. Keramati, M., Gutkin, B.S.: A reinforcement learning theory for homeostatic regulation. In: Shawe-Taylor, J., Zemel, R.S., Bartlett, P., Pereira, F.C.N., Weinberger, K.Q. (eds.) Advances in Neural Information Processing Systems 24, pp. 82–90 (2011)
10. Konidaris, G.D., Hayes, G.M.: An architecture for behavior-based reinforcement learning. Adaptive Behavior 13(1), 5–32 (2005)
11. Oja, E.: Principal components, minor components, and linear neural networks. Neural Networks 5(6), 927–935 (1992)
12. Peng, D., Yi, Z., Luo, W.: Convergence analysis of a simple minor component analysis algorithm. Neural Networks 20(7), 842–850 (2007)
13. White, R.W.: Motivation reconsidered: The concept of competence. Psychological Review 66(5), 297 (1959)
14. Luciw, M., Kompella, V.R., Kazerounian, S., Schmidhuber, J.: An intrinsic value system for developing multiple invariant representations with incremental slowness learning. Frontiers in Neurorobotics 7 (2013)
15. Shirinov, E., Butz, M.V.: Distinction between types of motivations: Emergent behavior with a neural, model-based reinforcement learning system. In: IEEE Symposium on Artificial Life, ALife 2009, pp. 69–76. IEEE (2009)
16. Sprague, N., Ballard, D.: Multiple-goal reinforcement learning with modular sarsa (0). In: IJCAI, pp. 1445–1447 (2003)
17. Singh, S., Jaakkola, T., Littman, M.L., Szepesvári, C.: Convergence results for single-step on-policy reinforcement-learning algorithms. Machine Learning 38(3), 287–308 (2000)
18. Sutton, R.S., Barto, A.G.: Reinforcement learning: An introduction. MIT Press, Cambridge (1998)
19. Lagoudakis, M.G., Parr, R.: Least-squares policy iteration. The Journal of Machine Learning Research 4, 1107–1149 (2003)
20. Mahadevan, S., Maggioni, M.: Proto-value functions: A laplacian framework for learning representation and control in markov decision processes. Journal of Machine Learning Research 8(16), 2169–2231 (2007)
21. Schmidhuber, J.: Formal theory of creativity, fun, and intrinsic motivation (1990–2010). IEEE Transactions on Autonomous Mental Development 2(3), 230–247 (2010)
22. Guedalia, I.D., London, M., Werman, M.: An on-line agglomerative clustering method for nonstationary data. Neural Computation 11(2), 521–540 (1999)
23. Kompella, V.R., Luciw, M., Schmidhuber, J.: Incremental slow feature analysis: Adaptive low-complexity slow feature updating from high-dimensional input streams. Neural Computation 24(11), 2994–3024 (2012)

Unsupervised Learning of Sensory Primitives
from Optical Flow Fields

Oswald Berthold* and Verena V. Hafner

Cognitive Robotics Group, Dept. of Computer Science
Humboldt-Universität zu Berlin
Rudower Chaussee 25, 12489 Berlin, Germany
{oberthol,hafner}@informatik.hu-berlin.de
http://koro.informatik.hu-berlin.de

Abstract. Adaptive behaviour of animats largely depends on the processing of their sensory information. In this paper, we examine the estimation of robot ego-motion from visual input by unsupervised online learning. The input is a sparse optical flow field constructed from discrete motion detectors. The global flow field properties depend on the robot motion, the spatial distribution of motion detectors with respect to the robot body and the visual environment. We show how online linear Principal Component Analysis can be applied to this problem to enable a robot to continuously adapt to a changing environment.

Keywords: adaptive behaviour, source separation, feature learning, neural network, optical flow, primitives, redundancy, representation learning, sensor array, unsupervised, vision.

1 Introduction

Moving around in the world is *the* prime ability agents need for accomplishing things in a physical world. Many organisms have evolved to use some form of vision for sensing the motion of their bodies with respect to the environment and in relation to their own motor signals. The reason this works so well for animals also holds for robots. Their vision is fast, lightweight, passive and reliable through a large amount of redundancy.

Our approach to adaptive robot control is defined by learning data-driven primitives from raw sensorimotor channels [1]. These can be used for synthesis of behaviour in real world scenarios. We are motivated in this approach by the likely presence of similar organizational principles in biological nervous systems [2], [3].

The sensory information considered here is vision. A vision sensor is, at a fundamental level, an array, not necessarily homogenous, of photosensitive elements. This is true for both biological and technical systems. Motion is reflected in such an array as the propagation of a stable structure yielding spatio-temporally correlated excitation of the single elements. The role of motion detection in the visual sense, its implementation in early vision and the neural mechanisms underlying motion detection have been studied extensively in the literature [4]. Inspired by these ideas, many algorithms and circuits

---

* Oswald Berthold is funded by the DFG Research Training Group METRIK.

A.P. del Pobil et al. (Eds.): SAB 2014, LNAI 8575, pp. 188–197, 2014.

have been proposed that are able to locally detect elementary visual motion. An array of Elementary Motion Detectors (EMDs) comprises an Optical Flow (OF) field. While elementary motion is always local and planar, full egomotion can be estimated through wide-field integration. This is the reconstruction of the full 6 Degree of Freedom (DoF) motion parameters of the vision sensor (traveling with the animal or robot) in $\mathbb{R}^3$.

The problem can be solved through analysis of geometric properties of the sensor and environmental statistics. While the first part of this approach is straightforward [5], the latter part is not so easy to deal with because of large environmental variabilities. Another approach could be the computational modeling of known biological egomotion circuits and the implantation of these models [6] into an appropriate sensorimotor system (robot). We propose to follow an unsupervised learning approach on optic flow fields to solve this problem which make use of the high redundancy in the visual input to extract the underlying regularities which are imprinted on the raw sensory stream by camera geometry, viewing direction, motion type and environment all at once.

The paper is structured as follows: In section 2 we review related work. We go into more detail about the methods used for motion detection, signal acquisition, basis field extraction and recombination in section 3. We pick one method suitable for online learning and apply it in section 4 in simulation and on a real robotic car equipped with an onboard camera. We briefly discuss the results in section 5 and conclude with a summary in section section 6.

The main contribution of this paper is a demonstration of general unsupervised online learning of optical flow subspaces and respective component estimation on both real and simulated monocular cameras on different robotic vehicles.

2   Related Work

There are several research directions that contribute with respect to this problem, neurobiology, biorobotics, computer vision and machine learning. We will roughly group our quick survey of existing work according to these categories.

2.1   Biology and Biorobotics

Above we have mentioned neurophysiological work on decoding parts of the vision apparatus of insects leading to the concept of Elementary Motion Detectors (EMD). A summary on the topic is given in [4]. Here we are interested in properties of the global flow field, the total combined output of all EMDs in a vision system. In [7] the question of the principal resolvability of arbitrary 6 DoF motion through the visual input alone is brought up and answered affirmatively. The existence of specialized channels (primitives) in biological vision for basic orthogonal flow field components is hypothesized.

The question of ambiguity in motion fields is considered in [8] and found to be non-critical for practical concerns. Other work later expanded on these results [9] and compared the ideal motion field and the optical flow field. Their main argument is, that while quantitative equivalence can hardly be accomplished, its is only qualitative similarity which is of practical interest. The qualities there refer to the attractors of planar dynamical systems, which are used to model the basis flow fields.

In [10] a mapping and activity analysis of the role of interneurons in the fly's motion processing pathway is presented. Neurons specializing in specific flow field subspaces are identified and wide-field integration is found essential for ambiguity resolution resulting from local motion detection. The receptive field organization of these integrating neurons has been shown to resemble self-motion induced optical flow fields. They are hypothesized to implement matched filters on the input stream. This is corroborated in [11], and in [12] the notion of environmental distance distributions is picked up.

2.2 Feature Learning for Vision

We now move our focus from biological analysis to learning based approaches. While the geometry of vision with regard to projection and motion is in general analytically tractable, this is not so with environmental statistics. This justifies the need to learn flow field decompositions from the vision data of a situated agent.

Several approaches have been proposed. The most relevant one to our approach is [13]. Although egomotion is not explicitly considered there, other more complex motion phenomena are examined and a general methodology is proposed for parsing these flow fields. Detection of specific motions is realized by finding linear combinations of orthogonal basis flow fields,

$$F(x,c) = \sum_{j=1}^{n} c_j BF_j(x) \tag{1}$$

with coefficients c_j corresponding to the strengths of the motion components. The applicability of Principal Component Analysis (PCA) to learning the basis flow fields is established and the general notion of *motion features* (as compared to static image features) is introduced. This is taken further in [14] by including mechanisms for stabilizing the motion perception through inclusion of models which help in outlier rejection and anomaly detection.

Other egomotion related work is not as directly connected but still worth mentioning. For example [15] presents an active vision mechanism that measures motion parallax and uses that to point the camera into the direction of motion. In [16] the detection and classification of externally observed motion of other agents is investigated. [17] used an evolutionary approach to optimize an artificial compound eye for obstacle distance estimation based on motion parallax. In [18], on the other hand, the viewing direction of discrete MDs is calibrated by comparing the vision input with Inertial Measurement Unit data during random body motions. [19] also investigates optimal visual sensor topologies in relation to the sensor/environment interaction patterns and in [20] a plenoptic (multi-camera) setup which also exploits the cross-redundancy in multiple visual channels to estimate egomotion is considered.

Apart from specifically vision related work, an even larger body of work exists that is concerned with the general issue of representation learning. A comprehensive review is given in [21]. Another directly related line of research is that of autonomous mapping of sensorimotor configurations. These works are more general with respect to modality but otherwise contain more explicit reasoning regarding the interaction of several learning processes [22–24] or are focused on finding the sensorimotor dimensionality alone [25].

3   Methods

3.1   Problem Statement

We first restate the problem. We have an array E of n EMDs that generate a field of quasi-local 2-dimensional motion vectors. We want to find a set of p orthogonal basis flow fields $\{BF_i\}_{i=0,\dots p-1}$, each corresponding to, and induced by, a single basic motion type. The BF_i can be used both for matched filtering of the combined input or can be linearly combined to yield a resulting flow field. An example expansion of Equation 1 is given below, as

$$c_0 \cdot \boxed{} \quad + \quad c_1 \cdot \boxed{} \quad = \quad \boxed{} \tag{2}$$

with $c_0 \propto$ translational velocity and $c_1 = [1.2, 0.6, 0.25] \propto$ rotational velocities, each for a single body axis respectively. Each arrow corresponds to the output of one EMD and the placement is taken from 1(a).

(a) EMD placement on the real robot.   (b) Random EMD placement in simulation.

Fig. 1. 1(a) shows the EMD placement within the camera frame and an example activation for forward translation. The camera is mounted upside down on the robot, which is why the inline EMD numbering is upside down too. In this image the inhomogenous depth distribution is clearly visible. An analogous example for the simulated camera is given in 1(b).

3.2   Preprocessing

The most important step in preprocessing is the computation of motion components from the raw pixel input. The resulting flow field components are the input to the learning system. Thus, we compute the optical flow for the n manually or randomly placed regions (EMDs) of interest within the camera image and sum the u and v image plane motion components of the dense flow field for each region. This results in $2n$ signals representing the spatial average of the u and v image motion components in the image subregions. No other processing is applied to the motion signals. On the real car we use the non-pyramidal Lucas-Kanade method and in the simulation experiments we use the Farneback method, both taken from the OpenCV [26] library.

Earlier experiments have shown that it is difficult to compute the optical flow for the entire image at frame rates exceeding 30 Hz, while we would like to use the 60-100 Hz the camera is capable of delivering. Computing the OF for discrete subregions (EMDs) helps to alleviate this problem.

3.3 Autoencoder and Principal Component Analysis

The Autoencoder (AE) [27] is an instructive way of looking at dimensionality reduction. Linear autoencoders have been shown to be equivalent to PCA [28] thus in the following we focus on that latter technique. PCA transforms the correlated inputs into a set of of uncorrelated output signals that are ordered by the amount of variance they explain in the original data. The PCA transformation matrix is the matrix of eigenvectors of the covariance matrix $S_Z = ZZ^T$ of the concatenated input column vectors Z. The result of the transform has the same dimensionality as the original input but the dimensionality can now be reduced by selecting only a subset of the principal components. Empirically, batch PCA on our data showed very good results. In order to extend the system for online learning, we used the Generalized Hebbian Algorithm [29] (GHA, also: Sanger's rule). GHA provides the following weight update rule, in matrix form

$$\Delta w = \eta \left(h \cdot z^T - \mathrm{LT}[hh^T]w \right) \tag{3}$$

Here, η is a learning rate parameter, z is the network input, h is the hidden unit activation (the features) and LT is the lower triangular matrix operator. We used an $\eta = 0.02$ throughout all the experiments.

4 Experiments

In the experiments we use three types of rigid body robots. One is a real R/C model car with onboard forward facing camera and onboard computing for realtime estimation of optical flow. The others are an ATRV, a six-wheeled differential drive car-like vehicle and a quadrotor. The latter two are used in simulation. The simulated vehicles also have a camera mounted whose output is computed within the simulation. The general procedure is to apply a suitable motor pattern to the actuators of the robot and collect the signals from the motion detectors implemented in the visual system. We then apply PCA to the input stream and compare the derived motion components with the motor pattern and analyze the resulting basis fields embedded in the respective weight matrices. The network size (number of hidden neurons) is chosen equalling the number of expected DoF of motion for each particular robot, two for the cars and six for the quadrotor. The visual scenery is assumed to be static and contain no moving objects.

In all experiments we design a simple motor pattern to generate all motion types of interest. In the case of the car, both possible motions occur simultaneously, in the quadrotor case angular and translatory motion is combined for each body axis (as dictated by the underacutation) and sequenced over the three axes.

4.1   Two Motion Components from Real Robot Data

In this scenario we recorded optical flow information from four regularly placed EMDs, motor output and other sensor information while writing a randomly modulated pattern to the motors. This results in 8 channels of interleaved u_{ij}, v_{ij} local motion information. We assume 2 external motion components, translation along x-axis and rotation around z-axis (yaw). We perform batch PCA on the visual motion data alone. The results can be seen as a temporal trace in Figure 2 and as extracted basis fields for two different episodes in Figure 3.

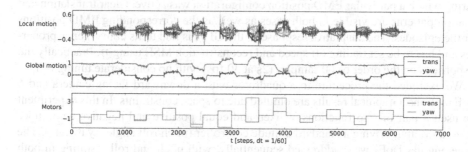

Fig. 2. A typical episode of our experiment. The car is undergoing motion generated by the motor signals in the bottom graph. "trans" effects translation and "yaw" effects turning of the car. They are only active together. The amplitudes of both components are randomly modulated but fixed for each pair of forward and reverse translation. In the top graph all eight raw motion signals are plotted (the network input). In the center graph the hidden unit activation, that is, the global motion of the robot as given by the first two principal components is drawn.

Looking at the weight matrices for different runs consisting of separate recordings of the R/C car moving back and forth in the same environment we can extract the basis flow fields, some of which are rendered in Figure 3. The acquired flow field differs from an ideal (isotropic) environment flow field due to the environmental statistics. In Figure 1(a) we saw that the EMDs in the lower half-image generally see much smaller depths than those in the upper half-image and thus get saturated from translation alone. This is reflected in the acquired basis fields. This means, that the environmental circumstances can contribute to particular kinds of separation of the two motion types.

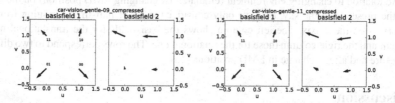

Fig. 3. Basis flow fields corresponding to the two possible motions of the car: translation (basisfield 1) and turning (yaw, basisfield 2). Note how the different depth levels seen by the upper and lower motion detectors are exploited for separation.

4.2 Online PCA on Two Motion Components

Here we use a small car-like vehicle (the ATRV) from the MORSE [30] simulator robot library. The images are provided as a ROS image stream. Here we use random and dynamically changeable positions for the EMDs in order to emulate both different sensor configurations as well as a changing environment (EMD position induces different depth to surface). An example configuration is displayed in Figure 1(b).

A variation of the experiment consists in changing the position of the EMDs during learning. As expected, GHA recovers from that and relearns the new mapping. Figure 4 shows two respective basis fields at two points in time, each taken from a subepisode during which a particular EMD position configuration was active. Clear translation and rotation patterns are visible in both cases as well as the corresponding EMD positions for the episodes. The adaptative response of the GHA is tied to its convergence properties and has to be set trading off speed and reconstruction MSE using η. Practically the response is on the order of 60 samples (2s at 30 fps) with no considerate tuning of η.

We extended the procedure to a quadrotor with a downward facing camera and 6 DoF motions. Graphical results are omitted due to space constraints. In this experiment we used a pair of step functions of fixed and equal positive and negative amplitudes as motor output driving a standard attitude controller (pitch/roll angles, yaw rate). The three angular DoFs were addressed sequentially, with pitch and roll resulting in both rotations and subsequent horizontal translation. Vertical translation was present all of the time as a byproduct of the PID altitude controller with noisy measurement input. Applying the GHA to the output of six EMDs (12 inputs to the network) resulted in six basis fields corresponding to the helicopter's six DoF of motion.

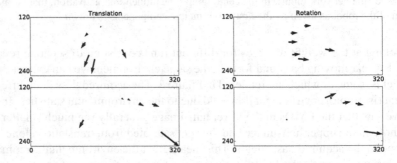

Fig. 4. Adaptation to changing environment (emulated by changing EMD position) on the ATRV. Due to the presence of the sky, here we only consider the lower half-image ranging from 120 to 240 pixels on the y-axis. The left column shows the basisfields for the translational motion component and the right column those for the rotational one. The rows correspond to two different times, before and after a change in EMD positions.

5 Discussion

In this section, we discuss the role of the motor signals and the number of principal components. We disregard the scale estimation problem in our approach as we are not aiming for metrically precise motion control. Rather, as pointed out earlier, we are only interested in the qualitative adequacy of the basis fields.

It is possible to integrate additional sensory channels such as the motor and gyro signals to improve the egomotion estimation. While for the gyros this is straightforward, the robot responds as a delayed first order system to the motor commands. That means, the response is delayed and temporally smeared. This requires the use of a model capable of handling the dynamics. The question remains then, what is the optimal point at which to introduce such an internal model. Another perspective on motor signals is that the as yet unidentified features can be assigned relations with particular actions by correlation.

The number and order of the extracted principal components in our case depends only on the vision input, but exactly that signal is generated by a particular motor signal. In general there is a relation between variance in the motor signal and variance in the sensory consequences. This relation might be linear or include e.g. integrating effects. We do not in any way treat here the question of how to autonomously establish a suitable motor pattern.

6 Conclusions

We have presented a simple and lightweight robotic vision system can be set up such that the egomotion parameters can be reconstructed from wide-field optical flow detectors in an unsupervised manner. During learning, the basis flow fields are extracted with PCA techniques which correspond to the matched filters model proposed for fly vision and which match the characteristic flow fields induced by basic robot motions. A requirement for this to happen is of course that a suitable motor pattern is provided which actually elicits all the basic motions that the robot is capable of. The environmental statistics are seamlessly integrated into the extracted basis fields, thus producing overall an environmentally tuned system. Two dominating, grossly different depth levels in the scene are exploited for separating translational and rotational optical flow. Finally, by the use of a learning rule for PCA, the system is able to adapt itself online to changing circumstances and learn transient mappings for different environments.

Future work will be concerned with using these sensory primitives in closed-loop motor learning tasks. An interesting extension includes consideration of dynamic placement of the EMDs.

References

1. Berthold, O., Hafner, V.V.: Neural sensorimotor primitives for visioncontrolled flying robots. In: Workshop on Vision-based Closed-Loop Control and Navigation of Micro Helicopters in GPS-Denied Environments at IEEE/RSJ International Conference on Intelligent Robots and Systems, IROS 2013 (2013),
   http://rpg.ifi.uzh.ch/docs/IROS13workshop/Berthold.pdf
2. Lettvin, J.Y., et al.: What the Frog's Eye Tells the Frog's Brain. In: Proceedings of the IRE 47.11, pp. 1940–1951 (1959), doi:10.1109/JRPROC.1959.287207
3. Mussa-Ivaldi, F.A., Solla, S.A.: Neural Primitives for Motion Control. IEEE Journal of Oceanic Engineering 29, 640 (2004)

4. Borst, A., Egelhaaf, M.: Principles of visual motion detection. Trends in Neurosciences 12(8), 297–306 (1989)
5. Bruss, A.R., Horn, B.K.P.: Passive navigation. Computer Vision, Graphics, and Image Processing 21(1), 3–20 (1983)
6. Franz, M.O., Krapp, H.G.: Wide-field, motion-sensitive neurons and matched filters for optic flow fields. Biological Cybernetics 83(3), 185–197 (2000),
    http://www.kyb.tuebingen.mpg.de/fileadmin/user_upload/files/
    publications/pdf81.pdf, doi:10.1007/s004220000163
7. Longuet-Higgins, H.C., Prazdny, K.: The Interpretation of a Moving Retinal Image. Royal Society of London Proceedings Series B 208, 385–397 (1980)
8. Horn, B.K.P.: Motion fields are hardly ever ambiguous. International Journal of Computer Vision 1(3), 259–274 (1988), http://dx.doi.org/10.1007/BF00127824, doi:10.1007/BF00127824
9. Verri, A., Poggio, T.: Motion field and optical flow: Qualitative properties. IEEE Transactions on Pattern Analysis and Machine Intelligence 11(5), 490–498 (1989), doi:10.1109/34.24781
10. Krapp, H.G., Hengstenberg, B., Hengstenberg, R.: Dendritic structure and receptive-field organization of optic flow processing interneurons in the fly. Journal of Neurophysiology 79, 1902–1917 (1998)
11. Dahmen, H.-J., Franz, M.O., Krapp, H.G.: Extracting Egomotion from Optic Flow: Limits of Accuracy and Neural Matched Filters. In: Motion Vision, pp. 143–168. Springer, Heidelberg (2001), http://dx.doi.org/10.1007/978-3-642-56550-2_8, doi:10.1007/978-3-642-56550-2_8, ISBN: 978-3-642-62979-2
12. Franz, M.O., Chahl, J.S.: Linear combinations of optic flow vectors for estimating self-motion: A real-world test of a neural model. In: Advances in Neural Information Processing Systems (NIPS), vol. 15, pp. 1319–1326. MIT Press (2002)
13. Fleet, D.J., et al.: Design and Use of Linear Models for Image Motion Analysis. International Journal of Computer Vision 36(3), 171–193 (2000),
    http://dx.doi.org/10.1023/A:1008156202475,   doi:10.1023/A:1008156202475,
    ISSN: 0920-5691
14. Roberts, R., Potthast, C., Dellaert, F.: Learning general optical flow subspaces for egomotion estimation and detection of motion anomalies. In: CVPR, pp. 57–64. IEEE (2009), http://dblp.uni-trier.de/db/conf/cvpr/cvpr2009.htmlRobertsPD09,   ISBN: 978-1-4244-3992-8
15. Barth, M., Ishiguro, H., Tsuji, S.: Determining Robot Egomotion from Motion Parallax Observed by an Active Camera. In: Proceedings of the 12th International Joint Conference on Artificial Intelligence, IJCAI 1991, vol. 2, pp. 1247–1253. Morgan Kaufmann Publishers Inc. (1991), http://dl.acm.org/citation.cfm?id=1631552.1631644, ISBN: 1-55860-160-0
16. Guthier, T., Eggert, J., Willert, V.: Unsupervised Learning of Motion Patterns. In: European Symposium on Artificial Neural Networks, Computational Intelligence and Machine Learning, vol. 20, pp. 323–328. Bruges (April 2012),
    http://tubiblio.ulb.tu-darmstadt.de/57795/
17. Lichtensteiger, L., Eggenberger, P.: Evolving the morphology of a compound eye on a robot. In: 1999 Third European Workshop on Advanced Mobile Robots, Eurobot 1999, pp. 127–134 (1999), doi:10.1109/EURBOT.1999.827631
18. Briod, A., Zufferey, J.C., Floreano, D.: Automatically calibrating the viewing direction of optic-flow sensors. In: 2012 IEEE International Conference on Robotics and Automation (ICRA), pp. 3956–3961 (2012), doi:10.1109/ICRA.2012.6225011

19. Ruesch, J., Ferreira, R., Bernardino, A.: Self-organization of Visual Sensor Topologies Based on Spatiotemporal Cross-Correlation. In: Ziemke, T., Balkenius, C., Hallam, J. (eds.) SAB 2012. LNCS, vol. 7426, pp. 259–268. Springer, Heidelberg (2012), http://dblp.unitrier.de/db/conf/sab/sab2012.html#RueschFB12
20. Dong, F., et al.: Plenoptic cameras in real-time robotics. The International Journal of Robotics Research 32(2), 206–217 (2013), doi:10.1177/0278364912469420
21. Bengio, Y., Courville, A.C., Vincent, P.: Representation Learning: A Review and New Perspectives. IEEE Trans. Pattern Anal. Mach. Intell. 35(8), 1798–1828 (2013)
22. Pierce, D., Kuipers, B.: Map Learning with Uninterpreted Sensors and Effectors. Artificial Intelligence 92, 169–227 (1997), http://dblp.org/db/journals/ai/ai92.html#PierceK97
23. Olsson, L., Nehaniv, C.L., Polani, D.: From unknown sensors and actuators to actions grounded in sensorimotor perceptions. Connection Science 18(2), 121–144 (2006), http://dblp.org/db/journals/connection/connection18.html#OlssonNP06
24. Kaplan, F., Hafner, V.V.: Information-theoretic framework for unsupervised activity classification. Advanced Robotics 20(10), 1087–1103 (2006)
25. Philipona, D., O'Regan, J.K., Nadal, J.P.: Is there something out there?: Inferring space from sensorimotor dependencies. Neural Computation 15(9), 2029–2049 (2003)
26. Bradski, G.: The OpenCV Library. Dr. Dobb's Journal of Software Tools (2000)
27. Hinton, G.E., Salakhutdinov, R.R.: Reducing the dimensionality of data with neural networks. Science 313(5786), 504–507 (2006), doi:10.1126/science.1127647
28. Bourlard, H., Kamp, Y.: Auto-association by multilayer perceptrons and singular value decomposition. Biological Cybernetics 59(4-5), 291–294 (1988), doi:10.1007/BF00332918
29. Haykin, S.: Neural networks - A comprehensive foundation. Pearson (1999)
30. Echeverria, G., Lemaignan, S., Degroote, A., Lacroix, S., Karg, M., Koch, P., Lesire, C., Stinckwich, S.: Simulating Complex Robotic Scenarios with MORSE. In: Noda, I., Ando, N., Brugali, D., Kuffner, J.J. (eds.) SIMPAR 2012. LNCS, vol. 7628, pp. 197–208. Springer, Heidelberg (2012), http://morse.openrobots.org

Reinforcement-Driven Shaping of Sequence Learning in Neural Dynamics

Matthew Luciw[1], Sohrob Kazerounian[1], Yulia Sandamirskaya[2],
Gregor Schöner[2], and Jürgen Schmidhuber[1]

[1] Istituto Dalle Molle di Studi sull'Intelligenza Artificiale (IDSIA),
Manno-Lugano, Switzerland
[2] Institut für Neuroinformatik at the Universitätstr, Bochum, Germany
{matthew,sohrob,juergen}@idsia.ch,
{yulia.sandamirskaya,gregor.schoener}@ini.ruhr-uni-bochum.de

Abstract. We present here a simulated model of a mobile Kuka Youbot which makes use of Dynamic Field Theory for its underlying perceptual and motor control systems, while learning behavioral sequences through Reinforcement Learning. Although dynamic neural fields have previously been used for robust control in robotics, high-level behavior has generally been pre-programmed by hand. In the present work we extend a recent framework for integrating reinforcement learning and dynamic neural fields, by using the principle of shaping, in order to reduce the search space of the learning agent.

Keywords: Neural Dynamics, Elementary Behaviors, Reinforcement Learning, Shaping.

1 Introduction

In the past few years, there has been a renewed interest in Dynamic Field Theory (DFT) for robust control of robotic agents [32,28,25]. In DFT, attractor dynamic based behaviors stably deal with noisy and time-continuous sensory input. making it a desirable candidate for a method of sensory processing and motor control.

To enable an agent to perform high-level, goal-directed action sequences, the behavioral repertoire of an agent can be organized into Elementary Behaviors (EBs). Each EB has an "intention", a stable attractor state persisting during the behavior, and a "condition of satisfaction" (CoS; the desired perceptual outcome of a behavior), a stable attractor state which destabilizes the intention, and therefore sits between EBs. EBs can be chained together to perform action sequences. Although preprogrammed behavioral sequences may suffice in certain environments, a more general autonomous agent should be able to learn new rewarding behavioral sequences, and adapt to different environments, online and in real-time.

In order to show how goal-directed sequences of EBs could be learned from reward, we recently introduced a model [17] which blended Dynamic Neural Fields, and the Reinforcement Learning (RL; [37,16]) algorithm, SARSA(λ). This system could autonomously learn sequences through random exploration, and the model operated in real-time, continuous environments.

A.P. del Pobil et al. (Eds.): SAB 2014, LNAI 8575, pp. 198–209, 2014.

One drawback with our previous model is that, as the number of available behaviors increases, waiting for such an agent to randomly explore action sequences in real-world environments becomes untenable. Building upon our previous framework, we introduce here a study of how the concept of shaping [35,22], from the field of animal learning can be used in order to speed up training time for robotic and artificial agents operating in our learning framework. Shaping has elsewhere been applied to robot learning [13,20,2,30,5], but not before within a DFT-based framework. DFT-based EBs provide a robust interface to noisy and continuous environments, RL provides autonomous learning through exploration, and shaping accelerates learning without abandoning our inspiration: a developmental narrative that goes back to Piaget [23].

2 Background

2.1 Dynamic Field Theory

While classical neural network architectures make use of computational units at the level of individual neurons, Dynamic Field Theory (DFT; [32]) is a framework built on Amari dynamics [1], which mathematically describe the continuous-time dynamics of activitions over a field of neurons. The activity of any given Dynamic Neural Field (DNF) is defined over continuous dimensions (e.g., color or space), which characterize the sensorimotor systems and task space of the agent. Fields aggregate neural activity by simulating excitatory inputs, as well as lateral patterns of connectivity, such as local excitatory, and long-range inhibitory connections. As a result of the non-linearities in the DNF's dynamics, and the lateral interactions within the fields, stable localized *peaks* of activation emerge from distributed, noisy, and transient input. These activation peaks represent perceptual objects or motor goals in the DFT framework.

This ability to form and stabilize robust categorical outputs, makes DFT architectures particularly well suited for robotic control systems. Multiple coupled DNFs spanning different perceptual and motor modalities can be composed into complex DFT architectures to organize robot behavior. The building blocks of these architectures are known as Elementary Behaviors.

2.2 Elementary Behaviors and Behavior Chaining

An Elementary Behavior (EB) is an organizational structure in DFT which not only defines the actions associated with a behavior, but also the mechanisms for initiating and terminating that behavior.

The key elements in a DFT EB are the intention and the condition of satisfaction. Both the intention to act and the associated condition of satisfaction are represented by attractor states within dynamic neural fields. Because the amount of time needed to complete an action may vary unpredictably in dynamic and partially unknown environments, the intention to achieve the behavior's goal is maintained as a stable state until completion of the goal is signaled, so it is not necessary to model how long it is expected for the behavior to take. The condition of satisfaction is a neural representation of the sensory conditions that index that an intended action has been completed. The CoS serves two roles: 1. it terminates the associated intention, and 2. as a stable state, it serves as a breakpoint between behaviors — once satisfaction is achieved, the agent can decide what behavior to do next.

A standard DNF-based EB [27] consists of a set of DNFs, as well as intention and CoS nodes. While the nodes play a role at the level of inter-behavior dynamics (i.e., switching between behaviors by initiating and terminating a given EB), the DNFs in the EB determine the intra-behavior dynamics (e.g., how the motor system responds in real-time, to changing perceptual stimuli).

In previous work, we have shown how EBs may be chained according to rules of behavioral organization [25,27], serial order [29,7,6], or the value-function of a goal-directed representation [17]. Multiple EBs can be composed into chains [28], where a sequence of behaviors execute one after another, in parallel and/or in response to sensory information [27].

In order to introduce learning into the scheme, adaptive weights can be placed between CoS nodes and intention nodes, representing transitions between a just completed behavior (CoS), and possible next behaviors (intention). These weights serve as values in the RL sense.

2.3 Dynamic Neural SARSA

The recently introduced Dynamic Neural SARSA(λ) [17] model integrates the well known SARSA(λ) model of reinforcement learning [26,37] with the mathematical language of neural dynamics. The model makes use of EBs for sensorimotor control, while simulating the eligibility traces (λ) of the SARSA model with an Item and Order Working Memory [11].

Although the model successfully learns behavioral sequences from delayed rewards, random exploration with the fully connected search space (any EB can transition to any other EB) can become prohibitively time consuming. Not only does random exploration lead to a combinatorial explosion of the search space with increasing numbers of behaviors, but because each behavior is a continuous real-time action, any given action will require a variable amount of time to terminate before exploration can continue. For such a learning mechanism to work in a more efficient, and time-friendly manner, shaping is used.

2.4 Shaping

Shaping, introduced by B.F. Skinner [35,22], is well-known in both the psychological and reinforcement learning literature as a method of conditioning. Shaping involves teaching a desired behavior by *successive approximations*, where the teacher or trainer invents and rewards subgoals, which bring the agent's behavior closer to that of the desired behavior. For example, in a classic shaping experiment, Skinner trained a pigeon to strike a wooden ball, by successively rewarding the pigeon turning towards the ball, then stepping towards the ball, then moving within a certain distance of the ball, etc. Skinner described the effect of shaping as "altering the general distribution of behavior", noting "in this way we can build complicated operants which would never appear in the repertoire of the organism otherwise". Critically, one of the defining characteristics in shaping, is successive and shifting *positive* rewards, rather than the use of negative punishments (which can certainly also be used to "alter the general distribution of behavior").

With respect to artificial agents, RL researchers realized that difficulties could arise from some reward functions, such as those with a single goal state in a large search space, when combined with undirected exploration methods, such as ϵ-greedy or purely random search [38,37]. Undirected exploration methods rely on random actions, resulting in 1. redundancy in the search due to lack of a memory structure and 2. search bias centralized on the starting position, making it more difficult to discover far away rewards. *Informed*, directed exploration methods (such as *optimistic initialization* or *artificial curiosity* [31]) are more effective in accelerating learning. But the learning speed with directed exploration pales in comparison to guided learning, wherein one knowledgable about how to achieve rewards is able to transfer this knowledge to the agent. Guided learning manifests in RL under various guises and names, some of which are, sometimes (but not always), referred to as shaping. These include chaining [39] or chunking of actions into macro-actions [21], manipulating the reward function to guide the agent [13,20], and knowledge transfer over tasks [33,18].

Reinforcement learning is, in theory, an attractive framework for autonomous learning. Autonomous robots present difficulties however: they are slow, and prone to breakage [8], and, of course, they have to operate in real-time. Undirected and even directed exploration presents prohibitive challenges for autonomous robots, especially with larger state spaces. Dorigo and Colombetti [5] introduced the term *robot shaping*, wherein a trainer, providing guidance and support, was found to be greatly effective in speeding up the robot's learning. Various methods have been introduced to allow the teacher to reinforce the robot in a timely and useful manner, such as a reinforcement sensor [4], "good" and "bad" buttons [41], as well as related methods such as Learning from Easy Missions (LEM; [2]).

3   Methods

Robot and Environment. The Kuka Youbot was our experimental robotic platform for our system, implemented in the Webots simulator [40]. The Youbot combines a omnidirectional mobile base (via Mechanum wheels [14]) with a one degree of freedom (DOF) rotating base platform, upon which is a standard three DOF RRR arm [36] with a two pronged gripper, with force feedback. The Youbot provides flexibility to move around untethered on a flat surface, and to reach for and grasp small objects. It is a good "far-ranging" pick and place robot, compared to an arm with an immobile base. The Youbot was enhanced with a RGB and kinect sensor on the front, to detect and localize targets for reaching, and infrared range (IR) sensors around the robot, to detect obstacles. The Youbot is placed in an environment with a few differently colored blocks upon boxes, some obstacles, and a deposit location — the container near the oven. A reward is given when the robot transports a object of a specific color into the container at the deposit location. See Fig. 1. Our implementation used seven different elementary behaviors, which we will discuss further below. First we describe EBs in general in terms of attractor dynamics and neural fields.

Attractor Dynamics EBs. As modeled by Bicho, Mallet, and Schöner [3], each EB involves controlling one or more behavioral variables (e.g., heading direction), which

Fig. 1. Left. The YouBot. Right. The environment.

represent the state of the system, particular to that EB. The behavioral variable values are continually mapped to control the robot's effectors. The behavioral dynamics are differential equations updated via attractive and repulsive forcelets. The attractor solutions are the asymptotically stable states, and the achievement of one of these is the goal of the behavior. Example attractive forces are changing the alignment of heading direction until a target is directly in front of the robot, and diminishing the distance between the robot and the target until it is below a threshold. Example repulsive forces are from obstacles, which effectively perturb heading direction and distance so that the robot moves away from them. The definitions and strengths of the attraction, repulsions, and their ranges are hand-selected.

Field-Based EBs. The above attractor dynamics approach is effective but limited. In some cases, such as with a real robot using information from its sensors to represent its world, the necessary variables (such as the target location) are not directly available; instead the robot needs to leverage its sensory information into usable representations. Dynamic neural fields are used to overcome this limitation. Instead of behavioral variables, DNFs use behavioral dimensions (i.e., a selection of sensory input), over which there is a field of activation. Field activations have input from the environment, lateral input (self-excitation, and a localized activation kernel), and EB-specific "top-down" biases (certain dimensions are boosted, to preferably choose a target associated with those dimensions). Stable peaks emerge as output from the activation dynamics, and those peaks are used as *de facto* behavioral variables.

The activation level of a DNF uses the following differential equation (analyzed by Amari [1])

$$\tau \dot{u}(x,t) = -u(x,t) + h + S(x,t) + \int \omega(x-x')\sigma(u(x',t))dx', \qquad (1)$$

over spatial dimension x at each time t, where $h < 0$ is a negative resting level and $S(x,t)$ is the sum of external inputs, for instance from sensors or other DNFs. The local activation kernel $\omega(\Delta x)$ determines the lateral interaction within the field, e.g., local excitation and long-range inhibition. There is also self-excitation, in the form of σ, an output function, typically a sigmoid. A high output value leads to a stable peak of activation, the unit of representation in DFT. Field-based EBs use three fields, namely perceptual, condition of satisfaction, and motor, and include a perceptual field bias (for target representation), and a CoS field bias (for goal representation).

EBs used.

- **Visual search** is a field-based behavior, which controls the robot's base, and which stabilizes when the target object is central in the robot's vision. The perceptual field's input is a color dimension at all input image columns [29]. The target's color is biased in the perceptual field, such that only that color's appearance in the field can produce an output peak. The perceptual output feeds into the CoS and motor fields (which controls heading direction). The CoS bias is over central image columns, and the CoS only creates a peak if the target is centered. If the target is not visible, a default pseudo-random movement behavior takes over.
- **Approach target** moves the robot towards the target, which must have been found with visual search beforehand (as a precondition [25]) Behavioral variables are heading direction and speed. The IR sensors provide repulsive forces. The CoS is that the distance between the target and robot is small.
- **Orient arm to target** rotates the arm platform until that the angle between the base-gripper vector and the base-target vector becomes nearly zero. This provides an excellent angle of approach for grasping.
- The **reaching** EB uses the Jacobian (which relates joint angle changes to the velocity of the end effector) of the three DOF RRR arm to continually move the point in between the gripper prongs to a point just above the target (a closed form inverse kinematics solution exists for such a manipulator, but does not suit an attractor dynamics framework).
- The **close gripper** EB closes the gripper prongs until the force feedback, resulting from the gripper pressing on the object, surpasses a threshold.
- The **open gripper** EB moves the gripper prongs in the opposite direction until the joint limits are reached.
- **Approach deposit location** has the same dynamics as **approach target**, but uses the deposit location as the target.

Failure State. These behaviors can fail, either due to the lack of a precondition, or something going wrong during execution (like the object not being grasped properly and falling down). We added a **failure** state for such cases. To detect failure, conditions of *dissatisfaction* (CoD) were built into each EB. All behaviors used timer-based CoD's, set to 200 time steps, where each time step in simulation lasted 64 ms. After failure, the robot pose is reset, as is the environment's state (e.g., any displaced objects are placed back in their starting positions).

Reinforcement Learning. We use a particular RL method, called T-learning [10], in which value is associated with transitions between states, instead of states or state-action pairs. Assigning value to transitions is appropriate in our framework because an elementary behavior itself is an attempted transition between two stable states (attractors), and the agent's decision constitutes choosing the next elementary behavior when it is in one of these stable states. In other words, the agent needs to pick its next ideal transition. T-learning is the simplest RL method for this type of setup. With T-learning and EBs, there is no need to define a separate action set.

Further, T-learning is a more efficient learning method than standard SARSA or Q-learning when some actions are failure-prone, as is the case in many robotic learning environments. In our setup, the rewarding transitions are reinforced when accomplished successfully, but when they fail (e.g., the object slips out of the robot's gripper during an attempted grasp), a different transition is credited — one which goes to a "failure" state. If state-action values were used, and if "grasp" were an action, a failure would de-value this action. T-learning suits the learning of "skilled" behavior, where learning to make difficult transitions is highly rewarding. By difficult, we mean that only a small percentage of possible actions reliably transition to a state associated with high reward. The T-learning agent will continue to try to make that transition after experiencing it just once.

The T-learning update rule is

$$T(s, s') \leftarrow T(s, s') + \alpha \left[r + \gamma T(s', s'') - T(s, s') \right] \tag{2}$$

where s, s', and s'' are three successive stable states (either CoS of an EB, or the failure state), r is a reward, α is the learning rate, and γ is the discount factor. In our implementation, T-learning is combined with eligibility traces, in the same way SARSA becomes SARSA(λ) [37].

4   Experimental Results

In the sort of behavioral chaining task we are considering here, we need to reinforce a *sequence* of behaviors, which led to a reward. This is not a Markovian setup. In the rewarding sequence $A \rightarrow B \rightarrow C$, the reward is delivered after C, but C is only a valuable behavior to select after B and A. If we reinforce the selection of C, the robot will often wrongly select it. One way to deal with this is to use composite states such as AB, BC, or ABC, which causes an explosion in the number of states, but can be tractable if we know the necessary chaining limit. Another way is to use an eligibility trace [19,15], which is what is done in our implementation.

In our previous implementation, using DN-SARSA(λ), the agent needed to discover the rewarding sequence, through random search, before any reinforcement, i.e., learning of the value node weights, could be done. For n behavior nodes, the chance that a sequence of length m is discovered randomly is $1/(n^m)$, which becomes prohibitively small as the number of EBs and/or the length of the sequence increases. Learning, while theoretically guaranteed, becomes too slow for real world agents.

With shaping, the teacher's input modifies the reward function by providing positive reinforcement for successfully completed intermediate steps. We expect shaping decreases *both* the search time to discover the rewarding sequence (i.e., perform it for the first time), and to *learn* the policy that allows the robot to accomplish the sequence reliably. To test this, we compared two RL setups, in which 100 learning trials were run in each. In both, there were four behaviors, and the rewarding sequence was 5 items long (e.g., $A \rightarrow D \rightarrow C \rightarrow B \rightarrow A$). In one case (with shaping), the agent received rewards after each step in the sequence (besides the first was completed). In the other (without shaping), the agent only received a reward after the entire sequence was completed. In each case, ϵ-greedy action selection was used, and we tested two *exploration settings* of $\varepsilon = \{0.999, 0.996\}$, where the random action chance starts from $\epsilon = 1$ (100%) and is multiplied by ε after each behavioral transition. In all cases, the learning rate for T-learning $\alpha = 0.1$, the eligibility trace parameter $\lambda = 0.6$, and the discount factor $\gamma = 0.9$.

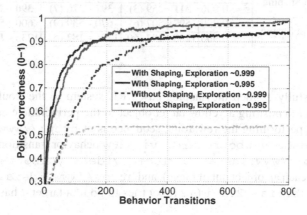

Fig. 2. Shaping improves the speed of policy learning, with an appropriate exploration setting

In order to measure policy correctness, we measured the deviation of the optimal policy from the policy at every time step. To do this, the maximum valued action of each state was compared with the correct action. If they matched, the agent scored 0.25 points. A perfect policy, where the agent does the best thing in each state, scores 1, and the worst policy scores 0. Mean policy correctness for the four methods at each decision point, or behavior transition point, are shown in Fig. 2. One can see that on average, the two variants with shaping learn much faster. The variants with a quicker decreasing exploration factor are more prone to catastrophic failure runs, where the agent never learns the rewarding sequence. If one can tolerate a chance of failure, the variant with shaping and quicker exploration decrease can learn a bit faster than the other shaping variant. The variant without shaping and quick exploration decrease is very prone to failures.

In Table 1, we can see the average time each variant *first* discovered the rewarding sequence. We also try a few different learning rates, here. The number to the left of the dash in each table cell shows the mean sequence discovery time, while the number to the right of the dash shows the mean time, if all failure runs are removed. In parentheses is how many failure runs there were (out of 100). One can see the shaping variants usually find the sequence first. The variant without shaping and fast exploration decrease fails more often than not, but the runs that don't fail find the sequence very quickly. This however, is simply due to sampling bias (namely, by throwing out all long-run trials that do not complete). The only way this variant can learn the correct sequence is if it gets lucky with the random number generator, and finds the correct sequence early on.

Table 1. Format: a-b (c). (a): Mean number of decisions before the rewarding five-item sequence was first discovered. (b) Each run was stopped after 2000 decisions, and "catastrophic runs" never find the sequence. The second number shows the average without including catastrophic runs. (c): The number of catastrophic runs, out of 100.

		Learning Rate		
		0.1	0.25	0.5
With Shaping	$\varepsilon = 0.999$	401 - 401 (0)	**372** - 372 (0)	400 - 400 (0)
	$\varepsilon = 0.995$	**311** - 259 (3)	391 - 270 (7)	**390** - 287 (6)
Without Shaping	$\varepsilon = 0.999$	597 - 507 (6)	670 - 539 (9)	600 - 511 (6)
	$\varepsilon = 0.995$	1280 - **197** (*60*)	1291 - **182** (*61*)	1233 - **173** (*58*)

We successfully applied the shaping-based RL system to the Youbot, to produce the behavior of depositing a yellow target object in the periwinkle container. A video of the youbot performing the rewarding sequence is at http://www.idsia.ch/~luciw/videos/youbotreward.avi. A few behavior transition failures can be seen at http://www.idsia.ch/~luciw/videos/youbotfail1.avi (the robot tries to reach an object out of range), and http://www.idsia.ch/~luciw/videos/youbotfail2.avi (the robot tries to go to a target it has not located visually, yet).

5   Discussion and Conclusions

Without shaping, the robot had to explore, either randomly, or over every possible sequential path. Although this could be effective in discovering and reinforcing basic organizational constraints between behaviors, the speed of learning the overall goal would be significantly slower. With shaping, the goal was reached faster. Both of these modes could be appropriate in different situations. While a naive robot may need to explore broadly to discover what it can and cannot do at a low level (assuming it is protected from harming itself [8]), it can be desirable to allow a teacher to guide learning for particular tasks. In such scenarios, shaping becomes an efficient and effective method of learning.

A potential drawback of imposing shaping or some other guided learning method on an autonomous agent is that the agent loses some autonomy by being guided. In other words, the agent might not only learn to do what we want it to do, but also how to do it. Skinner's pigeon could not be directly programmed, but our robots can be. What is the utility of learning? Why don't we just program the robot to do what we want?

The same arguments supporting RL over direct programming apply to shaping, except at a lower level of granularity. Shaping, in the form suggested by Skinner's experiments, involves constructing "waypoints", in the reward function, without imposing the exact path to get to each waypoint. Adaptive algorithms can take advantage of unforeseen environmental quirks and find surprising (to the teacher) paths. And some agent-environments are not straightforward to hand-program (i.e., bicycle [24], cart-pole [9]).

Further, shaping does not have to be the only method of learning available. Shaping can be an important piece of the learning repertoire of any autonomous agent that will interact with teachers/trainers in real time. The robot can use other forms of learning (i.e., curiosity-driven exploration) when it has time to do so, and when it won't hurt itself. In other cases, the teacher can play a very important role.

Future Work. A deficiency of our architecture is that it cannot learn a sequence with multiple instances of the same item in it, such as $A \to B \to A \to C$. This is a known issue of sequence learning with an Item and Order working memory [12], which is what we used for the eligibility trace. Any method where a temporal sequence becomes a spatial pattern via decay will be unable to represent a sequence with repeated elements, without using duplicated but unique elements, sometimes called *rank cells* (e.g., $A - 1$, $A - 2$ can represent two instances of A [34]).

A simple method to deal with the repeated items problem, in the context of this work, is to ensure that no rewarding sequence includes repeated elements. Of course, this will diminish the sequence space that is searched over. It is sensible that, given such a shortcoming, we should not allow exploration of sequences with repeated items either, but our current system has no such restrictions. We are currently exploring neural dynamics mechanisms for disabling exploration over repeated items. We note this will improve the learning speed of the current system, as the probability of randomly getting the right sequence of m items in n possibilities increases greatly, from $1/(n^m)$ to $1/(n!/(n-m)!)$.

Acknowledgments. This work was funded through the 7th framework of the EU in grant #270247 (NeuralDynamics project).

References

1. Amari, S.: Dynamics of pattern formation in lateral-inhibition type neural fields. Biological Cybernetics 27, 77–87 (1977)
2. Asada, M., Noda, S., Tawaratsumida, S., Hosoda, K.: Purposive behavior acquisition for a real robot by vision-based reinforcement learning. In: Recent Advances in Robot Learning, pp. 163–187. Springer (1996)
3. Bicho, E., Mallet, P., Schöner, G.: Target representation on an autonomous vehicle with low-level sensors. The International Journal of Robotics Research 19(5), 424–447 (2000)
4. Colombetti, M., Dorigo, M.: Training agents to perform sequential behavior. Adaptive Behavior 2(3), 247–275 (1994)
5. Dorigo, M.: Robot shaping: an experiment in behaviour engineering. The MIT Press (1998)
6. Duran, B., Sandamirskaya, Y.: Neural dynamics of hierarchically organized sequences: a robotic implementation. In: Proceedings of 2012 IEEE-RAS International Conference on Humanoid Robots, Humanoids (2012)
7. Durán, B., Sandamirskaya, Y., Schöner, G.: A dynamic field architecture for the generation of hierarchically organized sequences. In: Villa, A.E.P., Duch, W., Érdi, P., Masulli, F., Palm, G. (eds.) ICANN 2012, Part I. LNCS, vol. 7552, pp. 25–32. Springer, Heidelberg (2012)
8. Frank, M., Leitner, J., Stollenga, M., Förster, A., Schmidhuber, J.: Curiosity driven reinforcement learning for motion planning on humanoids. Frontiers in Neurorobotics 7 (2013)
9. Gomez, F., Miikkulainen, R.: 2-D pole-balancing with recurrent evolutionary networks. In: Proceedings of the International Conference on Artificial Neural Networks, pp. 425–430. Citeseer (1998)

10. Graziano, V., Gomez, F.J., Ring, M.B., Schmidhuber, J.: T-learning. CoRR abs/1201.0292 (2012)
11. Grossberg, S.: Behavioral contrast in short-term memory: Serial binary memory models or parallel continuous memory models? Journal of Mathematical Psychology 3, 199–219 (1978)
12. Grossberg, S., Kazerounian, S.: Laminar cortical dynamics of conscious speech perception: Neural model of phonemic restoration using subsequent context in noise. The Journal of the Acoustical Society of America 130(1), 440–460 (2011)
13. Gullapalli, V.: Reinforcement learning and its application to control. PhD thesis, Citeseer (1992)
14. Indiveri, G.: Swedish wheeled omnidirectional mobile robots: kinematics analysis and control. IEEE Transactions on Robotics 25(1), 164–171 (2009)
15. James, M.R., Singh, S.: Sarsalandmark: an algorithm for learning in pomdps with landmarks. In: Proceedings of The 8th International Conference on Autonomous Agents and Multiagent Systems-Volume 1, pp. 585–591. International Foundation for Autonomous Agents and Multiagent Systems (2009)
16. Kaelbing, L.P., Littman, M.L., Moore, A.W.: Reinforcement learning: A survey. Journal of Artificial Intelligence Research 4, 237–285 (1996)
17. Kazerounian, S., Luciw, M., Richter, M., Sandamirskaya, Y.: Autonomous reinforcement of behavioral sequences in neural dynamics. In: International Joint Conference on Neural Networks, IJCNN (2013)
18. Konidaris, G., Barto, A.: Autonomous shaping: Knowledge transfer in reinforcement learning. In: Proceedings of the 23rd international conference on Machine learning, pp. 489–496. ACM (2006)
19. Loch, J., Singh, S.: Using eligibility traces to find the best memoryless policy in partially observable markov decision processes. In: Proceedings of the Fifteenth International Conference on Machine Learning. Citeseer (1998)
20. Mataric, M.J.: Reward functions for accelerated learning. ICML 94, 181–189 (1994)
21. McGovern, A., Sutton, R.S., Fagg, A.H.: Roles of macro-actions in accelerating reinforcement learning. In: Grace Hopper celebration of women in computing, vol. 1317 (1997)
22. Peterson, G.B.: A day of great illumination: Bf skinner's discovery of shaping. Journal of the Experimental Analysis of Behavior 82(3), 317–328 (2004)
23. Piaget, J.: The origins of intelligence in children. International Universities Press, New York (1952)
24. Randlov, J., Alstrom, P.: Learning to drive a bicycle using reinforcement learning and shaping. In: Proceedings of the Fifteenth International Conference on Machine Learning, pp. 463–471 (1998)
25. Richter, M., Sandamirskaya, Y., Schöner, G.: A robotic architecture for action selection and behavioral organization inspired by human cognition. In: IEEE/RSJ International Conference on Intelligent Robots and Systems, IROS (2012)
26. Rummery, G., Niranjan, M.: On-line Q-learning using connectionist systems. University of Cambridge, Department of Engineering (1994)
27. Sandamirskaya, Y., Richter, M., Schöner, G.: A neural-dynamic architecture for behavioral organization of an embodied agent. In: IEEE International Conference on Development and Learning and on Epigenetic Robotics, ICDL EPIROB 2011 (2011)
28. Sandamirskaya, Y., Schöner, G.: Dynamic field theory of sequential action: A model and its implementation on an embodied agent. In: Scassellati, B., Deak, G. (eds.) International Conference on Development and Learning ICDL 2008, paper 53, 8 pages (2008)
29. Sandamirskaya, Y., Schöner, G.: An embodied account of serial order: How instabilities drive sequence generation. Neural Networks 23(10), 1164–1179 (2010)
30. Sasksida, L.M., Raymond, S.M., Touretzky, D.S.: Shaping robot behavior using principles from instrumental conditioning. Robotics and Autonomous Systems 22(3), 231–249 (1998)

31. Schmidhuber, J.: Curious model-building control systems. In: Proceedings of the International Joint Conference on Neural Networks, Singapore. Volume 2, pp. 1458–1463. IEEE Press (1991)
32. Schöner, G.: Dynamical systems approaches to neural systems and behavior. In: Smelser, N.J., Baltes, P.B. (eds.) International Encyclopedia of the Social & Behavioral Sciences, Oxford, Pergamon, pp. 10571–10575. Pergamon Press, Oxford (2002)
33. Selfridge, O.G., Sutton, R.S., Barto, A.G.: Training and tracking in robotics. In: IJCAI, pp. 670–672. Citeseer (1985)
34. Silver, M.R., Grossberg, S., Bullock, D., Histed, M.H., Miller, E.K.: A neural model of sequential movement planning and control of eye movements: Item-order-rank working memory and saccade selection by the supplementary eye fields. Neural Networks 26, 29–58 (2012)
35. Skinner, B.F.: The behavior of organisms: An experimental analysis (1938)
36. Spong, M.W., Hutchinson, S., Vidyasagar, M.: Robot modeling and control. John Wiley & Sons, New York (2006)
37. Sutton, R., Barto, A.: Reinforcement learning: An introduction, vol. 1. Cambridge Univ. Press (1998)
38. Thrun, S.B.: The role of exploration in learning control. In: Handbook of Intelligent Control: Neural, Fuzzy, and Adaptive Approaches. Van Nostrand Reinhold, New York (1992)
39. Touretzky, D.S., Saksida, L.M.: Operant conditioning in skinnerbots. Adaptive Behavior 5(3-4), 219–247 (1997)
40. Webots: Commercial Mobile Robot Simulation Software, http://www.cyberbotics.com
41. Weng, J.: Developmental robotics: Theory and experiments. International Journal of Humanoid Robotics 1(02), 199–236 (2004)

Rapid Humanoid Motion Learning
through Coordinated, Parallel Evolution

Marijn Stollenga, Jürgen Schmidhuber, and Faustino Gomez

IDSIA, USI-SUPSI
Galleria 2
Manno-Lugano, CH 6928
{marijn,juergen,tino}@idsia.ch

Abstract. Planning movements for humanoid robots is still a major challenge due to the very high degrees-of-freedom involved. Most humanoid control frameworks incorporate dynamical constraints related to a task that require detailed knowledge of the robot's dynamics, making them impractical as efficient planning. In previous work, we introduced a novel planning method that uses an inverse kinematics solver called Natural Gradient Inverse Kinematics (NGIK) to build task-relevant *roadmaps* (graphs in task space representing robot configurations that satisfy task constraints) by searching the configuration space via the Natural Evolution Strategies (NES) algorithm. The approach places minimal requirements on the constraints, allowing for complex planning in the task space. However, building a roadmap via NGIK is too slow for dynamic environments. In this paper, the approach is scaled-up to a fully-parallelized implementation where additional constraints coordinate the interaction between independent NES searches running on separate threads. Parallelization yields a $12\times$ speedup that moves this promising planning method a major step closer to working in dynamic environments.

Keywords: Robotics, planning, parallel search, NES.

1 Introduction

The difficulty in planning coordinated motion for high-DOF robots, like the iCub humanoid (see figure 1), is that while the trajectory, of say the right hand, connecting point a to point b in the 3D *operational* workspace, $\mathcal{P}$, may be easy to compute, the trajectory in n-dimensional configuration space, $\mathcal{Q}$, (41-dimensional in the case of the iCub upper-body) that produces the hand movement by controlling the joints is generally not known. Determining the *configuration* $q \in \mathcal{Q}$ for each *pose* $p \in \mathcal{P}$ along the trajectory requires solving the Inverse Kinematics (IK) problem which is ill-posed due to the many-to-one nature of the forward kinematics, $f : Q \to P$, i.e. there are an infinite number of joint configurations that produce the same pose. Therefore, in order to solve the IK problem, the space of functions $f' : P \to Q$ must be constrained so that each pose maps to a unique configuration.

A.P. del Pobil et al. (Eds.): SAB 2014, LNAI 8575, pp. 210–219, 2014.

In previous work [17], a method called Natural Gradient IK (NGIK) was introduced that solves the IK problem by using Natural Evolutionary Strategies (NES; [7]) to search for configurations that minimize arbitrary cost-functions. NGIK is applied repeatedly to incrementally build a Task-Relevant Roadmap (TRM): a collection of configurations whose corresponding poses uniformly fill a user-defined *task space*, where poses related to a particular task are easily represented. Starting with a single configuration (point), new points are added by searching in the neighborhood of points already in the map.

While this approach yielded TRMs for the 41-DOF iCub (upper-body) that could then be used to plan sophisticated motion, the amount of time it takes to build a map limits its use to static environments. If the state of the world changes, for example because an object in the workspace has moved, some points may now violate hard constraints (they now collide the with object), or soft constraints (the repositioning of the object has altered the task). If the map cannot be rebuilt or repaired efficiently before the world undergoes more change, the planner will not be able to keep up.

In this paper, TRM construction is sped up by implementing it in parallel so that the map is grown from many points simultaneously (one for each processing core). Parallelization requires more than just a multi-threaded re-implementation; the independent NES searches must be coordinated by incorporating additional constraints (fitness terms) that prevent them from interfering with each other in task space if their search distributions overlap.

The ultimate goal is to accelerate the map building process to the point where the map can be reconstructed fast enough to cope with dynamic environments. Our preliminary experiments show that a significant speedup can be achieved that, while not yet at the level necessary to deal with dynamic environments, is still encouraging given the potential to increase the level of parallelization in the future.

The next section discusses the concept of a task space and TRMs. Sections 3 and 4 describe how TRMs are evolved using NGIK, and how coordinated parallel version is realized, respectively. Finally, section 5 presents our preliminary results using the simulated iCub robot.

2   Task-Relevant Roadmaps

Well known robot planning methods [14], such as Rapidly Exploring Random Trees [9] and Probabilistic roadmap planning [12] are able to build non-colliding motion plans by randomly sampling configuration space. However, the plans they produce often generate unnatural movement, especially with high-DOF robots, because they are not constrained.

Recent work has acknowledged the lack of control over how the configuration space is searched, and that to gain control the notion of a task space is required: a specialized coordinate system that often reduces the dimensionality of how poses are defined and provides a way of easily comparing poses in terms of the

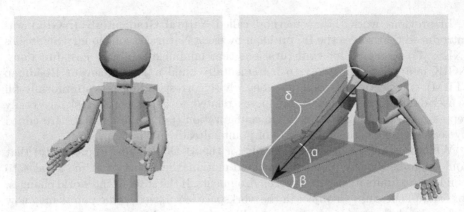

Fig. 1. The iCub Humanoid Robot. (left) the iCub, simulated in MoBeE, shown in its *home pose*. (right) an example task space designed to inspect an object from different angles and distances, formed as $\{\alpha, \beta, \delta\} = t \in \mathcal{T}$, where δ is the distance to the point, and α and β are angles that the head makes with respect to the object.

Table 1. Several examples of task-maps

Type	Task Space Dimension(s)	Formula
Position	The position of a body part. Can be masked to select only a certain dimension of the position.	$g_{position} = v_{bodypart}$
Rotation	The rotation of a body part. Can be masked to select only a certain rotation.	$g_{rotation} = u_{bodypart}$
Distance	The distance between a body part v_1 and another body part or object v_2.	$g_{distance} = \|v_1 - v_2\|$
Angle	The angle of the vector from a body part v_1 to another body part or object v_2, projected on a plane defined by u_{dim1} and u_{dim2}.	$g_{angle} = \arctan(u_{dim1}^T(v_1 - v_2), u_{dim2}^T(v_1 - v_2))$

features (angles, distances) that are most relevant to the task (see figure 1). Formally a task space is defined by a real-valued map of the form:

$$g : \mathcal{P} \times \mathcal{Q} \times \mathcal{W} \to \mathcal{T} \subseteq \mathbb{R}^m,$$

where $\mathcal{P}, \mathcal{Q}, \mathcal{W}$ are the poses of the body parts, the configuration space, and the world state respectively. $\mathcal{T}$ is a task space of m dimensions. Examples of task-maps are shown in Table 1. The task space guides the search to a sub-space of configurations that correspond to poses which relate to a given task. For example if the task is to hold an object at a fixed distance from the head.

The STOMP algorithm [10] allows for flexible, arbitrary cost-functions and plans a path that minimizes these costs. However, it plans directly in the configuration space, without considering how a selected path maps to task space.

CBiRRT [4] uses a rapidly exploring random tree on a constrained manifold; a subset of the configuration space defined by constraints, and can create impressive movements. While CBiRRT has been augmented with the concept of task space regions [5] to focus the search to feasible regions of the configuration space, it can only use a restricted set of constraints that are projectable to task space. Berenson et al. [5] mention that they use a direct sampling algorithm that allows for "arbitrarily complex" constraint parameterization, but only use it to sample goals and *not* to plan paths as it "can be difficult to generate samples in a desired region".

Clearly it is desirable to have a maximum flexibility in the defining constraints and task spaces, but current approaches either cannot handle such flexibility, use it only in a part of their algorithm, or find only *one* posture and not a full movement. Recently several methods have approached both IK and planning, aiming to be generic and flexible to use [3, 8, 11, 16]. These methods have impressive results, but always put certain restrictions on constraints that can be used and often have difficulty with high degrees of freedom.

In [17], we tackled complex IK and planning at the same time, by combining a sample-based inverse kinematics solver with an iterative roadmap construction strategy. The resulting Task-Relevant Roadmaps (TRMs) provide a graph of poses that are evenly spread over the task space, and can be used to plan natural, constrained motions. The next section describes how TRMs are evolved using NGIK.

3 Evolving TRMs

The goal of the method is to build a map of between configurations and points in task space: $\{(q_1, t_1), (q_2, t_2), .., (q_k, t_k)\} \subset \mathbf{M}$ that have a maximum coverage of the task space $\mathcal{T}$. TRMs are constructed incrementally by repeatedly applying Natural Gradient Inverse Kinematics (NGIK) to discover configurations which satisfy task constraints, and adding them to an initially empty map. NGIK searches the configuration space, using Natural Evolution Strategies (NES;[7]), in a neighborhood around points already in the map to minimize a cost or fitness function:

$$h(p, q, w) = \sum_i \alpha_i h_i(p, q, w), \tag{1}$$

where $h_i : \mathcal{P} \times \mathcal{Q} \times \mathcal{W} \to \mathbb{R}^+$ is the i-th cost-function which has as input the poses of all body parts p, the joint-state vector q, and world state w, and outputs a non-negative cost. Each function is weighted by α_i.

The NES family of black-box optimization algorithms use parameterized probability distributions over the search space, instead of an explicit population (i.e. a conventional ES). Typically the distribution is a multivariate Gaussian parameterized by $\theta = (\mu, \Sigma)$, where μ is the mean vector, and Σ is the covariance matrix. Each generation, a set of samples is taken from the distribution and evaluated. The distribution is then updated the direction of the natural gradient, in order to minimize/maximize the expected fitness of the distribution.

Algorithm 1 describes the map building procedure in pseudo-code. First, the empty map is initialized and the map-building constraint,

$$h_{map} = \sum_{\{q',t'\} \in NN(m,t,\mathbf{M})} \underbrace{|d - \|t - t'\||}_{construction} + \underbrace{c\|q - q'\|}_{smoothness}, \qquad (2)$$

is added to the given constraints h which describe the desired task for the particular robot in question, where t is the task-vector calculated by the task-map $t = g(p, q, w)$, and $NN(m, t, \mathbf{M})$ calculates the m nearest neighbors to t in map $\mathbf{M}$. The first term *constructs* the map by pulling the solution close to the previous points in task space, but keeps it at a certain distance d, growing the map. The second term enforces *smoothness* by minimizing the change in joint angles over neighboring points in the map, where c is a weighting constant.

Each iteration through the while loop attempts to search for a new configuration to add to the map, starting from an existing point that is selected by SELECTPROPORTIONAL($\cdot$). If the map is empty, the configuration of the home posture (see figure 1) is used. The returned configuration in the map, q_{start}, becomes the starting point for the evolutionary search conducted by NES.

At each generation, NES takes λ samples from the current search distribution over the configuration space (the 41-dimensional joint-space, in the case of the iCub). Each sample (candidate configuration), $q_i, i = 1..\lambda$, is evaluated by first computing its corresponding pose, p, in operational space, using the forward kinematics, f, and then plugging x, p, and the state of the world, w into fitness function $h()$ (equation (1)). After all samples are evaluated, the distribution parameters, θ, are updated.

The cycle terminates, returning a proposed configuration, q', when the search distribution has converged according to some pre-defined criteria. A converged distribution means that the search is in a local minima. q' is then mapped to task space by $g(\cdot)$ and added to the map if t' is outside the current map and is a non-colliding posture. These hard constraints must be checked because, even though they form part of the fitness function, they only penalize violations numerically, but do not prevent NES for accidentally converging to an unfeasible configuration. The process of adding points continues until the algorithm fails to generate a new, acceptable configuration after a predefined number of attempts, k.

Once the map is constructed, edges are added between elements using an n-nearest-neighbor connection strategy in the configuration space, which then can be used to plan motion using, e.g. an A^* planner (see [17] for further details).

4   Parallelizing E-TRM

Parallelizing E-TRM is not a simple matter of distributing Algorithm 1 over multiple cores. The independent searches in configuration space must be coordinated in order ensure that they do not duplicate work or interfere with each

---

Algorithm 1: E-TRM(h, k)

$i \leftarrow 0$
$\mathbf{M} \leftarrow \{\}$ // initialize an empty map
$h^* \leftarrow h + \alpha_{map} h_{map}$ // add the map-build cost function
while $i < k$ **do**
    $q_{start} \leftarrow$ SELECTPROPORTIONAL($\mathbf{M}$)   // choose element from map
    $q' \leftarrow$ NES(h^*, q_{start})   // minimize h^*, return optimized config
    $t' \leftarrow g(q')$ // compute corresponding point in task space
    if CHECK(q', t') **then** // check hard constraints and if t' not in map
        $\mathbf{M} \leftarrow \mathbf{M} \cup (q', t')$
    else
        $i{+}{+}$
    end
end

Procedure selectProportional($\mathbf{M}$)

if EMPTY?($\mathbf{M}$) **then**
    return q_{home}
end
$scores \leftarrow \{\}$
for $p \in \mathbf{M}$ **do**
    $scores \leftarrow scores \cup$ COUNTNEIGHBOURS($\mathbf{M}, p$) $+ fails[p]$
end
$selection \leftarrow \{\}$
for $p \in \mathbf{M}$ **do**
    if $scores[p] = \min_p scores$ **then**
        $selection \leftarrow selection \cup p$
    end
end
return SELECTRANDOM($selection$)

---

other in building the map. This coordination is implemented by introducing an additional *repulsion* constraint for each of the active NES searches:

$$h^i_{repel} = \sum_{i \neq j} \max[0, d - \|g(\mu_j) - g(\mu_i)\|], \tag{3}$$

which penalizes the fitness of an individual from the i-th NES if the center of the distribution from which it was drawn, μ_i, is close to other centers $\mu_j, i \neq j$. This constraint pushes the separate NES distributions away from each other so that they move into uncharted parts of task space rather than search in the same region. Algorithm 2 shows Parallelized E-TRM in pseudocode. The most important differences from the non-parallel version (Algorithm 1) are lines 4, where the repulsion constraint is added, 6-10, where the separate NES algorithms are initialized, and 11-12, where the NES searches are updated (one generation) in parallel.

Algorithm 2: Parallel E-TRM(h, k, P)

1   $M \leftarrow \{\}$ `// initialize an empty map`
2   $S \leftarrow \{\}$ `// initialize an empty set of NES algorithms`
3   $h^* \leftarrow h + \alpha_{map} h_{map}$ `// add the map-build cost function`
4   $h^* \leftarrow h^* + \alpha_{repel} h_{repel}$ `// add repulsion cost function`
5   **while** $i < k$ **do**
6   **while** $size(S) < \min(P, size(M))$ **do**
7         $q_{start} \leftarrow$ SELECTPROPORTIONAL(M)
8   INITIALIZE (s,q_{start})   `// start a new NES`
9         $S \leftarrow S \cup s$ `// add it to already active set`
10   **end**
11   **parallel_foreach** $s \in S$ **do**
12   UPDATE(s)
13   **endfor**
14   **foreach** $s \in S$ **do**
15   **if** CONVERGED?(s) **then**
16           $S \leftarrow S \setminus \{s\}$ `// remove s from the set`
17           $q' \leftarrow$ GETMEAN(s)
18   **if** CHECK(q', t') **then**
19             $M \leftarrow M \cup (q', t')$
20   **else**
21   i++
22   **end**
23   **end**
24   **end**
25 **end**

---

5   Experiments

5.1   Setup

The iCub robot [18], with the full 41 degrees-of-freedom, was simulated using MoBeE [6] which performs fast forward kinematics calculations and collision detection, using the SOLID 3.5.6 [2] collision detection library. Parallelization was implemented using the Threading Building Blocks library, which is responsible for spawning threads and assigning them to each core [15]. The constraints rely on fast nearest neighbours searches, thus we use the Approximate Nearest Neighbors library, which uses kd-trees for efficient search [1].

    The method was evaluated on a reaching task, where the task space is formed by the (x, y, z) coordinates at the center of the right-hand palm of the iCub. A collision constraint and homepose constraint prevent the iCub from hitting itself and guide the robot into more natural postures. Two more constraints are added to keep the left hand oriented straight and close to a certain position, to keep it out of the way of the right hand (see [17] for complete details). The distance parameter d was set such that the points in the constructed map are spaced roughly 2.5cm from each other in task space.

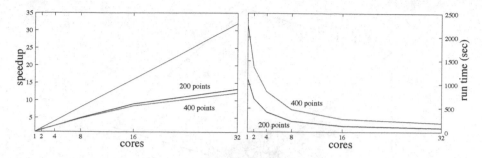

Fig. 2. Parallel speedup. The curves show the speedup achieved for each number of cores when building a map with 200 points (upper curve), and 400 points (lower curve)

The population size for every NES, λ, was set to 30 and the covariance matrices were initialized with values of 0.03 on the diagonal. In other words, NES initially searches using a standard deviation of 0.03 for every joint. For the very first point of the map, different values are used as there is no other point to start from, and thus the search needs to be more thorough. We use a population of 150 and a standard deviation of 0.15 in this case.

The stopping criterion (the CONVERGED?() function in Algorithm 2) used to decide when an individual NES should stop searching and return a new point, works by maintaining two moving averages, one averaging the last 20 fitness values of an individual at the center, μ, of the distribution, and one averaging the last 40. If the average of the last 20 is higher than the that of the last 40, the search is considered to have stagnated, and is terminated. The parameters were determined experimentally to lead to a good tradeoff between quality of results and speed.

A set of 10 simulations was run for each of six levels of parallelization: 1, 2, 4, 8, 16, and 32 cores. All simulations were run until the map contained 400 points, on a 64-core Dell PowerEdge C6145[1].

5.2   Results and Discussion

Figure 2 shows the average performance gain afforded by Parallel E-TRM over (serial) E-TRM . The graph on the left plots the speedup for each number of cores for reaching the first 200 and 400 points. The black diagonal line represents the ideal, where speedup equals the number of cores. The graph on the right shows the performance in terms of the amount of real time required to reach 200 and 400 points, for a given level of parallelization. Parallelization at 32 cores reduces the time to generate a 400-point graph from 2267 seconds ($\approx$ 37 minutes) to 186 seconds. While this is a far cry from what would be required to allow for planning in even very slowly changing dynamic environments, the speedup of 12$\times$ is significant. Moreover, the difference between the speedup for 200 and

---

[1] with 4 AMD Opteron 6376 16-core CPUs running at 2.3 GHz, and 128 GB of RAM (16 $\times$ 8 GB modules).s

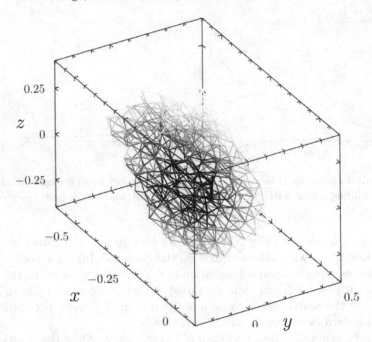

Fig. 3. Evolved TRM. The plot shows one for the evolved TRMs plots in 3D task space (see figure 1). Each point int the graph represents a pose in which the right hand of the robot is at location (x, y, x).

400 was not found to be statistically significant ($\rho = 0.05$), which indicates that the rather modest parallel efficiency is not due to the increasing size of the map. Instead, the hardware architecture seems to suffer from a memory hierarchy that is not well suited to high-throughput parallel access [13] Future experiments will migrate the system to new hardware with substantially larger L3 caches.

References

[1] libann: A library for approximate nearest neighbor searching, http://www.cs.umd.edu/~mount/ANN/
[2] Solid: Collision detection library, http://www.dtecta.com/
[3] Badger, J.M., Hart, S.W., Yamokoski, J.D.: Towards autonomous operation of robonaut 2 (2011)
[4] Berenson, D., Srinivasa, S.S., Ferguson, D., Kuffner, J.J.: Manipulation planning on constraint manifolds. In: Proceedings of the IEEE International Conference on Robotics and Automation (ICRA), pp. 625–632. IEEE (2009)
[5] Berenson, D., Srinivasa, S., Kuffner, J.: Task space regions a framework for pose-constrained manipulation planning. The International Journal of Robotics Research 30(12), 1435–1460 (2011)
[6] Frank, M., Leitner, J., Stollenga, M., Harding, S., Förster, A., Schmidhuber, J.: The modular behavioral environment for humanoids and other robots (MoBeE). In: ICINCO, pp. 304–313. SciTePress (2012) ISBN 978-989-8565-22-8

[7] Glasmachers, T., Schaul, T., Yi, S., Wierstra, D., Schmidhuber, J.: Exponential natural evolution strategies. In: Proceedings of the 12th Annual Conference on Genetic and Evolutionary Computation, pp. 393–400. ACM (2010)

[8] Hauser, K., Ng-Thow-Hing, V., Gonzalez-Baños, H.: Multi-modal motion planning for a humanoid robot manipulation task. Robotics Research, 307–317 (2011)

[9] Hsu, D., Latombe, J.-C., Motwani, R.: Path planning in expansive configuration spaces. In: Proceedings of the IEEE International Conference on Robotics and Automation (ICRA), vol. 3, pp. 2719–2726 (1997)

[10] Kalakrishnan, M., Chitta, S., Theodorou, E., Pastor, P., Schaal, S.: Stomp: Stochastic trajectory optimization for motion planning. In: Proceedings of the IEEE International Conference on Robotics and Automation (ICRA), pp. 4569–4574. IEEE (2011)

[11] Kallmann, M., Huang, Y., Backman, R.: A skill-based motion planning framework for humanoids. In: Proceedings of the International Conference on Robotics and Automation (ICRA), pp. 2507–2514. IEEE (2010)

[12] Kavraki, L.E., Svestka, P., Latombe, J.C., Overmars, M.H.: Probabilistic roadmaps for path planning in high-dimensional configuration spaces. IEEE Transactions on Robotics and Automation 12(4), 566–580 (1996)

[13] Desktop-HPC Lab. First results for swift on a 64-core amd opteron 6376, https://community.dur.ac.uk/pedro.gonnet/?p=269

[14] LaValle, S.M.: Planning algorithms. Cambridge University Press (2006)

[15] Reinders, J.: Intel threading building blocks: outfitting C++ for multi-core processor parallelism. O'Reilly Media, Inc. (2010)

[16] Sentis, L., Khatib, O.: A whole-body control framework for humanoids operating in human environments. In: Proceedings of IEEE International Conference on Robotics and Automation (ICRA), pp. 2641–2648. IEEE (2006)

[17] Stollenga, M., Pape, L., Frank, M., Leitner, J., Förster, A., Schmidhuber, J.: Task-relevant roadmaps: A framework for humanoid motion planning. In: IEEE International Conference on Intelligent Robots and Systems (IROS), pp. 5772–5778 (2013)

[18] Tsagarakis, N.G., Metta, G., Sandini, G., Vernon, D., Beira, R., Becchi, F., Righetti, L., Santos-Victor, J., Ijspeert, A.J., Carrozza, M.C., et al.: iCub: the design and realization of an open humanoid platform for cognitive and neuroscience research. Advanced Robotics 21(10), 1151–1175 (2007)

Programmable Self-assembly with Chained Soft Cells: An Algorithm to Fold into 2-D Shapes

Jürg Germann, Joshua Auerbach, and Dario Floreano

Laboratory of Intelligent Systems, EPFL - IMT - STI - LIS
Station 11, 1015 Lausanne, Switzerland
{jurg.germann,joshua.auerbach,dario.floreano}@epfl.ch
http://lis.epfl.ch

Abstract. Programmable self-assembly of chained modules holds potential for the automatic shape formation of morphologically adapted robots. However, current systems are limited to modules of uniform rigidity, which restricts the range of obtainable morphologies and thus the functionalities of the system. To address these challenges, we previously introduced "soft cells" as modules that can obtain different mechanical softness pre-setting. We showed that such a system can obtain a higher diversity of morphologies compared to state-of-the-art systems and we illustrated the system's potential by demonstrating the self-assembly of complex morphologies. In this paper, we extend our previous work and present an automatic method that exploits our system's capabilities in order to find a linear chain of soft cells that self-folds into a target 2-D shape.

Keywords: Self-Assembly, Soft Robotics, Modular Robotics.

1 Introduction

Modular robots have the potential to adapt their morphologies to achieve desired behaviors upon command [1]. Compared to fixed-morphology robots, modular robots offer greater adaptability and versatility. However, a major challenge for modular robots is to have constituent modules interact in such a way that they self-assemble into a target morphology.

Programmable self-assembly of chained modules is a promising strategy for automatically generating complex robot morphologies. Inspired by protein-folding, it provides a means of constructing morphologically and functionally diverse structures from a minimal set of building blocks. This method has several benefits. First, it is superior to other self-assembly strategies in terms of yield[1] and the range of achievable morphologies [2,3]. Second, modules can be relatively simple because there is a permanent connectivity constraint between all modules, which reduces hardware complexity (e.g. for communication or attachment/detachment between modules) [4]. Third, because of the system's intrinsic modularity, it is especially well-suited for in-silico optimization of morphology and functionality using stochastic meta-heuristics such as evolutionary algorithms [5].

---

[1] Yield being the difference between actual and desired outcome [3].

A.P. del Pobil et al. (Eds.): SAB 2014, LNAI 8575, pp. 220–229, 2014.

Programmable self-assembly of chained robotic modules has previously been investigated by Griffith [6], who suggested a two-dimensional system composed of serially connected square tiles. These tiles could move around their connection-points, resulting in a flexible chain that could fold into different geometric configurations. Through the use of four tile-types with different magnetic patterns, their system could approximate any two dimensional shape. More recently, this work was extended to three dimensions, along with algorithms to approximate any three dimensional shape [7]. Inspired by this work, Knaien et al. [8] developed a system called "MilliMoteins" that consisted of a chain of electropermanent magnetic motors that could dynamically fold into different configurations. In another work [9], it was shown that serially connected soft cubes could self-assemble into a previously designed 3-D shape by being stretched by an external tension. Finally, Risi et al. [10] presented software results of a custom "printer" that folds a long ribbon of material bearing additional elements such as virtual motors and sensors. The authors evolved and optimized robots that had different morphologies and could perform different forms of locomotion.

All of these systems have demonstrated the potential of programmable self-assembly for robotics. However, the use of modules with pre-defined shapes and uniform rigidity has limited the range of morphologies that these systems could produce. In our previous work, we combined the concepts of programmable self-assembly and soft robotics [11]. We showed that by introducing components that can obtain different softness states, the diversity of achievable morphologies at a given resolution is enhanced. Also, we demonstrated that such a system could programmatically self-assemble into complex and curvilinear morphologies that other systems would require significantly more modules to produce. However, the increased design space of potential morphologies made available by this system has, as of yet, been unexplored.

In this paper, we present an automatic method that solves the problem of how to exploit this newly available design space when a target 2-D shape is given. In order to approximate any shape with high accuracy, we put emphasis on matching a 2D hamiltonian path of target shapes. As the search for a hamiltonian path through shapes is part of other research [7], we avoid this step and focus on surface shape matching here. Hence, we provide an algorithm that can approximate the surface of any 2-D shape with high accuracy using a programmatically self-assembling system composed of soft modules.

In the following, we start by briefly introducing our previous work before presenting the newly developed algorithm in detail. Subsequently, we explain the methods and experimental setup used. Finally, we characterize the performance of the implemented algorithm on randomly generated 2-D benchmark shapes.

2   Soft Cells

In our previous work [11], we introduced a model system composed of "soft cells" that can obtain different mechanical softness pre-settings. These soft cells are initially interconnected at permanent points and arranged as a linear chain. Every

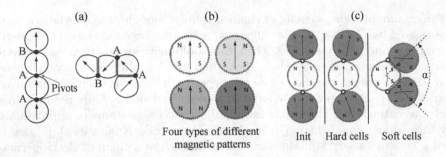

Four types of different
magnetic patterns

Init   Hard cells   Soft cells

Fig. 1. (a) The basic working principle of programmable self-assembly of linear chains: modules are aligned in series and connected through permanent pivot joints. Local interactions determine the folding of the chain. (b) Design of soft cells: each cell has four magnetic sections. According to the distribution of the magnetic regions, four different cell types have been designed. (c) Schematic representation of local folding of adjacent soft cells at their initial configuration (left), at the final configuration for three hard cells (middle), and at the final configuration for three soft cells (right).

cell possesses specific characteristics in terms of softness and magnetic properties. The specific characteristics of individual cells in a sequence determines their local interactions, and ultimately defines how the self-assembly process develops. Figure 1 displays an example of the basic self-assembly or self-folding process: cells fold about each joint once the system is released from the initial state. Joint A specifies the direction of the fold to be counterclockwise and joint B specifies the direction of the fold to be clockwise. Hence, by setting the folding sequence to be AAB the system self-assembles into the structure shown on the right of Figure 1(a).

Soft Cells: For simplicity, we model a soft cell as a two dimensional object. A cell consists of a thin flexible membrane with an operating inner pressure, which defines its softness.

Local Interactions: Each cell's membrane features specific connection areas that allow the cell to interact with other cells. In our system, these local interactions depend on magnetic connection areas. A minimal set of four different cell types has been designed, with four connection areas per cell type (Figure 1(b)).

Folding Process Assuming a frictionless environment, self-assembly occurs as a consequence of the equilibration of magnetic interaction forces and contact mechanics between adjacent cells (Figure 1(c)).

Contact Area and Folding Angle: Due to contact mechanics the contact area in equilibrium after folding between two highly soft cells will be larger compared to the contact area between two harder cells (Figure 1(c)). As a consequence, the angle between three adjacent cells after folding in equilibrium is also influenced by the softness of the cells (Figure 1(c)). Hence, the system's equilibrium state and final morphology is controllable through varying the softness of the cells.

3   Algorithm Description

Assumption - Sequential Folding

The contact mechanics of mechanically soft, self-assembling components are typically highly non-linear [11]. In our system, composed of chains of soft cells, the non-linear effects are further compounded if the self-assembly process happens in parallel, i.e. all the local interactions between all components occur at the same time. However, in order to develop a robust algorithm that is capable of predicting the folding of a system with many components, it is essential to find a way to cope with these non-linear interactions.

One way of reducing the effects of these non-linear interactions is to force the folds to occur sequentially, e.g. by using a time-delay or a printing system such as the one presented in [6]. Because the cells then assemble one-by-one, the folds are isolated in time and cannot influence each other. This greatly limits the extent of non-linear interactions.

Modeling

Previously, we investigated and quantified the relation between cell softness, contact area and folding angle α (Figure 1(c)) of adjacent folding cells. Here, in order to predict the outcome of a single fold, we make use of these previously obtained results. We use a cubic spline interpolation to model the interplay between the contact area and the softness of a pair of folding cells.

In order to compare the algorithm to state-of-the-art systems, we also model a system comprised of cells with uniform hardness. In this system, the contact area between adjacent cells is always constant.

Algorithm Overview

The main goal of the algorithm is that for a desired resolution (i.e. number of cells or cell dimension) the cell centers match a given 2-D path as closely as possible after folding. As we assume sequential folding for the self-assembly process, we have developed an iterative search algorithm, which aims to set one soft cell after the other on the given path. In the following, we provide a more detailed description on the algorithm.

1. Read in a 2-D image. For simplicity we assume that this image contains a single shape, which can be approximated with a Hamiltonian path.
2. Process the image and extract the surface path. The surface path is extracted using common image processing techniques: canny edge detection, boundary tracing and smoothing using a 5-point moving average [16].
3. Set the softness and magnetic pattern of the first two cells: the first cell is placed at a random position on the surface path and is given a random magnetic pattern. The orientation of the first cell is set in such a way that the second cell's center is on the surface path as well. According to the distance between the two cell centers, the softness of these cells is determined. The magnetic pattern is set depending on the folding direction of the second cell.

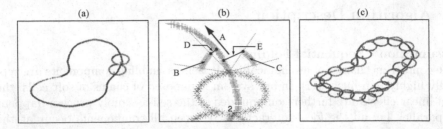

Fig. 2. Example of the algorithm intermediate steps: (a) Placement of the first two cells; (b) Finding the properties of the next cell: 'A' represents the search direction vector, 'B' depicts potential cell positions when folding counter clockwise, 'C' depicts potential cell positions when folding clockwise, 'D' = minDistCounterClockwise and 'E' = minDistClockwise. See text for details. (c) Output of the algorithm: a sequence of cells that matches the given surface.

4. Loop over the entire surface path in order to find the softness and magnetic pattern of the remaining cells. This step is further described in the next section "Algorithm details".
5. Once all of the cells have been set, i.e. their softness and magnetic patterns defined, the algorithm is finished. The result is a 1-D sequence of cells with specified softnesses and magnetic patterns.

Algorithm Details

In order to find the softness and the magnetic pattern of the next cell such that its center comes as close to the surface path as possible, the following steps are executed (see Figure 2):

1. All possible cell positions for the next cell are computed based on the softness of the previous cell. Varying the potential properties of the next cell (softness, magnetic pattern) can lead to a range of cell positions (Figure 2(b)).
2. For all potential cell positions the shortest distance to the discretized surface path is computed.
3. Two cell positions are retained: the one with the shortest distance to the surface when folding clockwise (minDistClockwise), and the one with the minimal distance to the surface when folding counterclockwise (minDist-CounterClockwise)(see Figure 2(b)).
4. Check if the found cell positions are in the search direction of the surface path (see Figure 2(b)). The search direction is defined as the vector that spans from the last cell (pivot point on surface path) to the point on the surface path that is one cell diameter away. A potential cell center is assumed to be in the search direction if the angle between the surface direction vector and the vector from a cell position to the closest surface path point is smaller than 90°. If one of the two positions is not in line with the search direction, its corresponding minimal distance is set to infinite.
5. Check for the cell position with the smallest minimal distance to the surface path and return that position.

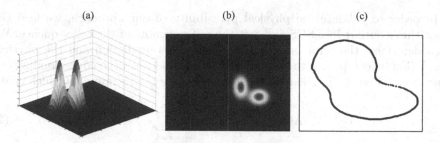

Fig. 3. Randomly generated Gaussian mixture models. Two Gaussian density points (a) shown in 3-D, (b) shown in 2-D. (c) Thresholding at an arbitrary level yields a non-uniform shape.

4   Methods

Implementation and Testing
The algorithm as described in the previous section is implemented in MATLAB® (Matlab). In order to test the algorithm, its output is tested both in Matlab as well as in our custom developed physics-based simulation tool "Soft Cell Simulator" (SCS) [12]. Using our simulation framework enables us to assess the performance in a physically more plausible and accurate way.

Experimental Setup
In order to evaluate the performance of the algorithm in a fair manner, we generate randomly shaped benchmarks upon which the algorithm is tested. Random but plausible robot shapes can be obtained when using Gaussian Mixture Models [13]. In this method, a 2-D workspace contains a list of Gaussian points. Each point has an associated density and standard deviation. In order to generate a 2-D shape, the linear sum from all Gaussian points is taken and thresholded. Figure 3 illustrates an example of the method. Two Gaussian points result in a non-uniform shape. In our experiments, up to five Gaussian points are used, whereas the points may have different standard deviations. This choice of parameters typically leads to smooth, freeform shapes that potentially could be robot morphologies, as has been shown in [17].

Analysis
For assessing the correctness of the algorithm's output, we compute the geometrical accuracy between a resulting morphology and a target shape (similar to the geometric accuracy of 3-D printed models [14]):

$$\text{Geometric Accuracy} = \frac{A_{\text{target}} - A_{\text{error}}}{A_{\text{target}}} \times 100\% \tag{1}$$

where A_{target} is the surface-area of the target object and A_{error} is the surface between the centers of the folded cells and the target object. See Figure 4 for an illustration of this computation.

In order to validate the physical plausibility of our approach, we feed the algorithm's output into SCS and test the self-assembly of the cell sequence. We then determine the error between the algorithm's prediction and the physical simulation by computing the Euclidean distance between the corresponding cell centers (see Figure 7). The individual errors ϵ_i are then summed up such that:

$$\text{Accumulated Error} = \sum_{i=1}^{n} \epsilon_i \qquad (2)$$

5 Results

Ten complex 2-D shape models, which were first created by Gaussian mixture models and then processed using common image processing tools, were tested to validate the effectiveness and robustness of the developed algorithm.

Geometric Accuracy for Randomly Generated Benchmarks

Figure 4 plots the geometric accuracy of the algorithm output for the randomly generated benchmarks obtained at different resolution settings (number of cells). As can be observed in the figure, the accuracy generally increases with a higher number of cells. This is because, if resolution is low, the cell centers may lay close to the desired path, but many details of the actual given shape are lost. An example of this effect is shown in Figure 5, where the approximation of the snail shape is illustrated at different resolution settings.

In order to illustrate the advantages of our system composed of cells with non-uniform softness settings, we also run the algorithm with uniform softness settings (which is the case in state-of-the-art systems [6-10]). This result is also plotted in Figure 4(b). As this plot makes clear, the geometric accuracy of the output with uniform softness settings is always lower compared to the case with non-uniform softness settings. This demonstrates the increased capabilities of the system with non-uniform softness settings to approximate shapes at lower resolution and with higher geometric accuracy.

Algorithm Validation in Physics-Based Simulation

To further validate the output of the algorithm in a physically more accurate environment, we feed the obtained cell sequences for the ten benchmarks into SCS. We then asses the error between the Matlab prediction and the physics-based simulation. Figure 6 shows an example of the difference between Matlab and SCS output. Figure 7 plots the quantified accumulated error when increasing the number of cells. As the figure makes clear, there is a linear increase of the accumulated error with each added cell. This error has two potential sources. First, because of the non-linear interactions between folding cells and the interpolation used to approximate this process in Matlab, some error occurs with each fold. Second, because of energy drift in the physics-engine (i.e. there is a gradual change in the total energy of a closed system over time, due to numerical

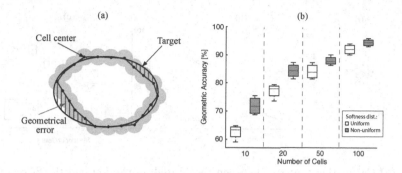

Fig. 4. (a) Calculation of geometric accuracy, (b) geometric accuracy of the algorithm's output for ten randomly generated benchmarks when allowing either a uniform or a non-uniform cell softness distribution

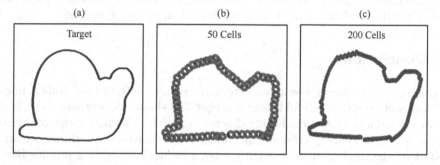

Fig. 5. Algorithm output to match the target shape of a snail. (a) Target, (b) output with resolution of 50 cells, (c) output with resolution of 200 cells

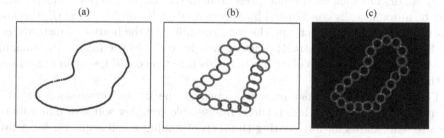

Fig. 6. Example of difference between Matlab prediction and physics based simulation environment. (a) Target, (b) Matlab prediction, (c) SCS simulation.

integration artifacts that arise with the use of a finite time step [15]), there is additional error introduced at every computational step.

Finally, we compute the geometric accuracy of the result of the self-assembly process in the physics-based simulation. The result is plotted in Figure 7(c). Despite the linear increase of accumulated error between Matlab and SCS, the geometric accuracy of the physics-based simulation remains high and follows the same profile as the Matlab prediction. Thus, from this result we conclude that

228   J. Germann, J. Auerbach, and D. Floreano

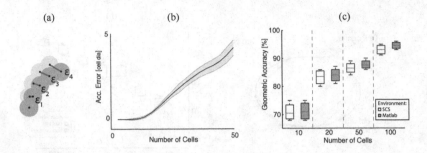

Fig. 7. (a) Calculating the error between the Matlab prediction and the SCS simulation, (b) accumulated error for an increasing number of cells, (c) geometric accuracy of benchmarks in SCS for different resolutions (number of cells)

the algorithm, despite its simplistic modeling, is capable of predicting sequences that fold with a relatively high accuracy into desired target shapes.

6   Conclusion

In this paper, we have presented an iterative search method that finds a linear chain of soft cells that self-folds into a target 2-D shape. We evaluated the algorithm's capability of approximating diverse shapes by measuring the geometric accuracy for randomly generated benchmarks. As we have shown, the algorithm's output reaches high geometric accuracy both in Matlab and in a physics-based simulation environment.

The algorithm presented here is well-suited to be combined with a space-filling algorithm such as the one presented in [7]. Then, a robot's morphology may be automatically constructed by approximating its surface using the method described here and by specifying the required filling of the body (for instance according to functional constraints such as weight, etc.). In the future, by stacking 2-D building blocks on top of each other, this principle could be further extended to the third dimension.

The results in this paper present a cornerstone in our progression towards an automatic method to design and self-assemble complex soft modular robots, because this allows for automating the step of finding a cell sequence for a target morphology while exploiting the soft characteristics of our system. As this method allows one to obtain robotic structures with high morphological complexity from a small number of components, we believe that it will be possible to create functionally complex, self-assembling robots that are well-adapted to a given task or environment.

Acknowledgements. The research leading to these results has received funding partially from the Swiss National Foundation through the National Center of Competence in Research Robotics and from the European Union Seventh Framework Programme (FP7/2007-2013) under grant agreement n° 308943.

References

1. Murata, S., Kurokawa, H.: Self-Organizing Robots. Springer Tracts in Advanced Robotics, vol. 77 (2012)
2. Whitesides, G.M., Grzybowski, B.: Self-assembly at all scales. Science 295, 2418–2421 (2002)
3. Pelesko, J.A.: Self assembly: the science of things that put themselves together. CRC Press (2007)
4. Gross, R., Dorigo, M.: Self-Assembly at the Macroscopic Scale. Proceedings of the IEEE 96, 1490–1508 (2008)
5. Pfeifer, R., Lungarella, M., Iida, F.: Self-Organization, Embodiment, and Biologically Inspired Robotics. Science 318, 1088–1093 (2007)
6. Griffith, S.: Growing Machines. PhD Thesis. MIT (2004)
7. Cheung, K.C., Demaine, E.D., Bachrach, J.R., Griffith, S.: Programmable assembly with universally foldable strings (Moteins). IEEE Transactions on Robotics 27, 718–729 (2011)
8. Knaian, A.N., Cheung, K.C., Lobovsky, M.B., Oines, A.J., Schmidt-Neilsen, P., Gershenfeld, N.A.: The milli-motein: A self-folding chain of programmable matter with a one centimeter module pitch. In: IEEE International Conference on Intelligent Robots and Systems, pp. 1447–1453 (2012)
9. Yim, S., Sitti, M.: SoftCubes: Towards a Soft Modular Matter. In: IEEE International Conference on Robotics and Automation, pp. 530–536 (2013)
10. Risi, S., Cellucci, D., Lipson, H.: Ribosomal Robots: Evolved Designs Inspired by Protein Folding. In: GECCO 2013, pp. 263–270 (2013)
11. Germann, J., Maesani, A., Pericet-Camara, R., Floreano, D.: Soft Cells for Programmable Self-Assembly of Robotic Modules (Under review)
12. Germann, J., Maesani, A., Stöckli, Floreano, D.: Soft Cell Simulator: A tool to study Soft Multi-Cellular Robots. In: IEEE International Conference on Robotics and Biomimetics, pp. 1300–1305 (2013)
13. Pernkopf, F., Bouchaffra, D.: Genetic-based EM algorithm for learning Gaussian mixture models. IEEE Transactions on Pattern Analysis and Machine Intelligence 27, 1344–1348 (2005)
14. Jin, G.Q., Li, W.D., Gao, L.: An adaptive process planning approach of rapid prototyping and manufacturing. Robotics and Computer-Integrated Manufacturing 29, 23–38 (2013)
15. Gans, J., Shalloway, D.: Shadow mass and the relationship between velocity and momentum in symplectic numerical integration. Physical Review E 61, 4587–4592 (2000)
16. Gonzalez, R.C., Woods, R.E., Eddins, S.L.: Digital Image Processing Using MATLAB. Pearson Prentice Hall, New Jersey (2004)
17. Hiller, J., Lipson, H.: Automatic design and manufacture of soft robots. IEEE Transactions on Robotics 28(2), 457–466 (2012)

Voxel Robot: A Pneumatic Robot with Deformable Morphology

Mark Roper, Nikolaos Katsaros, and Chrisantha Fernando

SBCS, EECS, Queen Mary University of London,
Mile End Road, UK
mark.roper@qmul.ac.uk
http://www.eecs.qmul.ac.uk/people/view/20110

Abstract. The Voxbot is a cubic (voxel) shaped robot actuated by expansion and contraction of its 12 edges designed for running evolutionary experiments, built as cheaply as possible. Each edge was made of a single 10ml medical syringe for pneumatic control. These were connected to an array of 12 servos situated on an external housing and controlled with an Arduino microcontroller from a laptop. With twenty motor primitive commands and the slow response of its pneumatics this robot allows real time controllers to be evolved in situ rather than just in simulation. With simple combinations and sequencing of motor primitives the Voxbot can be made to walk, rotate and crab crawl. The device is available in kit form and is very easy to build and replicate. Other morphologies can be built easily.

Keywords: Arduino, Soft Bodied Robotics, Evolutionary Robotics, Robustness.

1 Introduction

Traditional robots are typically composed of hard fixed components linked together by hinges, joints and powered by motors and gears. These have success in may areas but lack the adaptability and robustness to perturbations, lesions, and construction errors, that we see in the natural world. In recent years work has progressed on a new range of 'soft body' robots that use new composite materials and manufacturing methods to create more biologically inspired robots. The most notable of these is the robot tentacle [1] with potential use for bomb disposal, surgery, cleanup tasks in hazardous environments. As impressive as this design is, it is still crafted and controlled by the human hand and can only ever be as good as it's human inventor.

A parallel line of research evolves soft body robots in virtual worlds [2]. These are able to utilise a number of simulated materials and produce designs optimally evolved for a given fitness function within their environment. Karl Sims is probably the father of this field producing evolved creatures back in 1994 [3]. Hardware and software have moved on since then and recent techniques use the VoxCAD voxel simulator as a testbed [4]. A voxel is a 3D simulated cube that

A.P. del Pobil et al. (Eds.): SAB 2014, LNAI 8575, pp. 230–239, 2014.

can be given particular material properties (stiffness, stretch, periodic inflation) these voxels are stacked together and due the the periodic inflating nature of some of these voxels the whole structure can move. Simple controllers modify the volume of each voxel and using evolved morphologies to alter the structure of the creature different motion can be produced. Voxels within a simulated environment can be created to perform a range of motion tasks and can be tuned via a fitness function to generate designs optimised for speed, energy use or specific environmental factors.

However, as advanced as these virtual worlds have become they can never replicate the complexity and variance of the real world. There have been several examples of real world voxel robots, these have either used fixed voxel connections producing motion through actuating servos and motors [5], [6], or self assembling cubes that can move independently of each other or join up to form new shapes [7]. However even the most advanced of these self contained cubes 'Cubli' [8] which can step and hop on a single corner still has a fixed rigid shape, locomotion of these devices at their current scale will never resemble the movements of living creatures.

We set out to design a simple-to-build soft robot that still presented a sufficient range of motor actions that would be robust enough to run for long periods. As a demonstration we begin with a single cubic morphology. A cube might not seem the most logical design for a locomotion robot however the shape does have some intriguing properties, with twelve independently expandable and retractable edges it has twelve degrees of motion. In addition a cube has eight corners each composed of three edges, six faces composed of four edges and three planes (x, y, z) again composed of four edges, and finally the entire cube composed of all twelve edges (see figure 2). The ability to fully expand, retract, relax or oscillate any of these regions provides a repertoire of twenty primitive motor action controls. These actions can be combined to produce a single synchronous motion of the cube, or sequenced to provide a complex range of movements.

2   Materials and Methods

Our goal was to produce voxel like device cheaply with easily obtainable parts. These are to be made available to the general public in kit form, and therefore need to be simple to construct and without the need for any special tools or equipment. These constraints together are not trivial to satisfy. The final Voxbot design fulfils almost all of these requirements with most components connecting with push fit joints and only rudimentary hardware skills required to build the Voxbot and its external servo control system. From the kit manufacturing perspective the design has the advantage that it uses a limited number of components and the required parts can be manufactured in bulk using a 3D-printer.

A variety of prototypes were designed. The project consisted of two main design areas; the robot and the servo control system. The first design for a robot "SpongeBot" is shown in Figure 1a. The control system containing 12 servo syringe modules each of which would be connected to a voxel cube edge

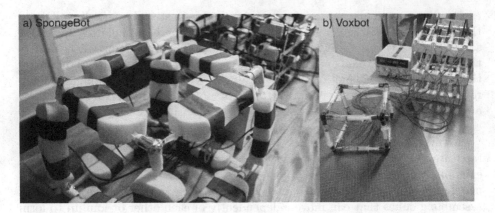

Fig. 1. Development stages of the robot cube and servo control system. Left: SpongeBot and original servo control system. Right: Voxbot and smaller updated servo controller.

was very bulky and had a Heath Robinson flavour. Each servo syringe module followed an old fashioned Texas oil rig design however the arm was extended to provide better power transfer. To allow for easy wiring, all of the twelve modules were attached together to form a 3 x 4 cube. All of the servos were connected to an AdaFruit servo controller board and from there to an Arduino Mega control board. The control system now allowed twelve hydraulic syringes to be powered simultaneously and with adjustment of the servo timing and rotation rate a smooth motion of all syringes could be maintained. One issue that did arise was if a servo got stuck or drew to much current then all other servos would behave erratically until the mechanism freed itself. The system also continually looked for the weakest point with screws, nuts and Lego parts often working loose. SpongeBot in the foreground was constructed not with pneumatics but a hydraulic dual syringe set up for each edge, the corners were made from plumbing parts to give stability, and the edges were made from car wash sponges to allow each edge to bend and flex as required. Video 1 in Supplementary Material shows SpongeBot in operation.

Voxbot, see Figure 1b. is an attempt to make the robot more robust for continual use and easy to store, move and assemble. The corners were replaced with injection moulded 3 way 90 degree joints which fitted perfectly into a standard off the shelf 19mm flexible PVC tube. This tubing provided enough stability to hold the syringes firmly yet allowed the flexibility required in the robot during motion. With the use of these components there was a substantial reduction in weight from 700g to 300g, this allowed Voxbot to be run pneumatically making assembly quicker, easier and much less messy. The updated version of the servo control system was reduced in size, used a much sturdier support frame to hold everything firmly in place, and the syringes could be easily removed from the cube if necessary (especially useful when using hydraulics). It also used two AdaFruit servo control boards instead of just one as this allowed two power supplies to be installed which gave much better servo responses if all Voxbot edges were active simultaneously.

The dynamics of the pneumatics are slower and less accurate than that of the original hydraulic system, however this inaccuracy did present some unexpected and useful dynamics. To extend or retract an edge the servos needed to make a rapid movement from fully extended to fully retracted, or vice-versa, it could then take over a second for the Voxbot syringes to finish reacting. By initiating a subsequent move before this was complete we could significantly change the robots movements, equally a longer pause would allow gravity to take effect and modify the shape of the Voxbot so again producing alternate movements when the following action commands were executed. The final property of the pneumatics actually became one of the primitive motor action sets. A reset mode was built into the original software to rotate the servos to a fixed central start and end position, this prevented rapid movements and current drain during power up and initialisation stage. In this central servo position we found the corresponding edges of the Voxbot were able to expand and contract with relative ease when being pulled by adjoining edges, this in turn allowed even greater flexibility of movement within the Voxbot. Video 6 in Supplementary Material shows Voxbot in operation.

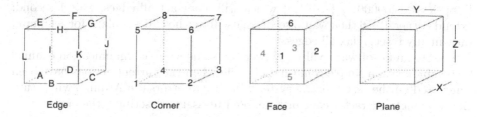

Fig. 2. Schematic view of Voxbot regions; edges (A-L), corners (1-8), faces (1-6) and planes (x,y,z). Pneumatic tubing to servo control system lay across edge B.

2.1 Control Architecture

The Voxbot project was conceived as a way of providing a real world, real time robot for developing evolving systems. For this reason we wanted to hide all complexities of the servo control from the researcher and instead provide a number of motor actions that could be called from any development language (C++, Python, etc.). The use of the Arduino Mega control board means that all communication can take place over a serial connection (via usb cable, or wifi with extra hardware). The Arduino processes a simple text based language composed of custom words and scripts. The twenty primitive motor actions (called words) are subdivided into four motor classes; expand, contract, reset/relax and oscillate. Each of these can determine which cube type is referenced; edges, corners, faces, planes or whole cube. The word defines which of these is to be acted upon, for example if you wish to expand corners 5, 6 you would write the word <xc|56>or to oscillate edges 1 and 12 you would write <oe|AL>(see Figure 2). Although this allows you to modify more than one edge in a single command it would not allow you to expand some edges while contracting others, to do this the words can be combined into a script tag "{...}" all word commands within the script are performed synchronously. For example {<re|*><xe|AD><se|B>} would relax all edges apart from extending edges 1 & 4 and contracting (shrink) edge 2 (Within a script word commands to the right will overwrite preceding commands relating to the same edge).

With the move from hydraulics to pneumatics the delay between subsequent command scripts became very important. By default there is a one second delay from the servos completing the current movement and processing the next. As this may be a useful parameter to adapt while creating evolutionary systems the ability to change these settings was built into the language. To change the delay between scripts you simply write <ds|3000>i.e. update default script delay to three seconds. There is a similar command for the delay a servo will wait while oscillating, this also ensures all oscillating edges which were started simultaneously will remain synchronised at the start of the subsequent movements (<do|4000>). This now allows the researcher to build a complex set of commands that can be constructed in the their native programming language and then sent to the Voxbot. A multi-script example: {<se|*><xc|46><ds|3000>} {<op|X><ds|60000>} {<re|*>} which will: contract all edges, wait 1 second; extend corner 4 & 6 then wait 3 seconds; oscillate the cubes x plane for 1 minute; then finally reset/relax all edges.

The Arduino software will reply over the same serial communication channel (usb cable) with a simple confirmation code when the current actions have been completed on the servo control system. In case of errors the Arduino will return either a single character code or a detailed messages describing the error.

3   Results

The primary aim of the project was to build a robot robust enough to perform evolutionary algorithms on a real world model. Simply put, the Voxbot and servo control system should stand up to continual experimental use. This was overall achieved successfully and by performing a sequence of relax, extend and contract of all edges between each experiment the Voxbot also managed to maintain a true cubic shape without excessive human interaction.

From manual experiments we knew that the cube could be walked forward by adjusting individual edges but this was slow and hardly biological. These initial experiments performed without the servos but by hand squeezing the appropriate syringes did however show that it was possible to shift the centre of weight of the cube such that the opposing corner could be lifted and then freely moved forward. Video 2 in the Supplementary Material shows the (very) slow motion of the cube one edge at a time. Although one syringe movement is possible, and was successfully repeated with the servo control system connected it did not make for particularly interesting dynamics. To begin full testing we began by generating random movements by setting out of phase oscillations in the cube edges. This provided the first evidence that synchronous movement of the

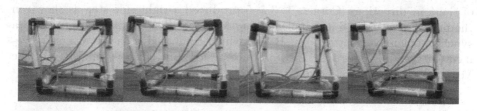

Fig. 3. Sample of Voxbot positions and edge orientations during random out of phase edge oscillations

cube edges could provide real, easily repeatable locomotion. These movements produced the required shift in the cube's centre of gravity and the extension and contraction of edges allowing corners to move while they were relieved of weight. However due to the out of phase oscillations the movement produced would first move in one direction and then oscillate in a new direction, or non at all, changing as the oscillation dynamics of the cube altered. Figure 3 shows examples of the cube positions and edge orientations that were exhibited while executing random movements. Video 5 in Supplementary Material shows a full example of one of the random movement experiments.

In the second batch of experiments we wished to show that more precise and reliable movements could be produced before attempting to execute an evolution algorithm. Using intuition and trial and error we manually configure edge alignments and oscillations that could produce a basic set of movements.

The first reliable movement to be produced was achieved by simply contracting all cube edges and then expanding corners 1 & 7 (see Figure 2), after a short delay all edges were made to oscillate. The initial configuration forced corners 2 & 4 to take most of the cube weight, during the first oscillation edge B would contract and edge D extend moving corners 1 & 3 forward, on the next oscillation the process was reversed moving corners 2 & 4 forward. This produced a fast efficient crab like movement diagonally across the table. Due to the beautiful symmetry of the cube it was possible to quickly change the direction of the diagonal walk in any of the four directions. Clip 2 in video 6 of the Supplementary Material shows the cube moving in one diagonal direction and then a seamless change of direction of the crab crawl.

Rotation, or more precisely a reverse pirouette around a base corner, was accomplished by expanding two base corners and a corresponding top corner. For a clockwise rotation corners 1, 2 & 7 should be expanded, for anticlockwise simply expand the adjacent top corner giving corners 1, 2 & 8. This rotation was significantly slower than the crab crawl managing only a few degrees each iteration. Again using symmetry corners 2, 3 & 5 also produced rotation, in this case it was slightly faster, however this may simply be due to the additional weight of the pneumatic cables on the edge while rotating around the original corner. Video 6 of Supplementary Material clip 3 shows the rotation.

The final manual movement produced was a step or hop in the direction of a cube face, again by expanding just three corners the Voxbot could be moved any of the four directions. Corners 1, 3 & 5 produced a right side step as shown in the final clip of video 6 in Supplementary Material. The oscillations produced a synchronous movement of edges B & D which combined with the reverse movement in the top edges H & F to produce a slow but effective mini hop of the Voxbot in the given direction.

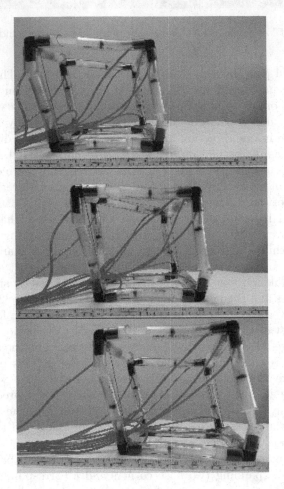

Fig. 4. Voxbot movement after ten generations of the microbial genetic algorithm experiment. Although slow the Voxbot has sufficient power in this gait to pull the pneumatic tubes behind it.

The Voxbot had proved that locomotion and a variety of gaits was possible through manual manipulation. It was essential to show that it was also possible to run real time genetic algorithms (GA) on the platform. A simple interactive microbial genetic algorithm [9],[10] experiment was carried out, with fitness being attributed by hand to each controller. Two controllers were evaluated and the best controller chosen to overwrite the loser with mutation. The human observer chose the controller that produced the most displacement over the table surface. A GA program was written in C++ that generated the Voxbot script code to be sent to the Arduino, it then prompted the human experimenter to enter the distance traversed. The genome consisted of simple twelve integer array defining the start position of each edge (0-relaxed, 1-extended, 2-contracted) followed by a command to oscillate all edges with state 1 or 2. In the first experiment even after ten generations very little movement had been accomplished. The Voxbot did establish a large shift in its centre of gravity which enabled it to lift corner 3 significantly off the ground and a movement on edge D did make a small rotation possible but the genome never discovered a reciprocal movement on the other cube face to move it forward. An inspection of the genome at each generation showed that the best fitness was created when more of the edges were oscillating (i.e. in state 1 or 2). In many of the generations the genomes would only encode oscillation of seven or eight edges. To resolve this issue on the second experiment we made a minor adjustment to the C++ program such that all edges would be instructed to oscillate, this provided three oscillation states that a cube edge could be in. After ten generations the displacement of the Voxbot increased from virtually no forward motion to 7.5cm within the one minute experiment. This movement was as efficient, if not better, than the previous side step motion discovered during manual configuration. The final generation did not produce a direct forward motion but would slowly bare to the right during the run, as can be seen in Figure 4 as it slowly approaches the camera. Interestingly the gait produced for this stepping motion was completely different to that of the manual configuration, in this instance the nearside horizontal edges C & G are synchronised and opposite to the vertical edges J & K, while the far-side edge oscillations are the reverse, this shows an opposing left / right gait seen in many natural systems. Video 7 of the of Supplementary Material shows the full motion produced by the winning genome of the 1st, 5th and 10th generations.

4   Discussion

The Voxbot robot was designed to perform evolutionary experiments in the real world. Our first trials of this new device show that not only is it able to run for extended periods of time with little human interaction, but even when configured into a cube one of the least mobile and least naturally inspired shapes it is still able to produce interesting locomotion and show a variety of complex gaits. The evolutionary experiment although only run for ten generations shows a noticeable progression towards a more efficient design and this was accomplished with the most basic of genomes. With the addition of a more complex genome of multiple cube orientations and the use of delay constraints already built into the Voxbot language even more sophisticated movements should be possible.

The core design works well however the servo controller still needs some refinement. The current control system uses a metal frame and wooden supports for the syringes and servos, although this allowed for easy construction and was useful during prototyping the connection between the pull arm and the syringe pistons did occasionally wear loose or get stuck. The next generation of the device will use 3D printed parts producing much more accurate alignment of the components. These changes should in turn allow the new version to use cheaper plastic gear servos rather than the more expensive metal gear high torque servos required for the original hydraulic robot. Each development iteration intends to make the Voxbot both cheaper to manufacture and easier to construct. The continual project aim is to develop a system that can not only be used for effective research into soft body robots in our own lab but also as an educational tool cheap and reliable enough to be used to introduce a new generation of researchers and students to; computer hardware interfaces, software languages and artificial intelligence techniques.

Soft robotics are slowly making an impact into the mainstream robotics community as new materials and manufacturing techniques become available. The recent publicity of the soft NASA 'Super Ball Bot' [11] shows there is a real need and use for these soft robots. Our Voxbot provides an easily replicable and durable experimental platform for those organisations without a NASA space mission budget.

Acknowledgements. We thank FP-7 TRUCE and FP-7 FET OPEN INSIGHT grants for funding this work. Also thanks to EPSRC Innovation grant from QMUL. We thank Daphne Lai and Martyn Amos for organising the TRUCE Hackademia event in November 2013. We thank Kok Ho Huen, David Wilkinson and Chris Jack from QMUL for all their technical and equipment advice. A special thanks to Boris Mitavskiy and Rollo Hollins for their many hours sawing and nut fastening while at the TRUCE Hackademia retreat.

Supplementary Material

http://www.robozoo.co.uk/robots/voxbot/

References

1. Martinez, R.V., Branch, J.L., Fish, C.R., Jin, L., Shepherd, R.F., Nunes, R.M.D., Suo, Z., Whitesides, G.M.: Robotic Tentacles with Three Dimensional Mobility Based on Flexible Elastomers. Advanced Materials 25(2), 205–212 (2013)
2. Cheney, N., MacCurdy, R., Clune, J., Lipson, H.: Unshackling Evolution: Evolving Soft Robots with Multiple Materials and a Powerful Generative Encoding. In: Proceedings of the Genetic and Evolutionary Computation Conference (2013)
3. Sims, K.: Evolving 3D morphology and behavior by competition. Artificial life 1(4), 353–372 (1994)
4. Hiller, J.D., Lipson, H.: Multi material topological optimization of structures and mechanisms. In: Proceedings of the 11th Annual Conference on Genetic and Evolutionary Computation, pp. 1521–1528. ACM (2009)
5. Yim, M., et al.: Connecting and disconnecting for chain self-reconfiguration with PolyBot. IEEE/ASME Trans Mechatron 7(4), 442–451 (2002)

6. Festo Moecubes (2009), http://www.festo.com/cms/en_corp/9617.htm
7. Romanishin, J.W., Gilpin, K., Rus, D.: M-blocks: Momentum-driven, magnetic modular robots. In: 2013 IEEE/RSJ International Conference on Intelligent Robots and Systems (IROS), pp. 4288–4295. IEEE (2013)
8. D'Andrea, R., http://raffaello.name/dynamic-works/cubli/
9. Harvey, I.: The microbial genetic algorithm. In: Kampis, G., Karsai, I., Szathmáry, E. (eds.) ECAL 2009, Part II. LNCS, vol. 5778, pp. 126–133. Springer, Heidelberg (2011)
10. Goldberg, D.E., Holland, J.H.: Genetic Algorithms and Machine Learning. Machine Learning 3(2), 95–99 (1988)
11. NASA Super Ball Bot (2013), http://www.nasa.gov/directorates/spacetech/niac/2012_phase_I_fellows_agogino.html

Task-Driven Evolution of Modular Self-reconfigurable Robots*

Vojtěch Vonásek[1], Sergej Neumann[2], Lutz Winkler[2], Karel Košnar[1],
Heinz Wörn[2], and Libor Přeučil[1]

[1] Czech Technical University in Prague, Faculty of Electrical Engineering,
Dept. of Cybernetics, Technicka 2, 166 27, Prague, Czech Republic
vonasek@labe.felk.cvut.cz
[2] Karlsruhe Institute of Technology, Institute for Process Control and Automation,
Engler-Bunte-Ring 8, 76131 Karlsruhe, Germany
{neumann,winkler,woern}@kit.edu

Abstract. In future space missions, versatile, robust, autonomous and
adaptive robotic systems will be required to perform complex tasks. This
can be realized using modular robots with the ability to reconfigure to
various structures, which allows them to adapt to the environment as
well as to a given task. As it is not possible to program beforehand the
robots to cope with every possible situation, they will have to adapt autonomously. In this paper, we introduce a novel framework which allows
modular robots to adapt physically (i.e., to change the structure) as well
as internally (i.e. to learn the behavior) to achieve high-level tasks (e.g.
'climb-up the cliff'). The framework utilizes evolutionary methods for
structure adaptation as well as to find a suitable behavior. The main
idea of the framework is the utilization of simple motion skills combined
by a motion planner to achieve the high-level task. This allows to achieve
complex task easily without need to optimize complex behaviors of the
robot.

1 Introduction

In space missions such as colonization of planets, robots are envisaged to set a
foundation for human expeditions [7]. Flexible and robust autonomous robotic
systems are required to operate in these hostile environments with low temper-
atures and high radiation. As not all the tasks can be pre-programmed before
a mission, nor the robots can be designed to cope will all possible situations,
an ability to autonomously adapt for a given task and environment is necessary.
The robots have to adapt both physically (i.e., to change the structure) as well
as internally (i.e., to adapt the behavior).

Modular Self-reconfigurable Robots (MSR) are potential candidates for such
missions. These robots consist of basic building blocks, which themselves are
fully functional robots [13]. Each module can move by its own or more modules

---

* The work in this paper was supported by MSMT grant No. 7AMV14DE007.

A.P. del Pobil et al. (Eds.): SAB 2014, LNAI 8575, pp. 240–249, 2014.

can be connected into a robot organism. The high reconfigurability of MSRs makes them very flexible for different tasks as they can adapt their structure to better fulfill a given goal. Furthermore, broken modules can be exchanged, which increases the robustness of the robots.

In this paper, we present a novel framework for the task-driven evolution of MSR systems. The core of the proposed framework is an evolutionary method combined with a planning process. The evolutionary part provides candidate solutions, i.e. robot structures and possible behaviors. To estimate quality (fitness) of a candidate solution, motion planning is utilized to create a plan to achieve the desired high-level task using these behaviors. The fitness of a solution is then computed as the cost of the plan. The utilization of the planning process allows to use simple motion skills and combine them to achieve the given task, instead of evolving a single behavior specialized for the task. These simple skills can be learned faster, than learning the single complex behavior. Furthermore, such an approach is more robust, as possible disturbances or imprecision of command execution can be easily compensated by the planning process, that runs on the robot.

1.1 Related Work

The evolution of structure and behavior can be done simultaneously or separately. Due to many parameters to be optimized, usually genetic or evolutionary algorithms are employed for these tasks. In first case, a single genotype contains both structure of the robot as well as parameters of the controllers [15,14]. However, such a co-evolution only allows to evolve one behavior and not several behaviors. Moreover, run-time of these methods may be considerable high especially when a complex behavior is required. Such an approach is thus suitable especially for simple robots with simple behaviors.

In the second approach, where the structure and behavior are evolved separately, first the structure is evolved and then, the motions are optimized. A motion of a modular robot can be realized using pattern generators. A Central Pattern Generators (CPGs) [5] producing periodical signals for the actuators are widely used. CPGs can model various types of locomotion such as crawling or walking and they have been employed also for humanoids or legged robots. To achieve a desired locomotion, parameters of the CPGs need to be optimized, which can be solved using genetic algorithms [12], genetic programming [3], evolutionary approaches [16,10] or meta-heuristics [2].

As the methods for simultaneous evolution of structure and behavior can be time consuming and computational intensive, they are not suitable for space missions, where the computational power is limited. Therefore, separated evolution of structure and behavior is preferred. While many papers have been presented for structure evolution, motion is usually realized as a single behavior such as crawling of walking in a desired direction. Such methods may become ineffective, when a complex task such as 'climb-up the cliff' has to be achieved.

To evolve a robot suitable for a given high-level task, we propose the framework for Evolved Learning Organisms (ELO), which adapts the structure and the behavior separately. The framework is based on the idea, that a complex high-level goal can be achieved using simple motion patterns combined by a high-level planning technique.

2   The Framework

The ELO framework is motivated by the Mars mission, where modular robots will operate on the landscape. They communicate via a radio channel with the main station, which solves computationally intensive tasks. Let us consider a situation, where a robot needs to traverse into a valley, as depicted on Fig. 1b. The base station is asked to suggest a new structure and plan to fulfill the goal. The ELO utilizes a physical simulation with a terrain model to find a suitable robot organism, its behavior and a plan to achieve the goal.

The schema of the framework is depicted of Fig. 1a. Here, an evolutionary engine is used to find new robot structures. To evaluate the fitness of a candidate solution, two main aspects need to be considered: a) the cost of reconfiguration from actual structure to the new one; b) the cost of achieving the desired goal. The cost of the reconfiguration is estimated using a reconfiguration planner, which is described in [1] in details. To evaluate the second part of the fitness, simple motion primitives are first optimized. These primitives represent basic skills such as 'move-left' or 'stand-up' and they are then combined using a motion planning to find a feasible plan to achieve the desired goal.

The found solution (i.e., robot structure with suitable motion primitives, re-configuration and motion plan) is sent to the robot, which reconfigures to the target structure. Due to possible reality gaps of the simulation, the robot may behave differently when controlled directly by the primitives evolved in the simulation. Therefore, before the plan is executed, the simulated primitives are first verified on the real robot. The on-board planner is then used to revise the plan considering the real performance of the primitives. The plan, which consists of sequence of motion primitives, is then executed. When the robot deviates from

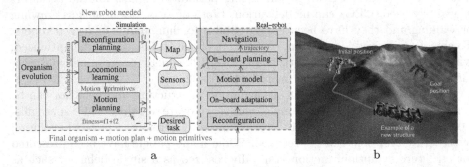

a   b

Fig. 1. The schema of the ELO framework (a). Example of a Mars scenario: the robot needs to descend into the crater (b). The Organism evolution component test many candidate robot structures (e.g. the snake-like robot). The Motion planning component creates a plan (green) to reach the goal, which is then used to compute the fitness.

the plan, e.g. due to slippage or imprecise execution of the primitives, a new plan is generated on-board. The process is terminated if the high-level goal is achieved, or when the on-board planner cannot find a feasible plan to achieve it. In such a case, the base station is asked to provide a new structure and plan.

2.1 Organism Evolution

The task of organism evolution is to generate feasible robot structures. These structures are described by a string (a RFL word) which follows the Robot Formation Language (RFL) notation [8]. It consists of symbols for module types, symbols for the spatial relationship between two modules and symbols describing the beginning and the ending of a branch. Let X be a module type which denotes a CoSMO robot [6]. This robot can dock at four different sides, which are denoted as A, B, C and D and they can be rotated to each other with a multiple of 90°. These rotations are denoted by 0, 1, 2 and 3. In most cases, 0 may be omitted. To describe the beginning and the ending of a branch, the symbols [and] are used. For example: $XABX$ describes an organism with two modules which are connected with their A respectively B side to each other. $X[ABX][BCX]$ describes a module to which two other modules are connected.

RFL words can be easily modified, e.g the connection between two modules can be altered or a sub-organism can easily be extracted from or attached to an RFL word. Hence, these words are ideal as genomes for individuals in an Evolutionary Algorithm [9]. In the organism evolution task different mutation and crossover operators are applied on these RFL words to create a new generation. For mutating an organism, the spatial relationship between two organisms is changed, a module or a branch is removed from the organism or a new module is attached to the organism. The crossover operator takes two branches from two organisms and attaches them together to create a new organism. While applying these operators it is necessary to ensure that the resulting genome describes a valid organism structure, e.g. that two modules are not connected to the same side of the same module. Therefore, a parser (which is based on the RFL grammar) is used to check this structural integrity. A second test is based on the geometry of the organism and is used to ensure that the modules in this organism are not colliding with each other.

To evaluate the fitness of the evolved structures, its suitability for a given high-level task needs to be estimated. The fitness has to consider a cost of reconfiguration into the new structure, which is computed in the reconfiguration planner [1]. To estimate the suitability of the candidate structure for the given high-level task, simple motion primitives are first learned and then used in a motion planning.

2.2 Locomotion Learning

The locomotion learning component has the task to develop different motion behaviors for a given organism using a physical simulation. Motion of the modular robots can be realized using CPGs. By finding parameters of the CPGs, various motion primitives can be prepared. Depending on the robots structure and a selected CPG, many parameters need to be tuned, which can be solved using an evolutionary approach. This requires to define fitness function for each of the motion primitives. As the primitives being learned are further utilized in a motion planner, they can be relatively simple, i.e. they should provide motion of a robot in its vicinity, For example, to achieve 'move-forward' behavior, the fitness can be computed using traveled distance. If the organism needs to rotate, the fitness is based on the angle of the rotation. To learn climbing a stair, the fitness function could count the number of steps the organism can climb.

As has been shown in our previous works [10,16], Particle Swarm Optimization (PSO) can be used to find the parameters in a short time. In the PSO approach, each particle represents the vector of CPG's parameters. Fitness of the particles is evaluated using the physical simulation, which simulates motion of the robot driven by the selected CPG. As the fitness evaluation may be time consuming, an extension of PSO called fPSO [4], that evaluates the particles less frequently, can be used. In the fPSO, the fitness is estimated together with a reliability value. If this value drops below a certain threshold, the particle is fully evaluated in the simulation. As the estimations are much faster than an evaluation in simulation, fPSO finds optima in less time than the standard PSO algorithm.

2.3 Motion Planning

The task of the motion planning module is to combine the motion primitives learned by the above described approach to achieve the high-level goal. Motion planning for modular robots can be solved using sampling-based methods such as with Rapidly Exploring Random Trees (RRT). The RRT algorithm iteratively builds a tree of feasible configurations, which is rooted in the initial configuration. Each configuration contains 3D position and rotation of a pivot module and angles between the connected modules. When the tree approaches the goal configuration, the resulting path can be found in the tree. To find plans for modular robots equipped with the motion primitives, we have proposed the RRT-MP (Rapidly Exploring Random Tree with Motion Primitives) [16] algorithm. Here, the primitives are considered as atomic actions, which reduces complexity of the planning task, as the planner does not need to derive the low-level control signals for the actuators. Fitness of an organism can be computed e.g. according to length of the plan or it can be based on the consumed energy.

2.4 On-Board Motion Planning

The slowest part of the RRT-MP method is the physical simulation, which cannot be run on the on-board computer. To enable fast on-board motion planning with low computational and memory demands, the concept of of Simplified Motion Model (SMM) was proposed [17]. The SMM describes only final rotation and translation of the robot without modeling intermediate states during the motion. This approximation is useful, as the robot moves using short primitives, therefore the details about the motion can be avoided. The SMM contains only

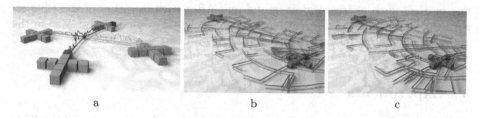

a   b   c

Fig. 2. Difference between full motion model (jerky trajectories) and SMM (straight lines) (a). The SMM assumes, that robot moves on a straight line when controlled by the primitives (solid straight lines). This assumption is satisfied when the primitives are applied for a short time. Examples of motion plans generated using SMM (b,c).

few parameters, that are estimated during the on-board locomotion adaption. For each motion primitive, a single SMM is created. The evaluation of SMM is very fast and it allows to create plans with hundreds of nodes even on slow computers.

2.5   On-Board Locomotion Verification and Adaptation

Due to possible imprecision of the physical simulation (reality gap), the motion primitives provided by the Locomotion learning component may lead to different results when applied on a real robot. This could complicate reaching of the desired goal, as the robot will not follow the plan exactly. Therefore, the primitives derived in the physical simulation need to be verified on the real robot. This requires to execute each primitive on the robot and measure parameters of the SMM based on the change of robot's state. The motion plans generated on-board using the SMM are thus more realistic than the plans provided by the physical simulation.

However, even utilization of SMM with real robot's parameters cannot ensure, that the execution of the plan will lead to exactly same states as is predicted by the planner. This can be caused by imprecision of commands execution or due to a slippage between the robot and the terrain. Small deviations from the plan are not problematic, as they can be compensated by fast re-planning. However, such a compensation might not be enough when behavior of the robot significantly differs from the expected behavior. In such a case, the problematic motion primitives should be optimized directly on the real robot.

Such an optimization can be realized similarly to the optimization described in Section 2.2. The task is to find parameters of a selected CPG to control the robot in a desired way. For the optimization, the PSO method can be utilized. Contrary to the Locomotion learning, where the fitness is computed using physical simulation, here, the fitness is based on real motions of the robot. Depending on the desired primitive, the fitness can be computed using global localization (e.g. as a distances traveled by the robot) or it can be computed using the internal sensors (e.g. angles of the joints). The former case is useful for the rough primitives (e.g. 'move-forward' or 'walk-back'), while latter case can be used for fine motions such as 'rise-leg' or 'stand-up'. After each iteration of the PSO algorithm, new particles representing the primitives are evaluated and used in the on-board planner to generate a new plan. The on-board adaptation is terminated when the on-board planner provides a feasible plan to reach the goal.

3 Experiments

This section shows examples of current state of selected components of the ELO framework. Due to space limit, we only show achieved goals and we refer to our publications for technical details. The simulation part of the ELO is realized by Robot3D simulator [11], which simulates CoSMO (Collective Self-Reconfigurable Robot Organism) modular robots [6]. CoSMO consists of cube shaped modules equipped with four docking mechanisms. They exhibit a powerful main hinge capable of lifting up to four other modules. The modules also possess a 2D drive with which they can move by their own. Furthermore, the robots can exchange energy and can communicate via Ethernet with each other while connected. They are equipped with a small PC with Blackfin BF561 processor, 30 MB of RAM with μCLinux.

3.1 Organism Evolution

In the experiments each individual had 100 seconds to move. After that time its fitness has been calculated. For a new generation, the best 10% are taken unchanged as elitists from the previous generation, 20% of the individuals are created by cross-over and the rest is mutated. For mutation, the probability to add one module is 40%, to remove a module is 20%, to rotate a connection is 30% and to swap two branches on the same module is set to 30%. In former experiments this setup was used for different selection strategies (i.e. Rank Selection vs. Fitness Proportionate (FP)), on different terrain and with different module behavior rules [9]. However, these experiments were realized for only 30 generations.

Though, good results have already been achieved after that time, it was not clear, how many generations were required to find almost optimal solutions (due to the huge search space, an optimal solution cannot be guaranteed). Therefore, one of those experiments has been repeated with 200 generations and 20 experiments. In these experiments FP has been used as selection strategy, the organisms had to move over uneven terrain, where the obstacles had the size of a robot module and the fitness was measured by traveled distance. Furthermore, the evolution was restrained by one rule: when attaching a new module to an organism (i.e. to the parent module, which is part of that organism), the phase of the module was set to $\phi_{child} = \phi_{parent} + 0.25$. One goal of this experiment was to figure out, if with this rule caterpillar like organism are evolved.

Figure 4 shows the fitness of the best solution found so far of those experiments. There, the results of the experiments have been summarized as three curves, which describe the median, the lower and the upper quartile. The highest maximum fitness in an experiment was 700 cm, the lowest was 410 cm, which was reached by most of the experiments after 60 generations. Figure 3 shows the four best organisms in all these experiments. Most of those evolved organisms exhibit caterpillar like structures with additional modules at their sides. These modules prevent the organism from falling aside which would happen with a pure caterpillar organism. Another result of this experiment is, that it is likely that the evolution sticks in a local minimum, which can be prevented by raising the mutation rate or running several evolution runs in parallel.

Fig. 3. Examples of evolved organisms

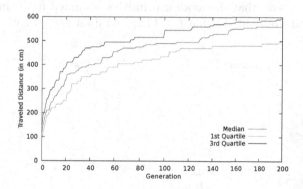

Fig. 4. Fitness values (traveled distance after 100s) of the best solutions found so far

3.2 On-Board Motion Planning and Motion Adaptation

The RRT-MP planner utilizing the SMM model was implemented for the Blackfin CPU. Construction of a motion plan between arbitrary positions in an arena of size 4x5 m takes $\sim$ 1 s. Comparing to the time required to execute the plan (order of minutes), the on-board planning is fast enough. Example of a generated plan and screen shot from the navigation are depicted on Fig. 5. The video record is available at: http://www.youtube.com/watch?v=fCy3grSRC9k.

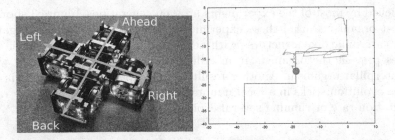

Fig. 5. The Cross organism described by string $X[AAX][BAX][CAX][DAX]$ (left). The plan (red lines) with actual position of the robot (blue circle) and with its real performance (green curve) (right).

During the on-board motion adaptation, the desired motions can be learned from scratch (particles in the PSO algorithm are initialized by random values) or the best parameters obtained in the simulations can be used for the initialization. The importance of the proper initialization has been verified for the snake-like robot with three modules. The results are shown on Fig. 6. As can be seen, the random initialization (Fig. 6b) led to longer optimization with final value $f \doteq 13$ cm after 140 iterations, while the adaptation initialized with results obtained in the simulation provided $f \doteq 24$ cm in 40th iteration (Fig. 6c). In the 40th iteration, the randomly initialized solution was only $f = 10$ cm. The adaptation with properly initialized particles is thus significantly faster. The graphs also show, that the motion primitive obtained from simulation was further improved from initial value $f = 17$ cm to final $f = 24$ cm.

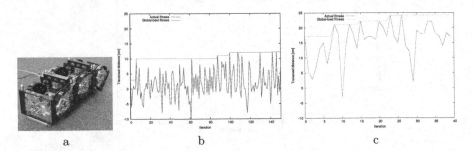

a   b   c

Fig. 6. A simple snake-like robot (the RFL string is $XACXACX$) (a) The progress of fitness with randomly initialized particles (b) and with particles initialized with solutions provided by the simulation (c)

4   Conclusion and Future Work

The experiments have shown, that both simulated as well as on-board parts of the ELO framework can adapt structure and behavior of the robots. In the future work, the remaining components have to be integrated into the framework and then, the whole system will be tested on real robots.

References

1. Bihlmaier, A., Winkler, L., Wörn, H.: Automated Planning as a New Approach for the Self-Reconfiguration of Mobile Modular Robots. In: Robot Motion and Control (RoMoCo) (2013)
2. Blum, C., Roli, A.: Metaheuristics in combinatorial optimization: Overview and conceptual comparison. ACM Computing Surveys (CSUR) 35(3), 268–308 (2003)
3. Černý, J., Kubalík, J.: Co-evolutionary Approach to Design of Robotic Gait. In: Applications of Evolutionary Computation (2013)
4. Cui, Z.H., Zeng, J.C., Sun, G.J.: A fast particle swarm optimization. International Journal of Innovative Computing, Information and Control 2(6), 1365–1380 (2006)
5. Ijspeert, A.J.: Central pattern generators for locomotion control in animals and robots: A review. Neural Networks 21(4), 642–653 (2008)
6. Liedke, J., Matthias, R., Winkler, L., Wörn, H.: The Collective Self-Reconfigurable Modular Organism (CoSMO). In: Proceedings of IEEE/ASME International Conference on Advanced Intelligent Mechatronics (AIM 2013) (2013)
7. Landis, G.A.: Robots and humans: synergy in planetary exploration. Acta Astronautica 55(12), 985–990 (2004)
8. Winkler, L., Kettler, A., Szymanski, M., Wörn, H.: The Robot Formation Language - A Formal Descriptions of Formations for Collective Robots. In: Proceedings of IEEE Symposium on Swarm Intelligence 2011 (SIS 2011), pp. 102–109 (2011)
9. Winkler, L., Wörn, H., Friebel, A.: A Distance and Diversity Measure for Improving the Evolutionary Process of Modular Robot Organisms. In: Proceedings of IEEE Int. Conf. on Robotics and Biomimetics, ROBIO (2011)
10. Winkler, L., Neumann, S., Wörn, H.: A Framework for the Automatic Generation of Self-Reconfigurable Robot Organisms and the Optimization of the Gait for these Organisms. In: Proceedings of the IEEE Conference on Control, Systems & Industrial Informatics(ICCSII 2013) (2013)
11. Winkler, L., Vonasek, V., Wörn, H., Preucil, L.: Robot3D - A Simulator for Mobile Modular Self-Reconfigurable Robots. In: IEEE Conference on Multisensor Fusion and Integration for Intelligent Systems (MFI) (2012)
12. Marbach, D., Ijspeert, A.J.: Online optimization of modular robot locomotion. In: Proceedings of the IEEE International Conference on Mechatronics and Automation, ICMA (2005)
13. Moubarak, P., Ben-Tzvi, P.: Modular and reconfigurable mobile robotics. Robotics and Autonomous Systems 60(12), 1648–1663 (2012)
14. Pouya, S., Aydin, E., Möckel, R., Ijspeert, A.J.: Locomotion gait optimization for modular robots; coevolving morphology and control. Procedia Computer Science 7 (2011)
15. Sims, K.: Evolving virtual creatures. In: Proceedings of the 21st Annual Conference on Computer Graphics and Interactive Techniques, pp. 15–22. ACM (1994)
16. Vonásek, V., Saska, M., Košnar, K., Přeučil, L.: Global motion planning for modular robots with local motion primitives. In: ICRA (2013)
17. Vonásek, V., Winkler, L., Liedke, J., Saska, M., Košnar, K., Přeučil, L.: Fast onboard motion planning for modular robots. In: ICRA (accepted, 2014)

A Bacterial-Based Algorithm
to Simulate Complex Adaptive Systems

Diego Gonzalez-Rodriguez[1] and Jose Rodolfo Hernandez-Carrion[2]

[1] Carlos III University of Madrid, Spain
xmunch@xmunch.com
[2] University of Valencia, Spain
rodolfo.hernandez@uv.es

Abstract. Bacteria have demonstrated an amazing capacity to overcome environmental changes by collective adaptation through genetic exchanges. Using a distributed communication system and sharing individual strategies, bacteria propagate mutations as innovations that allow them to survive in different environments. In this paper we present an agent-based model which is inspired by bacterial conjugation of DNA plasmids. In our approach, agents with bounded rationality interact in a common environment guided by local rules, leading to Complex Adaptive Systems that are named 'artificial societies'. We have demonstrated that in a model based on free interactions among autonomous agents, optimal results emerge by incrementing heterogeneity levels and decentralizing communication structures, leading to a global adaptation of the system. This organic approach to model peer-to-peer dynamics in Complex Adaptive Systems is what we have named 'bacterial-based algorithms' because agents exchange strategic information in the same way that bacteria use conjugation and share genome.

Keywords: Complexity, Artificial Society, Bacterial-based Algorithms, P2P Society, Complex Adaptive Systems, CAS.

1 Introduction

Bacteria have demonstrated an amazing capacity to overcome environmental changes by collective adaptation through genetic exchanges. By using a distributed communication system and sharing individual strategies, bacteria propagate mutations as innovations that allow them to survive in different scenarios [1,2,3,4,5]. Resilience is the capacity of a system to absorb changes in an environment, adapting its properties to disturbance but retaining its basic structure [6]. In this paper we will introduce our agents-based approach to model resilience in artificial societies. Even though similar approaches have been previously reported, such as MBFOA [7], MGA [8], OBBC [9] or BEA [10], we have developed a proof-of-concept inspired by bacterial conjugation that allows us to show how, in artificial societies based on interactions among agents with bounded rationality, optimal results emerge by incrementing heterogeneity levels and decentralizing communication structures [11]. Bacterial conjugation is a distributed communication system used by bacteria to exchange strategies of survival,

A.P. del Pobil et al. (Eds.): SAB 2014, LNAI 8575, pp. 250–259, 2014.
© Springer International Publishing Switzerland 2014

implemented on genetic code. It matches the kind of dynamics we want to model because of several reasons. First of all, we conceive both natural and artificial societies as Complex Adaptive Systems (CAS) [12] which evolution depends on interactions among autonomous agents. Secondly, we sustain that collective adaptation is related to decentralized communications [13], relying on information exchanges by using P2P networks to share codified blocks of information. Third, heterogeneity in population and variation (or mutation) of strategies is also a factor of evolution even though communication and P2P dynamics play an important role.

2   Model

2.1   Definition

Following an agent-based modeling approach, we want to simulate and analyze the impact of both peer-to-peer connections and heterogeneity on strategies optimization, that is, on distributed generation of knowledge. In agent-based modeling, agents with bounded rationality interact in a common environment guided by local rules, leading to Complex Adaptive Systems that are named 'artificial societies' [14,15]. These simplified models of biological societies grow from the bottom up in computational environments and can be used as laboratories to test some hypotheses. In our case, we will use a special type of agent-based model, a bacterial-based algorithm that is inspired by bacterial conjugation and that matches with our purpose of simulating emergence of collective intelligence. In this model, we have a set A with N agents (a_i). Each agent owns a genome that contains a specific strategy (s_i) to optimize a function. Depending on an agent's strategy, its knowledge level will be greater or lower. Then if an agent is able to optimize a given function in order to get a result with 70% of accuracy by using its own strategy, its knowledge level will be set to 70 and so on. Knowledge levels determine an agent's position in a social structure. So agents with a more successful genome will dominate the cultural life of society.

During simulation agents move randomly through a bi-dimensional grid. When two agents have the same coordinates (x,y) they meet to each other and compare their knowledge levels. After that, the one with a lower knowledge (a_a) tries to get a copy of genome from the more successful (a_b). If the owner of the best strategy (a_b) does not share its strategic knowledge we will say that conjugative machinery to send plasmids is inhibited. Otherwise a_b will offer a plasmid with a copy of his genome to agents in the same coordinates and lower knowledge. Even though if the owner (a_b) allows the other agent (a_a) to get a copy of its genome and then improve its strategic knowledge, a_b can impose two restriction policies to that copy:

- *Inhibit Reproduction:* The receiver of a plasmid (a_a) is allowed to use the strategy that is contained in the copy but it does not own the intellectual property of that strategy. Then plasmid cannot be sent to others once it is received. In this case the first owner (a_b) is the only one with reproduction rights on that strategy.

- *Inhibit Mutation:* The receiver (a_a) can use the strategy but cannot modify it. Genome only can be used as a unit of privative software or as a behavioral dogma, following the exact strategy proposed by first owner (a_b). Otherwise, if mutation is not inhibited, strategies may be modified or mixed with other ones by the receiver (a_a).

With this model we want to show that centralized and homogeneous societies, those with greater number of agents that follow restrictive behaviors, lead to lower levels of knowledge and higher levels of inequality than distributed and heterogeneous ones. We will do it by comparing bacterial-based societies with different configurations and observing how inhibiting plasmid conjugation, reproduction or mutation modifies the statistical results. Only in a "P2P Society", by sharing individual information among agents without communication constraints, optimal strategies and social development are achieved.

2.2   Agent Genome

As we have explained above, in our model each agent (a_i) of the agents set A has its own strategy (s_i) coded as a part of its genome. Considering a set Sec containing several strategies (s_i), its cardinality |Sec| (number of different strategies) will be equal or bigger than unity and equal or smaller than cardinality of A. We will denote it as:

$$\forall\ a_i \in A\ \exists\ s_i \in Sec : 1 \leq |Sec| \leq |A| \tag{1}$$

If by default the value of |Sec| was one, simulation would start in a completely homogeneous society. If this value was near to |A| (number of agents) it would be a heterogeneous society.

Agent genome has a segment denominated "S" which contains a coded strategy (s_i) of the set Sec. Genome also can include another three sequences (P, R and O) which are related to the three constraints that we have described:

1. Inhibit original plasmid conjugation (P)
2. Inhibit copy reproduction (R)
3. Inhibit code mutation (O)

Depending of the presence of each one of these three segments, agents behavior will catalyze or constraint the arrival of the optimal scenario, the one in which knowledge is generated in distributed societies with low inequality among agents.

If there is P then the genome will not be released by conjugation, that is, that strategy will be private. So only the absence of P enables the first owner of the genome to act as a donor; that is, to send a copy of genome as a plasmid to another agent by using conjugation. If possibility of that P occurs is high then the society will follow a centralized paradigm, that is, just some nodes will be able to send information. P implies that original genome will be never copied and sent to anybody else. Then, strategies of nodes without P and a successful strategy coded on S will dominate the culture.

If there is R this means that receivers of a copy of a genome are not allowed to resend the replicated plasmid to another agent. It avoids decentralized propagation of strategies, considering that the original owners of a genome are the only ones which can distribute copies. High possibility of R implies a constraint to diffusion of received strategies, because receiver will be able to use the successful strategy but will not be allowed to propagate them and share its knowledge with others.

Decentralization is inversely related to these two parameters. High P and R rates imply centralized societies without P2P communication and without reproduction rights. Oppositely, low P and R rates lead to P2P exchanges of information without limits of copies.

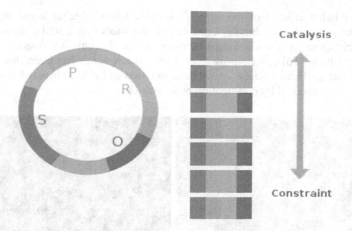

Fig. 1. Social behavior of agents depending on their genome

During a conjugation process, when one agent sends a plasmid to another, the S sequence (which contains a copy of the strategy of the donor) could be modified. This means that mutation of any strategy is allowed by default. But mutation can be inhibited if O is present in the genome. O sequence implies that a plasmid cannot be modified. So only low levels of O presence lead to an open society in which variation of bad strategies in short time is guarantee. However, high presence of O in the population genome implies that strategies are closed and invariant. So once an agent follows a specific strategy it cannot change this until it receives another genome from a more successful agent.

Differentiation of strategies is another important variable in this model. Cardinality of Sec is related to the number of different strategies by default, so if |Sec| is near to |A| and there is a low presence of O segments in population genome then it implies more heterogeneity.

2.3   Local Rules and Complex Dynamics

The main characteristic of complex phenomena is that it emerges from local interactions among simple agents which have not global information about the whole system. In complex science, global dynamics are considered a result of local rules. Following that approach, our agents behave according to their own internal states by following single algorithmic rules.

Each agent's decision takes into account two values, its own knowledge and neighbors' knowledge. Each iteration agents compare both values by using their internal evaluator, which is the function that constitutes their bounded rationality. There is a different internal evaluator to every single agent, assuming variability of cognitive skills within a population. After positive evaluation, if it is worth to learn a new strategy according to that internal criteria (and if any inhibitor impede it), conjugation between two agents occurs. When an agent receives a new genome it replaces the previous one. This replacement can be complete or not, depending of mutation inhibition. In this version of our model, mutation implies a recombination of 50% of both genomes. After replacement of genome, the receiver tests the new strategy by using it to optimize a fixed selection function. Accuracy of function optimization determines the new knowledge level of the agent. The more knowledge an agent achieves, the more social reputation it obtains. Considering our model as a social network we can define each agent as a node linked to other nodes through information exchanges. Network analysis [16] can help us to evaluate which agent has been dominating the culture of our artificial society, so we have decided to build a directed graph with all the connections created by conjugation processes (Fig. 2).

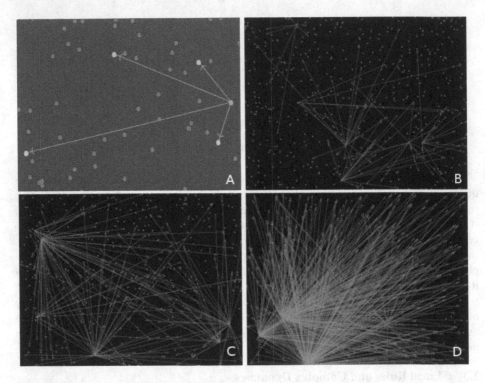

Fig. 2. Growing social structures. Four agents have decided to learn from a fifth one after comparing their knowledge levels. These conjugation processes have increased the node out-degree to 4. (B, C, D) Emergence of centralized social network with high presence of O, R and P segments in genome.

3   Experimental Results

3.1   Simulation Conditions

In order to analyze the influence of specific variations on initial conditions, we have simulated $|Z|^3$ different environments considering the set $Z = \{0,1\}$. The focus of this study is how probabilistic distribution of Boolean genes (P, R, O) affects social structure, that is, the role of cultural constraints. We have fixed $|Sec| \sim |A|$ and recombination to 0.5 when mutation is allowed. For any of those $|Z|^3$ setup configurations, we have executed our model during 10^4 iterations. Repeating each one of these experiments with random populations between 10^3 and 10^4 agents we have observed common patterns that are related to P, R and O presence in population genome. We have tested the emergence of different global configurations, from centralized societies with low levels and unequal distribution of knowledge to "P2P societies" in which heterogeneity and decentralization lead to collective success. We have used NetLogo 5.0.4 to implement our model and Java 6 to extend it.

We have defined a selection function with ten variables. Every iteration agents replace each one of those variables with the values of the S segment. If these ten genes optimize the function and the result is equal or greater than 70, we consider that the owner of that Si segment has a good level of knowledge. Results between 50 and 70 means a medium level of knowledge and lower than 50 a bad one.

As we can see (Fig. 3) our artificial societies are Complex Adaptive Systems that evolves through agent interactions. The adaptive behavior of the system as a whole consists in increasing the distribution of good strategies and the elimination of bad ones. But the speed of that propagation is mainly related to P presence, that is, with the number of agents that are allowed to share strategies.

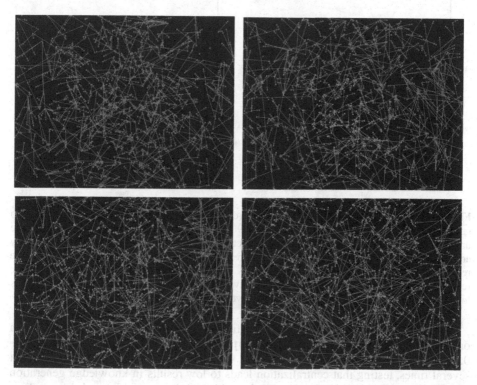

Fig. 3. Propagation of strategies. Low P and R rates (P ~ 0.19, R ~ 0.24) in a population with 10^3 agents leading to decentralization and vertical propagation of successful strategies. Red agents have knowledge levels lower than 70, otherwise they are colored with green.

3.2   Emergence of Equality in Distribution of Knowledge

After reproducing several scenarios with random initial knowledge-level distributions, we have observed that worse results are achieved in centralized and homogeneous societies; for example, a society with presence of O and R in the whole of population genome. O presence means that we will not see strategy modifications, that is, the maximum level of knowledge will be static during the 10^4 iterations. Then the best strategy will depend only on initial configuration, when random S_i segments are generated; this simulation will only take into account the propagation of those initial strategies. R implies that there is not any reproduction of received genome, so only the original owner will be able to propagate it.

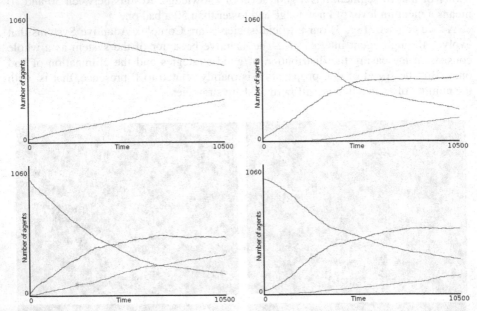

Fig. 4. Evolution of knowledge levels. These results show how medium knowledge tends to grow slowly in centralized societies with P ~ 0.90 and R ~ 0.83. The number of agents per time unit that use strategies that satisfy a given selection function with less than 50 % of accuracy are plotted in red, those with more than 70% are in green, and others are in blue. Each picture reproduces a 103 agents simulation that has been executed during 104 iterations. Blue represents agents with strategic knowledge between 50 and 70, red means knowledge levels lower than 50 and green implies a knowledge level higher than 70.

We have studied how P presence modifies the global behavior of this system. In order to compare two variations of that artificial society, one with P probability ~ 0.90 (Fig. 4) and other with P probability ~ 0.19, we have repeated the experiment several times, testing that centralization leads to low results in knowledge generation (Fig. 5). We have also simulated scenarios with high heterogeneity and decentralization levels by reducing P, R and O probabilities and we have seen that with a whole elimination of O sequences (O probability ~ 0), that is, activating mutation of strategies, generation of knowledge not only is faster but also richer in variety. As picture 6 shows, different focus of improvement are found in population when diversity occurs. In this heterogeneous scenario, good strategies come from different agents with different initial locations. Agents evolve in creative ways because of modification of strategies is allowed and innovative knowledge is propagated because of decentralization, leading to an egalitarian and optimal artificial society.

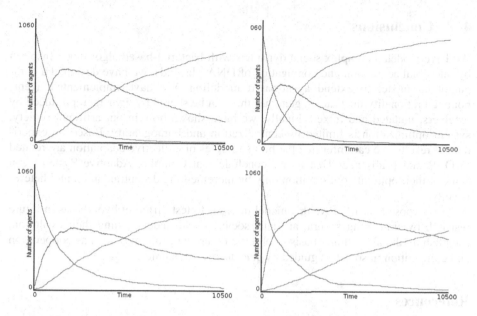

Fig. 5. In these four simulations P probability ~ 0.19 rather than P probability ~ 0.90 (Fig. 4). This change produces an acceleration of knowledge propagation. Bad strategies are removed early and competition is between medium and good strategies. The best options reach almost the whole population in only 10^4 iterations. The colors applied are the same as in Fig. 4.

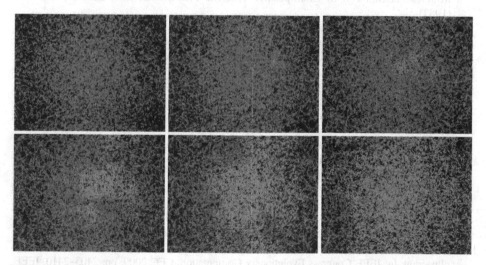

Fig. 6. Distributed production of knowledge in a "P2P Society". Low P, O and R rates (P ~ 0.03, R ~ 0.14, O ~ 0.27) in a population with 10^4 agents during 10^3 iterations. This Complex Adaptive System evolves faster because of heterogeneity and connectivity. Through peer-to-peer exchanges, reproduction and modification rights, bad strategies (red) are replaced or mixed with medium strategies (blue) that are recombined and distributed, leading to this map of successful strategies (green). Each picture represents a snapshot of the same simulation in time.

4   Conclusions

We have modeled complex social dynamics with bacterial-based algorithms. Inspired by microbial adaptation and conjugation of DNA plasmids, we have designed a computational model to extend agent-based modeling. We have implemented agent-bounded rationality in strategic genomes that can be shared by owners, reproduced by receivers, mutated and mixed. Finally, we have shown how in our artificial society, system optimization is limited by centralization and homogeneity. Based on experimental results, we can infer that the best strategies of collective adaptation are related to O, R and P absence. That is, we conclude that Complex Adaptive Systems can achieve their optimal configuration only by incrementing decentralization and heterogeneity.

Our purpose is to improve this model in order to test different hypotheses in future research by simulating several artificial societies and understanding their evolution, establishing the algorithmic basis to observe emergent properties such as cooperation and competition in societies guided by *peer-to-peer* dynamics.

References

[1] Smith, P.: Conjugation-a bacterially inspired form of genetic recombination. In: Pap. Genet. Program. 1996 Conf., pp. 1–8 (1996)

[2] Trieu-Cuot, P., Carlier, C., Martin, P., Courvalin, P.: Plasmid transfer by conjugation from Escherichia coli to Gram-positive bacteria. FEMS Microbiol. Lett. 48, 289–294 (1987)

[3] Llosa, M., Gomis-Rüth, F.X., Coll, M., de la Cruz Fd, F.: Bacterial conjugation: a two-step mechanism for DNA transport. Mol. Microbiol. 45, 1–8 (2002)

[4] Thomas, C.M., Nielsen, K.M.: Mechanisms of, and barriers to, horizontal gene transfer between bacteria. Nat. Rev. Microbiol. 3, 711–721 (2005)

[5] Waters, V.L.: Conjugation between bacterial and mammalian cells. Nat. Genet. 29, 375–376 (2001)

[6] Deffuant, G., Gilbert, N.: Viability and Resilience of Complex Systems. Springer, Heidelberg (2011)

[7] Mezura-Montes, E., Hernández-Ocaña, B.: Modified Bacterial Foraging Optimization for Engineering Design. In: Intelligent engineering systems through artificial neural networks, ASME Press (2009)

[8] Harvey, I.: The microbial genetic algorithm. In: Kampis, G., Karsai, I., Szathmáry, E. (eds.) ECAL 2009, Part II. LNCS, vol. 5778, pp. 126–133. Springer, Heidelberg (2011)

[9] Muller, S.D., Marchetto, J., Airaghi, S., Kournoutsakos, P.: Optimization based on bacterial chemotaxis. IEEE Trans. Evol. Comput. 6(1), 16–29 (2002)

[10] Das, S., Chowdhury, A., Abraham, A.: A bacterial evolutionary algorithm for automatic data clustering. In: IEEE Congress Evolutionary Computation, CEC 2009, pp. 2403–2410. IEEE Press, Trondheim (2009)

[11] Heylighen, F.: The growth of structural and functional complexity during evolution. Evol. Complex., 1–18 (1999)

[12] Lansing, J.S.: Complex Adaptive Systems. Annu. Rev. Anthropol. 32, 183–204 (2003)

[13] Baran, P.: On distributed communications: Introduction to distributed communications networks. Vol. IXI RAND Corp. Res. Doc. 12, 51 (1964)

[14] Epstein, J.M., Axtell, R.: Growing artificial societies: social science from the bottom up. Brookings Institution Press, Cambridge (1996)
[15] Meyer, J.A.: Artificial Life and the Animat Approach to Artificial Intelligence. Artificial intelligence, 325–354 (1996)
[16] De Lejarza, I.M., Hernández-Carrión, J.R.: Ranking-based Ties' Social Networks. An illustration based on a system of Fashion Capital Cities in the world. Bus. Syst. Rev. 1(1) (2012)

Online Evolution of Deep Convolutional Network for Vision-Based Reinforcement Learning

Jan Koutník, Jürgen Schmidhuber, and Faustino Gomez

IDSIA, USI-SUPSI
Galleria 2
Manno-Lugano, CH 6928
{hkou,juergen,tino}@idsia.ch

Abstract. Dealing with high-dimensional input spaces, like visual input, is a challenging task for reinforcement learning (RL). Neuroevolution (NE), used for continuous RL problems, has to either reduce the problem dimensionality by (1) compressing the representation of the neural network controllers or (2) employing a pre-processor (*compressor*) that transforms the high-dimensional raw inputs into low-dimensional features. In this paper we extend the approach in [16]. The Max-Pooling Convolutional Neural Network (MPCNN) compressor is evolved online, maximizing the distances between normalized feature vectors computed from the images collected by the *recurrent neural network* (RNN) controllers during their evaluation in the environment. These two interleaved evolutionary searches are used to find MPCNN compressors and RNN controllers that drive a race car in the TORCS racing simulator using only visual input.

Keywords: deep learning, neuroevolution, vision-based TORCS, reinforcement learning, computer games.

1 Introduction

Most approaches to scaling neuroevolution to tasks that require large networks, such as those processing video input, have focused on indirect encodings where relatively small neural network descriptions are transformed via a complex mapping into networks of arbitrary size [4, 7, 10, 13, 15, 23].

A different approach to dealing with high-dimensional input which has been studied in the context of single-agent RL (i.e. TD [25], policy gradients [24], etc.), is to combine action learning with an unsupervised learning (UL) preprocessor or "compressor" which provides a lower-dimensional feature vector that the agent receives as input instead of the raw observation [5, 8, 12, 17, 19–21]. The UL compressor is trained on the high-dimensional observations generated by the learning agent's actions, that the agent then uses as a state representation to learn a value function.

In [3], the first combination of UL and evolutionary reinforcement learning was introduced where a single UL module is trained on data generated by

A.P. del Pobil et al. (Eds.): SAB 2014, LNAI 8575, pp. 260–269, 2014.
© Springer International Publishing Switzerland 2014

entire population as it interacts with environment (which would normally be discarded) to build a representation that allows evolution to search in a relatively low-dimensional feature space. This approach attacks the problem of high-dimensionality from the opposite direction compared to indirect encoding: instead of compressing large networks into short genomes, the inputs are compressed so that smaller networks can be used.

In [16], we scaled up this Unsupervised Learning – Evolutionary Reinforcement Learning (UL-ERL) approach to the challenging reinforcement learning problem of driving a car in the TORCS simulator using vision from the driver's perspective as input. The high-dimensional images were compressed down to just three features by a Max-Pooling Convolutional Neural Network (MPCNN; [2,22]) that allowed an extremely small (only 33 weights) recurrent neural network controller to be evolved to drive the car successfully. The MPCNN was itself trained separately off-line using images collected previously while driving the car manually around the training track.

In this paper, the feature learning and control learning are interleaved as in [3]. Both the MPCNN, acting as the sensory preprocessor (compressor), and the recurrent neural network controllers are evolved simultaneously in separate populations, with the images used to train the MPCNNs being taken from the driving trials of the evolving controllers rather than being collected manually *a priori*.

The next section describes the MPCNN architecture that is used to compress the high-dimensional vision inputs. Section 3 covers our method—the UL-ERL framework applied to visual TORCS race car driving domain. Section 4 presents the experiments in the TORCS race car driving, which are discussed in section 5.

2   Max-Pooling Convolutional Neural Networks

Convolution Neural Networks [6, 18] are deep hierarchical networks that have recently become the state-of-the-art in image classification due to the advent of fast implementations on graphics card multiprocessors (GPUs) [1]. CNNs have two parts: (1) a deep feature detector consisting of alternating *convolutional* and *down-sampling* layers, and (2) a classifier that receives the output of the final layer of the feature detector.

Each convolutional layer ℓ, has a bank of $m^\ell \times n^\ell$ filters, F^ℓ, where m^ℓ is the number input maps (images), I^ℓ, to the layer, and n^ℓ is the number of output maps (inputs to the next layer). The i-th output map is computed by:

$$I_i^{\ell+1} = \sigma \left(\sum_{j=1}^{m^\ell} I_j^\ell * F_{ij}^\ell \right), \quad i = 1..n^\ell, \ell = 1, 3, 5...,$$

where $*$ is the convolution operator, F_{ij}^ℓ is the i-th filter for the j-th map and σ is a non-linear squashing function (e.g. sigmoid). Note that ℓ is always odd because of the subsampling layers between each of the convolutional layers.

The downsampling layers reduce resolution of each map. Each map is partitioned into non-overlapping blocks and a value from each block is used in the output map. The *max-pooling* operation used here subsamples the map by simply taking the maximum value in the block as the output, making these networks Max-Pooling CNNs [2, 22].

The stacked alternating layers transform the input into progressively lower dimensional abstract representations that are then classified, typically using a standard feed-forward neural network that has an output neuron for each class. The entire network is usually trained using a large training set of class-labeled images via backpropagation [18]. Figure 2 illustrates the particular MPCNN architecture used in this paper. It should be clear from the figure that each convolution layer is just a matrix product where the matrix entries are filters and convolution is used instead of multiplication.

3   Method: Online MPC-RNN

The Online MPC-RNN method for evolving the controller and the compressor at the same time is overviewed in figure 1. The controller is evolved in the usual way (i.e. neuroevolution; [26]), but instead of accessing the observations directly, it receives feature vectors of much lower dimensionality provided by the unsupervised compressor, which is also evolved.

The compressor is trained on observations (images) generated by the actions taken by candidate controllers as they interact with the environment. Here, unlike in [16] where the compressor was pre-trained off-line, the loop is closed by simultaneously evolving the compressor using the latest observations (images) of the environment that are provoked by the actions taken by the evolving controllers.

For the compressor, a deep *max-pooling convolutional neural network* (MPCNN) is used. These networks are normally trained to perform image classification through supervised learning using enormous training sets. Of course, this requires *a priori* knowledge of what constitutes a class. In a general RL setting, we may not know how the space of images should be partitioned. For example, how many classes should there be for images perceived from the first-person perspective while driving the TORCS car? We could study the domain in detail to construct a training set that could then be used to train the MPCNN with backpropagation. However, we do not want the learning system to rely on task-specific domain knowledge, so, instead, the MPCNN is *evolved* without using a labeled training set. A set of k images is collected from the environment, and then MPCNNs are evolved to maximize the fitness:

$$f_\mathrm{k} = \min(D) + \mathrm{mean}(D), \tag{1}$$

where D is a list of all Euclidean distances,

$$d_{i,j} = \|\mathbf{f}_i - \mathbf{f}_j\|, \forall i > j,$$

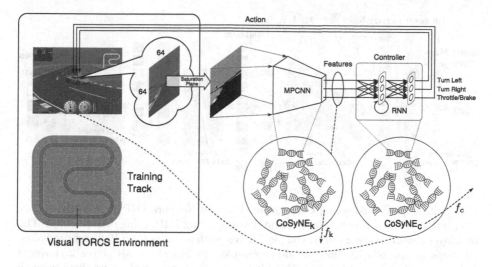

Fig. 1. Overview of the online TORCS controller evolution in the online UL-ERL scheme. At each time-step, a raw 64×64 grayscale (saturation plane) pixel image, taken from the driver's perspective, is transformed to features by the Max-Pooling Convolutional Neural Network (MPCNN) compressor. The features are used by the candidate RNN controller to drive the car by steering, accelerating and braking. Two evolutionary algorithms are interleaved to simultaneously optimize both the controller and compressor. The current implementation uses the CoSyNE algorithm: $CoSyNE_k$ for the MPCNN, $CoSyNE_c$ for the RNN controllers, using the best MPCNN found by $CoSyNE_k$.

between k normalized feature vectors $\{\mathbf{f}_1 \ldots \mathbf{f}_k\}$ generated from k images in the training set by the MPCNN encoded in the genome.

This fitness function forces the evolving MPCNNs to output feature vectors that are spread out in feature space, so that when the final, evolved MPCNN processes images for the evolving controllers, it will provide enough discriminative power to allow them to take correct actions.

4 Visual TORCS Experiments

The goal of the task is to evolve a recurrent neural network controller and MPCNN compressor that can drive the car around a race track.

The visual TORCS environment is based on TORCS version 1.3.1. The simulator had to be modified to provide images as input to the controllers (a detailed description of modifications is provided in [16]). The most important changes involve decrease of the control frequency from 50 Hz to 5 Hz, and removal of the "3-2-1-GO" sequence from the beginning of each race.

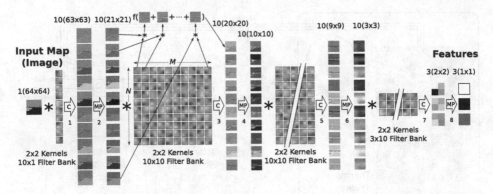

Fig. 2. Example Max-Pooling Convolutional Neural Network (MPCNN) with 8 layers alternating between convolution (C) and downsampling (MP; using max-pooling). The first layer convolves the input 64×64 pixel image with a bank of 10×10 filters producing 10 maps of size 63×63, that are down-sampled to 21×21 by MP layer 2. Layer 3 convolves each of these 10 maps with a filter, sums the results and passes them through the nonlinear function f, producing 10 maps of 20×20 pixels each, and so on until the input image is transformed to just 3 features that are passed to the RNN controller, see Figure 1.

4.1   Setup

The MPCNN compressors and RNN controllers are evolved in a coupled system, alternating every four generations between two separate CoSyNE [9] algorithms, denoted $CoSyNE_k$ for the MPCNNs, and $CoSyNE_c$ for the RNN controllers.

The process starts by first evolving the controllers. In each fitness evaluation, the candidate controller is tested in two trials, one on the track shown in figure 1, and one on its mirror image. A trial consists of placing the car at the starting line and driving it for 25 s of simulated time, resulting in a maximum of 125 time-steps at the 5 Hz control frequency. At each control step a raw 64×64 pixel image (saturation plane only), taken from the driver's perspective is passed through an initially random MPCNN compressor which generates a 3-dimensional feature vector that is fed into a simple recurrent neural network (SRN) with 3 hidden neurons, and 3 output neurons (33 total weights). The first two outputs, o_1, o_2, are averaged, $(o_1 + o_2)/2$, to provide the steering signal (-1 = full left lock, 1 = full right lock), and the third neuron, o_3, controls the brake and throttle (-1 = full brake, 1 = full throttle). All neurons use sigmoidal activation functions.

The fitness of the controllers use by $CoSyNE_c$ is computed by:

$$f_c = d - \frac{3m}{1000} + \frac{v_{max}}{5} - 100c \,, \tag{2}$$

where d is the distance along the track axis measured from the starting line, v_{max} is maximum speed, m is the cumulative damage, and c is the sum of squares of

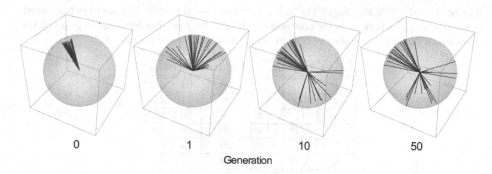

Fig. 3. Evolving MPCNN features. Each plot shows the feature vectors for each of the 40 training images collected at the given generation of CoSyNE$_k$ on the unit sphere. Initially (generation 0), the features are clustered together. After just a few generations spread out so that the MPCNN discriminates more clearly between the images. The features stabilize after generation 50.

the control signal differences, divided by the number of control variables, 3, and the number simulation control steps, T:

$$c = \frac{1}{3T} \sum_i^3 \sum_t^T [o_i(t) - o_i(t-1)]^2. \tag{3}$$

The maximum speed component in equation (2) forces the controllers to accelerate and brake efficiently, while the damage component favors controllers that drive safely, and c encourages smoother driving. Fitness scores roughly correspond to the distance traveled along the race track axis. Each individual is evaluated both on the track and its mirror image to prevent the RNN from blindly memorizing the track without using the visual input. The original track starts with a left turn, while the mirrored track starts with a right turn, forcing the network to use the visual input to distinguish between tracks. The final fitness score is the minimum of the two track scores (equation 2).

After four generations of CoSyNE$_c$, CoSyNE$_k$ starts. First, a population of MPCNNs with 8 layers, alternating between convolution and max-pooling operations (see figure 2 and Table 1) is initialized with random kernel weights uniformly distributed between -1.5 and 1.5). The MPCNNs are then evolved for four generations using 40 randomly selected images from the previous CoSyNE$_c$ phase to compute the fitness function f_k (equation 1).

Each 64×64 pixel image is processed by a candidate MPCNN by convolving it with each of the 20 filters in layer 1, to produce 20 63×63 feature maps, each of which is reduced down to 21×21 by the first max-pooling layer (2). These 20 features are convolved again by layer 3, max-pooled in layer 4, and so on, until the image is reduced down to just 3 1-dimensional features which are fed to the controller. This architecture has a total of 3583 kernel coefficients (weights). All MPCNN layers used scaled *tanh* transfer function.

Table 1. MPCNN topology. The table summarizes the MPCNN architecture used; type of a layer, where C is for convolutional, MP for max-pooling, dimensions of the filter bank m and n, number of output maps and their resolution.

Layer	Type	m	n	#maps	map size
1	C	1	20	20	63×63
2	MP	-	-	20	21×21
3	C	20	20	20	20×20
4	MP	-	-	20	10×10
5	C	20	20	20	9×9
6	MP	-	-	20	3×3
7	C	20	20	3	2×2
8	MP	-	-	3	1×1

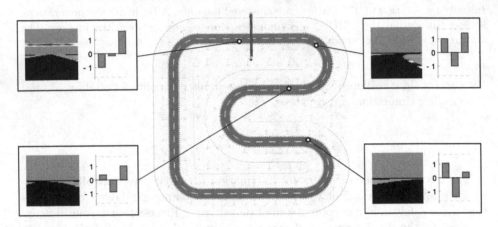

Fig. 4. Evolved visual features. Each inset shows the image at a particular point on the track and the 3-dimensional feature vector produced by the MPCNN after its evolution finished.

At the end of the four generations, the best compressor in the population becomes the compressor for the controllers in the next round of $CoSyNE_c$. $CoSyNE_k$ and $CoSyNE_c$ continue to alternate until a sufficiently fit controller is found, with 20% of the training images being replaced by new ones selected at random in each iteration of $CoSyNE_k$. Both MPCNN compressors and controllers are directly encoded into real-valued genomes, and the population size of both CoSyNEs was 100, with a mutation rate of 0.8.

4.2   Results

We report just 2 runs because a single run of 300 generations of both $CoSyNE_c$ and $CoSyNE_k$ takes almost 80 hours on an 8-core machine[1] (running 8 evaluations in parallel). The fitness, f_c, reached 509.1 at generation 289 for run no.

---

[1] AMD FX 8120 8-core, 16 GB RAM, nVidia GTX-570.

Table 2. Maximum distance, d, in meters and maximum speed, v_{max}, in kilometers per hour achieved by hand-coded controllers that come with TORCS which enjoy access to the state variables (the five upper table entries), a million-weight RNN controller that drives using pre-processed 64×64 pixel images as input, evolved indirectly in the Fourier domain, MPC-RNN, where the MPCNN is trained offline from manually collected images [16] and the Online MPC-RNN agent that collects the MPCNN training images automatically.

controller	d [m]	v_{max} [km/h]
olethros	570	147
bt	613	141
berniw	624	149
tita	657	150
inferno	682	150
visual RNN [14]	625	144
MPC-RNN [16]	547	97
Online MPC-RNN	489	91

1 and 495.5 at generation 145 for run no. 2, where a generation refers to one generation of each CoSyNE. Table 2 compares the distance travelled and maximum speed of the best controller with the offline-evolved MPCNN controller [16], a large RNN controller evolved in frequency domain [14], and the hand-coded controllers that come with the TORCS package.

The performance of Online MPC-RNN is not as good as its offline variant, but the controllers still approach a fitness of 500, which allows them to complete a lap and continue driving without crashing. The controllers with the pre-trained MPCNN drive slightly better because of possibly two reasons (1) the MPCNN compressor, that improves online does not reach the optimum and (2) as the compressor evolves together with the RNN controller, the weights of the controller have to be updated after each compressor change due to different features that it provides. The hand-coded controllers are much better since they enjoy an access to the car telemetry and features like distances to the track edges.

Figure 3 shows the evolution of the MPCNN feature vectors for each of the 40 images in the training set, in one of the two runs. As the features evolve they very quickly move away from each other in the feature space. While simply pushing the feature vectors apart is no guarantee of achieving maximally informative compressed representations, this simple, unsupervised training procedure provides enough discriminative power in practice to get the car safely across the finish line.

5 Discussion

The results show that it is not necessary to undertake the complicated procedure of collecting the images manually by driving the car and training the compressor beforehand. The MPCNN compressor, trained online from images gathered is good enough for a small RNN with 33 weights to be evolved efficiently to solve the driving control task.

Another approach would be to combine the controllers and compressors within a single directly-encoded genome, but one can expect this to run even longer. Also, instead of using an MPCNN with fitness f_k, the collected images could be used to train autoencoders [11] that would be forced to generated suitable features.

The presented framework is more general than just a TORCS driving system. It remains to be seen whether the agents can be plugged into some other environment, collect the images on the fly and train the controllers to perform the desired task. The TORCS control signal is only 3-dimensional, future experiments will apply Online MPC-RNN to higher-dimensional action spaces like the 41-DOF iCub humanoid, to perform manipulation tasks using vision.

Acknowledgments. This research was supported by Swiss National Science Foundation grant #138219: "Theory and Practice of Reinforcement Learning 2", and EU FP7 project: "NAnoSCaleEngineering for Novel Computation using Evolution" (NASCENCE), grant agreement #317662.

References

1. Ciresan, D.C., Meier, U., Gambardella, L.M., Schmidhuber, J.: Deep big simple neural nets for handwritten digit recognition. Neural Computation 22(12), 3207–3220 (2010)
2. Ciresan, D.C., Meier, U., Masci, J., Gambardella, L.M., Schmidhuber, J.: Flexible, high performance convolutional neural networks for image classification. In: Proceedings of the International Joint Conference on Artificial Intelligence (IJCAI), pp. 1237–1242 (2011)
3. Cuccu, G., Luciw, M., Schmidhuber, J., Gomez, F.: Intrinsically motivated evolutionary search for vision-based reinforcement learning. In: Proceedings of the IEEE Conference on Development and Learning, and Epigenetic Robotics (2011)
4. D'Ambrosio, D.B., Stanley, K.O.: A novel generative encoding for exploiting neural network sensor and output geometry. In: Proceedings of the 9th Conference on Genetic and Evolutionary Computation (GECCO), pp. 974–981. ACM, New York (2007)
5. Fernández, F., Borrajo, D.: Two steps reinforcement learning. International Journal of Intelligent Systems 23(2), 213–245 (2008)
6. Fukushima, K.: Neocognitron: A self-organizing neural network for a mechanism of pattern recognition unaffected by shift in position. Biological Cybernetics 36(4), 193–202 (1980)
7. Gauci, J., Stanley, K.: Generating large-scale neural networks through discovering geometric regularities. In: Proceedings of the Conference on Genetic and Evolutionary Computation (GECCO), pp. 997–1004. ACM (2007)
8. Gisslén, L., Luciw, M., Graziano, V., Schmidhuber, J.: Sequential constant size compressors for reinforcement learning. In: Schmidhuber, J., Thórisson, K.R., Looks, M. (eds.) AGI 2011. LNCS, vol. 6830, pp. 31–40. Springer, Heidelberg (2011)

9. Gomez, F.J., Schmidhuber, J., Miikkulainen, R.: Accelerated neural evolution through cooperatively coevolved synapses. Journal of Machine Learning Research 9, 937–965 (2008)
10. Gruau, F.: Cellular encoding of genetic neural networks. Technical Report RR-92-21, Ecole Normale Superieure de Lyon, Institut IMAG, Lyon, France (1992)
11. Hinton, G., Salakhutdinov, R.: Reducing the dimensionality of data with neural networks. Science 313(5786), 504–507 (2006)
12. Jodogne, S.R., Piater, J.H.: Closed-loop learning of visual control policies. Journal of Artificial Intelligence Research 28, 349–391 (2007)
13. Kitano, H.: Designing neural networks using genetic algorithms with graph generation system. Complex Systems 4, 461–476 (1990)
14. Koutník, J., Cuccu, G., Schmidhuber, J., Gomez, F.: Evolving large-scale neural networks for vision-based reinforcement learning. In: Proceedings of the Genetic and Evolutionary Computation Conference (GECCO), Amsterdam (2013)
15. Koutník, J., Gomez, F., Schmidhuber, J.: Evolving neural networks in compressed weight space. In: Proceedings of the Conference on Genetic and Evolutionary Computation, GECCO (2010)
16. Koutník, J., Schmidhuber, J., Gomez, F.: Evolving deep unsupervised convolutional networks for vision-based reinforcement learning. In: Proceedings of the 2014 Genetic and Evolutionary Computation Conference (GECCO). ACM Press (2014)
17. Lange, S., Riedmiller, M.: Deep auto-encoder neural networks in reinforcement learning. In: International Joint Conference on Neural Networks (IJCNN), Barcelona, Spain (2010)
18. LeCun, Y., Bottou, L., Bengio, Y., Haffner, P.: Gradient-based learning applied to document recognition. Proceedings of the IEEE 86(11), 2278–2324 (1998)
19. Legenstein, R., Wilbert, N., Wiskott, L.: Reinforcement Learning on Slow Features of High-Dimensional Input Streams. PLoS Computational Biology 6(8) (2010)
20. Pierce, D., Kuipers, B.: Map learning with uninterpreted sensors and effectors. Artificial Intelligence 92, 169–229 (1997)
21. Riedmiller, M., Lange, S., Voigtlaender, A.: Autonomous reinforcement learning on raw visual input data in a real world application. In: Proceedings of the International Joint Conference on Neural Networks (IJCNN), Brisbane, Australia, pp. 1–8 (2012)
22. Scherer, D., Müller, A., Behnke, S.: Evaluation of pooling operations in convolutional architectures for object recognition. In: Diamantaras, K., Duch, W., Iliadis, L.S. (eds.) ICANN 2010, Part III. LNCS, vol. 6354, pp. 92–101. Springer, Heidelberg (2010)
23. Schmidhuber, J.: Discovering neural nets with low Kolmogorov complexity and high generalization capability. Neural Networks 10(5), 857–873 (1997)
24. Sutton, R.S., McAllester, D.A., Singh, S.P., Mansour, Y.: Policy gradient methods for reinforcement learning with function approximation. In: Advances in Neural Information Processing Systems 12 (NIPS), pp. 1057–1063 (1999)
25. Tesauro, G.: Practical issues in temporal difference learning. In: Lippman, D.S., Moody, J.E., Touretzky, D.S. (eds.) Advances in Neural Information Processing Systems 4 (NIPS), pp. 259–266. Morgan Kaufmann (1992)
26. Yao, X.: Evolving artificial neural networks. Proceedings of the IEEE 87(9), 1423–1447 (1999)

A Swarm Robotics Approach to Task Allocation under Soft Deadlines and Negligible Switching Costs

Yara Khaluf[1], Mauro Birattari[2], and Heiko Hamann[1]

[1] Department of Computer Science, University of Paderborn
Zukunftsmeile 1, 33102 Paderborn, Germany
{yara,heiko.hamann}@uni-paderborn.de
http://upb.de/cs/si
[2] IRIDIA, Université Libre de Bruxelles
B-1050 Brussels, Belgium
mbiro@ulb.ac.be
http://iridia.ulb.ac.be/

Abstract. Developing swarm robotics systems for real-time applications is a challenging mission. Task deadlines are among the kind of constraints which characterize a large set of real applications. This paper focuses on devising and analyzing a task allocation strategy that allows swarm robotics systems to execute tasks characterized by soft deadlines and to minimize the costs associated with missing the task deadlines.

Keywords: Soft deadlines, Time-constrained tasks, Swarm robotics, Multi-agent systems.

1 Introduction

Considering the large number of real-world applications where swarm robotics represents an efficient system to be investigated, real-time tasks represent a remarkable category of these applications. Deadlines are often enough associated with real-world tasks, such as data gathering in large sensor networks (datamules), recycling systems and pollution cleaning. A task is referred to as real-time task, when the correctness of the task results is not related only to the logical correctness, but also to the time at which these results are delivered. The point in time before which the real-time task should be executed is referred to as the task *deadline*. There are two main types of deadlines, as categorized in traditional real-time systems [20]. *Hard deadlines* are deadlines, that when missed, can lead to catastrophic consequences. *Soft deadlines* are deadlines, that affect the quality of the results, if not met. Thus, missing this type of deadlines is associated with specific costs. This paper focuses on soft-deadline tasks which can be considered as suitable tasks to be executed by a stochastic system such as a swarm of robots. Also natural systems need to cope with related task allocation problems but rather based on priorities than explicit deadlines. For example

A.P. del Pobil et al. (Eds.): SAB 2014, LNAI 8575, pp. 270–279, 2014.
© Springer International Publishing Switzerland 2014

feeding the larvae of honey bees requires appropriate task allocation. Larvae have different hunger levels and stimulate nurse bees that react with different visiting rates [10]. In the following, a task allocation strategy is developed to allow the robots to assign themselves autonomously to tasks and to execute them in parallel under the considerations of their soft deadlines. The developed strategy is tested using the biologically inspired *foraging* task. To the best of our knowledge, there are only few works which did concentrate on task allocation in swarm robotics under time constrains. The auction strategy is one of the most frequently used, see [7,6]. In addition to the well established auction strategy, heuristics are introduced in the context of robot allocation to tasks with time constraints as in [1]. In [19] and [11], market-based task allocation strategies are introduced, where time is the main critical constraint. This is considered together with a reward mechanism associated to tasks which are successfully completed. Mathematical modeling is not intensively investigated in the context of swarm robotics, still some examples can be found in [16,8,15,2,14].

In this paper we present a novel approach based on mathematical modeling to analyze the performance of swarm robotics and the behavior of individual robots. The goal is to develop an appropriate task allocation under the constraints of the different tasks. The rest of the paper is organized as follows: Section 2 describes the problem on which we are focusing. Section 3 presents the mathematical models used in analyzing the swarm performance in addition to the behavior of individual robots. The developed allocation strategy is presented in details and verified using Monte-Carlo simulations in Section 4. In Section 5 a physics-based simulation is established using the robot simulator ARGoS to verify the allocation strategy and the paper is concluded in Section 6.

2   Problem Description

In this paper we focus on the problem of assigning a swarm of N homogeneous robots to a set of tasks which are characterized by their soft deadlines. A task deadline is the point in time up to which the task should be executed and it is referred to as *soft* when missing it is not catastrophic, but associated with specific costs.

Consider a set of M soft-deadline tasks $\{T_1, T_2, \ldots, T_M\}$ which need to be executed in parallel. Each of these tasks consists of discrete sub-tasks referred to as the task *parts*, where a single part requires one robot to execute it. Executing task T_i is achieved when a specific number S_i of its parts is accomplished. The robots' cooperation is necessary for any task execution, as the number of parts required to be accomplished within the task deadline, is not achievable using one robot. The parts of the different tasks are regenerated periodically, therefore after the execution of a part, a new part will replace it. The switching costs among the tasks, which represent the costs associated with the time required by a robot to stop the execution of one task and to start to work on another one, are assumed to be negligible. This condition is verified when the tasks are located on the same physical area or when the time required to travel among the different tasks is negligible in comparison to the task execution times, see [12].

Let us denote the number of parts that has been accomplished on task T_i up to the deadline D_i by $\rho_i(D_i)$. The costs associated with missing the deadline of task T_i are directly related to the part of the task which remains unprocessed at its deadline. Therefore, we can define the cost function ζ_i as the difference between the number of parts required to be achieved S_i and the number of parts $\rho_i(D_i)$ executed up to the deadline D_i

$$\zeta_i = S_i - \rho_i(D_i). \tag{1}$$

The goal, as mentioned above, is to design an allocation strategy that allows the robots to assign themselves autonomously to the different tasks under their time constraints (deadlines). This technique is efficient when switching costs between tasks are negligible. Robots select their tasks autonomously using a *decision matrix*, that defines the robots' behaviors probabilistically. It holds the transition probabilities $p_{i,j}$ to switch from task T_i to task T_j. Controlling the behavior of the individual robots probabilistically is a common approach in stochastic systems such as swarm robotics. The decision matrices are designed to minimize the costs associated with missing the task deadlines.

3   System Modeling

In this section we present the techniques used to model both the performance of the robots swarm and the behavior of the individual robot. These techniques are exploited later for the development of the allocation strategy.

3.1   Swarm Performance Modeling

We define the swarm performance as the amount of work (task parts) accomplished by the swarm within the deadline of the task. Based on our task specification, the amount of work accomplished on any task within a specific time duration represents a discrete random variable. The swarm performance, as defined, is the sum of the individual contributions of all robots that worked on the task up to its deadline. The total number of completed parts increases over time as the robots succeed in accomplishing their individual parts.

The process associated with the evolution of the amount of work accomplished on task T_i over time up to its deadline D_i represents a time-continuous stochastic process $X(t)$. This process is modeled as a Poisson process [18] with a task-specific rate λ_i for task T_i. The Poisson process is, by definition, a stochastic process that counts the events within a specific time period. By mapping the occurrence of an event to the completion of an individual task part, the Poisson process represents an appropriate modeling technique for the work progress on any of the considered tasks over time. When the amount of work that is accomplished on any task over time is modeled using a Poisson process, the swarm performance ρ_i obtained within the deadline D_i will follow the Poisson distribution with the parameter $\lambda_i D_i$

$$\rho_i \sim Poisson(\lambda_i D_i). \tag{2}$$

In general, when the robots finish executing some task, they become available to be assigned to other tasks. As the tasks we are focusing on in this paper are time-constrained tasks, the deadline of the task represents the point in time at which the task should be accomplished and the assigned robots become available again. Therefore, we divide the execution time of the tasks into periods called activation periods. The task stays active over all the periods which are included in its deadline. The i-th period is defined as

$$\eta_i = D_i - D_{i-1} \qquad \forall i \in \{2, \ldots, M\} \qquad (3)$$

where $\eta_1 = D_1$.

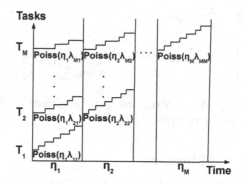

Fig. 1. The Poisson processes modeling the progress of the accomplished amount of work on different tasks over their different activation periods

As the number of robots working on a task may change during its activation periods, the rate of accomplishing work of that task may change consequently. Therefore, individual Poisson processes are used to model the work progress on a specific task over its different activation periods. The evolution of work accomplished on task T_i during the jth activation period is modeled as a Poisson process with the rate λ_{ij}. This random amount of work follows the Poisson distribution with the parameter $\lambda_{ij}\eta_j$.

Furthermore, it is well-known that the sum of Poisson processes is a Poisson process with the rate equal to the sum of the rates associated with the summed up processes. Therefore, the Poisson process modeling the evolution of work accomplished on task T_i until its deadline D_i has the rate $\lambda_i = \sum_{j=1}^{i} \lambda_{ij}$. The random amount of work that was achieved until the deadline D_i of task T_i is distributed following the Poisson distribution with the parameter $\sum_{j=1}^{i} \lambda_{ij}\eta_j$

Hence we have

$$\rho_i \sim \mathcal{P}oisson(\sum_{j=1}^{i} \lambda_{ij}\eta_j) \qquad \forall i \in \{1, \ldots, M\}. \qquad (4)$$

The expected value of a random variable which follows a Poisson distribution with the parameter λ is equal to λ. Hence based on Eq.(4), the expected value of the performance that was achieved until the deadline D_i is given by

$$\mathbb{E}(\rho_i(D_i)) = \sum_{j=1}^{i} \lambda_{ij}\eta_j.$$

However, the performance required to be achieved at the deadline D_i is S_i parts. Consequently, the expected value of the cost function defined in Eq.(1) can be written as

$$\mathbb{E}(\zeta_i) = S_i - \mathbb{E}(\rho_i(D_i))$$

$$= S_i - \sum_{j=1}^{i} \lambda_{ij}\eta_j$$

$$= \begin{cases} S_i - \sum_{j=1}^{i} \lambda_{ij}\eta_j & \text{when } \sum_{j=1}^{i} \lambda_{ij}\eta_j < S_i \\ 0 & \text{when } \sum_{j=1}^{i} \lambda_{ij}\eta_j \geqslant S_i. \end{cases} \tag{5}$$

As we can notice in Eq.(5), no costs are associated with tasks on which more parts than their sizes are accomplished.

3.2   Individual Robot Modeling

The behavior of the individual robots can be described as follows. Each robot selects one of the tasks to work on and each time it finishes executing one part, it has the possibility to switch to another task or to continue on the same task.

The tasks are mapped to the states of a Markov chain and each robot is modeled as an individual process with the above described behavior over the M states of the chain. The robot continues to work on the task it has selected for a random time, namely, the time required to accomplish one part of the current task. This represents a random time with a task-specific mean denoted by $\hat{\mu}_i$, which is assumed to be easily estimated over short-term experiments as it is performed in Section 5. After executing one part of the current task, the robot chooses its next task to visit where the choice is made among the available tasks including its current one. A specific probability matrix referred to as the *decision matrix* is used by the robots to select autonomously their next tasks. The described process associated with each robot, represents by definition a *semi-Markov* process [18], which has an invariant (limiting) probability measure, π_i, that can be obtained by solving the following system

$$\pi_i = \sum_{j=1}^{M} \pi_j p_{j,i} \qquad \text{where } \sum_{i=1}^{M} \pi_i = 1. \tag{6}$$

π_i represents the proportion of transitions that take the robots into task T_i. The proportion of the time that the robot spends working on task T_i in comparison to its total working time is given by Eq.(7). For time-constrained tasks, we are interested in the time spent by the robot on task T_i within the deadline D_i. Let us denote this time by $\tau_i(D_i)$. Based on Eq.(7), $\tau_i(D_i)$ can be obtained by Eq.(8).

$$\tau_i = \frac{\pi_i \hat{\mu}_i}{\sum_{j=1}^{M} \pi_j \hat{\mu}_j} \qquad (7) \qquad \tau_i(D_i) = \frac{\pi_i \hat{\mu}_i}{\sum_{j=1}^{M} \pi_j \hat{\mu}_j} D_i \qquad (8)$$

When a swarm of N robots is used to execute M tasks and each single robot is modeled as a semi-Markov process with the above described behavior, the total time spent on task T_i up to its deadline D_i can be calculated using Eq.(9). Consequently, the number of times $n_i(N, D_i)$ that T_i is expected to be visited by a swarm of N robots within its deadline D_i, is calculated using Eq.(10).

$$\tau_i(N, D_i) = \frac{\pi_i \hat{\mu}_i}{\sum_{j=1}^{M} \pi_j \hat{\mu}_j} D_i N \qquad (9) \qquad n_i(N, D_i) = \frac{\pi_i}{\sum_{j=1}^{M} \pi_j \hat{\mu}_j} D_i N \qquad (10)$$

The rate of the visits to task T_i within its deadline D_i by the swarm of N robots, which represents the number of the parts expected to be processed within the task deadline, is obtained by dividing Eq.(10) by the task deadline yielding

$$\lambda_i = \frac{\pi_i}{\sum_{j=1}^{M} \pi_j \hat{\mu}_j} N. \qquad (11)$$

4   Task Allocation Strategy

The expected value of the cost function associated with the swarm performance was calculated in Section 3.1 using Eq.(5)

$$\mathbb{E}(\zeta_i) = \begin{cases} S_i - \sum_{j=1}^{i} \lambda_{ij} \eta_j & \text{for } \sum_{j=1}^{i} \lambda_{ij} \eta_j < S_i \\ 0 & \text{for } \sum_{j=1}^{i} \lambda_{ij} \eta_j \geqslant S_i. \end{cases}$$

The rate λ_{ij} of the Poisson process in the j-th activation period of task T_i, can be written in terms of the transition probabilities based on Eq.(11)

$$\lambda_{ij} = \frac{\pi_{ij}}{\sum_{k=j}^{M} \pi_{kj} \hat{\mu}_k} N \qquad \forall i \in \{1, \ldots, M\}, \forall j \in \{1, \ldots, M\}.$$

So the expected value of the cost function associated with task T_i can be written in terms of the transition probabilities, as

$$\mathbb{E}(\zeta_i) = \begin{cases} S_i - \sum_{j=1}^{i} \frac{\pi_{ij}}{\sum_{k=j}^{M} \pi_{kj} \hat{\mu}_k} N \eta_j & \text{for } \sum_{j=1}^{i} \frac{\pi_{ij}}{\sum_{k=j}^{M} \pi_{kj} \hat{\mu}_k} N \eta_j < S_i \\ \\ 0 & \text{for } \sum_{j=1}^{i} \frac{\pi_{ij}}{\sum_{k=j}^{M} \pi_{kj} \hat{\mu}_k} N \eta_j \geqslant S_i \end{cases} \qquad (12)$$

where $i \in \{1, \ldots, M\}$.

The developed allocation strategy aims to minimize the costs associated with the part left unprocessed at the task deadline. Minimizing the costs is required for all tasks based on their priorities. The task priority is related, in our case, to the tightness of the task deadline. Therefore, the task with an earlier deadline or a larger size has a higher priority. A simple way to define the priority of task T_i is given by

$$\beta_i = \frac{S_i/D_i}{\sum_{j=1}^{M} S_j/D_j}. \tag{13}$$

The sum of the task priorities is always 1.

The minimization problem, that we consider, represents a multi-objective optimization problem with M objective functions.

$$\underset{\pi_{ij}}{\text{minimize}} \begin{cases} \mathbb{E}(\zeta_1) = f(\pi_{11}) \\ \mathbb{E}(\zeta_2) = f(\pi_{21}, \pi_{22}) \\ \vdots \\ \mathbb{E}(\zeta_M) = f(\pi_{M1}, \pi_{M2}, \ldots, \pi_{MM}) \end{cases} \tag{14}$$

It is solved using the well-known methodology of scalarizing the multi-objective optimization problem and formulating a single-objective optimization problem. We sum the M objective functions, where each is weighted by the priority of its task and the obtained objective function is

$$\underset{\pi_{ij}}{\text{minimize}} \sum_{i=1}^{M} \beta_i \mathbb{E}(\zeta_i). \tag{15}$$

The described optimization problem is solved *off-line* and the robots are provided with the resulting decision matrices (one per activation period) which hold the transition probabilities between tasks. After that, each robot can start to use the decision matrix of the current period, independently, to assign itself and switch among the different tasks.

Let us consider an example of 3 tasks which are characterized by their soft deadlines $\{500, 750, 1000\}$ time units and their sizes $\{1500, 1000, 500\}$ parts. The size of the swarm, used to execute these tasks, varies over the range $N \in [5, 50]$ robots with an increment step of 2 robots. The task priorities are calculated using Eq.(13). The optimization problem is solved for the different swarm sizes. Hence, the decision matrices are obtained and then used to predict and simulate the costs of missing the deadlines. Figure 2 shows the value of the cost function over all examined sizes of the swarm. The cost is estimated using Eq.(12), after that it is averaged over 100 runs of Monte-Carlo simulation. The figure shows a high level of consistency between the calculated cost and the simulated one.

5   Physics-based Simulation

In this section we consider the task of *multi-foraging* to verify the developed allocation strategy through performing physics-based simulations. Foraging behavior, in its simple form, is the behavior of exploring the environment searching

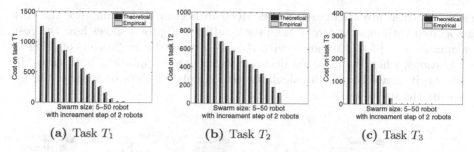

(a) Task T_1 (b) Task T_2 (c) Task T_3

Fig. 2. Cost function theoretically calculated based on Eq.(12) and compared with its value averaged over 100 runs of Monte-Carlo simulation

for food items and retrieving them to a safe area referred to as the nest. It can be observed in a large number of social insect colonies and animal societies [5]. Foraging was intensively investigated in swarm robotics systems [13,4,15,9]. Multi-foraging refers to the task of retrieving different types of items.

For our simulations we use the robot simulator $ARGoS^1$, where a homogeneous swarm of foot-bot[2] robots is simulated. We consider three types of items 500 *red* parts, 300 *black* parts and 150 *white* parts, which are uniformly scattered. The nest is marked with a set of lights which can be sensed by the working robots. The robots apply the *diffusion* behavior [3] combined with obstacle avoidance to maximize the exploration of the arena. The robot's motion is governed by a *light-repulsion* behavior to move out of the nest towards the arena. As soon as it finds some part to retrieve, it starts to apply a *light-attraction* behavior to move towards the nest. Both light-attraction and light-repulsion behaviors are combined with obstacle avoidance. As the three types of items are uniformly scattered on the arena, the switching costs among the tasks can be considered as negligible. We use a homogeneous swarm with a varying size between [5, 50] robots, with an increment step of 5 robots. The time required by a single robot to retrieve one part of each of the three types is averaged over 10 runs of *AR-GoS* simulations each for a duration of 500 seconds. In our scenario, the average of this time differs for the different types of items due to the different number of parts available of each type. The average of the time required by a single robot to retrieve one part increases by increasing the swarm size due to the spatial interferences among the robots. We use the average measured when the largest swarm is used (50 robots). This design decision is based on performing a worst case estimation of the swarm performance and consequently of the cost function. The average time of retrieving one part of each of the three items is respectively {98.5, 130, 197}. The soft deadlines associated with the tasks are: {500, 1500, 3000} seconds and the task sizes are {150, 300, 500} parts. The de-

---

[1] ARGoS is a state-of-the-art, open source $3D$ robot simulator. Its design allows for the simulation of large homogeneous and heterogeneous swarms of robots [17].

[2] Foot-bot is a wheeled robot with 17 cm diameter × 29 cm hight and weights 1.8 kg. It is equipped with a set of sensors and actuators in addition to an on-board CPU.

cision matrices are calculated, as described in Section 4, to minimize the cost associated with missing any of the task deadlines. Figure 3 shows how the cost calculated using Eq.(12) agrees with the one averaged over 20 runs of ARGoS simulations, when the designed decision matrices are applied in both cases. In addition it shows how both calculated and simulated costs decrease while increasing the size of the swarm.

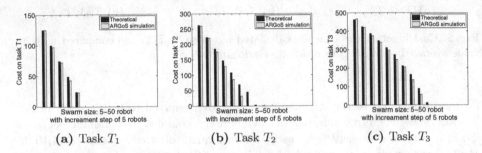

(a) Task T_1 (b) Task T_2 (c) Task T_3

Fig. 3. Cost function theoretically calculated based on Eq.(12) and compared with its value averaged over 20 runs of *ARGoS* simulation

6 Conclusion

This paper focuses on developing a task allocation approach that allows a swarm of robots to execute a set of tasks under the consideration of soft deadlines. The resulting behavior of the robots can adapt itself efficiently to dynamic changes such as changes in the swarm size (e.g. robots failures). The probabilistic design of this behavior allows for a higher level of self-adaptivity than for example the one obtained by assigning fixed-size groups of robots to the tasks. Addressing robot-to-robot communication as a part of our future work may increase significantly the self-adaptivity of the system, as exchanging knowledge about dynamic changes in the environment, tasks or swarm, will be possible. In addition, a part of our future work is the estimation of the mean time $\hat{\mu}_i$ as a function of the number of robots working on task T_i.

References

1. Acebo, E.D., de la Rosa, J.: Introducing bar systems: A class of swarm intelligence optimization algorithms. In: AISB Convention Communication, Interaction and Social Intelligence, Aberdeen, Scotland, pp. 18–23 (2008)
2. Agassounon, W., Martinoli, A.: A macroscopic model of an aggregation experiment using embodied agents in groups of time-varying sizes. In: Proceedings of the IEEE Conference on System, Man and Cybernetics (SMC), Hammamet, Tunisia, pp. 250–255 (2002)

3. Beal, J.: Superdiffusive dispersion and mixing of swarms with reactive Levy walks. In: IEEE 7th International Conference on Self-Adaptive and Self-Organizing Systems, SASO 2013, pp. 141–148 (2013)
4. Campo, A., Dorigo, M.: Efficient multi-foraging in swarm robotics. In: Almeida e Costa, F., Rocha, L.M., Costa, E., Harvey, I., Coutinho, A. (eds.) ECAL 2007. LNCS (LNAI), vol. 4648, pp. 696–705. Springer, Heidelberg (2007)
5. Danchin, E., Giraldeau, L., Cézilly, F., et al.: Behavioural ecology. Oxford University Press, Oxford (2008)
6. Guerrero, J., Oliver, G.: Multi-robot task allocation method for heterogeneous tasks with priorities. In: Distributed Autonomous Robotic Systems 6, pp. 181–190. Springer, Berlin (2007)
7. Guerrero, J., Oliver, G.: Auction and swarm multi-robot task allocation algorithms in real time scenarios. In: Yasuda, T. (ed.) Multi-Robot Systems, Trends and Development, pp. 437–456. InTech (2011)
8. Hamann, H.: Space-Time Continuous Models of Swarm Robotics Systems: Supporting Global-to-Local Programming. PhD thesis, University of Karlsruhe, Germany (November 2008)
9. Hamann, H., Wörn, H.: An analytical and spatial model of foraging in a swarm of robots. In: Şahin, E., Spears, W.M., Winfield, A.F.T. (eds.) Swarm Robotics Ws. LNCS, vol. 4433, pp. 43–55. Springer, Heidelberg (2007)
10. Huang, Z., Otis, G.: Inspection and feeding of larvae by worker honey bees (hymenoptera: Apidae): Effect of starvation and food quantity. Journal of Insect Behavior 4(3), 305–317 (1991)
11. Jones, E., Dias, M., Stentz, A.: Learning-enhanced market-based task allocation for oversubscribed domains. In: IEEE/RSJ International Conference on Intelligent Robots and Systems, IROS, pp. 2308–2313 (2007)
12. Khaluf, Y.: Task Allocation in Robot Swarms for Time-Constrained Tasks. PhD thesis, University of Paderborn, Germany (2014)
13. Labella, T., Dorigo, M., Deneubourg, J.: Division of labor in a group of robots inspired by ants' foraging behavior. ACM Transactions on Autonomous and Adaptive Systems 1(1), 4–25 (2006)
14. Lerman, K., Galstyan, A.: Mathematical model of foraging in a group of robots: Effect of interference. Autonomous Robots 13(2), 127–141 (2002)
15. Lerman, K., Galstyan, A., Martinoli, A., Ijspeert, A.: A macroscopic analytical model of collaboration in distributed robotic systems. Artificial Life 7(4), 375–393 (2001)
16. Lerman, K., Martinoli, A., Galstyan, A.: A review of probabilistic macroscopic models for swarm robotic systems. In: Şahin, E., Spears, W.M. (eds.) Swarm Robotics 2004. LNCS, vol. 3342, pp. 143–152. Springer, Heidelberg (2005)
17. Pinciroli, C., Trianni, V., O'Grady, R., Pini, G., Brutschy, A., Brambilla, M., Mathews, N., Ferrante, E., Caro, G., Ducatelle, F., Birattari, M., Gambardella, L., Dorigo, M.: ARGoS: A modular, parallel, multi-engine simulator for multi-robot systems. Swarm Intelligence 6, 271–295 (2012)
18. Ross, S.: Applied probability models with optimization applications. Dover Publications Inc., New York (1992)
19. Schneider, J., Apfelbaum, D., Bagnell, D., Simmons, R.: Learning opportunity costs in multi-robot market based planners. In: Proceedings of the 2005 IEEE International Conference on Robotics and Automation, ICRA 2005, pp. 1151–1156 (2005)
20. Stankovic, J.: Deadline scheduling for real-time systems: EDF and related algorithms. Springer (1998)

Supervised Robot Groups with Reconfigurable Formation: Theory and Simulations

Zoltán Szántó[1], Lőrinc Márton[2], and Sebestyén György[1]

[1] Dept. of Electrical Engineering, Sapientia Hungarian University, Romania
{zoltan.szanto,marton1}@ms.sapientia.ro
[2] Dept. of Computer Science, Technical University of Cluj Napoca, Romania
gheorghe.sebestyen@cs.utcluj.ro

Abstract. In this paper we propose a control approach for teleoperated robot groups in which the shape of the formation can be reconfigured by a supervisor. To implement the formation control, the supervisor uses two haptic devices: the first haptic device is used to control the leader of the formation; the second is used to modify the formation. The haptic (force) feedbacks reflect the presence of obstacles: the first reflects the proximity of the obstacles from the formation leader; the second reflects the nearness of the obstacles from the center of the formation. An obstacle avoidance algorithm was also proposed for the members of the robot group. A simulation environment was developed to analyze the behavior of the proposed robot formation control approach. The simulated formation can be controlled through the Internet using real haptic devices.

Keywords: Formation Control, Obstacle Avoidance, Robot Simulation, Internet, Teleoperation.

1 Introduction

The formation control problem has received a lot of attention by the robotics and control community over the last decade, see surveys: [1] and [2]. In many applications, like exploration of wide areas or search and rescue operations, having a group of mobile robots is proven to be more effective than relying on a single agent. In this context, teleoperation systems can harvest the human intelligence while providing a safe environment for the operator who can remotely supervise the task execution. However, due to the physical limitations of the operator, such algorithms are needed that allow operator to control a team of robots.

In the study [3] a team of mobile robots is controlled based on virtual and behavioral structures. The robots are modeled as identical charges and due to the repulsive forces they avoid each other. A virtual robot which has the same magnitude charge but opposite sign is placed in the center of the formation which holds the formation together.

The authors of [4] use the Proportional-Derivative (PD) control to enforce motion coordination of multiple slave vehicles and complement it with avoidance functions. Here too a virtual robot is placed in the center of the formation.

A.P. del Pobil et al. (Eds.): SAB 2014, LNAI 8575, pp. 280–289, 2014.

In [5] a decentralized control strategy for bilaterally teleoperating heterogeneous groups of mobile robots is proposed. Using passivity based techniques, the behavior of the group is allowed to be as flexible as possible with arbitrary split and join events (e.g., due to inter-robot visibility/packet losses or specific task requirements) while guaranteeing the stability of the system.

In the leader-follower control algorithm presented in [6] the follower tracks a reference trajectory based on the leader position and a predetermined formation without the need for leader's velocity and dynamics. A virtual vehicle is constructed in such a way that its trajectory converges with the reference trajectory of the follower. Position tracking control is designed for the follower to track the virtual vehicle using Lyapunov and back stepping synthesis.

In all the papers above the shape of the formation was predetermined, it could not be controlled or reconfigured by a supervisor during task execution.

In this paper we discuss the problem of coordinating a group of robots in which the participants are required to follow an on-line reconfigurable formation while avoiding potential obstacles. We propose a teleoperation based formation control using two haptic devices as control interfaces. In this context our contribution can be summarized as follows. Firstly, a formation structure and a control algorithm is developed for the formation control of groups of robots. The controller uses the input from the two haptic devices, one for the leader and one for the formation shape, to generate the velocities for each robot. Secondly, a new obstacle avoidance algorithm is proposed which is based on the Lyapunov theory. The algorithm calculates the velocities in such a way that the robots avoid the obstacles even if this means temporary leaving the reference trajectory, i.e. the formation adapts its behavior in function of the presence or absence of obstacles. If obstacles are present in the proximity of a robot (i.e the robot is inside the obstacle's safety region), then it switches to another control strategy instead of direct leader following. In case of complex environments, when the obstacles can be near to each other, multiple obstacles can be put in one safety region. Finally, a simulation environment developed to study the effectiveness of the proposed algorithm is evaluated in experiments. The developed simulator is directly adapted to the haptic based teleoperation and it can also transmit direct video feedback from the simulated environment.

2   Algorithm for Teleoperated Formation

2.1   Controllable Formation Structure

The control of the formation is accomplished using two haptic devices (H_1 and H_2). Assume that both of them can be moved along two axes (x, y) by the human operator and that they can generate forces along these axes (F_{Hix}, F_{Hiy}, $i = 1, 2$). The positions and velocities of the haptic devices (x_{Hi}, y_{Hi}, v_{Hix}, v_{Hix}, $i = 1, 2$) are assumed to be available for the control design.

The haptic devices are connected to a master computer which receives the position and velocity signals of the controlled robot and sends the velocities (control signals) for each mobile robot in the group.

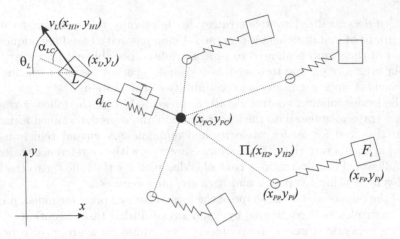

Fig. 1. Teleoperated robot formation

The concept of the proposed control system is presented in Fig. 1. Consider a group of fully actuated robots that consists of one leader (L) and N followers (F). The leader is teleoperated directly by the first haptic device. It also "pulls" a non-rigid predefined reference structure consisting of N vertices. A center (C) for the formation is set relative to the leader. The relative leader-center position is defined by the distance between the leader and the center (d_{LC}), and by the angle between the leader robot's heading and the line which connects the center of the robot and the center of the structure (α_{LC}).

The positions of the structure's vertices are chosen relative to this center. The vertices of the prescribed structure represent the reference positions for the followers. Each follower robot is associated to one vertex. Π_i is a parameter vector that defines the relative vertex-center position. The elements of the vector (Π_i) are considered modifiable using the second haptic. The position of the second haptic (x_{H2}, y_{H2}) determines the relative position of a vertex and the predefined center:

$$\Pi_i = \Pi_i(x_{H2}, y_{H2}). \tag{1}$$

For each fully actuated robot the velocity along the x and y axis can be predefined. The kinematic model of the leader robot is considered as:

$$\begin{cases} \dot{x}_L = v_{Lx}, \\ \dot{y}_L = v_{Ly}. \end{cases} \tag{2}$$

The leader's velocity is considered to be proportional to the position of the first haptic device:

$$\begin{cases} v_{Lx} = k_{x_{H1}} \cdot x_{H1}, \\ v_{Ly} = k_{y_{H1}} \cdot y_{H1}. \end{cases} \tag{3}$$

The orientation of the leader is given by:

$$\theta_L = \arctan\left(\frac{v_{Lx}}{v_{Ly}}\right). \tag{4}$$

The relative leader-center position is defined by a distance (d_{LC}) and an angle (α_{LC}), as it is shown in Fig. 1:

$$\Pi_{Cx} = d_{LC}\sin(\theta_L - \alpha_{LC}), \tag{5}$$
$$\Pi_{Cy} = d_{LC}\cos(\theta_L - \alpha_{LC}), \tag{6}$$
$$\Pi_C = (d_{LC}, \alpha_{LC}). \tag{7}$$

The coordinates of the structure's predefined center are denoted by x_C and y_C. A non-rigid contact between the leader and the structure's center is used to assure a smooth prescribed motion for the followers. The leader - center coupling is defined using the following second order dynamics:

$$\dot{x}_C = v_{Cx} \tag{8}$$
$$\dot{v}_{Cx} = k_{C1}x_C + k_{C2}v_{Cx} + k_{C1}(x_L - x_C - \Pi_{Cx}).$$

The parameters k_{C1} and k_{C2} are chosen such that the matrix $\begin{pmatrix} 0 & 1 \\ k_{C1} & k_{C2} \end{pmatrix}$ has strictly negative, real eigenvalues. On the y axis the position and velocity are generated using the same filter.

The prescribed positions of the ith follower is the ith vertex of the structure that is given by the coordinates x_{Pi} and y_{Pi}. It is considered that the position of each vertex is defined analytically with regards to the position of the predefined center:

$$x_{Pi} = X_{Pi}(x_C, y_C, \Pi_i), \tag{9}$$
$$y_{Pi} = Y_{Pi}(x_C, y_C, \Pi_i). \tag{10}$$

Based on (1), (9) and (10) the velocity components of the vertex can be computed as:

$$v_{Pxi} = \frac{\partial X_{Pi}}{x_C}v_{Cx} + \frac{\partial X_{Pi}}{y_C}v_{Cy} + \frac{\partial X_{Pi}}{x_{H2}}v_{H2x} + \frac{\partial X_{Pi}}{y_{H2}}v_{H2y}, \tag{11}$$
$$v_{Pyi} = \frac{\partial Y_{Pi}}{x_C}v_{Cx} + \frac{\partial Y_{Pi}}{y_C}v_{Cy} + \frac{\partial Y_{Pi}}{x_{H2}}v_{H2x} + \frac{\partial Y_{Pi}}{y_{H2}}v_{H2y}. \tag{12}$$

The follower robots are also considered to be described by the same kinematic model as the leader robot:

$$\begin{cases} \dot{x}_{Fi} = v_{Fxi}, \\ \dot{y}_{Fi} = v_{Fyi}. \end{cases} \tag{13}$$

The control signals for the followers can be computed as:

$$v_{Fxi} = K(x_{Pi} - x_{Fi}) + v_{Pxi}, \tag{14}$$
$$v_{Fyi} = K(y_{Pi} - y_{Fi}) + v_{Pyi}. \tag{15}$$

By substituting the control laws above into (13), it can be seen that the velocities computed above assure that the trajectories of the follower robots converge to the reference points (x_{Pi}, y_{Pi}).

2.2   Haptic Forces

The role of the haptic feedback is to support the operator during the navigation amongst obstacles. The force feedback from the haptic device H_1, which drives the leader, can be calculated based on the distance between the leader and the sensed obstacles [7]. Consider that the position of the nearest obstacle (O) to the leader is given by (x_O, y_O). In this case the sensed haptic force by the human operator can be computed as $F_{H1x} = K_{F1}|x_L - x_O|$ and $F_{H1y} = K_{F1}|y_L - y_O|$. It is assumed that the relative positions of the robots and obstacles are measurable.

In the case of the second haptic device, the force feedback can be computed similarly by considering the position of the formation center instead of the leader position: $F_{H2x} = K_{F2}|x_C - x_O|$ and $F_{H2y} = K_{F2}|y_C - y_O|$.

2.3   Obstacle Avoidance

In many real formation control scenarios the formation moves amongst obstacles, which should be avoided by the members of the formation. Moreover, during formation reconfiguration, the inter-robot collision has to be avoided. It is why the control laws (14) and (15) have to be extended in such way to assure the safe motion in the presence of obstacles. Around each obstacle a safety region is defined:

$$\Delta_j = \{(x, y)|d_j(x, y) \leq R_j\}, \quad \Delta_O = \cup \Delta_j, \tag{16}$$

where $d_j(x, y) = \sqrt{(x - x_{Oj})^2 + (y - y_{Oj})^2}$ and R_j defines the radius of Δ_j.

If the ith follower robot is in the safety region of an obstacle, the computed velocity of the corresponding robot has to be redefined to assure that the robot leaves the safety region. To tackle this problem, a repulsive force with x and y components is defined $\delta_{ij} = (\delta_{ij}(x_i),\ \delta_{ij}(y_i))$, which acts between the ith robot and jth obstacle. It is considered that δ_{ij} is differentiable if $(x_i, y_i) \in \Delta_j$ and it has the following properties:

$$\delta_{ij}(x_i) > 0,\ \delta_{ij}(y_i) > 0,\ \text{if}\ (x_i, y_i) \notin \Delta_j, \tag{17}$$

$$\delta_{ij}(x_i) = 0,\ \delta_{ij}(y_i) = 0,\ \text{if}\ (x_i, y_i) \in \Delta_j, \tag{18}$$

$$\delta_{ij}(x_1) < \delta_{ij}(x_2) \text{ and } \delta_{ij}(y_1) < \delta_{ij}(y_2),\ \text{if}\ d_j(x_1, y_1) > d_j(x_2, y_2), \tag{19}$$

$$\delta_{ij}(x_1) = \delta_{ij}(x_2) \text{ and } \delta_{ij}(y_1) = \delta_{ij}(y_2),\ \text{if}\ d_j(x_1, y_1) = d_j(x_2, y_2). \tag{20}$$

Consider that the ith robot is in the safety region of obstacle j. For this case the following Lyapunov like function can be defined for the robot:

$$V_{ij} = \delta_{ij}(x_{Fi}) + \delta_{ij}(y_{Fi}). \tag{21}$$

The time derivative of the Lyapunov-like function is given by

$$\dot{V}_{ij} = \frac{\partial \delta_{ij}(x_{Fi})}{\partial x_{Fi}} \dot{x}_{Fi} + \frac{\partial \delta_{ij}(y_{Fi})}{\partial y_{Fi}} \dot{y}_{Fi}. \tag{22}$$

From (22) and (13) yields that $\dot{V}_{ij} < 0\ \forall\ (x_{Fi}, y_{Fi}) \in \Delta_j$.

Consider the control law for the follower robot, when it moves inside a safety region:

$$v_{Fxi} = -\frac{\partial \delta_{ij}(x_{Fi})}{\partial x_{Fi}} + v_{Rxi}, \text{ where } \frac{\partial \delta_{ij}(x_{Fi})}{\partial x_{Fi}} v_{Rxi} \leq 0, \tag{23}$$

$$v_{Fyi} = -\frac{\partial \delta_{ij}(y_{Fi})}{\partial y_{Fi}} + v_{Ryi}, \text{ where } \frac{\partial \delta_{ij}(y_{Fi})}{\partial x_{Fi}} v_{Ryi} \leq 0. \tag{24}$$

The control laws (23), (24) assure that the repulsive force decreases if the robot is inside the safety region i.e. it leaves the safety region over time. The second terms of the velocity control signals assure that the robot leaves the safety region not necessarily along the gradient of the repulsive force. If the robot leaves the safety region near the entrance point, limit cycle in the motion of the robot can appear presuming that the reference velocity, applicable outside the safety region, does not change its direction. In this work a random extra velocity term is introduced into the control signal. It assures a randomized search for a better obstacle avoidance path near the obstacle.

According to (14) and (23), the control velocity along the x axis for the ith follower can be summarized as follows:

$$v_{ix} = \begin{cases} K(x_{Pi} - x_{Fi}) + v_{Pxi}, & \text{if } (x_{Fi}, y_{Fi}) \notin \Delta_O, \\ -\frac{\partial \delta_{ij}(x_{Fi})}{\partial x_{Fi}} + v_{Rxi}, & \text{otherwise.} \end{cases} \tag{25}$$

$$\text{where } v_{Rxi} = \begin{cases} r, & \text{if } \frac{\partial \delta_{ij}(x_{Fi})}{\partial x_{Fi}} r < 0, \\ 0, & \text{otherwise.} \end{cases} \tag{26}$$

Here r is a random real number generated in a predefined, bounded interval: $r = \text{rand}(-v_M, v_M)$. The control velocity of the follower robot along the y axis can be formulated in the same way.

If the robot enters into the safety regions of more than one obstacle, the safety region of the nearest obstacle is taken to calculate the control velocity. If the obstacles are close to each other, a single safety region can be considered for the neighboring obstacles.

3   Experiments with Simulated Robots

3.1   Simulation Environment

The control framework introduced in Sec. 2 was tested in a single master simulated multi-robot environment. The testbed on the master side consists of a two Phantom Omni haptic devices, H_1 and H_2. For each haptic device the update rate used was 1 kHz. The H_1 is used to operate the leader robot directly: the position commands (x and y axis) are used to calculate reference velocities, see (3). Using H_2 the operator can modify the formation layout by changing the Π or Π_C parameter vectors.

During the experiments, the communication between the master and the simulator was implemented over the Internet. In the case of communication noise

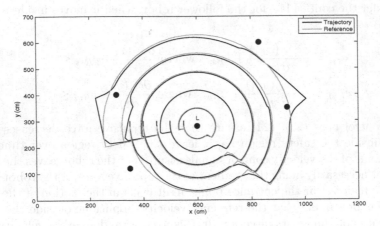

Fig. 2. Follower robot trajectories during sweep motion

the data structures in the communication environments can be regulated in order to achieve good communication performance in the haptic channels of the teleoperation system [8]. The simulator executes the received commands from the master computer, calculates and sends the force feedback on both x and y axis for each haptic device. The simulator also sends video feedback about the motion of the robots to the operator situated on the master side.

For the evaluation of the formation control a virtual 2D simulation environment was implemented. A simulated robot is modeled as a vertex around which the safety region is defined by (16), where $R = 20$ cm. For every robot the other robots represent obstacles. Similarly, the stationary obstacles are modeled the same way using $R = 100$ cm. In the simulated environment every robot and obstacle position is considered known. In real applications the robots can be localized using e.g. GPS technology in outdoor environments, the obstacles can be detected using distance sensors such as ultrasound or LIDARs.

The ith follower's velocity is calculated using (25), where $K = 3.5$, $v_M = 10.0$, and $\delta_{ij} = \frac{1}{(x_i - x_j)^2}$ is chosen as the repulsive force function.

3.2   Simulation Results

In the first experiment the operator aligns $N = 5$ followers after the leader in a line formation and performs a sweeping motion among 4 stationary obstacles. During this experiment the leader robot's position does not change, i.e. the H_1 is not used. Using H_2, the formation is rotated counterclockwise and it is spread out or pulled together at will by the operator. During this experiment H_2 modifies the elements of parameter vector $\mathbf{\Pi}_C$, defined in (7), as follows: $d_{LC} = K_{dLC}x_{H_2}$, $\alpha_{LC}[k] = \alpha_{LC}[k-1] + K_{\alpha LC}y_{H_2}$, where $K_{dLC} = 3.5$ and $K_{\alpha LC} = 0.5$ are scaling parameters. The prescribed positions for the ith follower is calculated as:

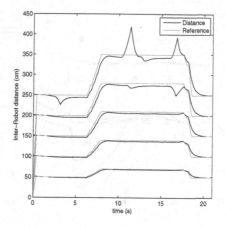

Fig. 3. Radius reconfiguration during sweep motion

$$\begin{cases} x_{P_i} = x_C + id_{LC}\sin(\theta_L - \alpha_{LC}), \\ y_{P_i} = y_C + id_{LC}\cos(\theta_L - \alpha_{LC}), \end{cases} \tag{27}$$

The path and reference path of each follower is presented on Fig. 2. The followers, as they follow their reference positions might come across stationary obstacles. In these case the velocities are calculated as such that the robot avoids the obstacle. However, this might cause the robot to quit the formation. As soon as the obstacle is not blocking the path of the robot it, resumes following the prescribed position. The reference distance and the real distance between L and each follower can be seen on Fig. 3. For example, the outer robot enters the safety region of all 4 obstacles resulting in a departure from the formation in the time intervals $2 - 4s$, $10 - 12s$, $12 - 14s$ and $16 - 18s$. On the same figure the reconfiguration, i.e. spread out and pull together, of the formation can be seen between $5 - 20s$.

During the second experiment a leader following test is performed by the operator among 3 stationary obstacles. A total of $N = 5$ followers are placed in random positions at the beginning of the experiment. Using the H_1 the operator guides the leader and H_2 is used to reconfigure the formation in the same way as described in the first experiment. Figure 4 illustrates the reference path and the real path of the followers. Figure 5 presents the feedback forces sent back to the haptic devices. The forces are sensed when robots are inside of an obstacle's safety zone. For example, during the rotation movement the leader was stopped (between $12 - 18s$) in the safety zone of the second obstacle causing a constant force value. The F_{H2}, which is related to the formation center and is sent to H_2, follows a similar pattern. The haptic feedback helps the human operator to avoid efficiently the obstacles near the robotic team.

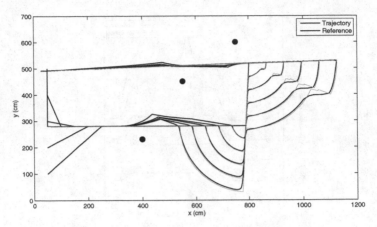

Fig. 4. Follower robot trajectories during leader-following

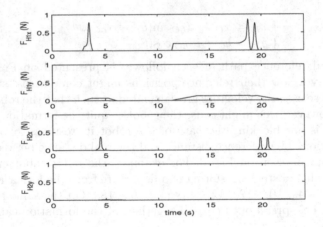

Fig. 5. The F_{H1} and F_{H2} forces during leader following

4   Conclusions

In this article, a formation controller is designed for coordinating a group of robots using a teleoperation based approach. The proposed method allows the operator, situated at the master side, to navigate and reshape the robot formation using two haptic devices. The leader robot is controlled directly by the operator using the first haptic device. The references of the followers are represented by a time-varying virtual structure. The shape of the structure can be reconfigured by the operator using the second haptic device. To calculate the control velocities of the follower robots, a switching control law was proposed. It combines a tracking control algorithm with an obstacle avoidance algorithm. Simulation were performed with $N = 5$ followers robots. Theoretically, the number of followers can be further increased with this teleoperation strategy, but the inter-robot distance should be set in function of the size (radius). Experiments performed demonstrate the applicability of the proposed formation control method. Using real haptic devices the operator can control a simulated formation over the Internet. In future works we consider moving to a decentralized control and adding some degree of intelligence to the robots.

Acknowledgments. This work was supported by a grant of the Romanian National Authority for Scientific Research, CNCS UEFISCDI, project number PN-II-RU-TE-2011-3-0005. The research was partially supported by TÁMOP-4.2.2.C-11/1/KONV-2012-0001 (FIRST) project.

References

1. Murray, R.: Recent research in cooperative control of multi-vehicle systems. In: International Conference on Advances in Control and Optimization of Dynamical Systems (2007)
2. Brambilla, M., Ferrante, E., Birattari, M., Dorigo, M.: Swarm robotics: A review from the swarm engineering perspective. Swarm Intelligence 7(1), 1–41 (2013)
3. Rezaee, H., Abdollahi, F.: A decentralized cooperative control scheme with obstacle avoidance for a team of mobile robots. IEEE Transactions on Industrial Electronics 61(1), 347–354 (2014)
4. Rodriguez-Seda, E., Troy, J., Erignac, C., Murray, P., Stipanovic, D., Spong, M.: Bilateral teleoperation of multiple mobile agents: Coordinated motion and collision avoidance. IEEE Transactions on Control Systems Technology 18(4), 984–992 (2010)
5. Franchi, A., Secchi, C., Son, H.I., Bulthoff, H., Giordano, P.: Bilateral teleoperation of groups of mobile robots with time-varying topology. IEEE Transactions on Robotics 28(5), 1019–1033 (2012)
6. Cui, R., Ge, S.S., How, B.V.E., Choo, Y.S.: Leader-follower formation control of underactuated autonomous underwater vehicles. Ocean Engineering 37(17-18), 1491–1502 (2010)
7. Marton, L., Szanto, Z., Haller, P., Sandor, H., Szabo, T., Vajda, T.: Bilateral teleoperation of wheeled mobile robots working in common workspace. IAES International Journal of Robotics and Automation (IJRA) 3(1) (2014)
8. Sandor, H., Szabo, T., Vajda, T., Haller, P., Szanto, Z., Marton, L.: Video supported bilateral teleoperation system: Design and implementation. In: 2013 IEEE 14th International Symposium on. Computational Intelligence and Informatics (CINTI), pp. 105–111 (November 2013)

Coupling Learning Capability and Local Rules for the Improvement of the Objects' Aggregation Task by a Cognitive Multi-Robot System

Abdelhak Chatty[1,2], Philippe Gaussier[2], Ali Karaouzene[2], Mohamed Bouzid[2], Ilhem Kallel[1], and Adel M. Alimi[1]

[1] REGIM: REsearch Groups on Intelligent Machine
National School of Engineers of Sfax (ENIS), Sfax University, Sfax, Tunisia
[2] ETIS: Neuro-cybernetic team, Image and signal Processing
National School of Electronics and its Applications (ENSEA),
Cergy-Pontoise University, Paris, France

Abstract. This paper aims to shed light on the benefits of the cognitive processes in the generation of emergent structures that allow the cognitive robots to succeed the objects' aggregation task. In the multi-robot system, every robot uses local rules and an on-line building and learning of its own cognitive map. This fusion alters the positive impact of the individual behavior in the improvement of the overall system performance. A series of simulations and experiments allowed us to present and discuss the system.

Keywords: Cognitive process, Learning Capability, Local rules, Emergent structures, Multi-robot system.

1 Introduction

The interaction between robots should not be complex [1]. Indeed, using a set of local rules with the stigmergy [2] allow the robots to produce emergent behaviors [3–7]. Based on this idea, researchers were able to design a number of successful experiments in the objects' aggregation task. A model relying on biologically plausible assumptions was proposed in [8] to analyse the phenomenon of dead bodies' aggregation by ants. The authors in [1] showed that interacting directly with objects simplifies the reasoning needed by multi-robot system and allows the aggregation of scattered objects. The aggregation and the sorting of colored frisbees by a multi-robot system is studied in [9]. The aggregation of small cylinders by a group of Khepera robots that use only contact sensors is also studied in [10]. In the experiments cited above, the robots do not have a navigation strategy; they move randomly using only local rules. Thus, the question that arises is to know what will happen if the robots would be able to use beside the local rules a bio-inspired navigation system which allows them to learn the objects' positions in their environment? The aim of this work is to show the positive result from coupling the learning capabilities with the local rules concerning the

A.P. del Pobil et al. (Eds.): SAB 2014, LNAI 8575, pp. 290–299, 2014.

performance improvement of the aggregation task by a multi-robot system. The goal is to accelerate the system convergence by allowing robots to pick up objects from the original source and to gather them in new a secondary source which we will call from now on a warehouse. This paper is organized as follows: in section 2 the robot's neural networks architecture is presented. Section 3 describes the robot's local rules. Section 4 and 5 are devoted to show the positive effect's of the local rules association with the learning capability in a multi-robot system.

2   The Robot's Neural Networks Architecture

Starting from neurobiological hypotheses on the role of hippocampus in the spatial navigation, several works [11–13] revealed special cells in the rats hippocampus that becomes active whenever the animal passes through a given place which it already visited. These neurons have been called place cells (PCs). We do not use PCs directly to navigate, plan or build a map, we rather use neurons called transition cells (TC) [14]. These cells represent the basis of the neurobiological model of temporal learning sequences in the hippocampus. A transition cell encodes a spatio-temporal transition between two PCs consecutively winning the place recognition competition, respectively at time t and δt. The set of PCs and TCs constitutes a non-cartesian cognitive map. The advantage of using transition cells is that their association with an action is univocal and quite straightforward and there is no need for an external algorithm to extract the action from the cognitive map. To develop the bio-inspired cognitive map, we took inspiration from the model presented in [15] which describes the role of the hippocampus. In practice, to create the PC the robot takes a visual panorama of the surrounding environment. The views are processed to extract visual landmarks. After learning these landmarks, a visual code is created by combining the landmarks of a panorama with their azimuths. This configuration serves as a code for PCs. The signals provided by the EC (the entorhinal cortex) are solely spatial and consistent with spatial cells activities. Spatial cells activities are submitted to a Winner-Take-All competition in order to only select the cell with the strongest response at a specific location. We will subsequently talk about the current location by indicating the spatial cell which has the highest activity at a given location. Thus, The temporal function at the level of the DG (dentate gyrus) is reduced to the memorization of past location. The acquired association at the level of CA3 (the pyramidal cells) is then the transition from a location to another aside from all of the information concerning the time spent on carrying out this transition. Once the association from the past location to the new one is learned, every new entry will reactivate the corresponding memory in the DG. A schematic view of our architecture is shown in Fig. 1. During the exploration of the environment each robot is able, independently of the other robots, to navigate, learn and create its own cognitive map on-line whose structure depends on the robot's own experience and discovery of the environment in which it lives [16]. After having explored the environment, the robots are able to predict, in each position the locations directly reachable.

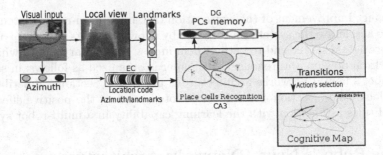

Visual input   Local view   Landmarks   DG
PCs memory

Azimuth   Location code   Place Cells Recognition
Azimuth/landmarks   CA3

Transitions

Action's selection

Cognitive Map

Fig. 1. From the construction of the visual code of place cells to the creation of the cognitive map [17]

The equations that govern learning in the cognitive map are 1 and reflearning2 where $T(t)$ is a binary signal (0 or 1) which is activated when a transition is made (moving from one place to another). This signal controls the learning of recurrent connections W^{CC}. γ is a parameter less than 1 which regulates the distribution of the motivation activity on the map. $\lambda 1$ and $\lambda 2$ are parameters of respectively active and passive forgotten on the recurrent connections. $S(t)$ is a signal marking the satisfaction of an objective. This signal controls the learning of synaptic connections between neurons in W^{MC} motivations activity X^M and neurons of the cognitive map of activity X^C.

$$\frac{dW_{ij}^{CC}(t)}{dt} = T(t).((\gamma - W_{ij}^{CC}).X_i^C(t).X_j^C(t) - W_{ij}^{CC}(t).(\lambda 1.X_j^C(t) - \lambda 2)) \qquad (1)$$

$$\frac{dW_{ij}^{MC}(t)}{dt} = S(t) \, for \, i,j = argmax_{k,l}(X_l^C(t).X_M^K(t)) \qquad (2)$$

3   Robot's Local Rules

In addition to the robots, the simulated environment contains three inexhaustible sources (A, B and C) and the real environment (with real robots) contains one source (G1). All sources are composed of a set of objects. The robots life cycles are linked to their supply levels from each source type. In fact, each robot possesses drives which corresponds to a source type. When the level of one supply decreases to a critical threshold level, the drive related to that type of supply triggers and the robot starts using its cognitive map to reach the source that allows the satisfaction of that need. If the robot fails to go back to that source or one of the warehouses of the same type before the corresponding satisfaction level reaches a very low level, it dies. Thus, the robots have two behaviors. The first one is the exploration mode which allows them to discover the environment without the need to satisfy their drives. The second behavior is manifested when the need arises and the drives triggers, the robots switch to the planning mode, using their cognitive maps to reach a source or a warehouse. Thereby, the robots are able to return to these sources or warehouses in order to pick up an object and deposit elsewhere in the environment. The grouping of two or more objects becomes a new warehouse which will be added to the cognitive map of the robots that they discover it and it will be used to create new warehouses, to satisfy robots's needs and it is going to be maintained by disposing objects on it as well. The pick up and the diposit local rules are functions of the number of robots perceived. The robot can indeed, tend to favor the location which contains other robots rather than empty regions in order to deposit the object. The pick up condition follows equation. 3, which means, that the probability to take an object from a source or a warehouse is inversely proportional to the number of robots surrounding the source , the more isolated is the source, the picking up probability is higher.

$$Pr_{(pick\_up)} = \exp^{-\lambda N_R} \tag{3}$$

where N_R is the number of robots in the neighborhood, λ is a positive constant. Equation. 4 describes the deposit conditions; the probability of deposit increases with time and distance from the original source or the warehouse from where the robot took the objects. It also depends on the number of the robots in the neighborhood, because when the current place of the robot is frequented by other robots it is suitable to be a refueling point.

$$Pr_{(Deposits)} = (1 - \exp^{-\alpha N_R}) * (1 - \exp^{-\beta t}) \tag{4}$$

where α, β are environmental factors, N_R is the number of robots in the neighborhood and t is the time since the taking.

4   Simulated Objects' Aggregation Task

We placed the three original sources (A, B and C) in the summits of an isosceles triangle knowing that the center of gravity is the relevant place. Indeed, when a new warehouse is created, it allows the optimization of the robots' traveling distance to go back to the sources and to deposit or to pick up more objects. The three original sources allow the creation of three different types of warehouses ("a" is from A, "b" from B and "c" is from C). In Fig. 2 (a), the 48 robots start moving randomly in the environment, with a limited field of view that restricts the ability to perceive the entire environment and let the robots detect only the close robots. While passing through a source or a warehouse, a robot increases its level of satisfaction and applies the local rule to pick up an object. The probability to pick up an object increases when the robot does not detect other robots next to the source. The probability of deposit increases when the robot detects other robots and it is sufficiently away from the original source as indicated by equation. 4. This means that the locations chosen for the deposit are often common to several robots. Fig. 2 (b) shows the creation of warehouses. Robots also have the possibility of refueling warehouses by adding objects to them. This provides stability for the warehouse in relevant locations which are close to several robots. However, warehouses that are abandoned or poorly visited will eventually disappear since the number of objects available will decrease rapidly (see Fig. 2 (c)). Finally, the system converges to a stable configuration (see Fig. 2 (d)) with a fixed number of warehouses in fixed places at 7587 time steps and remains the same for more than 20000 time steps (see Fig. 2 (e)). We note that the robots were able to create villages of warehouses, which consist of objects from the three different original sources in an appropriate location at the gravity center of triangles. Thus, Instead of browsing an Euclidean distance between the three original sources equal to 59.2 to look for objects, robots can reduce this distance (equal to 12.08) with the creation of near-perfect villages. This shows that the fusion of learning capability with the local rules can generate relevant warehouses, ensuring optimization of the distance traveled by the robots to return to sources, using the cognitive map (see Fig. 2 (f)), to solve the objects' aggregation task.

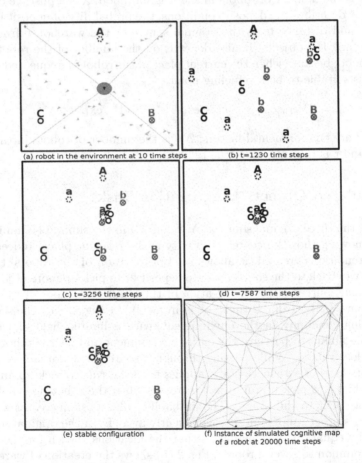

Fig. 2. Through the individual deposit process, the robots were able to create a village of different kinds of new stable warehouses in relevant places which allowed them to optimize the distance walked to return to the different kind of sources

5   Real Robots in the Objects' Aggregation Task

In order to verify the performance of the approach for the objects' aggregation task, we used a real multi-robot system composed of a reactive robot and another cognitive one which has already learned the environment and the location of the source (composed by 40 boxes see Fig. 6 (a)) in order to return back to pick up more objects. The robot's cognitive map is presented by Fig. 6 (d).

5.1   The Pick Up Operation

To allow robots to perform the pick up operation, we mounted on each robot a gripper (Fig. 3) equipped with a FSR pressure sensor to enable the objects detection by the robots. The application of an external force on the surface of the sensor indicates the presence of an object in the gripper. While keeping the same rules of the simulated multi-robot system, robots are not able to localize the objects in the environment. However, when using ultrasonic sensors, they are able to detect the presence of obstacles or other robots. Thus, robots are able to pick up objects from isolated sources. Therefore, the presence of other robots near to the robot will activate the obstacles avoidance procedure, which will prevent the robot to take objects in the occupied areas by other robots which satifies equation. 3.

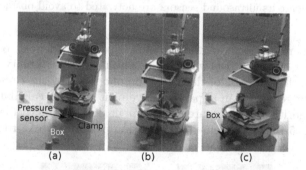

Fig. 3. (a) the random motion of the robot (b) the success of pick up operation by the activation of the pressure sensor, (c) followed by a change of the direction

5.2   The Deposit Operation

To deposit an object, the robot switches to a reverse gear for 3s and changes direction to release the object from the gripper fingers. In order to keep the same rules of simulated multi-robot system, we have equipped the robots with a FireWire camera which is mounted at the front of the robot and it is bent down to limit its field of view (50 cm between the robot and the other objects). This camera allows the robots to detect movement nearby which is estimated using a standard algorithm of Optical Flow [18]. Thus, each time a robot is in the camera's field of view, the deposit operation will be activated, which allows robots to place the object in areas frequently visited by other robots. For this reason we have reduced the scope of ultrasonic sensors when the deposit operation is triggered to prevent the confusion between robots and obstacles, and we also have reduced the linear speed of the robot in order to avoid the obstacles. To satisfy the second condition of the simulated multi-robot system of deposing far from the source, we disabled the deposit operation for 6s after taking the object. Fig. 4 shows the operation of deposit performed by a robot when it has detected another robot via the camera.

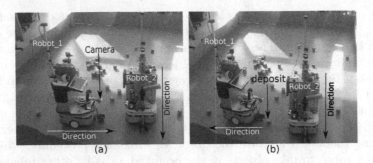

Fig. 4. Validation of the deposit operation. (a) the detection of the movement of the robot_2 via the camera (b) the deposit of the object through the backward movement of the robot_1 where its ultrasound sensors are activated to avoid obstacles.

The deposit operation includes the refueling operation (deposit objects in the warehouses that already exist) which is essential for the stability of the warehouses. Indeed, the detection of the collection of objects by the camera when the robot is moving generates an apparent movement which is calculated using the optical flow algorithm, this apparent movement detection activates the deposit procedure. Fig. 5 shows the refueling operation performed by a robot.

Fig. 5. Validation of the refueling operation. (a) the random motion of the robot. (b) the refueling operation followed by a learning phase of the new warehouse.

5.3   Experiments and Results

The robots start to move randomly with a high detection range of the ultrasound sensors, while passing through a source, the robot applies the pick up local rule to transport an object (see Fig. 6 (b)). Once the object is taken, the scope of ultrasonic sensors is reduced to allow the cognitive robot to place its object near to the frequented places by the other robot or next to another object (refueling warehouses). Once more than two objects are deposed at the same place, this place represents a new warehouse. When a new warehouse is discovered the robot tags this place as potentially interesting by setting a motivation to the corresponding TC (see Fig. 6 (d)). This labeling by motivation can guide the movements of the robot through its own cognitive map towards the warehouses' locations. Thus, when the need for a certain source is reached, the robot switches from an exploration behavioral state to a motivated state and the TCs which are associated to the corresponding drive are stimulated and eventually activated in order to make target locations pop-up. At that point, a path is planned through the cognitive map in the direction of the interesting target places for the purpose of picking up an objects or maintaining a warehouse (see Fig. 6 (c)). The experiments showed us the same observations about ambiguity of perception discussed in [1]. Indeed, in a pick up phase, where the scope of the ultrasound sensor of the robot is high, the warehouses are considered as obstacles. This allows the robots to take objects only from the isolated sources.

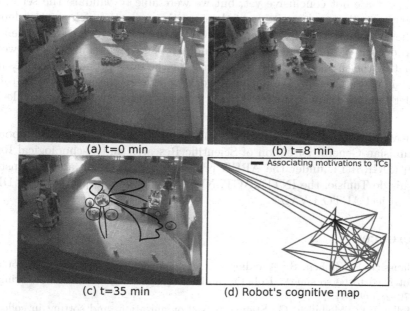

Fig. 6. The objects' aggregation task (a) the initial configuration, (b) robot tries to pick up a box (c) the emergence of five warehouses in fixed places. The black trajectories show some robot's paths to reach one of warehouses (using its cognitive map) (d) the association of the motivations in the robot's cognitive map.

The amplification of the local rules with the learning capability allows the emerging of five warehouses of different sizes in fixed places on the environment as shown in Fig. 6 (c). Thus, the evaluation of the approach through a real multi-robot system allowed us to show the feasibility of our bio-inspired architecture and the hypotheses tested through a simulated multi-robot system. However, among the major problems that we encountered are those related to either the size of the robots that push the objects off of their position or the error of the motion detection. Indeed, the reflection of light on the floor and the shadows of obstacles force the cognitive robots to deposit objects in non relevant places (like the isolated objects shown in Fig. 6 (c)).

6   Conclusion

We have shown in this paper how the fusion of the local rules with the learning capability gives birth to the creation of emergent structures which allow cognitive robots to resolve the objects aggregation task with the guarantee of a fixed number of warehouses in fixed places. In practice, we proposed a set of simulations that show through the cognitive processes, that the robots were able to speed up the convergence and to create a village of new stable warehouses in relevant places. In order to analyze the system in a real environment, we equipped the robots with the necessary tools and sensors that allow them to keep the same rules as the simulated multi-robot system. The first results of the experiment are not conclusive yet, but we were able to validate the set of elementary operations: construction of the cognitive map, the pick up, the deposit and the warehouse refueling operation. Our goals in the future experiments is to improve the performance of the real multi-robot system. Particularly, we are eliminating the engineered solutions by keeping the same probabilistic rules used in the simulated system. We will also work to develop the awareness of robots in order to allow them to detect, categorize and create news emergent rules.

Acknowledgment. The authors would like to thank the financial support of the Tunisian General Direction of Scientific Research and Technological Renovation (DGRSRT), under the ARUB program 01/UR/11 02, and the Institut Français de Tunisie, the INTERACT, NEUROBOT French project, and DIGITEO project AUTO EVAL.

References

1. Gaussier, P., Zrehen, S.: Avoiding the world model trap: An acting robot does not need to be so smart? Robotics and Computer-Integrated Manufacturing 11, 279–286 (1994)
2. Holland, O., Melhuish, C.: Stigmergy, self-organization, and sorting in collective robotics. Artif. Life 5, 173–202 (1999)
3. Mataric, M.J.: Designing Emergent Behaviors: From Local Interactions to Collective Intelligence. In: Meyer, J.A., Roiblat, H., Wilson, S. (eds.) Proceedings of the Second Conference on Simulation of Adaptive Behavior, pp. 1–6. MIT Press (1992)

4. Kube, C.R., Zhang, H.: Collective robotics: From social insects to robots. Adaptive Behavior 2, 189–218 (1993)
5. Brooks, R.A.: Coherent behavior from many adaptive processes. In: Proceedings of the Third International Conference on Simulation of Adaptive Behavior, pp. 22–29. MIT Press, Cambridge (1994)
6. Chatty, A., Kallel, I., Gaussier, P., Alimi, A.: Emergent complex behaviors from swarm robotic systems by local rules. In: IEEE Workshop on Robotic Intelligence In Informationally Structured Space (RiiSS), pp. 69–76 (2011)
7. Chatty, A., Gaussier, P., Kallel, I., Laroque, P., Florance, P., Alimi, M.A.: The evaluation of emergent structures in a "cognitive" multi-agent system based on on-line building and learning of a cognitive map. In: Proceedings of International Conference on Agents and Artificial Intelligence, ICAART 2013, pp. 269–275 (2013)
8. Deneubourg, J.L., Goss, S., Franks, N., Franks, A.S., Detrain, C., Chrétien, L.: The dynamics of collective sorting robot-like ants and ant-like robots. In: Proceedings of the First International Conference on Simulation of Adaptive Behavior on From Animals to Animats, pp. 356–363. MIT Press, Cambridge (1990)
9. Beckers, R., Holland, O.E., Deneubourg, J.L.: From local actions to global tasks: Stigmergy and collective robotics. In: In Articial Life IV. Proc. Fourth International Workshop on the Synthesis and Simulation of Living Systems, Cambridge, Massachusetts, USA, pp. 181–189 (1994)
10. Martinoli, A., Mondada, F.: Collective and cooperative group behaviours: Biologically inspired experiments in robotics. In: Khatib, O., Salisbury, J. (eds.) Experimental Robotics IV. LNCIS, vol. 223, pp. 1–10. Springer, Heidelberg (1997)
11. O'Keefe, J., Nadel, L.: The hippocampus as a cognitive map / John O'Keefe and Lynn Nadel. Clarendon Press, Oxford University Press, Oxford (1978)
12. Bachelder, I.A., Waxman, A.M.: Mobile robot visual mapping and localization: A view-based neurocomputational architecture that emulates hippocampal place learning. Neural Networks 7, 1083–1099 (1994)
13. Milford, M., Wyeth, G.: Mapping a suburb with a single camera using a biologically inspired slam system. IEEE Transactions on Robotics 24, 1038–1053 (2008)
14. Gaussier, P., Revel, A., Banquet, J.P., Babeau, V.: From view cells and place cells to cognitive map learning: processing stages of the hippocampal system. Biological Cybernetics 86, 15–28 (2002)
15. Banquet, J.P., Gaussier, P., Dreher, J.C., Joulain, C., Revel, A., Gunther, W.: Spacetime, order and hierarchy in fronto-hippocamal system: A neural basis of personality. In: Cognitive Science Perspectives on Personality and Emotion, pp. 123–189. Elsevier Science BV (1997)
16. Chatty, A., Gaussier, P., Kallel, I., Laroque, P., Alimi, M.A.: Adaptation capability of cognitive map improves behaviors of social robots. In: Proceedings of IEEE International Conference on Development and Learning and the Epigenetic Robotics. ICDL-EPIROB 2012, pp. 1–7 (2012)
17. Chatty, A., Gaussier, P., Hasnain, S.K., Kallel, I., Alimi, M.A.: The effect of learning by imitation on a multi-robot system based on the coupling of a low level imitation strategy and on-line learning for cognitive map building. Advanced Robotics, Special issue on Biologically Inspired Robotics 28(3), 1–13 (2014)
18. Horn, B.K.P., Schunck, B.G.: Determining optical flow. Artif. Intell. 17, 185–203 (1981)

Honeybee-Inspired Quality Monitoring of Routing Paths in Mobile Ad Hoc Networks

Alexandros Giagkos and Myra S. Wilson

Department of Computer Science, Aberystwyth University,
Aberystwyth, SY23 3DB, UK

Abstract. This paper discusses BeeIP, a reactive multipath routing protocol inspired by honeybees, and examines its performance for both connection-oriented and connectionless traffic within mobile ad hoc networks using a new modification to the algorithm for artificial swarming. Artificial agents follow concepts borrowed from the communication and foraging activities of real honeybees to detect new routing paths and maintain successful and robust data traffic. Paths are evaluated by constantly monitoring their quality based on a list of well-defined low-level parameters. The protocol is compared with the state-of-the-art DSR, AODV and its multipath version AOMDV using four benchmark performance metrics for both TCP and UDP traffic. The results suggest that BeeIP is able to achieve high packet delivery ratio, end-to-end delay and average receiving throughput, while it is shown second best in terms of control overhead for both transport layer protocols.

1 Introduction

Mobile ad hoc networks (MANETs) [9] are prone to the mobility of the nodes and their energy constraints. The former renders centralized control impossible while the latter dramatically affects the performance of the wireless network. Under these conditions, the nodes are expected to discover routing paths and forward data in an adaptive, optimal, self-healing and robust manner.

The characteristics above can be found in nature, in particular, in insect societies such as honeybees [3]. This paper illustrates how adaptive behaviours that are met in the natural system of the hive are applied in order to solve a complex routing problem. It discusses a reactive multipath routing protocol inspired by simple yet effective principles of honeybees, and presents an experimental comparison with state-of-the-art protocols for connection-oriented and connectionless traffic in MANETs.

In the next section a short description of the routing protocols used in this study is given followed by the discussion of BeeIP, the honeybee-inspired protocol, and its important internal mechanisms. The results from the experimental comparison are presented followed by the paper's conclusion and future work.

A.P. del Pobil et al. (Eds.): SAB 2014, LNAI 8575, pp. 300–309, 2014.

2   Reactive Protocols Used for Comparison

Ad hoc On-Demand Distance-Vector protocol (AODV) [10] is a well known reactive protocol for MANETs. In AODV, when the source does not have any previous routing knowledge for a specific destination, route request packets (RREQ) are broadcast to the network. If the RREQ is received by an intermediate node, the node updates its own routing table and broadcasts the RREQ further. The process repeats until the RREQ reaches its final destination, when the destination node responds by unicasting a route reply packet (RREP). The selection of the next hop is made at each node by using the shortest path metric. The reactive nature of AODV allows it to produce less control overhead, which compromises the time it requires to set up a connection when compared to proactive protocols.

AOMDV, a multipath protocol inspired by AODV, accepts duplicate copies of RREQ messages and examines them in order to find alternative reverse paths [13]. Each intermediate node can hold a cache of alternative paths which will be used as next hop in order to reach the appropriate destination. In terms of packet forwarding, AOMDV uses a simple approach; a link is used until it breaks, at which point an alternative is found from the cache. Being a multipath routing protocol, AOMDV is able to reduce both end-to-end delay and packet loss, and is able to utilize the network topology more efficiently as the load is distributed across multiple routes.

The Dynamic Source Routing protocol (DSR) [8] is designed to eliminate the periodic update messages between nodes, thus the bandwidth consumed for this control overhead. It uses source routing described in detail in [11]. A routing entry in DSR contains all intermediate nodes to be visited by a packet, rather than just the next hop information maintained by DSDV or AODV. DSR uses a similar route request mechanism to AODV. However, to reduce the cost of route discovery in terms of control overhead, each node in the network maintains a cache of source routes it has learnt or overheard by the previously incoming RREQ messages (promiscuous mode). The cache is then used aggressively in order to limit the message propagation. However, the major disadvantage of this protocol is that its aggressive use of caches, as well as its inability to locally repair broken links, lead to stale routing information and cache pollution.

3   BeeIP: A Reactive Bee-Inspired Protocol

This section provides an overview of BeeIP, a new multipath routing protocol for MANETs based on honeybees' interactions. More detailed descriptions of the elements of the protocol can be found in [5]. Its model consists of four types of agents (packets); scouts, foragers, ack_scouts and ack_foragers. The key concepts of the protocol are briefly presented below.

3.1   Scouting for Multiple Paths

A scouting process is initialized when a source requires a path to a destination and there is no sufficient routing knowledge available. A scout is broadcast and is propagated until it finally meets the destination, keeping in its header the addresses of the intermediate nodes it visits. When the scout is received by the destination an ack_scout is sent back to the source by following the reverse path of nodes already visited by the received scout. Each intermediate node that receives an ack_scout is not allowed to answer to others of the same scouting generation. Thus BeeIP is designed to find node-disjoint paths only. Node-disjoint paths are more resilient to failures than link-disjoint paths as they protect against both node and link failures. One or more ack_scouts may be sent from the destination allowing multiple paths to be found, each one marked with a unique identification number. While ack_scouts return, they collect data to measure the path's quality. This is an activity similar to the one performed by real honeybees in nature.

3.2   Artificial Foraging: Data Packet Delivery

The source node creates foragers in order to encapsulate real data, received from the transport layer. Each data packet is piggybacked to a forager which, in turn, asks for an appropriate path identification number to its destination. When it is received by the destination node, it delivers the data to the transport layer and converts to an ack_forager. Like the real honeybees, which take some time on the flower to collect the pollen or the nectar, the ack_forager stays at the destination node until some data packet needs to go back to the initial source.

While traversing a path from the destination to the source, the ack_forager collects low-level parameters that represent not only the current state of its senders, but also the network effectiveness of each intermediate link. These parameters are as follows. Firstly, the ack_forager's signal strength at the receiving node (Watts). When an ack_forager is received it carries a signal strength. A weak signal strength is an indication of long distance between the nodes and/or intermediate obstacles that affect the transmission. Secondly, the moving speed of the sender (velocity m/s). A moving node can easily go outside the transmission range and cause broken links. Thirdly, the sender's remaining energy level (Joules). Nodes with sufficient remaining energy are less vulnerable and better candidates for future packet transmissions. The forth parameter is the size of the MAC queue of the sender (bits). The queue size is an indication of how busy the sender is in terms of traffic and network congestion. Finally, the transmission delay between the sender and the receiver of a link in seconds. The use of time-stamps and synchronized clocks allows the measurement of the time an ack_forager requires to complete a transmission from the sender to the receiver of a link.

3.3   Path Quality Monitoring

A new quality value is calculated at every node visited by the ack_forager, and when it finally arrives home, the quality q of the path from the destination d to the source s can be expressed as:

$$Q_{ds} = \sum_{n=1}^{m-1} (q_{N_{n+1} \to N_n}), \quad [d = N_m, \; s = N_1] \tag{1}$$

where m is the total number of nodes in a numerically ordered path, and $N_{n+1} \rightarrow$ N_n the pair of nodes with direction towards the source node. The quality q of a link from node j to k as traversed by an agent b is shown in the following equation:

$$q_{jk} = sig'_b * w_{sig} + speed'_j * w_{speed} + energy'_j * w_{energy}$$
$$+ qd'_j * w_{qk} + txd'_{jk} * w_{txd} \tag{2}$$

where the prime numbers are the normalized values of the parameters (sig for signal's strength, etc), and the $w's$ are the appropriate weights. A more detailed explanation of the weighting system can be found in [4].

The result, obtained by Equation (1) is a number that can be used to represent the current quality of the path, in terms of the five low-level parameters. Results from a constant number of previous flights are collected, and based on them, the source is able to investigate whether there has been an improvement or deterioration to the path performance over time. Once there is sufficient amount of data available, the last step of the methodology is to apply regression analysis using Pearson's correlation coefficient [12] to catch any strong positive or negative correlation between the two variables, in this case: time and the quality of a path Q_{ds}. If the correlation is a strong positive, the foraging capacity is increased, whereas if it is a strong negative, the capacity is decreased. The foraging capacity is defined as the number of the remaining foragers for a path, i.e., the number of foragers allowed to use a path in the future.

3.4   Path Selection

The result as calculated by Equation (1), is used to compare each path's quality with its own previous findings, thus detecting improvements and deteriorations over time. Depending on the behaviour of the routing protocol that one may want to achieve, different selection metrics can be applied. On their way back, foragers collect this information and mark each path with a selection metric value. Traditional metric values are related to the number of hops in a path, the transmission speed of its links, the expected transmission count, the energy cost, the remaining energy, etc [1]. For the experimental comparison presented in this paper, a metric related to speed is used; the summation of the (half-round) transmission delay and queueing delay for each intermediate link of the path, from the destination towards the source. This ensures that the fastest path from the list is selected.

3.5   Broken Links Detection

Since BeeIP is designed to evaluate routing based on a 'path' level instead of 'link' level, link breakage within a path is detected when no foragers return to the source node within a period of time. In such a case, the source node sets the path's foraging capacity to 0 and marks the path as unacknowledged. The

first ensures that no future foragers will be given the broken path's unique identification number, whereas the latter allows the path to become available again,
if a forager eventually returns. Furthermore, internal timers are used to prune
any unacknowledged paths. This mechanism ensures that the control overhead
remains low as no special messages need to be sent to confirm nodes existence.
As the protocol is multipath, being able to switch quickly between routing alternatives allows it to be robust and resilient to bottlenecks and congestion.

3.6   Connectionless Transport Protocols

In TCP, acknowledgement packets, i.e., ack_scouts and ack_foragers are exploited
for free, as they piggyback the TCP acknowledgements and fly back. In UDP
this mechanism is not available. This problem is addressed by generating swarm
packets. A swarm is a control packet that carries the number of foragers that
return to the source and is released when one of two criteria is met. Either when
the number of waiting foragers has reached a predefined threshold (empirically
set to one third of initial colony population) or when a swarming timer has
expired. A swarm acts like an ack_forager in that it collects quality information
of the traversed path, which eventually affects its the foraging capacity at the
source.

4   Experiments and Results

BeeIP is compared with AODV, AOMDV, and DSR. Four performance metrics
are used for the comparison of the routing protocols; the packet delivery ratio
(PDR), the control overhead (CO), the average end-to-end delay (EED) and the
average receiving throughput (RTP) of the communication sessions during the
simulation. All experiments have been repeated 10 times using NS2 [7] and the
average results are presented. The set up of NS2 for both connection-oriented
(TCP) and connectionless (UDP) traffic experiments is given in Table 1.

Table 1. Summary of NS2 configuration

Number of nodes:	50
Terrain size:	1500 x 300 m^2
Simulation time and runs:	900 seconds, 10 runs
Initial energy:	100 to 1500 Joules
Movement model:	Random Waypoint (1 to 10 m/s)
Traffic generators:	FTP/TCP and CBR/UDP (packet size: 512 bytes)
Sending rate (UDP only):	3 packets per second
Active sources:	10 (both), 20 (UDP), and 30 (UDP)
Pause times:	0, 30, 60, 120, 300, 600, and 900
MAC layer:	IEEE 802.11b DCF (queue size 50 packets)
PHY layer:	914MHz Lucent WaveLAN
Transmission range:	150 metres

4.1   Connection-oriented Traffic

Figure 1 shows the PDR (%) as a function of the varying pause times. The error bars show the standard error from the mean. The first observation is that BeeIP shows the best PDR for highly dynamic networks and is rather insensitive to the pause time variations, whereas AODV's performance is slightly decreased as the network loses its dynamic characteristic. AOMDV is found to perform better than its single-path equivalent. On the other hand, due to its aggressive caching, DSR is able to perform better under less stressful situations, i.e., when the topology is less dynamic (pause time increases).

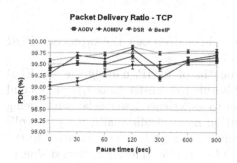

Fig. 1. PDR wrt. pause times   **Fig. 2.** CO wrt. pause times

Table 2. Route requests for different pause times, between multipath protocols AOMDV and BeeIP

	0	30	60	120	300	600	900
AOMDV:	5022	5219	5231	3854	5690	3542	2566
BeeIP:	848	1555	785	891	1164	746	732

Looking at the CO caused by the four routing protocols in figure 2, it is understood that as nodes lose their mobility, the number of control packets required to maintain routing is also reduced, especially with BeeIP, AODV and AOMDV. Between AODV and AOMDV, the latter is found to produce more CO due to its multiple RREP packets that are sent to support multipath discovery. Nonetheless, BeeIP is still able to keep the CO low, as it looks for node-disjoint paths, utilizing unicast scouting as well as the traditional broadcast. Also, compared to AOMDV, BeeIP is able to use the multiple paths in parallel, which not only distributes the traffic load across the alternative paths, it also mandates less number of route requests (scouting processes) for each communication session. Table 2 summarises the number of route requests incurred during the experiment between the multipath protocols. To conclude, DSR is shown to outperform all other protocols due to its lack of local repair mechanism, which reduces the CO dramatically. However, this strength's trade-off is to be prone to inactive

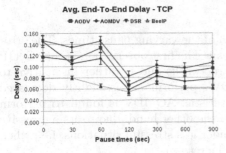

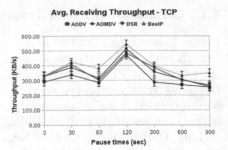

Fig. 3. EED wrt. pause times **Fig. 4.** RTP wrt. pause times

and out-of-date routing entries in cache, which decreases the protocol's PDR (figure 1) and EED (figure 3) for high mobility rates.

Figures 3 and 4 illustrate the two strengths of BeeIP, namely the low EED and average RTP. It is found that BeeIP is able to transfer more KB per second than the others, allowing each data packet to experience lower delay while being forwarded from the source to the destination node. Additionally, the protocol's small error from the mean is another indication that it is not sensitive to the increase of pause times when handling TCP traffic. This is reasoned due to the fact that BeeIP's buffering is always kept to a minimum. Firstly, being multipath the protocol uses more than one path to transmit packets for each session, spreading the data over the topology. Secondly, BeeIP shows balanced CO as fewer (as shown in Table 2) scouts are released. Thus, less packets flood the network and occupy the MAC interface queue of each of the nodes.

4.2   Connectionless Traffic

In this section, the performance of the protocols using connectionless traffic is under investigation. In order to provide a comprehensive comparative study between the protocols, two sets of experiments are presented; altering the pause times of the Random Waypoint movement model, and introducing low, medium and high traffic load to the network by changing the number of CBR active sources. Similar to the connection-oriented set up, 50 mobile nodes move within a $1500 \ x \ 300 \ m^2$ terrain for 900 seconds. Their initial energy level is a random number between 100 and 1500. In terms of traffic, 10 CBR active sources are constantly sending data packets of 512 bytes size, with a sending rate of 3 packets per second. Again, pause times of 0, 30, 60, 120, 300, 600 and 900 seconds are used.

Due to the constant bit rate traffic generator the numbers are lower. The results are similar to TCP. In figure 5, BeeIP is shown to achieve better PDR than the other protocols for all pause times. The CO (figure 6) is also shown to be better than AODV and AOMDV, with a deteriorated performance as the nodes tend to fixed positions. DSR is found to have the better CO score.

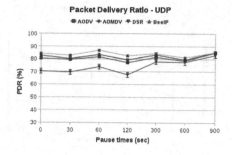

Fig. 5. PDR wrt. pause times

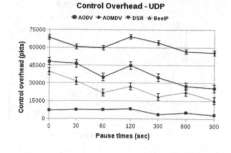

Fig. 6. CO wrt. pause times

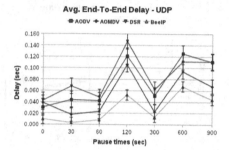

Fig. 7. EED wrt. pause times

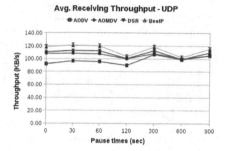

Fig. 8. RTP wrt. pause times

The average EED is proved to be the strength of BeeIP, as illustrated in figure 7 where, due to its fast packet switching mechanism, the proposed protocol outperforms the others. Interestingly, compared to the average EED for FTP/TCP data, the numbers are again very low. The reason for that is the extra overhead and delays TCP experiences because of its internal mechanisms at the transport layer [14]. Moreover, figure 8 summarises the performance of the protocols in terms of the average RTP for different pause times. The results again indicate that BeeIP has a better throughput performance than others, under static or moving nodes.

As mentioned before, in order to evaluate the performance of the protocols under various traffic loads the experiments have been repeated by using 10, 20 and 30 active CBR sources at a time, forming 15, 30 and 50 connections respectively. The pause time is kept to 30 seconds. Affecting the traffic load of the network emphasises the ability of the protocols in handling network congestion.

An initial observation from figure 9 is that as the number of active sources increases, the PDR is dramatically reduced. All protocols face a deterioration achieving higher ∼83% (BeeIP) and lower ∼69% (DSR) for 10 sources and higher ∼39% (BeeIP) and lower ∼34% (DSR) for 30 sources, as a result of the high traffic and congestions caused by bottlenecks. BeeIP is found to be competent especially when the number of active sources is 30. Increasing the number of active sources causes the performance of the protocols to follow a reversed pace

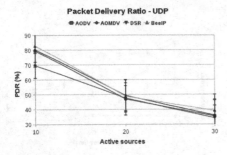

Fig. 9. PDR wrt. no of active sources

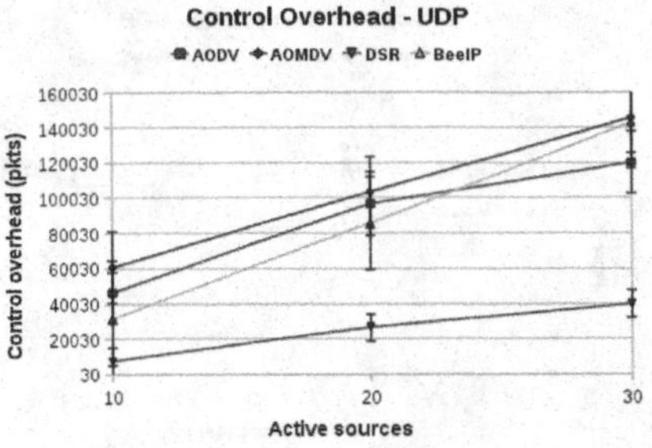

Fig. 10. CO wrt. no of active sources

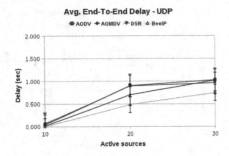

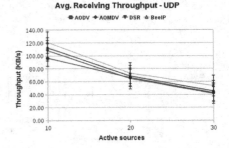

Fig. 11. EED wrt. no of active sources

Fig. 12. RTP wrt. no of active sources

in terms of CO; more control packets are sent as more sources send data packets to destinations. This is shown in figure 10, where DSR's design to reduce control packets proves fruitful. Finally, figures 11 and 12 present the average EED and RTP for all protocols. BeeIP is found to outperform the others in terms of delay and transfer more KB per second successfully.

5   Conclusion and Future Work

Adaptive behaviour inspired by honeybees is applied to dynamically discover and maintain routing solutions and forward data packets over wireless paths. BeeIP is discussed and compared to the state-of-the-art routing protocols for both connection-oriented and connectionless traffic. The latter is achieved by artificial swarming, the protocol's latest feature that allows foragers to aggregate and return to the source without the need of acknowledgements. The results indicate that a honeybee-inspired approach is able to outperform the other protocols, in terms of better packet delivery ratio (PDR), the average end-to-end delay (EED) and the average receiving throughput (RTP). The comparison with another nature-inspired and, in particular, bee-inspired routing protocol such as BeeAdHoc [2], would offer extra depth to the merits to BeeIP's design. However, no approved source code has been available in the public domain for the network simulator that was used in this project. Thus, these protocols are not included in this study and are instead seen as future work. Nevertheless, a qualitative comparison with BeeAdHoc is available in [6].

This research was funded by Aberystwyth University Postgraduate Research Fund.

References

1. Campista, M.E.M., Passos, D.G., Esposito, P.M., Moraes, I.M., de Albuquerque, C.V.N., Saade, D.C.M., Rubinstein, M.G., Costa, L.H.M.K., Duarte, O.C.M.B.: Routing metrics and protocols for wireless mesh networks. Computer Communications 22(1), 6–12 (2008)
2. Farooq, M., Pannenbaecker, T., Vogel, B., Mueller, C., Meth, J., Jeruschkat, R.: BeeAdHoc: an energy efficient routing algorithm for mobile ad hoc networks inspired by bee behavior. In: Proc. GECCO Genetic and evolutionary computation (GECCO 2005), pp. 137–172. ACM, New York (2005)
3. von Frisch, K.: The Dance Language and Orientation of Bees. Oxford University Press (1967)
4. Giagkos, A.: Protocol Design and Implementation for Bee-Inspired Routing in Mobile Ad hoc Networks. Ph.D. thesis, Aberystwyth University (2012)
5. Giagkos, A., Wilson, M.S.: Swarm intelligence to wireless ad hoc networks: adaptive honeybee foraging during communication sessions. Adaptive Behavior 21(6), 501–515 (2013), http://dx.doi.org/10.1177/1059712313500797
6. Giagkos, A., Wilson, M.S.: BeeIP - A Swarm Intelligence Based Routing for Wireless Ad Hoc Networks. Information Sciences (2014), http://dx.doi.org/10.1016/j.ins.2013.12.038
7. Issariyakul, T., Hossain, E.: Introduction to Network Simulator NS2. Springer (2009)
8. Johnson, D.B., Maltz, D.A.: Dynamic Source Routing in Ad-Hoc Wireless Networks. In: Imielinski, T., Korth, H. (eds.) Mobile Computing, pp. 153–181. Kluwer (1996)
9. Murthy, C.S.R., Manoj, B.S.: Ad Hoc Wireless Networks Architectures and Protocols. Prentice Hall, Upper Saddle River (2004)
10. Perkins, C.E., Belding-Royer, E., Das, S.: Ad hoc On-Demand Distance Vector (AODV) Routing IETF RFC3561 (July 2003), http://www.ietf.org/rfc/rfc3561.txt
11. Postel, J.: Internet Protocol - DARPA Inernet Programm, Protocol Specification, RFC 791 (September 1981), http://www.ietf.org/rfc/rfc791.txt
12. Read, T.R.C., Cressie, N.: Goodness-of-fit statistics for discrete multivariate data. Springer (1988)
13. Tarique, M., Tepe, K.E., Adibi, S., Erfani, S.: Survey of multipath routing protocols for mobile ad hoc networks. Journal of Network and Computer Applications 32(6), 1125–1143 (2009)
14. Xiao, H., Zhang, Y., Malcolm, J.A., Christianson, B., Chua, K.C.: Modelling and analysis of tcp performance in wireless multihop networks. Wireless Sensor Network 2(7), 493–503 (2010)

Human Inspiration and Comparison for Monitoring Strategies in a Robotic Convoy Task*

Silvia Rossi and Mariacarla Staffa

Department of Electrical Engineering and Information Technology D.I.E.T.I.
University of Naples - Federico II
via Claudio 21, 80125, Naples, Italy
{silvia.rossi,mariacarla.staffa}@unina.it

Abstract. Human-robot teamwork requires agents to pay attention to both surrounding environment and teammates. Bandwidth and computational limitations prevent an agent to continuously execute this monitoring activity. Inspired by the behavior of human beings, paying frequent attention to timers while approaching deadlines, we provide robots with general monitoring strategies based on attentional mechanisms, for filtering data and actively focusing only on relevant information. We consider a convoy task (led by a human or a robot) as a benchmark to evaluate and compare human and robot monitoring behaviors.

Keywords: Teamwork, Agent Monitoring, Attention, Human-Robot Interaction.

1 Introduction

In the last two decades Human-Robot Interaction (HRI) emerged as one of the main topics in service robotics development. In order to handle the human-populated environment dynamics, a robot should be endowed with autonomy, social skills and information exchange capabilities (both for direct or indirect communication [1]). Finally, it should act as a team member [2], thus take into account the roles of humans or robots belonging to the same team, their aims and goals, in order to accomplish common objectives. While HRI includes the possibility of interacting with robots as intelligent tools to be controlled (perhaps using speech or gesture), real human-robot collaboration and teamwork is a relatively unexplored field [3]. Human-robot teamwork requires agents to pay attention to both surrounding environment and teammates, in order to be "aware" of the interaction. Such awareness supports the robot controller in generating, selecting and modulating suitable behaviors [4] (i.e., a robot changes its action and movement by planning new trajectories depending on the teammates).

In order to monitor and to safely act in the surrounding environment, robots are fully equipped with sensors. However, this comes with the drawback of sensors data fusion and with the impossibility to continuously process such amount

---

* The research leading to these results has received funding from the EU FP7 as part of the project SAPHARI under grant 287513, and SHERPA under grant 600958.

A.P. del Pobil et al. (Eds.): SAB 2014, LNAI 8575, pp. 310–319, 2014.
© Springer International Publishing Switzerland 2014

of data in a sophisticated way. Bandwidth and computational limitations prohibit a monitoring agent from paying attention to all other agents for all the time [5]. Hence, monitoring agent policies rely on periodic monitoring, or ad-hoc policies [6,7] for updating the agent beliefs in a more efficient way. Currently, a few approaches rely on the adaptation of monitoring strategies [8] or on the evaluation of the monitoring frequencies starting from the dynamics of the environment [5]. Our working hypothesis is that adaptive monitoring strategies, inspired by attentional processes, that can be used to filter data and to actively focus on relevant information. Inspired by the behavior of human beings, paying frequent attention to timers while approaching deadlines [9], we aim at providing robots with general attentional monitoring strategies. These attentional policies allow to adaptively change the activation frequencies of the agent behaviors as well as the monitoring frequencies of the sensors used by these behaviors. In this way the agent is able to focus on the current relevant activities, aroused by salient stimuli, and to prevent unnecessary sensors processing by non-relevant behaviors.

In this work, we consider a convoy task (led by a human subject or a robot) as a benchmark to evaluate and compare natural human monitoring behaviors with those provided by the proposed attentional monitoring strategies. Convoy driving requires that both the leader and the follower accomplish the task. Namely, the leader (a robot or a human being), as well as the follower (a robot), has to monitor the teammates behavior and to adapt its own in order to not outdistance them. Moreover, the human subject monitoring strategy, while leading a convoy, can be observed. Our aim is to evaluate the monitoring strategies adopted by the different leader actors of the experiments, in order to see if there is a correspondence between the typical human behavior and the proposed attentional strategies used by the robot. We test our framework in a real world scenario.

2   Attentive Monitoring

In these last years some researchers started to pay attention to the role of attentional processes in order to achieve an adaptive emergent behavior for robotic systems. In previous papers, we highlighted the opportunity of managing the frequency of the sensory inputs processing and of the actions activation in an efficient way. This goal was achieved by introducing "internal clocks" in a robotic architecture to regulate such frequencies. We introduced a control system for the perceptual inputs that achieves a quasi-periodic activity (i.e., it possesses at least an active and inactive phase) and flexibility (i.e., dynamically adaptation of the clock period to external/internal states). The control architecture for the robot system was built according to *Reactive Paradigm* and *Schema Theory*. In particular, we connected a periodic control system to the activation of each single primitive behavior, and related this mechanism to the process of human beings attention [10]. Specifically, each time a primitive behavior is active, it evaluates the sensory inputs in order to produce the relative pattern of motor action, and calculates its new frequency of activation (i.e., how long it has to wait before activating again).

In the literature, different adaptive monitoring strategies, inspired by human behavior, have been proposed [11,9]. Application of such strategies to behaviors activation are related to the specific monitoring task the behavior is involved into. For example, a docking behavior that has a priori knowledge about the task to achieve (for example about the distance to cover for docking) may use strategies called of "Interval Reduction" [11,9]. Users involved in two simultaneous tasks, an engaging one (e.g., playing video-games) and another of monitoring (e.g., looking at the clock for checking the elapsed time), showed to adapt the frequency of monitoring the clock. In particular, they increase such frequency while the deadline is approaching following an interval reduction. This means that, while a continuous monitoring in time will produce T_{max} activations of a behavior, and a fixed periodical monitoring $\propto \frac{T_{max}}{const}$ activations, with an interval reduction strategy we have a number of activations equal to $\propto log_2(T_{max})$. It has been demonstrated that these strategies, asymptotically, are more effective than those characterized by a constant periodic monitoring [11,12] in a wide class of problems. Differently from these approaches, our attentional monitoring strategy can be designed in a way that the behavior activation frequency can change in accordance with specific laws which do not diverge too far from the optimum case (that with a priori knowledge), and that are related to the obtained information from the surrounding environment.

In previous work [8], we compared 4 possible monitoring policies (continuous, constant periodic, interval reduction with a priori knowledge and adaptive periodic monitoring), by showing that the adaptive periodic one is the most suitable in case of absence of a priori knowledge and dynamical environment. Moreover, we evaluated the performance of different adaptation strategies [8] and deployed learning algorithms to optimize such strategies [13] with the result that, even with simple adaptive mechanisms an increase of performance and a flexibility in the emergent behavior can be reached. However, in previous works, no evaluation of possible relationship between human abilities in monitoring and the robots behaviors strategies was performed. In this paper we aim at comparing the proposed attentional strategy, as customized for the robot behaviors, with the one naturally showed by human users while executing the same task.

2.1 The Convoy Problem

In this work, we consider a convoy task where a human or a robot could be involved in the leader role. Driving in a convoy is a teamwork activity and requires a monitoring (indirect communication) capability in order to keep the shared knowledge up-to-date. Typically, in such a kind of problem, two main *roles* defining the responsibilities within the team are considered: (i) the *leader* that takes up the heading position in the convoy and determines the way the environment is going to be explored; and (ii) the *follower* role that has to follow the leader and maintain a certain distance from it/her/him. It differs from a formation maintenance problem, that can be considered as a coordinated individual behavior, where there is a separate distinction between the leader agent, which is in charge to decide the path, and following agents that have to keep a predefined position with respect to the leader and the other agents. Driving in a convoy requires that both the leading and the following units accomplish the task, so the leader has to monitor the followers behavior and adapts its own in order not to lose them [14]. On the other hand, the following units must be able to follow the path set by the leader and to maintain a semi-static distance with the unit before them. Furthermore, the followers must also be able to deviate from the path in the case of dynamic conditions (i.e. an obstacle), and, after executing the deviation, they have to return to the path at the set distance. Hence, both the leader and the followers are aware of their own roles/behaviors and those of the other teammates. In this sense the tracking effort is a team-issue. Independently from its role, each robot has to adapt its own behavior with respect to the others and to monitor the external environment and the other agents' positions, while avoiding obstacles.

The convoy problem, with the human as a leader, allows to put the human in the robot framework: the human has to actively decide when to monitor the team activity and when to monitor the surrounding environment. Moreover, we can observe the monitoring strategies adopted by the human that is forced to turn his head back in order to look at the robot and to look forward to check for obstacles.

3   Case Study

We considered two different case studies, one with a team composed by two robots (case study A), and the other with a human being in the leader role (case study B). The team is required to autonomously navigate in a convoy through a straight corridor, while avoiding obstacles. The corridor is approximately 4.5 meters wide (with pillars and obstacles) and the navigation covers approximately 20 meters in length. In order to accomplish the task the robots are allowed to look at each other (as an indirect information exchange). A visual servoing approach is used for tracking robots and humans. Hence, robots and humans achieve a coordination that is observation-based [15].

Case study A. Figure 1a shows the robots during the execution of the convoy task. The multi-robot system, used in our experiments, is made up of two *Pioneer 3-DX* wheeled robots. Each robot is endowed with 16 sonar sensors, a computer–integrated webcam and a colorful landmark. The latter are necessary to make the robots capable of looking at each other in order to maintain the convoy. The control system is implemented on regular laptop computers via the *Robot Operating System* (ROS). We tested our approach by repeating the experiment 10 times for each setting (continuous monitoring, constant period monitoring, adaptive period monitoring).

Case study B. In the second case study we consider two settings. In one case the human is free to hear all sound signals (Figure 1b), while in the other, the human being (Figure 1c) is endowed with headphones (playing loud music). This

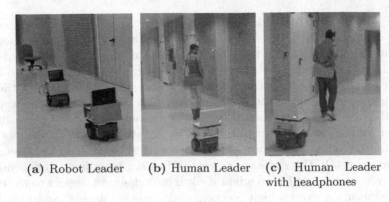

(a) Robot Leader   (b) Human Leader   (c) Human Leader
with headphones

Fig. 1. A snapshot of the convoy in different settings

was in order to cancel any sounds the human subject could hear coming from the robot, which can be used to indirectly infer the robot position/distance. Finally, the users were asked to walk looking ahead and turning their heads only to monitor the team behavior when they felt it was necessary. 13 male and 7 female graduate students participated in the experiments (divided into two sets of 10 subjects). The average age of the participants was 23.2 years. Each subject was asked to perform the task of leading the team one time only.

3.1 Robot Behaviors Description

In order to accomplish the task the following primitive behaviors have been implemented: *Wander, FollowCorridor, AvoidObstacles* and *FollowMate*. The coordination among the behaviors is realized via a particular combination (sum or subsumption) of the outputs of the primitive behaviors, depending on the robot role (Wander, FollowMate and AvoidObstacles for the follower; FollowCorridor, FollowMate and AvoidObstacles for the leader). At each control cycle possibly all the behaviors could be active at the same time. However, the behaviors activation frequencies produce outputs at different rates; hence, only the outputs of active behaviors are summed. This provides an emergent behavior such that the more active behaviors will have more influence in determining the output value.

Wander. The Wander behavior is for generating small rotations in the robot motion in order to find lost teammates. This behavior has a fixed frequency of activation $(p^w = \bar{p}^w)$.

FollowCorridor. This behavior allows the robot to keep itself as aligned to the corridor walls as possible. It uses the lateral sonar sensors for evaluating the robot orientation with respect to the corridor walls, and it assigns a "straightening" angular velocity. The difference between the minimum values perceived by the left frontal (s_f) and back (s_r) sonars (normalized with respect to the maximum detectable distance D_{max} by the sonar sensors) is used to establish the next activation waiting time (or activation period p^c). A higher difference triggers a greater urgency to put the robot in the straight direction, therefore the need of assigning a shorter waiting time as follows, where, p^c_{min} and p^c_{max} are respectively the minimum and maximum allowed waiting time for the FollowCorridor.

$$p^c = p^c_{max} - \frac{|s_f - s_r|}{D_{max}}(p^c_{max} - p^c_{min})$$ (1)

AvoidObstacles. This behavior is in charge to avoid obstacles. It provides different reactions, which are triggered according to the position h of the sonar detecting the current lower distance s^h from the obstacle. The activation period (p^a) of the AvoidObstacles behavior is computed in a way that the smaller the sonar sensor value, the smaller the period (thus, the higher the monitoring frequency). It is computed as follows:

$$p^a = p^a_{max} - \frac{s_{max} - s^h}{s_{max} - s_{min}}(p^a_{max} - p^a_{min})$$ (2)

This means that when an obstacle appears, the behavior increases its attention towards this stimulus by increasing its activation frequency. As in the previous case p^a_{min} and p^a_{max} represent respectively the allowed minimum and maximum value for the AvoidObstacles waiting time, while s_{min} and s_{max} the minimum and maximum perceivable value for a sonar.

FollowMate. This behavior is intended to make a robot follow/monitor another robot or human. The follow-mate attitude is accomplished via visual servoing. When a robot individuates the landmark it is supposed to follow (or monitor), it can adjust its linear and angular velocities according to the landmark position and dimensions in its field of view. A landmark is perceived as a blob of a specific color. A larger blob solicits deceleration, while a smaller blob solicits acceleration. At the same time, a blob perceived on either side of the field of view solicits a steering in the direction of the blob centroid (not for the leader role). This behavior has a variable frequency of activation. When the blob centroid is perceived on either side of the robot field of view, a greater urgency to put it back to the center is triggered, and then a shorter period is set. The period is computed as follows:

$$p^f = p^f_{min} + \frac{x_{max} - |x|}{x_{min} - x_{max}}(p^f_{max} - p^f_{min})$$ (3)

where, the absolute value x is the position of the blob centroid, x_{max} and x_{min} are thresholds, and p^f_{min} and p^f_{max} represent the range for the period values.

4 Experimental Results

In this section, we first describe a system running example. Figure 2 shows data produced by the FollowMate behavior of the follower robot during a run of the

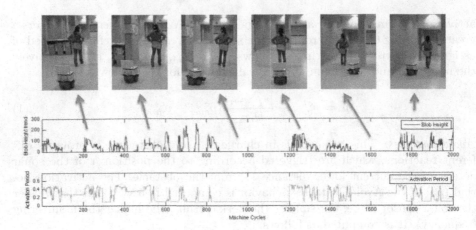

Fig. 2. FollowMate behavior of the Follower with respect to a Human Leader

case study B. The first plot in the figure represents the trend of the perceived blob height. In general, the more this height lies in the range 60-90px, the better the team member robot keeps a right distance from the companion (human/robot). High variation of this value is tolerable, since it depends on a number of factors that are hardly predictable and controllable, such as the diversity of brightness in different parts of the environment, and the orientation of the followed robot. In the second row, we show the trend of the FollowMate period. The snapshots of the interactions are related to salient events in the time line.

We notice that, during the first part of the navigation task, the values high variation corresponds to a first orienting phase. Then, the robot starts to correctly follow the human, but in correspondence of a barrier (the column in the corridor) it starts to turn causing the blob-camera to lose the blob for a while. After that, it is able to center the human again and follow him/her until the next narrow part of the corridor, where, again, the follower robot loses the leader for a while. Finally, the robot is able to identify the blob and follows the leader until the end of the path. For what concerns the activations of the FollowMate behavior, these are distributed over the time. In general, the follower robot has the attitude to decrease the monitoring period in dangerous situations (e.g., when an obstacle occurs) or when it is losing a teammate. In both cases the behavior is able to adaptively increase its monitoring activity by increasing its frequency of activation, while, when it is confident about the behavior of the leader, it relaxes the frequency of activation.

Case Study A. In order to assess the advantages introduced by the adoption of the attentional mechanisms, we report in Table 1 the performance produced by the FollowMate behavior of the leader robot considering three different attentional policies: 1) continuous monitoring (monitoring period set to 1); 2) constant monitoring period (monitoring period set to a fixed value $k = 3$); 3) adaptive monitoring period (monitoring period updated with respect to the behavior attentional

Table 1. Leader robot FollowMate performance while varying the attentive policies

	Case Study A		
Monitoring Policy	$p = 1$	$p = k$	$p = f(x)$
Time (m)	3.02 ± 0.36	2.86 ± 0.32	2.92 ± 0.24
Activations (#)	909 ± 138	435 ± 53	340 ± 26
Failures (%)	20	40	20
Monitoring Time (%)	100	48	37

Table 2. Human behavior data from video analysis

	Case Study B	
Monitoring Policy	$H - Headphones$	$H + Headphones$
Time (m)	1.42 ± 0.02	1.44 ± 0.03
Head Turns (#)	9.60 ± 1.14	9.20 ± 1.78
Failures (%)	18	14
Monitoring Time(%)	25	32

policy $f(x)$). Table 1 shows that, while the time (first row) to achieve the goal remains quite the same in the three cases, the number of activations of the FollowMate behavior (second row) is drastically reduced in the case of adaptive monitoring (third column). What is notable is that, in the case of periodic monitoring (second column), even if the number of activations decreases, the number of failures (e.g., the teammate is lost) increases. Instead, in the case of adaptive monitoring, the attentional inspired monitoring strategy allows to obtain the dual advantage of saving computational load, while maintaining the efficiency. The number of failures in this latter case is, in fact, comparable with the case of continuous monitoring. Last row of Table 1 shows the monitoring time percentage, evaluated as the average number of activations with respect to the average number of activations of the continuous monitoring case.

Case Study B. Data of the human behavior is extracted from a video analysis and results are summarized in Table 2. The two groups of human beings (with or without headphones) showed almost the same behavior in terms of the time to accomplish the task (first row). This could be due to the fact that human beings with the headphones compensate the lack of environmental sound awareness by checking the team for a longer time. In fact, while the average number of times the human beings turn their heads back, to monitor the team, are quite the same (second row), the average duration of the team monitoring activity (forth row) is greater for the subjects with headphones. In particular, the monitoring time is evaluated as the percentage of the time the subjects spent monitoring the team (i.e., time spent looking backward) with respect to the total time of the task. Failures, in the case of human with headphones, are slightly less than in the other case. Also this behavior is a consequence of the longer team monitoring time. The statistical correlation value, evaluated on the monitoring times for the two settings is equal to 0.0597, which means that in the 94% of cases this difference is not due to the case. This shows how the headphones affect the awareness of humans and consequently the performances of the team.

Comparison between A and B. Here, we compare the monitoring strategies adopted by the leader actors in the two case studies, from data in Tables 1 and 2. As we expected, the time to accomplish the task and the number of failures are reduced in the case study B. Intuitively, this may be due to the fact that the adaptation ability and the awareness of human beings allow the entire team to finish the task with better performances in terms of time to accomplish the task and a greater ability to maintain the convoy (hence, less failures). The number of head turns cannot be directly compared to the number of the robot behavior activations, because the human monitoring activities have different duration in time. In order to avoid this problem we refer to the monitoring time parameter. In particular, human participants without headphones spent only the 25% of their time in monitoring the team, with quick checks (4s in the average) from time to time, mainly in the process of avoiding obstacles. Most of their checks are right after an obstacles waiting for the team members. On the contrary, subjects with headphones spent 32% of the execution time monitoring the team. This is because they cannot infer any clue of the teammate behavior hearing the sounds made by the robot moving around. This human behavior is more similar to the robot behavior that spent the 37% of its time in monitoring the followers. Hence, our simple attentional policies allow an efficient use of the computational resources comparable with the human monitoring behavior with limited environmental awareness.

5   Conclusions

In this paper, we presented a comparison between an adaptive monitoring strategy of a robot leader with respect to the corresponding human behavior in a convoy task. One of the main problems, in such a kind of task, is the impossibility of continuously processing a great amount of data in a sophisticated way, especially when more parallel tasks (check the followers, while avoiding obstacles) have to be taken into account. Our working hypothesis is that an effective teamwork, in a convoy problem, can be achieved by adaptive periodic tracking strategies. Hence, inspired by the behavior of human beings, we designed a behavior based control architecture, where each behavior is endowed with attentional mechanisms to adapt the monitoring frequencies to the environment. Beyond the better global performances achieved by the human subjects, what is interesting, from our point of view, is to observe the monitoring strategies adopted by the different leader actors. In particular, we wanted to see if there was a correspondence between the typical human behavior and the attentional strategies used by the robot. We conclude that both refer to a capability of adaptively distributing over time the activations of the behavior of checking/monitoring the convoy (i.e., when and how to activate the FollowMate behavior). Naturally, in the case of human leader the awareness of the interaction is crucial in determining the task effectiveness and the smaller amount of time in the achievement of the task. Comparisons of the monitoring strategy showed, in fact, that the humans were more able to optimize their monitoring activities, especially in the case of contextual clues to infer the team behavior (as environmental sound). Humans with headphones showed a behavior, in terms of monitoring, more similar to the robot, while still keeping the task optimized.

References

1. Breazeal, C., Kidd, C., Thomaz, A., Hoffman, G., Berlin, M.: Effects of nonverbal communication on efficiency and robustness in human-robot teamwork. In: Proc. of Intelligent Robots and Systems, IROS, pp. 708–713 (2005)
2. Goodrich, M.A., Schultz, A.C.: Human-robot interaction: A survey. Found. Trends Hum.-Comput. Interact. 1, 203–275 (2007)
3. Hoffman, G., Breazeal, C.: Collaboration in human-robot teams. In: Proc. of the AIAA 1st Intelligent Systems Technical Conference, Chicago, IL, USA (2004)
4. Sisbot, E., Alami, R.: A human-aware manipulation planner. IEEE Transactions on Robotics 28, 1045–1057 (2012)
5. Kaminka, G.A., Tambe, M.: Robust multi-agent teams via socially-attentive monitoring. Journal of Artificial Intelligence Research 12, 105–147 (2000)
6. Elmaliach, Y., Kaminka, G.A.: Robust multi-robot formations under human supervision and control. Journal of Physical Agents 2, 31–52 (2008)
7. Zheng, K., Glas, D., Kanda, T., Ishiguro, H., Hagita, N.: Supervisory control of multiple social robots for navigation. In: Proc. of 8th ACM/IEEE International Conference on Human-Robot Interaction, HRI, pp. 17–24 (2013)
8. Burattini, E., Finzi, A., Rossi, S., Staffa, M.: Monitoring strategies for adaptive periodic control in behavior-based robotic systems. In: Proc. of the 2009 Advanced Technologies for Enhanced Quality of Life, pp. 130–135. IEEE Computer Society (2009)
9. Cohen, P., Atkin, M.S., Hansen, E.A.: The interval reduction strategy for monitoring cupcake problems. In: Proc. of the 3rd International Conference on the Simulation of Adaptive Behavior, pp. 82–90. MIT Press (1994)
10. Burattini, E., Rossi, S., Finzi, A., Staffa, M.: Attentional modulation of mutually dependent behaviors. In: Doncieux, S., Girard, B., Guillot, A., Hallam, J., Meyer, J.-A., Mouret, J.-B. (eds.) SAB 2010. LNCS (LNAI), vol. 6226, pp. 283–292. Springer, Heidelberg (2010)
11. Atkin, M.S., Cohen, P.R.: Monitoring strategies for embedded agents: Experiments and analysis. Adaptive Behavior 4, 125–172 (1995)
12. Ceci, S.J., Bronfenbrenner, U.: Don't forget to take the cupcakes out of the oven: Prospective memory, strategic time-monitoring, and context. Child Development 56, 152–164 (1985)
13. Di Nocera, D., Finzi, A., Rossi, S., Staffa, M.: Attentional action selection using reinforcement learning. In: Ziemke, T., Balkenius, C., Hallam, J. (eds.) SAB 2012. LNCS (LNAI), vol. 7426, pp. 371–380. Springer, Heidelberg (2012)
14. Cohen, P., Levesque, H.: Teamwork. Nous, Special Issue on Cognitive Science and AI 25, 487–512 (1991)
15. Kuniyoshi, Y., Kita, N., Rougeaux, S., Sakane, S., Ishii, M., Kakikua, M.: Cooperation by observation: The framework and basic task patterns. In: Proc. of IEEE International Conference on Robotics and Automation, ICRA, vol. 1, pp. 767–774 (1994)

Animal Social Behaviour: A Visual Analysis

Ester Martinez-Martin and Angel P. del Pobil

Robotic Intelligence Lab (RobInLab), Universitat Jaume-I, Castellón, Spain
{emartine,pobil}@uji.es

Abstract. Social activities are among the most striking of animal behaviours, providing knowledge about their intelligence, cognition and evolution. However, their observation in the field can be especially arduous. To address this, image processing methods have been developed. However, despite the extensively research on this topic, multiple object tracking still remains a very hard problem due to the wide variety of issues to be overcome (e.g. changes in illumination conditions, stopped colony member, occlusions, etc.). In this paper, we contribute a novel visual tracking application addressing the challenge of detecting and simultaneously tracking hundreds of animals in their habitat. For that, motion is used as primary cue. The system was validated in experiments with laboratory colonies of micro-robots and several example analysis of dewlap lizard's behaviour.

1 Introduction

Behaviour is one of the most important properties of animal's life because it allows animals to interact with their environment and other organisms. With the aim of understanding the causes, functions, development and evolution of behaviour, biologists try to answer one or more of the four questions to model the animal behaviour proposed by Niko Tinbergen [16]. Basically, the first question asks about the mechanisms of a behaviour. That is, what stimulates an animal to respond with the behaviour it displays and what the response mechanisms are. The second question concerns the translation of genotype to phenotype. In other words, as an individual grows from an embryo to an adult, there are developmental processes which allow the implementation of mature behaviours in their organism. The third question deals with the function of a particular behaviour to be successful in a specific task. Finally, the last question examines the evolutionary history of a behaviour along time, from ancestors up to the current species.

This study has been often supported by robots and computing systems. So, in the early twentieth century, the construction of robotic systems capable of dinamically and adaptively interacting with real-like scenarios contributed to encourage a mechanistic approach to the explanation of animal and human behaviours [5]. More recently, robotic reproductions of animal and insect-like behaviours have brought about developing general methodological guidelines for the study of intelligence and cognition and, in some cases, have helped to formulate hypotheses on particular aspects of animal behaviour [7,13,14]. The experimental validation of these hypotheses require a tedious, difficult task because of the high amount of data to be analysed, especially when cooperative behaviour is considered.

A.P. del Pobil et al. (Eds.): SAB 2014, LNAI 8575, pp. 320–327, 2014.

As a solution, computer vision systems for tracking moving targets are widely used. However, despite the existence of several approaches in tracking living societies, these approaches have many drawbacks when the number of *individuals* to track increases or when *individual* size is tiny. The last problem is not easy to solve because it is not viable to tag each colony member under study. The reason lies in the difficulty for choosing an appropriate tag since it must be very small in some cases. Consequently, sometimes, it cannot be possible to detect them in an image. In addition, the tags can become ambiguous when a swarm is composed of many individuals. Furthermore, tagging can alter individual behaviour.

Therefore, an application for tracking unmarked, unknown targets is required. In this regard, Balch et al. [2] presented a vision system for tracking ant colonies. The core idea is to detect ants by using colour classification to identify regions in the image that will be later scrutinized for indications of movement using more costly image differencing, and to *individually* track them from spatial information. Despite its good performance, that system has some limitations to be overcome such as occlusions, clumpling, splitting or motionless ants.

Going a step further, Correll et al. [6] implemented *SwisTrack*, a platform-independent, easy-to-use and robust tracking software developed to research swarm robotic and behavioural biology. It was part of the European project LEURRE [1] focused on building and controlling mixed societies composed of animals and artificial embedded agents (similar to Caprari's work [4], where a team of Insbots was introduced into a swarm of cockroaches and allowed for modification of the swarm behaviour). The colony under observation could be composed of insects, robots or both of them, and the *Swistrack* output is an image where their trajectories are drawn in world coordinates. Mainly, the *Swistrack* software detects the objects of interest by subtracting a background image from every video frame coming from a camera or a video. As mentioned in [6], the segmentation process fails when the *object*'s colour is too similar to the arena, there are changes in illumination, or when the objects move only a little (as a solution, they aggregated cockroaches to their experiments). Regarding tracking, *Swistrack* associates each individual position with the nearest object in the next processed frame, what cannot guarantee the maintenance of the trajectory-individual relations. Consequently, the *Swistrack* software is not adequate for real applications due to the high number of restrictions.

More recently, Kimura et al. [8] developed a computer-aided system for the identification and behavioural tracking of individual honeybees within a hive. This system successfully tracked hundreds of individuals without the need for marking, although there are some circumstances that make the system fail. Such cases are when an individual stands directly on top of another or when individuals hide in holes in the hive structure. Later being aware of the complexity of this issue, Marcovecchio et al. [10] created an application that performs the segmentation and tracking of multiple cockroaches running on Petri dishes. Among its drawbacks, it can be found the need of specifying the number of individuals, the impossibility of tracking individuals of some colours or individual swapping.

Motivated by these challenges, we present a visual tracking application to study micro-robots or social insect cooperative behaviour in their habitat without the risk of

322   E. Martinez-Martin and A.P. del Pobil

conditioning the results by tagging *individuals* or constraining the experimental settings. So, as depicted in Fig. 1, this application consists of two stages: (1) visually detecting individuals in their habitat without tagging them; and then, (2) estimating their trajectory overcoming the abovementioned tracking problems.

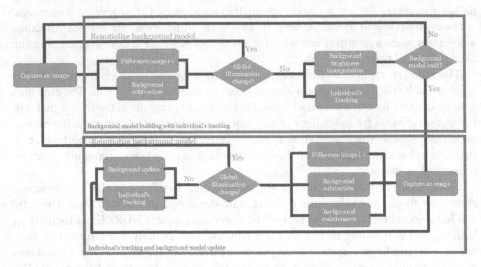

Fig. 1. Arquitecture of the presented visual tracking application

2   Image Segmentation

The first issue to be solved is to identify the set of pixels that represent all the *individuals* under study. To this respect, motion might be exploited as salient feature to attract the focus of the system towards the target moving entities (e.g. *colony members* as ants, honeybees, etc.) [11].

Keeping in mind animal's habitat, apart from dealing with multiple targets, the implemented application should be able of dealing with shadows, gradual changes in illumination (due to day time), sudden changes in illumination when any artificial lightning is switched on/off at any time, reflections on mirrors, the waving of trees and/or plants and occlusions.

Computer vision community has carried out a deep research on this topic in order to adapt detection approaches to those factors, although one of the most common is the *background subtraction* approach [9,15]. In that approach, a moving target is identified by using a background model obtained after observing several seconds the scene. Mainly, the background model consists of the estimation of a Gaussian distribution, or a mixture of them, such that pixels are classified as foreground when they do not fit the estimated background model. Nevertheless, this computer vision approach presents some drawbacks to be overcome such as everything observed during the training period is considered as background; no sudden illumination change occurs during the whole experiment; and/or, only non-stationary regions are highlighted, so individuals stopped during several seconds could be considered as part of background.

To address these issues, we propose a background maintenance technique which removes the constraint of observing a scene free of foreground elements during several seconds when a reliable initial background model is built, and copes with (gradual and global) changes in illumination, distinction between foreground and background elements in terms of motion and motionless, and non-uniform vacillating backgrounds.

For that, we developed a hybrid algorithm based on frame differencing and background subtraction along with a single-Gaussian background model and a mechanism for its effective maintenance. The underlying idea is to mutually reinforce frame difference and background subtraction so that the drawbacks of both approaches are overcome while keeping their original advantages.

Thus, in a first stage, an initial background model is built, while a surveillance task takes place. With the purpose of controlling the activity in the scene, image pixels are classified on the basis of a mixture of adjacent frame difference with background subtraction. Basically, a mixture of methods is necessary because, although frame difference provides an easy, fast motion detection, it only works on particular conditions. So, as background subtraction does not suffer from those disadvantages, it is possible to properly refine the raw classification obtained with frame difference. Note that at this stage the reference frame is set to the first frame of the visual input.

On the other hand, the second stage is composed of a mixture of three difference approaches: adjacent frame difference, background subtraction and background maintenance. The two first methods are combined as in the previous stage, but in this case, the reference frame used for the simple subtraction technique is set to the mean of the Gaussian distribution estimated for the background model built in the preceding phase. In both stages, thresholds are automatically established from histogram properties.

3   Individual's Tracking

Once the individuals are detected in an image, the next step is tracking them along time. Based on spatial information, the nearest neighbour approach could be used. However, the proximity criterion is not enough to determine the new individual's position as suggested in [6]. In addition, it should be also considered that individuals can meet, form groups, cross-over, etc.

With the aim of solving these situations and properly identifing individuals along time, we propose a method divided into three steps. The first step consists of labellingthe identified *blobs* in the previous step. A row-by-row labelling method is used to reduce the computational cost of the whole process. For that, the binary image is scanned twice: the first time to tag each foreground pixel based on the labels of its neighbours and to establish equivalences between different labels; the second, crossed scan will unify tags which belong to the same *blob*. Secondly, the application classifies the labelled *blobs* as targets to be tracked or as bad-segmented pixels, and detection of collisions inside a *blob* indentified as *colony member*. All targets are assumed as not touching in the first captured image. The number of targets to be tracked is specified by the user, and the application automatically estimates the minimal and maximal size allowed from the first captured image. This knowledge, together with the number of the detected *blobs* in each frame, allows to define a series of criteria to determine when a *blob* represents more than one object, and to reject all *blobs* that do not identify target individuals but are insted the result of a bad segmentation as it occurs with the set of noisy pixels. Finally, *blobs* that represent groups of more than one individual to be tracked are segmented.As it is difficult to identify several individuals at the same time, we have studied two different, possible situations by assuming that only two individuals are touching in a *blob*. It means that each *blob* will be divided into two new *blobs*: one will identify only one *colony member*, while the other can identify one or more individuals depending on the number of them represented by the *blob* to be split up. If the new blob represents several individuals, the split-up process is recursively applied until the obtained *blob* is composed of only one target. The two considered cases are: (1) two individuals are touching only in one point. In this case, a contour retrieval method is used. So, a chain code is obtained by considering that the contact pixel will be visited twice. Moreover, the contour irregularities have been taken into account to correctly determine the contact point; and, (2) two individuals are in touch in several points (the general case). The distinction between spaces between different objects in touch and the ones as result of segmentation errors, is the keypoint to solve this situation. A set of criteria together with a dimension criterion provide successful results.

4   Experimental Results

In order to evaluate the performance of the proposed approach, two different kind of experiments were performed. First, an analysis of dewlap lizard's behaviour is presented. Then, experiments with different laboratory colonies of micro-robots are presented.

4.1   Analysis of Dewlap Lizard's Behaviour

In this section, we present a work developed in collaboration with Sarah Partan from the Hampshire College [12] aimed at studying the behaviour of a dewlap lizard. A dewlap lizard is a reptile which has large skin dewlaps under its neck, such that it can extend and retract those dewlaps. The dewlaps are usually of a different colour from the rest of its body and can be enlarged to make the lizard seem much bigger than it really is, specially when warding off predators. Thus, the males use the dewlap to intimidate rivals and also to attract females during mating season. Despite the male dewlap lizard is much larger in size, the female anoles do indeed possess a dewlap as well. These uses for the dewlap work much in the same way as the neck frill on a frill-necked lizard, with the lizard extending its neck frill for much of the same reasons. Nevertheless, it is not known if the dewlap is used in thermo regulation like the neck frill is.

Therefore, our experiment consists of processing a video playback of a dewlap lizard with the goal of detecting its two mechanisms for communication: its movement up-down and the extraction and/or retraction of its dewlap. In particular, in this experiment we focused on the second communication way since we were analysing the application performance when almost transparent individual parts are considered, especially when they are within bright scenes. Fig. 2 illustrates some of the obtained results on the same image sequence. As it might be observed, only the dewlap is marked when it is extracted or retracted.

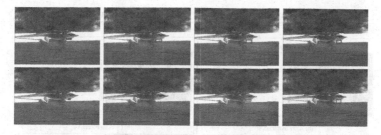

Fig. 2. Detection of dewlap lizard extraction and retraction

4.2 Swarm Robotics

The study of cooperative behaviour in insect swarms can be performed by using robotic systems. So, micro-robots can be used to emulate social insect behaviour [3] and their study involves detecting and tracking several miniature robots on a desktop table.

In agreement with that, the experimental set-up consists of a black arena on a desk, where micro-robots act, and a colour camera located on its centre, several centimetres higher, by pointing downwards, in order to capture the whole arena area. The distance between the camera and the arena can vary between experiments because there are no static parameters, as previously pointed out.

In our experiments, the colony under study is composed of micro-robots *Alice2002*. They are micro-engineering products designed by *École Polytechnique Fédérale de Lausanne (EPFL)* for research purposes. Each micro-robot is equipped with three active infrared sensors at the front and one in the back which allow the micro-robot to detect obstacles up to $3cm$ away. As white obstacles are better detected, the arena walls are white, despite black background.

Two different kinds of experiments were carried out. Firstly, the application performance was analysed when the number of the swarm individuals changes. In this case, we present two different experiments: (a) when three unmarked *Alice2002* are tracked and (b) when the trajectory study of a six untagged micro-robot swarm is done (results depicted in Fig. 3). Note that both of them have been obtained by using the same camera, a *STH-MD1-C Stereo head*, in order to properly make comparisons.

Both experiments, depicted in Fig. 3, start with a configuration without collisions between micro-robots. In that way, the application can estimate the parameters it needs to successfully perform its task: an initial interval of the allowed sizes for any object and the relationship between the image coordinates and the world ones. In the next step, the application obtains and provides the different estimated followed trajectories to the user.

So, when a colony of three members was considered, the micro-robots described a clockwise circular trajectory during the first 25 frames. Then, they changed to another circular movement, although the radius of the described trajectory is smaller, as shown in Fig. 3d. Finally, they navigated describing a straight-line trajectory in search of any wall to be followed and, when they found it, they travel parallel to it. On the contrary, when six micro-robots were used, a first circular trajectory was described by all of them. After a while, four individuals changed their trajectory to another circular trajectory with a larger radius, whereas the other two were in the wall following mode.

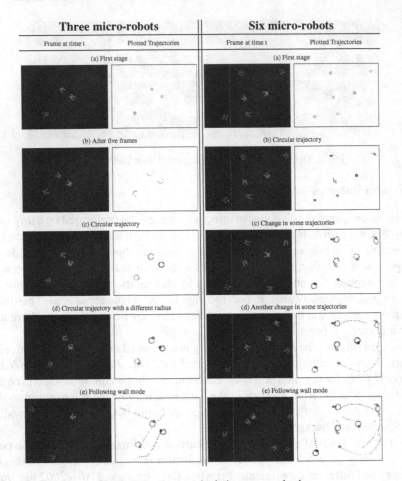

Fig. 3. Behaviour analysis in swarm robotics

At other time, two more micro-robot went in search of a wall to be followed. Note that, as shown in Fig. 3, the implemented application was able of detecting objects only partially visible.

5 Conclusions

In this work, we propose a visual application for the study of live animal colonies without the risk of conditioning the results tagging the colony members or changing their natural habitat. For that, a visual segmentation based on motion followed by a visual tracking algorithm is performed. This application has several advantages for individual identification and tracking. Firstly, individuals are robustly detected in a visual input without any constraint about the environment and lightning conditions. Secondly, the system succesfully tracks each colony member, even when their trajectories are merged and/or split up. In addition, the implemented application is also able of detecting objects even when their velocity is very slow or if they do not move, a case typically difficult for similar methods. Another advantage of the system is that, although a calibration method is not used, it is possible to estimate a correspondence between image coordinates and the world ones from the relationship between the real size of the colony members and their size in the image, which is automatically obtained by the application for each experiment. Finally, the application is transparent to the user such that they do not keed to know the implementation details to work with it.

Nonetheless, despite its good performance, there are still some issues to be solved. For instance, the assumption that the first taken image contains all the individuals without touching each other constrains the application to a large extent. For that reason, a new mechanism to determine visual individual's size should be developed. As a further achievement, we would like to add a post-procesing for behaviour analysis.

References

1. European project leurre (2006), http://leurre.ulb.ac.be
2. Balch, T., Khan, Z., Veloso, M.: Automatically tracking and analyzing the behavior of live insect colonies. In: AGENTS, Montréal, Quebec, Canada (2001)
3. Camazine, S., Deneubourg, J.L., Franks, N., Sneyd, J., Theraulaz, G., Bonabeau, E.: Self-Organization in Biological Systems. Princeton Studies in Complexity. Princeton University Press (2001)
4. Caprari, G., Colot, A., Siegwart, R., Halloy, J., Deneubourg, J.L.: Building mixed societies of animals and robots. IEEE Robotics and Automation Magazine 12(2), 58–65 (2005)
5. Cordeschi, R.: The Discovery of the Artificial: Behavior, Mind and Machines Before and Beyond Cybernetics. Kluwer Academic Publishers, Dordrecht (2002)
6. Correll, N., Sempo, G., de Meneses, Y.L., Halloy, J., Deneubourg, J.L., Martinoli, A.: Swistrack: A tracking tool for multi-unit robotic and biological systems. In: IROS, pp. 2185–2191 (2006)
7. Francesca, G., Brambilla, M., Trianni, V., Dorigo, M., Birattari, M.: Analysing an evolved robotic behaviour using a biological model of collegial decision making. In: Ziemke, T., Balkenius, C., Hallam, J. (eds.) SAB 2012. LNCS, vol. 7426, pp. 381–390. Springer, Heidelberg (2012)
8. Kimura, T., Ohashi, M., Okada, R., Ikeno, H.: A new approach for the simultaneous tracking of multiple honeybees for analysis of hive behavior. Apidologie 42, 607–617 (2011)
9. Liu, H., Pi, W., Zha, H.: Motion detection for multiple moving targets by using an omnidirectional camera. In: IEEE Conf. on Robotics, Intelligent Systems and Signal Processing, Changsha, China, vol. 1, pp. 422–426 (2003)
10. Marcovecchio, D., Stefanazzi, N., Delrieux, C., Maguitman, A., Ferrero, A.: A multiple object tracking system applied to insect behavior. In: CACIC, Argentina (2013)
11. Orabona, F., Metta, G., Sandini, G.: A Proto-object Based Visual Attention Model. In: Paletta, L., Rome, E. (eds.) WAPCV 2007. LNCS (LNAI), vol. 4840, pp. 198–215. Springer, Heidelberg (2007)
12. Partan, S.: (2009), http://helios.hampshire.edu/~srpCS/Home.html
13. Partan, S., Larco, C., Owens, M.: Wild tree squirrels respond with multisensory enhancement to conspecific robot alarm behaviour. Animal Behaviour 77(5), 1127–1135 (2009)
14. Pfeifer, R., Bongard, J.: How the body shapes the way we think: a new view of intelligence. The MIT Press, Cambridge (2007)
15. Stauffer, C., Grimson, W.E.L.: Adaptive background mixture models for real-time tracking. In: CVPR, pp. 246–252 (1999)
16. Tinbergen, N.: On aims and methods in ethology. Zeitschrift fur Tierpsychologie 20(4), 410–433 (1963)

Crowd Emotion Detection
Using Dynamic Probabilistic Models

Mirza Waqar Baig[1,2], Emilia I. Barakova[1], Lucio Marcenaro[2],
Matthias Rauterberg[1], and Carlo S. Regazzoni[2]

[1] Department of Industrial Design, Eindhoven University of Technology,
Eindhoven, Netherlands
[2] Department of Electronics Engineering, University of Genoa, Italy
{M.W.Baig,E.I.Barakova,G.W.M.Rauterberg}@tue.nl,
{Waqar,Lucio.Marcenaro,Carlo}@ginevra.unige.it

Abstract. Detecting emotions of a crowd to control the situation is an area of emerging interest. The purpose of this paper is to present a novel idea to detect the emotions of the crowd. Emotions are defined as evolving quantities arising from the reaction to contextual situations in a set of dynamic pattern of events. These events depend on internal and external interaction states in an already mapped space. The emotions of multiple people constituting a crowd in any surveillance environment are estimated by their social and collective behaviors using sensor signals e.g., a camera, which captures and tracks their motion. The feature space is constructed based on local features to model the contextual situations and the different interactions corresponding to different emergent behaviors are modeled using bio-inspired dynamic model. The changes in emotions correspond to behavioral changes which are produced to regulate behaviors under different encountered situations. Proposed algorithm involves the probabilistic signal processing modelling techniques for analysis of different types of collective behaviors based on interactions among people and classification models to estimate emotions as positive or negative. The evaluations are performed on simulated data show the proposed algorithm effectively recognizes the emotions of the crowd under specific situations.

Keywords: Crowd Emotions Detection, Collective Behavior, Dynamic Bayesian Networks, Autobiographical Memory, Dynamic event modeling.

1 Introduction

Emotion is a feeling evoked by environmental stimuli or by internal body states [1], which modulate human behavior in terms of actions in the environment or changes in the internal status of the body. The idea of emotional expressions as scientific subject was first recognized by Darwin, who found out that the natural selection process is not only applicable to anatomic patterns but also can be applied to animal's behaviors and mind. The detection of collective emotions of a crowd is a new research area that has not been explored systematically so far. Research has been carried out in single

A.P. del Pobil et al. (Eds.): SAB 2014, LNAI 8575, pp. 328–337, 2014.
© Springer International Publishing Switzerland 2014

person emotion detection and classification such as facial expressions systems using the distinctive facial features and calibrating them into emotions [2] of individuals. Voice expressions have also been used to detect emotions of individuals. The audio-based affect recognition using the features of pitch and context has been developed [3]. The body language and posture is also one of most useful feature in detection of emotion of people. The body language and posture guessed by the activity recognizers [4] [5]. Physiology based affect detection is quite broad approach, which requires the inclusion of delicate and calibrated sensors on body [6]. The physiology based methods are quite accurate but they require inclusion of delicate and calibrated sensors on body [7] and cannot be used in real life situations. Apart from these techniques, there are also multimodal techniques which fuse many features such as face, voice, and posture etc., the data coming from different sensors is fused to make a decision on type of emotion [8]. All the compact review mentioned above is in use for individual emotion detection, these systems cannot be employed in crowd emotion detection due to richness of features obtained with timing constraints of evaluation and calibration. The detection of emotions of the crowd is useful in crowd behavior management for safety and security and also in robot responses towards emotions of crowd.

The main contribution of this paper is to develop the first model to detect the emotions of the crowd. This paper presents the dynamic probabilistic modelling of behaviors that are being generated from autobiographical memory (AM). The AM is developed on modelling of events which got it concept from psychological theories. The evaluations have been performed for training and testing purposes. The paper explains the Emotion detection and classification algorithm in Section 2. The Section 3 consists of evaluations and results, Section 4 is conclusions, Section 5 consists of acknowledgement and Section 6 consists of references.

2   Crowd Emotion Computation

The proposed framework is based on Ortony, Clore and Collins (OCC) [17] theory of emotion. The estimation of emotions is based on Russell et al. [16] circumplex model of affect. The local features such as motion tracking and density of crowd are used to make the possible causal relationship based features space. This feature space after reduction is used to generate emergent possible behaviours in an unsupervised way. These behaviours are then trained into different models according to context and situation, which are used to detect emotions. The algorithm flow first shows the topology based partitioning of observation space and then using the local features to make event based memory. Using this event based memory model possible behaviours which are then used to estimate emotions of the crowd.

2.1   Topological Partitioning

In order to extract the effective information from the crowd, we need to discretize the space under observation into smaller acceptable areas, in which the rich data information should be preserved. The topology representing networks (TRNs) algorithms are possible solution to divide the observation space into discrete areas. The instantaneous topological map (ITM) is employed to divide the observation space into zones as shown in Figure 1. In [9], it has been demonstrated that ITM is an appropriate solution to discretize the zones of correlated trajectories.

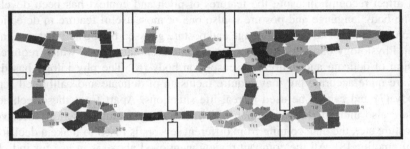

Fig. 1. With $\tau = 500$, τ defines the minimum distance between a given zone given all the observations for creating new zone

2.2 Modelling Events

The ability to predict the emotions requires understanding of actions in an area under surveillance in order to define the interactions and activities that represent emotions. To reach this goal, a probable technique is to memorize all possible interactions that occur in related area among people and environment and their reactions due to these actions. A bio-inspired technique is used which has been mentioned in [10][11][12][13]. These interactions are generated due to causal relationships that happen among persons and environment. These types of interactions can be learned using AM as mentioned by Damasio [14]. The two states proto (internal) and core (mirror of external) state based observations are defined as proto (entity) and core (crowd). This makes a chain of temporally and spatially aligned proto $\vec{x}_p$ and core state $\vec{x}_c$ vectors. The proto and core events can be defined as ε_p and ε_c using the probabilistic model to develop AM. The triplets of events for passive and active interactions are $\{\varepsilon_p^-, \varepsilon_c, \varepsilon_p^+\}$ and $\{\varepsilon_c^-, \varepsilon_p, \varepsilon_c^+\}$ respectively. These represents the causal relationship in terms of initial situation (first event$\varepsilon_{p,c}^-$), the cause (second event$\varepsilon_{c,p}$), and consequent effect of the examined entity (third event $\varepsilon_{p,c}^+$). This sequence of these states can be decided by using a probabilistic graphical model that describes the relationships among them using statistical and mathematical similarities among interactions. The interactions consist of temporal sequences of interdependent states described by two probability distributions: $p(\varepsilon_p^+|\varepsilon_c, \varepsilon_p^-)$ and $p(\varepsilon_c^+|\varepsilon_p, \varepsilon_c^-)$. The Dynamic Bayesian networks (DBNs) are used to model the interaction. The conditional probability densities (CPD) $p(\varepsilon_t^p|\varepsilon_{t-1}^p)$ and $p(\varepsilon_t^c|\varepsilon_{t-1}^c)$ simulates the motion tracking and crowdedness patterns. The interactions among the two interacting objects can be modelled using conditional probability densities (CPDs):

$$p(\varepsilon_t^p|\varepsilon_{t-\Delta t^c}^c); p(\varepsilon_t^c|\varepsilon_{t-\Delta t^p}^p) \tag{1}$$

The (1) represents the probability that events ε_c occurred at time $t - \Delta t^c$, by the interacting object which is related to the core context and vice versa. The casual relationships between the two interacting objects are modelled using two conditional probabilities (CPDs):

$$p\left(\varepsilon_t^p \middle| \varepsilon_{t-\Delta t}^c{}^c, \varepsilon_{t-\Delta t}^p{}^p\right); p\left(\varepsilon_t^c \middle| \varepsilon_{t-\Delta t}^p{}^p, \varepsilon_{t-\Delta t}^c{}^c\right) \tag{2}$$

The probability densities in (2) consider interaction of (1) as well as initial situation $\varepsilon_{t-\Delta t}^c{}^c$ and $\varepsilon_{t-\Delta t}^p{}^p$. The observations associated with proto and core are ε_t^p and $\varepsilon_t^c = [d_t]$. The proto and core states are $\vec{x}_p(t)$ and $\vec{x}_c(t)$. In order to represent these elements with respect to contextual information, a clustering technique of dimensionality reduction such as Self organized map (SOM) [15], unsupervised classifier is used to convert multidimensional proto $\vec{x}_p(t)$ and core vectors $\vec{x}_c(t)$ into low dimension W-Z, where W is the dimension of map (layer). The clusterization process, maps proto and core states into 2-D vectors, which correspond to the neurons of SOM map. These are called core super states S_{x_c} and proto Super states S_{x_p}. SOM allows clustering the proto $\vec{x}_p(t)$ and core vectors $\vec{x}_c(t)$ into corresponding neuron map as super states, which are then known as proto super-state S_{x_p} and core super-state S_{x_c}. The parameter M is to be tuned. The labels associated are given by:

$$S_{x_p}^i \mapsto l_p^i, \quad i = 1, \dots, n_p; \; S_{x_c}^j \mapsto l_c^j, \quad j = 1, \dots, n_c \tag{3}$$

where $S_{x_p}^i$ and $S_{x_c}^j$ are the ith and jth super states, and n_p and n_c are total number of proto and core states generated during mapping. The proto and core super-states are labelled with the semantic labels from the ITM zones. The event is defined as when a proto or core super-state changes its zone. This gives rise to AM associated with each zone. Using the SOM representation, it is possible to detect changes in the map through super states, where super-states are connected by local features for particular instances. This representation encompasses the changes in state vectors $\vec{x}_p(t)$ and $\vec{x}_c(t)$ for every time instatnt as movements in map. If changes in state vectors $\vec{x}_p(t)$ and $\vec{x}_c(t)$ do not imply changes in super-state labels $S_{x_p}^i \mapsto l_p^i$ and $S_{x_c}^j \mapsto l_c^j$, then the SOM mapping needs to be recalibrated as the semantics defined are not the correct representation of events. When super states $S_{x_p}^i$ and $S_{x_c}^j$ change during specific time instants, their contextual modification entails an event. Therefore, an event is defined as: $\theta_e^t = l_{p,c}^{i,j}(t-1) \mapsto l_{p,c}^{i,j}(t)$, where $i, j = 1, \dots, n_{p,c}$, with timing constraints T_{max}. There are also null events (null changes in super states $i = j$, can be defined as $\theta_e^t = \emptyset_e$. This gives rise to AM memory model, this is modelled by the events in which learning the changes from proto super-states to core-super-states and subsequent modification of core super-state is memorized. The following three types of events can be memorized. (i) $\theta_p^- = S_{x_p^0} \to S_{x_p^-}$ is the proto event at initial time instant. This represents the alteration of the proto super-state into $S_{x_p^0} \mapsto l_p^i$ to $S_{x_p^-} \mapsto l_p^j$ that can happen before the core event. The event θ_p^- also remembers the time window T_{max}^-. The two labels l_p^i and l_p^j and are related with super states $S_{x_p^0}$ and $S_{x_p^-}$. The event θ_p^- also remembers the time window T_{max}^-. (ii) $\theta_c^- = S_{x_c^-} \to S_{x_c^+}$

is the core event. This shows the alteration of external super-state into $S_{x_c^-} \mapsto l_c^m$ to $S_{x_c^+} \mapsto l_c^n$. (iii) $\theta_p^+ = S_{x_p^-} \to S_{x_p^+}$: is the proto event following the core event. It is also associated with the super states as $S_{x_p^-} \mapsto l_p^j$ to $S_{x_p^+} \mapsto l_p^k$. The following triplet $W = \{\theta_p^-, \theta_c, \theta_p^+\}$ represents the self-abstraction, which is related with AM. The AM represents the core conscious in Damasio work.

2.3   Emotion Modelling in Crowd

Emotion modelling in crowd is based on OCC theory [16], which states that the emotions are valanced reactions to events, agents and objects. These events, agents and objects can be either pleasing or displeasing to the subject under consideration. We use AM events which are already coupled by probability density of observations from agents and events. To scale the emotions into positive and negative, we use the Russell et. al. [17] two dimensional map of mental space of emotions. On this map, we only use valance coordinate to define emotions into positive and negative emotions. In order to cluster AM event stream triplets $\{\theta_p^-, \theta_c, \theta_p^+\}$ which are based on trajectory behavioral patterns, which is later used to classify into emotions. The triplet pattern for AM for trajectory behavior sequence is given by

$$W_N = \{w_1, \dots w_n\} \tag{4}$$

The training dataset consists of N triplet vectors

$$U = \{W_1, \dots. W_n, \dots. W_N\} \tag{5}$$

W_N is the total behavioral patterns gathered. In order to gather the natural clustering of training trajectories on which the model should be constructed, we need to cluster the data into classes. As number of clusters is unknown, we use the DBN modelling to cluster the data into behavioral patterns using affinity matrix approach. To calculate the affinity between two trajectory sequences, W_a and W_b, the D_a and D_b two DBNs, are trained using expectation maximization (EM) algorithm [18]. The affinity between W_a and W_b is:

$$Q_{ab} = \frac{1}{2}\{\frac{1}{s_a}\log p(W_a|D_b) + \frac{1}{s_b}\log p(W_b|D_a)\} \tag{6}$$

where $p(W_a|D_b)$ is the likelihood of perceiving W_a given D_b, s_a and s_b are the lengths of W_a and W_b respectively. A $N \times N$ infinity matrix is obtained $Q = [Q_{ab}]$, where $a, b \leq N$. This makes a new representation of dataset U as

$$Z_q = \{q_{k1}, \dots, q_{kn}, \dots. q_{kN}\} \tag{7}$$

where k is the cluster or class label. Each behavioural pattern is modelled by a feature vector which is dynamically warped by DBNs. This defines the scene/ situation based clusters in the model. Considering the different clusters, if we have only sparse data, then it will be difficult to fit the model. The training set Z_q in this case consists of K clusters. The distribution of behavioral patterns is modeled based on Gaussian mixture model (GMM). Given the K-th mixture component of GMM, the log likelihood of observing the training dataset Z_q is defined as:

$$\log p(Z_q|\partial) = \sum_{n=1}^{N}(\log \sum_{k=1}^{K} p(q_{kn}|\partial_k)) \qquad (8)$$

where $p(q_{kn}|\partial_k)$ is the Gaussian distribution of K-th mixture component. The parameters ∂ of the model are evaluated using EM algorithm. To design optimal number of classes for the mixture model, Bayesian information criterion [19]. For any given K, the BIC is given by:

$$BIC = -\log p(Q|\partial) + \frac{F_K}{2}\log N \qquad (9)$$

where F_K is the number of parameters required to model K-th component of GMM. Now N numbers of behavioral patterns are labelled to one of the behavioural clustered class. To define positive and negative emotional behaviors, we need to have labelled dataset for positive and negative emotions.

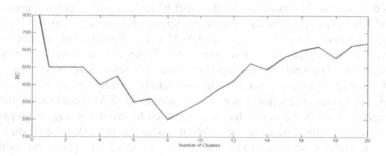

BIC versus cluster selection

Fig. 2. BIC model selection for optimal number of clusters of model, this BIC is modelled for negative emotion model E_n for affinity matrix of order N=60

For training initialization of positive E_p and negative emotion E_n models, the labelled dataset is used. The positive emotion E_p model is given for any behaviour O as:

$$p(O|E_p) = \sum_{q=1}^{Q_p} \delta_{pq} p(O|D_{pq}) \qquad (10)$$

where δ_{pq} is the mixing probability of qth mixture component with $\partial_{pq} = \sum_{q=1}^{Q_p} \delta_{pq} = 1$, and D_{pq} is the qth DBN corresponding to qth normal behavior. Similarly for negative emotions, the behavior O belonging to negative emotions model E_n is given by:

$$p(O|E_n) = \sum_{q=1}^{Q_n} \delta_{nq} p(O|D_{nq}) \qquad (11)$$

The models for both positive and negative emotions situations are trained separately using labelled data. An accumulative measure of online emotion classification is proposed in this task. Whenever an external observed behavior Q_{new} is detected, the probability distribution estimated by GMM of detected behavior and the positive and negative emotion models is evaluated by using the likelihood ratio test (LRT) [22].

$$\psi(Q_{new}) = \frac{p(Q_{new}|E_p)}{p(Q_{new}|E_n)} \begin{cases} \geq \propto_{th} & Positive\ Emotion \\ < \propto_{th} & Negative\ Emotion \end{cases} \qquad (12)$$

where $p(Q_{new}|E_p)$ and $p(Q_{new}|E_n)$ are calculated using equations, where α_{th1} and α_{th2} are the thresholds that are being tuned based on the model and false positive rate of detection of emotions. Using this procedure, several responses are calculated for time T_c and the decision is made with maximum response of people with positive and negative emotions based on detection of emotion of people detected in maximum in an area under observation.

3   Evaluation and Results

To evaluate the proposed computational model of crowd emotions, we design a simulation model in which we can produce the evacuation and panic situations. People are presented as agents that move under different behaviors and a realistic crowd behaviors and RBAS (Realistic Behavioral Agent Simulation) model is proposed [20]. The algorithm is based on social force model SFM [21], simulates the agents as ellipse with particular sizes. The agents have sense of environment and plan their own path to avoid collisions. The shaking and repelling effect in agents have been reduced using the body contact and sliding forces. The interactions among agents have been modeled based on personal reaction space. These changes in SFM model makes the model more realistic as every parameter has been modeled based on findings from psychology and video tracking. The crowd simulation model has been developed on C++. To train the negative emotions model, the following situations produced, which are common to panic and evacuation events was produced a) Herding b) Faster is Slower c) Turbulent flow d) Stop and go waves. The events have been captured and different kinds of behaviors have been detected during these flows according to the context such as passing through doors during high density, changing the motivation etc. The positive and negative emotion situations are labelled and normal behaviors are also labelled and two models for both positive and negative emotions have been trained. The labelled data for emotions produces the following clustered global negative behavior situations. The commonly observed behavior cluster classes are clustered at doors of rooms a) C_1 to C_3 b) C_2 to C_3 c) C_1 to C_4 d) C_1 to C_3 e) C_2 to C_4 f) C_3 to C_5 g) C_5 to C_6 h) C_4 to C_6, where C_1 to C_6 are the rooms in the simulation. There are also many other classes which are representation of sudden events. The optimal cluster selection is done using the BIC as shown in figure 2. The log likelihood ratio is plotted against frames which are taken at random. The emotions detected are then followed by comparison with the labelled data and it shows that detection ratio follows the actual labels as shown in figure 4.

To evaluate the performance of the algorithm, ROC (receiver operating curves) are obtained, these are obtained by 50 different trails of simulations with two different thresholds of likelihood ratios for both models of positive and negative emotions. The ROC curves evaluations in figure 3 and table 1 show the classification accuracy is quite acceptable.

4   Conclusion

A situation based emotion detection and classification technique has been proposed. Using the models for positive and negative emotions, the method utilizes a dynamic probabilistic clustering technique to model responses in different situations. The context based information is modeled based on the bio-inspired autobiographical memory. The likelihood ratio test used to classify emotions in crowds has been demonstrated. To our knowledge, the proposed model is the first one in the literature to present algorithm on detection of emotions of the crowd and results have shown that the model is capable of detecting the emotions of the people from individual level to collective level with high accuracy. This system could be useful in surveillance environment to predict the crowd situations before they happen. The future work includes the collection of datasets with the help of experts and making general context information for every kind of situation.

Table 1. Results from ROC for positive emotion model E_p and negative emotion model E_n

Parameters	Area under ROC curve for positive emotion model E_p	Area under ROC curve for negative emotion model E_n
$\propto_{th1}$	0.886	0.858
$\propto_{th2}$	0.845	0.812

Table 1. Results from ROC for positive emotion model E_p and negative emotion model E_n

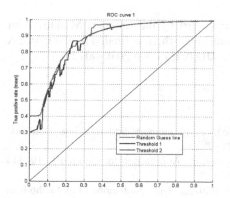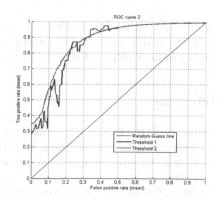

(a) ROC curve for positive emotion model E_p (b) ROC curve for negative emotion model E_n

Fig. 3. ROC curves obtained using 50 different experimental scenarios and using two different thresholds as in equation with $\propto_{th1}= -0.25$ and $\propto_{th2}= -0.30$. (a) Positive Emotion model E_p (b) Negative emotion model E_n.

(a) Positive Emotions Detected of the crowd at (350th frame)

(b) Herding Situation (Negative Emotions Detected) (850th frame)

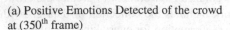
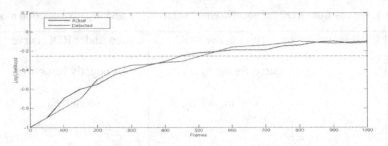

(c) Comparison of Log likelihood ratio and Frames

Fig. 4. Comparison of Log likelihood ratio and emotion deduced in different frames (a) Normal situation depicts positive emotion. The blue box represents the group of people whose emotions are averaged to give the result. (b) Herding behavior produced at C_3 to C_5 and negative emotions were detected on average in blue box. (c) Comparison of Log likelihood ratio and video frames using $\propto_{th} = -0.25$. The detected curve is by our model and actual curve is obtained by comparison of labelled data. The blue box shows the area under observation.

Acknowledgment. This work was supported in part by the Erasmus Mundus Joint Doctorate in Interactive and Cognitive Environments, which is funded by the EACEA Agency of the European Commission under EMJD ICE FPA n 2010-0012

References

1. Bower, G.H., Cohen, P.R.: Emotional influences in memory and thinking: Data and theory. In: Affect and Cognition, vol. 1 (1982)
2. Ekman, P.: Expression and the nature of emotion. Approaches to Emotion 3, 19–344 (1984)
3. Juslin, P.N., Scherer, K.R.: Vocal expression of affect. The new handbook of Methods in Nonverbal Behavior Research, 65–135 (2005)
4. Scherer, K.R.: Vocal communication of emotion: A review of research paradigms. Speech Communication 40, 227–256 (2003)
5. Mota, S., Picard, R.W.: Automated posture analysis for detecting learner's interest level. In: 2003 Conference on Computer Vision and Pattern Recognition Workshop, CVPRW 2003, vol. 5. IEEE (2003)

6. Villon, O., Lisetti, C.: A user-modeling approach to build user's psycho-physiological maps of emotions using bio-sensors. In: The 15th IEEE International Symposium on Robot and Human Interactive Communication, ROMAN 2006 (2006)
7. Villon, O., Lisetti, C.: A user-modeling approach to build user's psycho-physiological maps of emotions using bio-sensors. In: The 15th IEEE International Symposium on Robot and Human Interactive Communication, ROMAN 2006, pp. 269–276. IEEE (2006)
8. Bänziger, T., Grandjean, D., Scherer, K.R.: Emotion recognition from expressions in face, voice, and body: The Multimodal Emotion Recognition Test (MERT). Emotion 9(5), 691 (2009)
9. Jockusch, J., Ritter, H.: An instantaneous topological mapping model for correlated stimuli. In: International Joint Conference on. Neural Networks, IJCNN 1999, vol. 1. IEEE (1999)
10. Chiappino, S., et al.: Event based switched dynamic bayesian networks for autonomous cognitive crowd monitoring. In: Wide Area Surveillance, pp. 93–122. Springer, Heidelberg (2014)
11. Dore, A., et al.: A bio-inspired system model for interactive surveillance applications. Journal of Ambient Intelligence and Smart Environments 3(2), 147–163 (2011)
12. Dore, A., Regazzoni, C.S.: Interaction Analysis with a Bayesian Trajectory Model. IEEE Intelligent Systems 25(3), 32–40 (2010)
13. Dore, A., Cattoni, A.F., Regazzoni, C.S.: Interaction modeling and prediction in smart spaces: a bio-inspired approach based on autobiographical memory. IEEE Transactions on Systems, Man and Cybernetics, Part A: Systems and Humans 40(6), 1191–1205 (2010)
14. Damasio, A.R.: The feeling of what happens: Body and emotion in the making of consciousness. EBook (1999)
15. Kohonen, T.: Self-organizing maps, vol. 30. Springer (2001)
16. Ortony, A.: The cognitive structure of emotions. Cambridge University Press (1990)
17. Russell, J.A., Lewicka, M., Niit, T.: A cross-cultural study of a circumplex model of affect. Journal of personality and social psychology 57(5), 848 (1989)
18. Dempster, A.P., Laird, N.M., Rubin, D.B.: Maximum likelihood from incomplete data via the EM algorithm. Journal of the Royal statistical Society 39(1), 1–38 (1977)
19. Schwarz, G.: Estimating the dimension of a model. The annals of statistics 6(2), 461–464 (1978)
20. Baig, M.W., Barakova, E., Regazzoni, C.S., Rauterberg, M.: Realistic Modeling of Agents in Crowd Simulations. In: 2014 5th International Conference on Intelligent Systems Modelling & Simulation (ISMS), pp. 507–512. IEEE (2014)
21. Helbing, D., Molnar, P.: Social force model for pedestrian dynamics. Physical review E 51(5), 4282 (1995)
22. Neyman, J., Pearson, E.S.: On the problem of the most efficient tests of statistical hypotheses. Springer, New York (1992)

Author Index

Alimi, Adel M.   290
Auerbach, Joshua   220

Baek, SeungMin   98
Baig, Mirza Waqar   328
Barakova, Emilia I.   328
Barikhan, Subhi Shaker   65
Becerra, José A.   1
Bellas, Francisco   1
Berthold, Oswald   188
Birattari, Mauro   270
Boeddeker, Norbert   108
Bouzid, Mohamed   290
Braud, Raphael   154
Buhrmann, Thomas   21

Caussy, Ramesh   132
Chatty, Abdelhak   290
Christensen-Dalsgaard, Jakob   88

Dasgupta, Sakyasingha   121
Delarboulas, Pierre   132
del Pobil, Angel P.   320
Demazeau, Yves   88
Di Paolo, Ezequiel   21
Duro, Richard J.   1

Fedor, Anna   53
Fernando, Chrisantha   53, 230
Fischer, Christian   166
Floreano, Dario   220

Gaussier, Philippe   132, 154, 290
Germann, Jürg   220
Giagkos, Alexandros   300
Gomez, Faustino   210, 260
Gonzalez-Rodriguez, Diego   250
György, Sebestyén   280

Hafner, Verena V.   32, 188
Hallam, John   88
Hamann, Heiko   270
Hauser, Helmut   32
Hernandez-Carrion, Jose Rodolfo   250
Herreros, Ivan   76

Jahn, Luisa   32
Jeong, Eunseok   43
Jørgensen, Søren Vissing   88

Kallel, Ilhem   290
Karaouzene, Ali   154, 290
Katsaros, Nikolaos   230
Kazerounian, Sohrob   176, 198
Khaluf, Yara   270
Kim, DaeEun   43, 98
Kim, Dae-Shik   144
Kompella, Varun Raj   176
Košnar, Karel   240
Koutník, Jan   260

Lewis, Martha   53
Luciw, Matthew   198

Maffei, Giovanni   76
Mair, Elmar   108
Maniadakis, Michail   11
Manoonpong, Poramate   65, 121
Marcenaro, Lucio   328
Martinez-Martin, Ester   320
Martius, Georg   32
Márton, Lőrinc   280
Mostafaoui, Ghiles   154

Nagai, Yukie   144
Neumann, Sergej   240

Öllinger, Michael   53
Oubbati, Mohamed   166

Palm, Günther   166
Park, Jun-Cheol   144
Přeučil, Libor   240

Quoy, Mathias   132

Rauterberg, Matthias   328
Regazzoni, Carlo S.   328
Roper, Mark   230
Rossi, Silvia   310

Salgado, Rodrigo   1
Samet, Nermin   108

Sanchez-Fibla, Marti   76
Sandamirskaya, Yulia   198
Schmidhuber, Jürgen   176, 198, 210, 260
Schöner, Gregor   198
Staffa, Mariacarla   310
Stollenga, Marijn   210
Stürzl, Wolfgang   108
Szántó, Zoltán   280
Szathmáry, Eörs   53

Trahanias, Panos   11

Verschure, Paul F.M.J.   76
Vonásek, Vojtěch   240

Wilson, Myra S.   300
Winkler, Lutz   240
Wörgötter, Florentin   65, 121
Wörn, Heinz   240

Zeidan, Bassel   121
Zeil, Jochen   108